D0911737

Martin Scorsese, Woody Allen, and Spike Lee

Martin Scorsese, Woody Allen, and Spike Lee

Ethnicity, Race, and Identity in American Independent Film

James F. Scott

LEXINGTON BOOKS
Lanham • Boulder • New York • London

Published by Lexington Books
An imprint of The Rowman & Littlefield Publishing Group, Inc.
4501 Forbes Boulevard, Suite 200, Lanham, Maryland 20706
www.rowman.com

6 Tinworth Street, London SE11 5AL, United Kingdom

Copyright © 2019 The Rowman & Littlefield Publishing Group, Inc.

All rights reserved. No part of this book may be reproduced in any form or by
any electronic or mechanical means, including information storage and retrieval
systems, without written permission from the publisher, except by a reviewer
who may quote passages in a review.

British Library Cataloguing in Publication Information Available

Library of Congress Cataloging-in-Publication Data Available

ISBN 978-1-4985-4896-0 (cloth)
ISBN 978-1-4985-4898-4 (pbk.)
ISBN 978-1-4985-4897-7 (electronic)

For my daughter, Adrienne, and my son, Jamie,
together with all the film enthusiasts of the next millennium.

Contents

List of Figures

Preface

Since the early 1990s I have been following the respective careers of Martin Scorsese, Woody Allen, and Spike Lee, thinking that their work exhibited a common thread of interests, perhaps slightly obscured by the differences of surface phenomena that give each director his own terrain and personal voice. Though they have not yet completely fulfilled the creative agendas they once marked out for themselves, each has produced a remarkable body of work and established the broad directions that give coherence to their individual and collective energies. This imaginative coherence, inflected by race and ethnicity, is my subject.

The value of this long incubation is that it has allowed me to see race and ethnicity in light of the changes in emphasis and perspective that the altered demographic landscape of American culture has brought with it over the past two decades. In the early 1990s, few would have foreseen the increasing centrality of Hispanic, Latino, and Near Eastern immigration to the debate over national identity, nor imagined the level of anxiety and resentment that this debate would provoke. Now, as we approach the third decade of the new millennium, we witness a wave of xenophobia that not only inspires frantic cries for "protection" of our borders against a new generation of aliens, whether they be Islamic terrorists or Mexican drug dealers, but also harks back to ancient prejudices against Jews and African Americans that many thought were comfortably behind us. The violent cadre of right-wing protestors who intervened on behalf of the Confederate monuments in Charlottesville carried banners that were as likely to be anti-Semitic as antiblack. These phenomena give evidence of the ease with which ethnicity conflates with race and how easily both are absorbed into a blurred, but demonic "other." Such data also convince me of the continuing relevance of race and ethnicity to an understanding of the social system by which we define ourselves. Much to my regret, we are once again experiencing the stress of an immigration crisis more rancorous than anything since the firestorms of the 1920s, sparked by Madison Grant and the Anglo-Nordic polemicists of that era.

The extended gestation of my project has also enabled me to test its arguments on both sides of the Atlantic, and I much appreciate the opportunity I had on two occasions to present these three filmmakers to graduate students at Saint Louis University of Madrid, our sister campus in the Spanish capitol. The Iberian context somewhat neutralized the racial issue, but left anti-Semitism prominently in the foreground, opening old wounds from the Franco era. The other reference point was the status of the ethnic subcultures of Spain, particularly the Basques and the Catalonians, both eager to assert their own identity, even at the expense of the national culture. Not entirely to my surprise, I found the students returning frequently to language, religion, and diet as markers to designate particular spaces of race and ethnicity, where the children of Barcelona or Bilbao could provisionally set themselves apart from the Castilian inflections of Madrid. Most agreed that one could see in Spain tensions similar to those found in New York City, and the United States, ongoing friction between the hegemonic culture of class and status, and that of the various minorities, who perceived themselves as disadvantaged or disrespected, even when discrepancies of wealth and education were not obviously a factor. Teaching the same course in St. Louis, I found an audience more mindful of American racial binaries, particularly following the violence in Ferguson, which unfortunately spread to several other sites in the metropolitan area. Beyond the flashpoints of a particular moment, these events launched a conversation about the terms of cultural assimilation and whether a sense of national identity inevitably erases the awareness of ethnic roots. From these tensive exchanges came the conclusion that, with respect to ethno-racial identity, the word "integration" serves better than assimilation to describe the desired acculturation of minorities into the majoritarian consensus. The hope is that the preferred term allows for the agency of individuals who seek to determine their own ethno-racial assignment, even while acknowledging the hegemonic authority of affluence and historical privilege.

I have deliberately drawn on a considerable body of social science literature, intending to suggest a dialectical relationship between social anthropology and the perceptions of creative artists, who apprehend the same complex phenomena by intuitive rather than analytical and statistical means. I hope it is not imagined that the artists have been summoned to the court of rationality to be disabused of their partial perspectives and their incurable habit of fictionalizing fact. It seems greatly more meaningful to see both artists and scholars as partners in a search for insight into the complex web of relationships that build us into our social world. By my lights, the vivid portrait of loss and longing in Scorsese's *Taxi Driver* is as authentic as the cerebral detailing of alienation in Erich Fromm or C. Wright Mills.

As the project comes to completion, I'm also aware that I have inadvertently contributed to what might be called "canon formation." This springs from my decision to look closely at a relatively small number of films I admire, instead of trying to provide short-winded, incidental comments on all the films under the signature of these directors. But I don't mean to imply that my selections represent the eight "best" films of Scorsese, Allen, or Lee. Nor are they the only films that might be looked at from the standpoint of race and ethnicity. I would really prefer not to make value judgments about the worth or the flaws of particular films, though I know that I would much rather spend an evening looking more carefully at *Crimes and Misdemeanors* than sit through another screening of *Interiors*, though the latter is a well-intentioned effort on Allen's part to launch in a new direction. By the same token, I respect what Lee did recently in his Netflix update of *She's Gotta Have It*, but I don't feel that it was a successful effort. Suffice it to say that the films chosen for discussion offer access to themes I find most valuable in interpreting how these directors see the causes and consequences of ethno-racial conflict. If this approach accidentally occasions some sifting and winnowing of a very large body of work, that outcome does not seem entirely unwelcome. The same fate has overtaken Ibsen, Dickens, and Shakespeare.

Finally, I would like to thank my colleagues in the English Department and the Film Studies program at Saint Louis University (SLU) for their ongoing contribution to the refinement of my thinking about race and ethnicity as it expresses itself in the contemporary urban world. I am particularly indebted to Professor Ellen Crowell, who carefully read the introductory chapter of my manuscript and invited me to present my research to her graduate class in literary theory in the spring semester of 2017. I am also grateful for the invitation I received from Professor Hal Bush to make a similar presentation to the cadre of humanities scholars at SLU who inquire into cultural studies under the rubric of the "Textual Revolution." This presentation also produced a rich exchange of ideas and saved me from several missteps that I might not otherwise have avoided.

Both opportunities resulted in fruitful seminarial dialogues about race, ethnicity, and status in the new millennium. These topics, I suspect, will be much on our tongues for many years to come.

James F. Scott
Saint Louis University

Introduction

"God's Crucible"

This project began as an extended meditation upon the "melting pot," a metaphor the Zionist radical Israel Zangwill appropriated in 1908 for his play by that name. Though *The Melting Pot* is dramatically inept, its trademark phrase "God's crucible," a bubbling cauldron where "the fire of God" burns off ethno-racial differences, catches the danger, violence, and disruptive power of the assimilative process (Zangwill 1908). Like Zangwill, most commentators have invoked the metaphor positively, but obviously it has a more sinister side. If we take seriously this trope of molten metal, we see a threatening image of heat and pressure, which may produce a valuable alloy but will do so at the expense of individual elements in the mix. What happens to the personal self during this harrowing process of socialization? And what of the overseers who tend the seething mass? Who authorized them to play God and what exactly are God's tasks? The fiery cauldron is of a certain size, selectively filled with particular elements, and heated to a temperature decided by choice as well as chance. What about the bystanders who observe the cauldron from a respectful distance? Are they passive spectators or do they implicitly contribute to the forging process? Inevitably, there will be ongoing strife between immigrants (to say nothing of slaves, or indentured servants, or poverty-burdened outsiders of whatever complexion) and the majoritarian culture they are being compelled to join.

Looking at ethno-racial interaction from the vantage point of immigration and internal migration, we see a complex array of relationships that bear upon the formation of both personal and cultural identity, especially those oppressive forces that deform, dislocate, and sometimes defeat altogether the individual striving of marginalized peoples. The perspective of the outsider reveals the multiple fracture points at which personal will, or even the collective will of a particular subgroup, is thwarted or redirected by constellations of power too great to resist. Undoubtedly, American society is riven by various divisive forces, not least of which are gender, age, income, residency, and social status. But even though every individual identity is an unstable compound of contending elements, full of internal differences and dissonances, the construction of ancestry, especially when it approaches the color line, often undergirds the other divisions that mark our increasingly heterogeneous culture. These assumptions guide my efforts to reformulate Zangwill's melting pot metaphor and make it relevant to understanding three independent New York filmmakers of the last half-century: Martin Scorsese, Woody Allen, and Spike Lee.

The argument advanced in the following chapters is that assimilation and integration gain ground on all fronts during this period, but that the pace of this social transformation varies with the social capital of the three ethno-racial communities. The other variable is what we might call self-assignment. At this stage of the twenty-first century, the Jews have almost completely assimilated, which causes Alan Dershowitz in *The Vanishing Jew* (1998) to pose "the Jewish Question" in contemporary America as "can we survive our success?" (1–19). Woody Allen's Jews largely conform to the Dershowitz paradigm, though he does not share Derschowitz's insistence upon preserving Jewish identity. This said, two of Allen's best films from the 1980s, *Broadway Danny Rose* (1984) and *Radio Days* (1987), capitalize on nostalgia for a bygone era, before Jewish culture lost its distinctly ethnic texture. Scorsese's ethnics, or at least the ones he chooses to put at the center of his stage, are less perfectly assimilated, less rich in cultural capital, and less able to assign themselves privileged status on the pyramid of power. Whether it's the Sicilians, the Jews, or the nineteenth-century Irish, we see ethnics on the threshold of civic culture who still feel the powerful undertow of the family, the gang, and the clan. Lee's characters, of course, are the least assimilated, usually guarding their own spiritual turf, as in *Malcolm X* (1992) and *Get on the Bus* (1996). As they approach the threshold of the professional world, they integrate very cautiously, indeed suspiciously, fearing—like the ill-fated protagonist of *Bamboozled* (2000)—that in spite of their first-class intelligence and upscale wardrobe, they will still be seen as minstrel show figures or cartoon characters. Even Lee, however, approaches race more ambivalently in recent films like *25th Hour* (2002) and *BlacKkKlansman* (2018). Both films introduce racially ambiguous characters who attempt to self-assign their ethno-racial status, not always with complete success. We also see how ethno-racial categories increasingly blur into categories of class and culture.

Approaching the issues of ethno-racial identity themed into their respective films, I hope to find more refined tools for the analysis of complex cultural exchanges than Zangwill's bubbling cauldron affords, however vivid its poetry. At the outset, it seems advisable to employ a term like "interculturality" to describe ethno-racial interaction and replace the awkward word "assimilation," which inevitably implies the majoritarian and hegemonic culture swallowing up the outsiders who seek a place in the host society. The logic of this verbal adjustment is to more fully respect the identity of the marginalized subgroups in our midst, suggesting their capacity to resist an all-consuming assimilation as well as implying that they might join the national community without disowning their personal styles, habits, or values. In effect, this represents the assimilation process as something more like "integration," whereby a true cross-fertilization of social habits and practices is achieved. This acknowledges the fact that pizza and pasta are no longer thought of as exclusively "Italian food" and classical jazz has become more than "black music." Meanwhile, black athletes compete in and sometimes dominate what were once almost exclusively "white" sports, like intercollegiate and professional football or basketball.

But the improved nomenclature should not disguise the continued presence of multiple oppressive forces, nor cause us to pretend that authentic multiculturalism is a fully realized ideal. Waves of anti-Semitism continue to wash over us at unpredictable intervals, and African Americans remain disadvantaged in every theater of American life. Gender issues still complicate all aspects of cultural engagement. That disparate cultures might meet on a level playing field and negotiate as equals remains a utopic aspiration. Ethno-racial advancement has made its way in the face of strong resistances, which continue to compromise and deform the strivings of various subcultures. The majoritarian culture continues to be hegemonic, even though its norms and expectations have relaxed appreciably over the past half-century.

While this majoritarian culture is generically "American," the Founding Fathers explicitly stipulated, in the Naturalization Act of 1790, that the new nation would be a "white republic," with full-fledged citizenship reserved for the "free white person" (US Immigration Legislation Online). In other words, such privileges as the right to vote, or to hold public office, or in some cases even to own property, would be guaranteed only to persons who identified and performed as "white people." White people? Who are these "white people"? That was never absolutely clear. But for a considerable part of our national history, they seemed not to be Irish, or Sicilian, or Jewish. And certainly they were not African American, nor did they belong to the six tribes of the Iroquois Confederacy. These lingering doubts and preemptive exclusions, as articulated dramatically in the films of Scorsese, Allen, and Lee, are the object of my study.

I

My first real insight was the perception that something remarkable had happened to the American social order in the mid-1960s when President

Lyndon Johnson pushed through Congress two far-reaching pieces of legislation—the Civil Rights Act of 1964 and the Immigration and Nationality Act of 1965. Though in no sense formally related, except as part the president's ambitious "Great Society" agenda, these two initiatives sent shock waves through American culture that reverberated on into the next half-century, changing the social landscape in ways far more decisive than the Woodstock festival or even the tragedy at Kent State.

The Civil Rights Act invited African Americans to assert their claim to full equality and to seek a level of integration into the majority culture hardly imaginable in the Jim Crow era, or even immediately after WWII, when forced racial segregation was still the law of the land. The Immigration Act scuttled the racial and ethnic quotas that had largely denied citizenship to Asian, African, Middle Eastern, and Caribbean migrants, who had been largely excluded from our nation for more than 150 years by prevailing interpretations of what the Founding Fathers' "white republic" should look like. The far-reaching consequences of the 1965 immigration reform are set forth ably in Tom Gjelten's *A Nation of Nations: The Great American Immigration Story* (2015): "In 1960," he notes, "seven out of eight immigrants were white people from Europe. By 2010, Europeans accounted for barely one out of ten newcomers. Immigrants from other parts of the world dominated" (137–38). At first these were chiefly from Asia; later, the balance shifted toward Mexico and the Caribbean (see Gjelten 2015, esp. 161–238). As Tyler Anbinder emphasizes in *City of Dreams* (2016), New York City is the epicenter of these new demographics, now "more diverse than ever before," with a population in 2014 of "some 910,000 New Yorkers born in Asia, 860,000 . . . from Caribbean islands, 750,000 . . . from Central and South America, [and] 145,000 from Africa" (556–57). This huge infusion of immigrants from beyond Europe would inevitably have implications for the way our nation thinks about race and ethnicity.

In *Race and Immigration* (2014), Bowman, Kibrea, and O'Leary analyze the deeper consequences of this demographic shift, exploring "the race-immigration nexus" and tracing how "racial divisions both shape and are shaped by immigrant arenas and experiences" (5). Using a "race optic on immigrant identities" these scholars conclude that the masses of newcomers who identify as neither "white" nor "black" have forced the majority culture to see immigrants "in relational terms, as marked by the effort of immigrant groups to situate themselves in relation to others in the racial landscape" (122). In sum, this new complexion of metropolitan America radically destabilized ethno-racial boundaries and sent many in search of "available identity options" (129).

Unfailingly, the question of "identity options" touches upon our understanding of selfhood. Recent scholarship, as represented in antholo-

gies such as *Race, Ethnicity, and Self* (Koslow and Salet 2003), has emphasized "the ways in which culture surrounds, enmeshes, contextualizes,
moors, and pulls its citizens along," making it impossible to understand
individuals apart from the social energies that have worked upon them
since earliest childhood, principally through their families and whatever
subcultures have nurtured them (2003, 21). "Persons are embedded in
culture," says Carol Hoare, recognizing that "cognitive structures and
perceptual lenses are comprised of culturally built prisms through which
we sense and interpret" (21). Race and ethnicity are among the most
crucial of these "perceptual lenses," complicating the intercultural relationships of all ethno-racial minorities. Continuing her analysis, Hoare
claims that the white majoritarian culture "presumes itself as the norm
against which other identities are measured and evaluated," thereby opposing itself to "an ethic of care, connectedness, and relationships" more
characteristic of ethnic and tribal worlds (31). Another contributor to
this volume, Iris Martinez, constructs identity as "the consolidation of a
continuous interactive process between three integrating bonds: spatial,
temporal and social" (2003, 89). The spatial associates selfhood with a
particular place—Hester Street, Little Italy, Harlem. The temporal entails
value-laden objects—keepsakes, mementos, family albums, "the need to
relate to known familial and cultural objects." The social provides the
capstone, the sense of an "inner sameness," an integrity over time among
"a community of significant others" often affiliated through language
(89). Immigrants and racial minorities share an identity formation at odds
with the normative white identity formation that is recommended both
implicitly and explicitly throughout the acculturation process.

Approaching the issue of "identity formation," I am aware of the
danger implicit in conflating race and ethnicity and sense the need to
acknowledge the crucial differences between them, especially in the
American experience with its historical burden of black slavery. The problematic of this relationship is addressed very ably in Richard Alba's *Blurring the Color Line* (2009), which replaces race vs. ethnicity as absolutely
separate social categories with the understanding that "race and ethnicity
may be better viewed as poles in a multi-dimensional space" (40). This
new paradigm is anchored in the term "ethno-racial," whereby "most
African Americans are located at the racial pole since they are identifiable
solely on the basis of skin color [while] many individuals, including some
African Americans, are located in the middle of the space, where identifi-
ability depends on a bundled mix of characteristics, social and cultural
as well as physical" (40). This "bundle" includes language, accents, food
preferences, spiritual formation, dress, names, residential locations, and
schools, among other possible ethno-racial markers. Perceptively, Alba
notes, "the characteristics that go into the bundle can change over time, as

can the way they are seen." Furthermore, "intermarriage, it need hardly be said, can loosen the connection between phenotypic characteristics and group membership in the next generation" (40). These phenomena blur the lines between "ethnic" and "racial" difference.

Although both immigration reform and the civil rights initiative might well be understood as liberating, they begot tension in minority communities, which were thrown into conflict not only with the majority culture but also with each other. Perhaps even more importantly, their new political status propelled these various minorities toward extended self-scrutiny, as they gave themselves over to several decades of worry about their own ethno-racial identity. These new circumstances also affected better-situated ethnic minorities, like Jews and Italians, who were, in fact, better situated precisely because they had benefitted markedly from progressive social legislation of the 1930s, 1940s, and 1950s. Once derided as less than "white," they were now persuaded to complete a process of integration underway for most of the twentieth century. Ironically, much of the new energy within various minority cultures intensified their conflict with African Americans. This latter group not only had to compete with various immigrant cultures, some newly arrived and others going back to the nineteenth century, but had to meet the challenge of these rivals in the face of constraints from *The Urban Racial State* (2011). "In highly racialized societies such as the United States," says Cazenave, "one of the chief functions of cities and other urban governments . . . is the regulation of race relations within their geopolitical boundaries" (1). According to Cazenave, the institutions of the American urban world (meaning: the mayor's office, government agencies, courts, banks, the police, zoning boards, real estate interests, universities, etc.) were never racially neutral. Public housing projects were racially segregated and federal mortgage insurance was not readily available to prospective African American homeowners. Before and even during the civil rights era, Cazenave contends, these institutions sought to "manage race relations in ways that foster and sustain both [their] own immediate political interests, and ultimately, white racial supremacy" (see esp. 1–31). Information and entertainment media might easily be added to the list of institutions that have shaped and are shaping race relations in the United States. We seek to place the films of Scorsese, Allen, and Lee within this complex web of socio-cultural relationships.

My analysis of intercultural identity begins with the conjecture that whiteness is a "performance" more than an "essence," a powerful concept advanced by Gwendolyn Foster in *Performing Whiteness: Postmodern Re/constructions in the Cinema* (2003). Foster works from the assumption that racial divisions are understood intuitively, largely by reference to informal perceptions and cultural norms, a premise that allows her to construe "whiteness" as a dramatic enactactment more than a fixed attribute.

Though mindful of skin tones, she is equally alert to the way language, character, costume, and class impinge upon popular understanding of ethno-racial identity.

Exploring whiteness in the cinema, Foster contends that Hollywood in its classical period created a kind of "whiteface" in which stars of some-times quite various ethnicities strove to embody "whiteness" as a set of gestures, an array of signals, analogous to Jean Baudrillard's concept of a "simulacrum," in fact, "a copy lacking an original" (Foster 2003, 2). Armed with this semiotic code, she undertakes to describe the "white body" and even the "white space" in which we might expect to find this body establishing itself. "I suggest that this white space," she says, "where exchanges of identity are negotiated, is the space of whiteface, where class and ethnicity are homogenized, sterilized, and largely erased in motion pictures" (51). Her crowning example is the Busby-Berkeley musical "where the human body was reduced to a mind-numbing series of endless smiles, well-shaped legs and breasts, white-blond heads, and restless toe-tapping feet, complimented by the manufactured grace of a series of anonymous but immaculately clad leading men" (97). But it could also add, subtract, and exchange some of its parts, or enter into alien spaces, as did Mae West in *I'm No Angel* (1933). By "surrounding herself with black femaleness," says Foster, this transgressive Hollywood star found a way of "performing a site of contestation against stereotypes of white and black women" (39).

Taking Foster's point a bit further, we might look at instances when the ethnic body was transformed so as to occupy the "utopian space" of whiteness. Film star Rita Hayworth is a case in point. Born Margarita Carmen Cansino and trained as a Spanish dancer, she first gained at-tention as an extra in *Cruz Diablo* (1934) and soon after, while still per-forming under the stage name of Rita Cansino, became the sultry Latina heroine of *Under the Pampas Moon* (1935). But by 1940 she had disowned her Spanish name, signed with Columbia pictures, dyed her hair red, and anglicized her looks through cosmetic surgery, thus redefining herself as one of the most exciting "American" pin-up girls of the WWII period. Her well-rehearsed performance of whiteness was on display in *Strawberry Blonde* (1941) and *Cover Girl* (1944). Under an Argentinean moon or with *Charlie Chan in Egypt* (1935), she was ethnically ambigu-ous, a mysterious "other." But as a reddish-blond starlet flirting with Jimmy Cagney in the "white space" of romantic comedy, Cansino/Hayworth was 100 percent "American." Significantly, as in *Gilda* (1946), she could still call upon her ethnic gestures to channel the serpentine body language of the seductive *femme fatale*. But in a twist upon noir convention, Gilda turns out to be a good girl after all. In the last scene of the film, she walks away from South American decadence on the arm of her leading man, the all-American Glenn Ford. Here is an instance where ethno-racial identity is self-consciously invented, then performed, morphed, and continuously adjusted to fit a set of screen roles and the social circumstances that called them into being.

Ethno-racial performance continues to have relevance, as is evident in Wendy Roth's recent publication, *Race Migrations: Latinos and the Cultural Transformation of Race* (2012). In her study of Dominicans and Puerto Ricans who immigrated to the United States roughly since 1990, Roth discovered what she calls a tendency toward "performing race strategically," a topic to which she devotes a full chapter (151–75). The Latinos interviewed in depth for her research project spoke relentlessly of their racial ambiguity and even applied different constructs of racial identity to themselves, their neighbors, and their larger world. For some, race was binary, as in the historical American classification, while others racialized nationality and described their race as "Dominican" or "Puerto Rican," even when this required inventing a racial category outside the schematic of American census data. Most of the interviewees were conscious of "performing *latinidad*" (159) as a way of situating themselves in American national culture. As a highly relevant aside, Roth also notes that "many earlier immigrant groups, including Italian, Irish, Jews, and other European ethnics, followed such a pattern of cultural assimilation . . . into White America" (156).

This last point returns us to my own project. I want to investigate how three particular ethno-racial identities are represented in contemporary American cinema, using Martin Scorsese, Woody Allen, and Spike Lee to guide us through the conflicts that touch Sicilian Italians, Jews, African Americans, and—more marginally—Latinos. In Scorsese's case, this includes a historical sidebar about the Irish, the first case of contested assimilation, which lays out most of the paradigm before it is repeated and modified by the experience of other minorities. And in the case of Lee, race complicates the understanding of ethnicity in ways to which we will presently turn.

My thinking has its roots in the premises of the cultural studies movement, as these were articulated chiefly by Raymond Williams and Stuart Hall and reflected in the work of the Birmingham Centre for Contemporary Cultural Studies, whose agenda was conceived in the middle 1960s. In "The Future of Cultural Studies" (1996), Williams reminds his like-minded colleagues of the movement's founding principle, namely, that "you cannot understand an intellectual or artistic project without also understanding its formation" (168), that is, without taking hold of the complex of social processes which brought it into being. Simply put, the products of consciousness, like films and novels, are artifacts, literally "made" at a certain place and time to fulfill a set of social purposes. For

Williams, the process and the product are "two ways of materializing . . . what is in fact a common disposition of energy and direction" (168). Picking up this thread, Hall speaks of cultural production as a "signifying practice," fundamentally, the building of a set of signs that "represent" the world of experience, the "real" world. In this "symbolic domain," where all things are crafted into "discourse," the cultural artifact becomes our means of "organizing, clustering, arranging, and classifying concepts, and establishing complex relationships between them" (1996, 17). In the analyses to follow, I intend to examine the signifying practices of "ethnicity" and "race" as these are expressed in the filmmaking of Scorsese, Allen, and Lee. Together these directors have redefined the discourse of ethnicity and race as we now know them in the twenty-first century.

My work takes advantage of the abundant, high-quality research in ethno-racial studies published over the past quarter century, much of it focused upon the racialized "in-betweenness" that creates concepts like *Off White* (2004), the name and theme of a scholarly anthology on "power, privilege, and resistance" as seen from the standpoint of ethno-racial hybridity. Similar assumptions about hybridity govern the analysis of Guglielmo and Salerno, whose monograph asks *Are Italians White?* (2004). Their answer, unsurprisingly, is "yes," but it occasions a 250-page meditation on "how race is made in America." These essays build from Matthew Jacobson's *Whiteness of a Different Color* (1998), which foregrounds the "instability of race" (139), particularly in the later nineteenth century, noting the paradoxical status of certain immigrant ethnic groups, including the Irish, the Jews, and the southern Italians. The paradox is that they qualified for naturalization, as "white persons," automatically eligible for citizenship and generally experiencing social advantage in any situation where they might compete against Asians or African Americans for jobs, property, or public respect. But their racial status remained deeply problematic, as evidenced by a notorious lynching in New Orleans during the 1870s. On this occasion, eleven Italian prisoners were summarily executed by "the White League" (Jacobson 1998, 57). This racial taint upon Sicilians survived well into the twentieth century.

As noted, the analysis I am conducting is complicated by the inclusion of Spike Lee, an African American, whose filmic characters, both in fact and at law, represent "racial" as well as "ethnic" difference. In navigating these troubled waters, I follow the lead of immediately contemporary scholars like Ronald Fernandez in *America Beyond Black and White* (2007), Nell Painter in *The History of White People* (2010), William Frey in *Diversity Explosion* (2015), and especially in Emily Lee's valuable anthology *Living Alterities: Phenomenology, Embodiment, and Race* (2014). Troubled by the simplistic dichotomy of "black" and "white," particularly in the case of Hispanics who fit into neither category, Fernandez directly challenges the concept of racial difference and proposes that, "in a world without race, African Americans would be seen as an ethnic group with a unique and terrible history of oppression in the United States" (2007, 236). The key point here is that, however brutal and violent the abuses of slavery and its extended aftermath (and these brutalities are almost unparalleled), the victims of America's slave culture were created by a uniquely perverse acculturation, not by forces that altered their genes.

Recognizing that by the end of the twentieth century the American Society of Physical Anthropologists had disavowed "race" as a biological concept, Painter treats "the history of white people" as a series of demographic "enlargements," whereby in a series of steps or stages, "the category of whiteness—or we might say more precisely, a category of non-blackness—effectively expands" (2010, 396) to include first the Irish, then the Jews, the Slavs, and the Southern Europeans, finally Asians, and some children of the Caribbean. Given this degree of malleability, "black" is metamorphosed into a designation of class and caste: "For quite some time," says Painter, "many observers have held that money and inter-racial sex would solve the race problem, and indeed in some cases they have. Nonetheless, *poverty in a dark skin endures as the opposite of whiteness* driven by an age-old social yearning to characterize the poor as permanently other and inherently inferior" (396, my italics). William Frey in *Diversity Explosion* (2015) brings demographic expertise to bear on this issue, noting that racial hybridity is so prevalent in the new millennium that "the increase in multiracial marriages and births . . . almost certainly will lead to more blended populations in future generations" (191). Hence, he concludes, "the unmistakable trend toward a softening of racial boundaries that should lead to new ways of thinking about racial populations and race-related issues" (191). All this said, we should under no circumstances forget Charles Mills' point in "Materializing Race," the essay that constitutes the first chapter of Lee's *Living Alterities* (2014): "Socialized from birth to discern race, the marker of full and diminished personhood, we learn to apprehend this world through a sensory grid whose architecture has been shaped by blueprints still functioning independently of our will and conscious intent and resistant to our self-conscious redrawing" (37).

Omi and Winant in *Racial Formation in the United States* (1994) admirably contextualize the reason why race cannot simply be gathered up into ethnicity. Briefly, they argue that the ideology of racial privilege is peculiarly oppressive because the race myth, unlike the concept of ethnicity, was used to justify the massive plundering of Asia, Africa, and the Americas throughout the four hundred years of European colonial dominion. We should quickly add, however, that during the years (or perhaps centuries!) when Irish and Jewish ethnicity were constructed in racial terms, their "racial inferiority" was used to deprive them of land, property, and personal wealth. Witness the British preemptive seizure of land in eighteenth- and nineteenth-century Ireland and the theft of Jewish property at the hands of Hitler's Third Reich. This "racial project," directed against brown-skinned peoples, was designed, as Omi and Winant describe it, to build an impregnable barrier against any challenge to the legitimacy of the European conquest, "for never before and never again has an opportunity for the appropriation of wealth remotely approached that presented by the 'discovery'" of what was called 'the Indies'" (61). Hence, "just as the noise of the 'big bang' still resonates through the universe, so the over-determined construction of world 'civilization' as a product of the rise of Europe and the subjugation of the rest of us, still defines the race concept" (62). This line of argument reinforces the conclusions of Cara Bowman and her colleagues, namely that "racial boundaries are especially rooted in the efforts of dominant groups to create distinctions that affirm their power and superiority" (Bowman, Kibria, and O'Leary 2014, 4). For these reasons, Spike Lee understands his circumstances as special.

While the Omi/Winant argument points up "the limits of the immigrant analogy in addressing what was in many cases a qualitatively different historical experience—one which included slavery, colonialism, racially based exclusion and, in the case of Native Americans, virtual extirpation" (1986, 20), these scholars recognize that the ethnic paradigm is becoming the dominant discourse model for framing questions of race in the United States. In the concluding chapter of *Race Formation*, as they look specifically at racial discourse of the early 1990s, Omi and Winant see in "neoliberalism," the political preachments of the so-called "New Democrats," the attempt to form a bipartisan coalition that neutralizes right-wing race baiting by emphasizing "a new consensus with respect to race, a framework based on reforms and a rejection of group specific demands" (151). Whether the immigrant analogy will prevail in spite of its shortcomings cannot be confidently predicted at this time. What seems clear in the case of Lee, however, is that this is the paradigm he must implicitly accept in order to maintain working relations with the major Hollywood producers and distributors, like Warner Brothers, Disney, and, more recently, Home Box Office (HBO) and Netflix.

II

Actually, the ethnic paradigm serves quite well when it is deployed to examine the hybridized spaces where ethno-racial difference is likely to be represented with the greatest nuance. Already in *Whiteness Visible* (1998), Valerie Babb was charting this terrain, first setting up a highly categorical ethno-racial pyramid, but quickly adding detail that renders the categories more ambiguous and elastic. Babb finds her classical model at the Columbian Exposition of 1893, and a succession of World's Fairs of the period, where the anthropological exhibits ranked the "races" of the world in descending order from the Anglo-Nordic ideal, which was at once the most highly evolved human creature and the image of the "true American," because of the presumed racial stock of the Founding Fathers. "Cairo" was one of those off-white spaces of the Exposition where Egyptians were imagined as a race of exotic dancers, a reductionist image that seemed tenable because few fair-goers had firsthand acquaintance with the Middle East. Though the Asiatic, Oceanic, and Near Eastern peoples were explicitly caricatured, the "lesser" European races were spared the humiliation of becoming exhibits and allowed to pass in a broad and general way for "white." The other note of consequence, as Babb suggests at least by implication, is that the racial categories were not so much genetic as "biosocial," referencing language, literacy, religion, work habits, and even diet as bearing upon the construction of "whiteness." This approach left room for ethnics who were not "quite white" or not "bright white" to rearrange themselves on the ethno-racial pyramid both through substantive behavioral changes and artful role-playing.

The social historian who has looked at the "off-white" world in a particularly careful way is David Roediger, author of three books and several articles that address this issue from similar angles of entry. What he proposes, as in "White Looks, Hairy Apes, True Stories, and Limbaugh's Laughs" (1997), is a concept of mimicry, where to seem is to be. For Roediger, Eugene O'Neill's play *The Hairy Ape* furnishes the negative example of a proletarian ethnic who is mistaken for "black" because of where he is and what he does. In one scene of the play, Yank, a coal-handler on a steamship, is confronted by Mildred Douglas, a pale blond from the upper-class world who has decided to go slumming in the furnace room of the ship. At her first glimpse of the coal-handler, Mildred faints, says Roediger, "at the combination of his dirt, his ferocity, his power, and his 'gorilla face'" (M. Hill 1997, 37). Two points snap into crisp focus, immediately picked up in the language of Yank's shipmates: his look makes him "one of the bleedin' monkeys in the menagerie" but also, and perhaps more tellingly, an African American, "a piebald nigger," a "queerer kind of baboon than ever you'd find in darkest Africy," and finally one of the "slaves" who relentlessly push coal into the ship's boilers. What's more, says Roediger, the "rivulets of sooty sweat" that trickle down Yank's face turn the play into a "vicious parody of the blackface tradition of theatrical performance" (39), an instance where the mask is mistaken for the face.

Michael Rogin's analysis of black minstrelsy in *Blackface, White Noise* (1996) catches the complexity of American ethno-racial iconography as he chronicles how "whites in blackface acted out a racially exclusion-ary melting pot" (8). What he explores most successfully is the strategy by which ethnic undesirables (chiefly Irish, Jewish, Italian) deliberately foregrounded their racial difference from African Americans by adopt-ing "blackness" in the form of burnt cork, then removing it to prove it was a separable mask, not to be confused with anything intrinsic to their nature. Unlike Yank from *The Hairy Ape*, they never self-identified as black and they propelled themselves toward social acceptance by forcibly pushing off from the descendants of the slave culture with which they were sometimes deliberately elided. Rogin's summation highlights the ambiguities of American racial construction: "History, not biology, distin-guishes ethnicity from race, making the former groups (in the American usage) distinctive but assimilable, walling off the latter, legally, socially, and ideologically, to benefit those within the magic circle and protect the national body from contamination" (12). Although racial theory, at least until well into the twentieth century, claimed to find "inherent and immutable differences" (12) between racial groups, racial assignments were made inconsistently, almost arbitrarily, first excluding Irish, Jews, and Italians or Sicilians from full-fledged "whiteness," but later revising the constructions of race to make the children of Dublin, Jerusalem, and Palermo eligible to settle in the "white republic."

This set the stage for what Peter Schrag in *Not Fit for Our Society* (2010) calls "the Great Awhitening," which took place in the second quarter of the twentieth century (139–62). Assimilation was conditional, however, requiring that upwardly mobile ethnics give up most of their ancestral identity in order to advance into the privileged circle of whiteness. Through this process, the Eichelbaums turned into the Warner broth-ers, Benny Kubelski became Jack Benny, and Paolo Giuseppe DiMaggio became "Joltin' Joe DiMaggio," sometimes called "the Yankee Clipper." This was the moment when race theory stepped away from the Anglo-Nordic bias of Madison Grant to hesitantly embrace Americans who soon would be called "white ethnics" (139–52). Even the Anglicization of names eventually became optional, although as late as the 1950s, young Allen Konigsberg, still wary of WASP culture, launched his professional career under the Anglicized persona of "Woody Allen."

The reconfiguration of the American racial code, together with the civil rights movement and sweeping changes in national immigration policy, holds implications for the three directors whose work we are about to examine. Considering the films of Scorsese, Allen, and Lee, we find that each of these directors has examined his identity from the standpoint of his own ethno-racial roots, thus observing a particular stage of the assimi-lative process and grasping this process as someone within it, rather than outside of it. All of which gives us a study of the process of ethno-racial integration (Scorsese's Sicilian Italians, as well as his Irish), the outcome of this same process (Allen's almost fully assimilated Jews), and the still-unresolved debate over "assimilation," a deeply suspect term among Lee's African Americans. For particular historical reasons to which we will soon turn, each ethnic group stands in a layered relationship to the others and distinctly separate from other minorities, chiefly Asian and Latino, who are also making a mark on the American social landscape, especially in New York City after the liberalizing immigration reforms. Special contingencies dictate that Lee's African Americans still remain at the bottom of this ethno-racial pyramid, distrustful of the ethnic groups above them in the social hierarchy, and most reluctant to assimilate to a master class that they regard as at odds with their interests. Clearly Schrag's "awhitening" has not altered their pigment enough to relieve their sense of deeper grievances with the hegemonic culture than those exemplified by Scorsese's Sicilians and Allen's Jews.

These three filmmakers have fashioned their art from a special set of social conditions peculiar to the last three decades of the twentieth century. These are decades of paradox in the sense that public discourse of the period features "ethnicity" to an unprecedented degree, while the legal apparatus and macro-economic forces of the time undermine the bases of ethnic distinction, making social hierarchy more decisively dependent upon wealth, education, and class. The comprehensive civil rights legislation of the 1960s, the shift away from ethno-racial quotas in immigration, the post-industrial turn of the US economy, and especially the remarkable upward mobility of several Euro-American minorities (including the Italians and the Jews) are the crucial factors altering the ingredients and temperature of the American melting pot. But these same forces bring forward an exceptional concern for ethnic themes, noteworthy in everything from tabloid journalism to the most erudite scholarly monographs. They also create a film community willing to risk investment capital upon previously tabooed or stereotyped subjects and a film audience eager to explore these subjects as a means of inquiring into their own life worlds. This new frontier in American cinema was soon to be settled by the rising generation of "independent" filmmakers.

For our purposes, the most decisive macrofactor shaping the careers of these three directors (as well as legitimating their trademark themes) was the transformation of the American film industry that took place in the early 1970s. At this time, the Hollywood studios, stung by heavy losses from big budget disasters of the late 1960s, sensed their estrangement from the mass audience they had once taken for granted. In light of new market conditions, they sought fresh talent and alternative business models, which brought into being new production companies, like Miramax (f. 1979) and TriStar (f. 1982). Eventually, the studios reorganized themselves primarily as distributors, subcontracting many of their production costs to independent investors, who would develop their "properties" without studio supervision and would absorb most of the losses if things went wrong. The model proved so serviceable that the studios recovered from the lean 1970s and by the 1990s had made Miramax a sub-directorate of Disney and TriStar an affiliate of the Sony media empire. Early on, however, and through the seventies, there was an exceptional openness to experiment and innovation, which allowed the "Indie" film to take root.

"Indie" is a much-agitated term. Geoffrey King launches his painstaking analysis of independent production by noting that the term is "constantly under question, on a variety of grounds," none of them definitive. Among the considerations that come into play, he names the "industrial location" of the production facilities as well as "lower budgets and less marketing-driven filmmaking." But he also references aesthetic characteristics: "they adopt formal strategies that disrupt or abandon the smoothly flowing conventions associated with the mainstream Hollywood style; and they offer challenging perspectives upon social issues, a rarity in Hollywood" (see King 2005, 1–10). In King's judgment, these "alternative visions," which constitute the "social, political, and ideological dimensions of independent cinema" are more authoritative hallmarks of Indie status than production conditions considered in isolation (197–261).

During the first phase of this corporate transformation, would-be producers and directors reaped benefits from civic institutions that saw film as an important form of urban entrepreneurship. Changes in the federal tax code, particularly the Revenue Act of 1971, supported the restructuring of the film business by allowing a generous 7 percent tax credit on investments in film production. Although this tax advantage was rescinded in 1976, the five-year period of its availability helped media entrepreneurs through a particularly stressful period of reorganization. In New York, the Mayor's Office for Theater, Film, and Broadcasting (f. 1966) also committed itself wholeheartedly to the task of making the Big Apple a more film-friendly city, cutting regulations and facilitating access to the streets and sites of the five boroughs. The other element in the mix was the relaxation of the production code, which allowed a more frank representation of sex and violence than had been possible before the mid-1960s, giving motion pictures an edge in competing with television, which was more rigorously policed in the name of "family entertainment." The downsizing of theaters, whereby the great picture palaces of the studio era gave way to suburban cinema complexes with multiple screens, also made it possible for distributors to serve smaller niche markets while respecting the power of the big-budget blockbuster, which reasserted itself after the spectacular success of Stephen Spielberg's *Jaws* (1975). New art house sites, like the six-screen Lincoln Plaza complex on Manhattan's Upper

West Side, were specifically designed with American Indie product in mind (see Cook 1990, 9–66; Tzioumakis 2006, 167–212).

By the late 1970s, the image industry was ready to reclaim its place as a profitable form of post-industrial enterprise. New production and distribution arrangements also invited partnerships between the older studios with reliable distribution networks and independently owned production houses, like Orion (f. 1978), for which Allen worked almost exclusively throughout the 1980s, and Forty Acres and a Mule Filmworks, founded (1978) and utilized solely by Spike Lee. Scorsese's relationship to the Indie movement is more complicated, since he began making films before these new arrangements had been consolidated. Over the course of his career, he has worked on more cordial terms with the traditional film industry than either Lee or Allen. This point notwithstanding, in terms of an "alternative vision" and with respect to composition and editing, Scorsese has much more in common with Lee and Allen, or even Steve Soderbergh and Jim Jarmusch, than mainline talents like Spielberg and James Cameron. Michael Newman speaks relevantly in *Indie* (2011) when he says, "directors such as Martin Scorsese and Robert Altman," both slightly ahead of the Indie wave, "served as models for many Indie filmmakers" (24).

As the industry meditated upon its new circumstances, product imported from Europe advertised a more personal style of filmmaking, associated with directors like Federico Fellini, Jean-Luc Godard, and Francois Truffaut. Critic Andrew Sarris championed their cause, called them "*auteurs*," and used their example to enhance the prestige of the film director. Suddenly, *The Sound of Music* (1965) no longer seemed the inevitable template of success in the motion picture industry. With new doors opening for young directorial talent, the "film school generation" began to find its way into the profession. Young Martin Scorsese, a newly minted graduate of the New York University film program, was one of the brightest sparks to quickly kindle into full flame. But before this new stylistic mode could gain firm footing, the industry had to lock in place a more reliable business model. Much to the advantage of "ethnic" filmmaking, this was accomplished in Coppola and Puzo's production of *The Godfather*, the blockbuster hit of 1972.

"Multe grazie, Mario Puzo" (127) is Thomas Ferraro's heartfelt tribute to the author/scenarist of *The Godfather* in *Feeling Italian* (2005). This sentiment is misplaced only in the sense that it leans toward the personality cult in heaping all praise upon the author of the novel, when in reality the spectacularly successful film was the result of an opportunistic partnership between Paramount, Puzo, and another ambitious artist of the film school generation, Francis Ford Coppola. Coppola's business instincts were sometimes flawed, but the innovations he introduced into film editing and his streamlining of production teams were more forward-looking and cost-saving than anything that could have originated at Paramount (see Schumacher 1999, 67–86; Lewis 1995, 73–94). Together, the author, the director, and Paramount (principally the production chief, Robert Evans) created the formula for the new megahits of the post-studio era.

In its first week of exhibition *The Godfather* earned 8 million dollars, and by the end of the year, it had put 85 million dollars in the studio's coffers, about 10 percent of all the money earned by the American film industry in 1972. The publicity also foregrounded ethnicity, though the producers formally disclaimed references to the "Mafia" or "Cosa Nostra," assuring viewers that "no special connection with any group or subgroup is intended or should be inferred" (Ferraro 2005, 120). This concession sufficed to quiet the protests of the Italian American Civil Rights League and allowed the film to gain the advantage of its appeal to the mainstream culture's newfound interest in "off-white" ethnicity, particularly by way of its celebration of the extended family. That interest, it seems fair to say, was spurred in the early 1970s by widespread disenchantment with the national culture, expressed as suspicion of federal leadership and mounting resistance to the war in Indo-China. In the first scene of *The Godfather*, when the Don is asked by one of the ethnic underlings in the neighborhood for violent justice outside of statute law, Corleone's positive response resonated with a vigilante spirit that went well beyond the Sicilian clan.

Greatly less favored, but lifted by a rising tide, Scorsese profited remarkably from the success of *The Godfather*. According to his own account, his first efforts to secure funding for *Mean Streets* (1973) enjoyed little success. Though his friend John Cassavetes (another forefather of the Indie movement) had urged him to draw inspiration from his own experience, to chronicle what it was like to grow up in Little Italy, the American Film Institute had declined to support "Season of the Witch," the first version of *Mean Streets*. His mentor and adviser from NYU, Craig Manoogian, had dismissed his ethnic interests even more bluntly: "Hey, nobody wants to see films about Italian Americans" (Brunette 1999, 21). But this changed materially after Coppola had demonstrated that vividly imagined ethnics, especially when anchored to the romantic image of the gangster, could bring crowds of patrons to the box office. *Mean Streets*, of course, very little resembled *The Godfather* and never attracted an audience that in any way approached Coppola's numbers. Far from being a blockbuster, it became the model of the niche film that holds a much more modest place in the new Hollywood. But with its seeming kinship to Don Corleone's filmic family, Scorsese's project attracted enough investment to be viable, including a buy-in from the rock music promoter Jonathan Taplin, who brought at least one other large investor with him. Roger Corman, a master of low-budget production, supplied resources and technical assistance at bargain basement prices, and Warner Brothers was persuaded to act as distributor. In an earlier era, this studio had been associated with the edginess of film noir and more recently had marketed the genre-bending "gangster film" *Bonnie and Clyde* (1969). Reluctantly, Scorsese allowed *Mean Streets* to be stereotyped as "a junior Mafia picture" (Brunette 1999, 29) when it premiered in 1973 at the New York Film Festival. However ill defined, the "ethnic film" was now part of American artistic discourse and free to evolve in various directions.

III

In the cases of Scorsese, Allen, and Lee, this discourse evolved in keeping with a paradigm of assimilation articulated succinctly by Karen Brodkin in *How Jews Became White Folks* (1998). In this monograph she argues that, in the dialectic of ethno-racial advancement, "cultural capital" is played off against "racial taint" to establish the conditions under which a disadvantaged minority will be invited to emerge from its ghetto of social and psychic exclusion. Brodkin applies her template to two generations of twentieth-century American Jewry, noting that American Jews, especially the Jews of New York City, brought the most cultural capital to the bargaining table. Hence they became, along with the Irish, the City's most fully assimilated minority. Woody Allen's films study the consequences of this assimilative process, noting the price paid as well as the advantages gained, a price that may well include, at least implicitly, the obligation to guide and restrain less favored minorities. Scorsese's Italian-Sicilians are the next to assimilate and thus, in contrast to Allen, they provide us with the opportunity to see assimilation as a very gradual progress and one that acknowledges the power of the tribe to hold on to its own. Here Scorsese risks a hint of anachronism in flagship films like *Raging Bull* (1980), *GoodFellas* (1990), and *Casino* (1995), because he locates "the Italian experience" in a time frame about one generation removed from time present, the world of the forties, fifties, and sixties, rather than the decades of his own maturity. African Americans have proved the least disposed to assimilate, partly because the taint of slavery clings to them and partly because other disadvantaged minorities have moved themselves forward at African Americans' expense. In some instances, as reported by Lee in films like *Malcolm X* (1992), African Americans have more actively resisted assimilation, insisting on the claims of their own culture and their independent identity.

Two iconic books of the mid-1960s set the stage for the assimilative patterns we find dramatized in the films of Scorsese, Allen, and Lee. One of them, Milton Gordon's *Assimilation in American Life: The Role of Race,*

Religion and National Origin (1964), details the process of assimilation in its classical phase (from 1790 to 1964), when this term generally signified "Anglo-conformity," the expectation that the immigrant would adopt the language, dress, manners, and social habits of the majoritarian Anglo-Nordic culture, presumed to be the ethno-racial stock of the Founding Fathers, the authentic "100% Americans." (see, particularly, Gordon 1964, 84–114). The second work, Nathan Glazer and Daniel P. Moynihan's *Beyond the Melting Pot: The Negroes, Puerto Ricans, Jews, Italians, and Irish of New York City* (1963), makes a perfect companion piece to Gordon's argument, in no sense rebutting it, but undertaking to imagine how this assimilation paradigm might be projected into the foreseeable future. Though both books now seem seriously culture-bound (chiefly because the 1965 Immigration Act erased the ethno-racial quotas, shaking the system to its foundations), for exactly that reason each work provides a privileged window upon the turbulent 1960s, the first summing up past practices respecting assimilation, the second hesitantly speculating about the further products to be wrought from Zangwill's problematic "melting pot."

Writing in 1964, Gordon observed that, historically, most immigrants arriving before 1850 came from Northern Europe and resembled the original ethno-racial stock, while newcomers from the 1870s and after left behind homelands in Eastern and Southern Europe. The first group acculturated to their new homes largely without difficulty, the Irish constituting the only significant exception to that norm. It was otherwise with the later arrivals, chiefly Catholics from Poland and Italy, and Jews from Russia and the Ukraine. They clung to old world habits and resisted "assimilation," however it might be defined. During this century-long period, says Gordon, somewhat apologetically, the expectation was that the immigrants would adopt "the cultural patterns that have taken their major impress from the mold of the overwhelmingly English character of the dominant Anglo-Saxon culture or subculture in America, whose dominion dates from colonial times and whose cultural domination in the United States has never been seriously threatened" (1964, 73). Concisely put, they would be required to embrace the norm of "Anglo-Conformity." When they did not, this reluctance to be completely absorbed by the hegemonic class provoked the increasingly more insistent cry to curb immigration, particularly the intrusion of ethno-racial undesirables, like the Irish, the Jews, and the Southern Italians. The more flexible response, however, was to relax these cultural expectations, a turn of mind that encourages Gordon to sketch out two further models of assimilation—the "melting pot" and the practice of "cultural pluralism."

"Was it not possible," Gordon asks, "to think of the evolving American society not simply as a slightly modified England but rather as a totally new blend, culturally and biologically, in which the stocks and folkways of Europe were, figuratively speaking, indiscriminately mixed in the political pot of the emerging nation and melted together by the fires of American influence and interaction into a distinctly new type?" (1964, 115). Gordon's answer, like Zangwill's, was a resonant "yes." But the melting pot was susceptible to various interpretations, one in which "the melting pot concept may envisage the culture of immigrants as 'melting' completely into the host society without leaving any cultural trace at all" (125). Finding this outcome unsatisfactory, Gordon hurries on to propose a third model, which he calls "cultural pluralism." In this construction of the immigrant experience, "an approach to the immigrant which was sympathetic to his native cultural heritage and to his newly created ethnic institutions" (137), the goal of the assimilative process was a blending of cultures that allowed the newly minted American to maintain at least a modicum of the identity he had formed under the influence of his own culture. From this set of assumptions comes the ethnic church, the ethnic school, the ethnic neighborhood, the newspaper published in Yiddish, the Catholic Recreation Center, and the saint's image carried aloft in an Italianate street procession. Clearly, the pluralist model is the one Gordon is most eager to recommend, provided it does not encroach upon personal identity nor interfere with "the carrying out of standard responsibilities to the general American civic life" (158).

This seems the right moment to put the assimilation narrative in the hands of Glazer and Moynihan, whose *Beyond the Melting Pot: The Negroes, Puerto Ricans, Jews, Italians, and Irish of New York City* (1963) was published a year earlier than Gordon's *Assimilation*, but with the same fundamental concerns. What do these racialized cultural outsiders turn into? And under what circumstances? And within what time frame? Glazer and Moynihan deal much more concretely with specific ethnic groups, adding African Americans and Puerto Ricans to their account of American subcultures, even though they are technically not immigrants. With considerable acuity, they build a paradigm of acculturation that actually plays itself out over the next several decades, as they "trace the role of ethnicity in the tumultuous, varied, endlessly complex life of New York City" (xcvii). Though there is no hint of direct inspiration or influence, Scorsese, Allen, and Lee read the ethno-racial history of New York City very much in the same terms as Glazer and Moynihan.

Observing the New York of that particular historical moment, Glazer and Moynihan found it reasonable to fasten upon these particular minorities, because they were the dominant subgroups of the time. Furthermore, the Irish, the Jews, the Italians, the Puerto Ricans and the African Americans arranged themselves as a kind of hierarchy, almost like stair steps on the staircase of assimilation. Hence, though they called their work a "beginning book," they felt correctly positioned to "apply a higher level of intellectual effort and scholarly attention . . . to the persistence of ethnic ties in American society, a phenomenon that had not been forecast and had to be explained" (1963, lxxii). Ethno-racial identity, especially when reinforced by language, religion, custom, and the institutional structures which perform ethno-racial assignment, had proved much more durable than Zangwill's metaphor of the melting pot would suggest. That prompted these authors to explain why this was so and what countervailing forces would be required to move the assimilative process forward.

First of all, there is the template of the model minority, here the Irish and the Jews. Glazer and Moynihan treat the assimilation of the Irish as a *fait accompli,* though a cultural transformation charged with great historical significance. The Irish arrived, scorned and slovenly, after the famine of the 1840s, burdened by racialized Celtic stereotypes it took more than a generation to cast off. Were the despised Irish capable of anything beyond fighting, drinking, and womanizing? Yes, say Glazer and Moynihan, "by degrees the Irish style of the gaslight era became less and less Irish, more and more the style of the American city" (1963, 246). The authors point out that, "when the movies began to fashion a composite picture of the American people, the New York Irishman was projected to the very center of the national image" (246). What intervened, they conclude, was the Irish genius for politics, which first declared itself in the era of Tweed, when Irish power was constellated in the urban police force, but came forward to culminate in the presidency of John Kennedy, nearly a century later. By that later moment, "Irishness had come to represent some of the qualities the honest yeoman stood for in an earlier age, notably an undertone of toughness and practicality" (250). Both Scorsese and Lee, when they invoke Irish culture, adhere closely to this description.

For Glazer and Moynihan, the Jews represent a more complicated case, but perhaps for that reason provide a fuller paradigm of the assimilative process. Because the racial taint clung to them longer and English was not their native tongue, this group was obliged to push harder against structures of prejudice that denied them their rightful place. Yet "around the world, wherever they went, the Jews of Eastern Europe became in large proportions businessmen" (Glazer and Moynihan 1963, 143). Their relative economic success allowed them to indulge "a fierce passion to have their children educated and become professionals" (143). Thus "Jewish boys separate themselves from their playmates and devote themselves to studies, heading for the academic and specialized high schools" (145–46). This "passion for education that was unique in American history" (155) worked in conjunction with the tightly knit Jewish family to acculturate children who became almost ideally equipped to thrust themselves forward. This same family, however, and the array of community institutions that were also an integral part of Jewish culture discouraged marriage outside the Jewish world and conserved neighborhoods that were self-ghettoized. These impulses fostered the prevailing impression that the Jews were clannish and self-serving, disinclined to support the agendas of a larger "American" society. Quoting Erich Rosenthal, a Jewish sociologist, Glazer and Moynihan sum things up this way: "the basic function of Jewish education is to implant Jewish self-consciousness rather than Judaism, to 'inoculate' the next generation with that minimum of religious practice and belief that is considered necessary to keep alive a level of Jewish self-consciousness that will hold the line against assimilation" (164).

These upward-striving minorities are played off in contrast to less successful ethnic cultures, specifically the Italians, the Puerto Ricans, and the African Americans. Of these, the Italians stand highest on the rungs of success by virtue of their work ethic and their respect for family. But Italian culture is bedeviled by "amoral familism," the view that "one owes nothing to anyone outside one's family, and effort should advance only the family" (Glazer and Moynihan 1963, 195). Continuing, Glazer and Moynihan note that "the Italian family in some ways resembles the Jewish family in its strength, its heightened and uninhibited emotional quality, and even in some of its inner alliances" (197). But what is missing is the commitment to education and the impulse toward individual achievement. The consequence of this thinking, these authors argue, is a concept of success that anchors the individual to family and neighborhood, like a storefront lawyer or a family physician who lives within walking distance of the homes where he makes his house calls. These attitudes disadvantaged the Italian community in politics because "they had relatively few men of wealth and education," fewer still who were not "implicated in relations with underworld figures" (209). While "Jewish parents can be gratified symbolically by the accomplishment of a son who may be removed and even indifferent to them," South Italy was ruled by the proverb, "Do not make your child better than you are" (198–99).

If Italian ethnics failed for want of education, the Puerto Rican and African American communities were doubly disadvantaged because they lacked both education and a cohesive sense of family. Naturally, these were not personal faults, inhering in "race" or defective genes. They harked back to history, where sociologists like Franklin Frazier had "traced the history of the family, from slavery, to the Southern post-slavery situation, to the Northern city" (Glazer and Moynihan 1963, 52). The conclusion was clear: "There was no marriage in the slave family—husbands could be sold away from wives, children from parents. There was no possibility of taking responsibility for one's children, for one had in the end no power over them. One could not educate them, nor even, in many cases discipline them" (52). And the further tragedy was that "what slavery began, prejudice and discrimination, affecting jobs, hous-ing, self-respect, have continued to keep alive among many, many colored Americans" (52). From this history flows "the large mass of problems that are high up on the agenda of city government and civic groups—crime, delinquency, the breakdown of family responsibility" (83).

In the twenty-first century, *Beyond the Melting Pot* seems conspicuously dated, since it makes no mention of the Caribbean Latinos who now fill the far corners of Brooklyn and Queens, or the Korean green-grocers who peer out from storefronts throughout the five boroughs, much less the Eastern European crime syndicates, which play a major role in the city's drug trade. But for this very reason the book is a window upon the imaginative worlds of Scorsese, Allen, and Lee, as they emerge in the 1970s, then develop and transform themselves during the decades to fol-low. In the new millennium, all three directors would set new courses for themselves, leaving ethnic New York to a new generation of immigrants, who would contend with assimilation in terms of their own quite dif-ferent culture codes and the tensions these codes put in play. But at that moment when the favorite ethnics of Glazer and Moynihan were at the center of the bubbling cauldron, these directors forged a new cinematic language to define and describe the contentious, interactive struggle for full-fledged integration into the national culture.

This new language is my last theoretical reference point. In *Caliban's Voice: The Transformation of English in Post-Colonial Literatures* (2009), Bill Ashcroft argues that post-colonial writers like Salman Rushdie and Chi-nua Achebe have had to repurpose the "voice" of English in order to free it from Western imperialism and make it a fit vehicle to express the new cultural identities they would celebrate in India and Africa, respectively. In a similar fashion, these three New York directors, recognizing the apt moment when the studio system collapsed, took the new environment of independent filmmaking as the occasion to fashion new cinematic "voices," more conducive to express the nuances of ethnicity, as we find them in *Mean Streets*, or *Annie Hall* (1977), or *Do the Right Thing* (1989).

This new voice entails much more than attaching a positive valence to figures who had previously been apprehended negatively. Though both are professional gangsters, Paulie Cicero of Scorsese's *GoodFellas* is an entirely different character from Johnny Rocco of *Key Largo* (1946), a difference in some measure related to the fact that Paulie is played by Paul Sorvino, an ethnic Italian, and Rocco by Edward G. Robinson, a Romanian Jew. But in the imagery as well, there is masterful detail in the handling of Paulie: The delicacy with which he slices a clove of garlic is worlds removed from the violent bluster of Johnny Rocco. Similarly, Flipper Purify (Wesley Snipes), Lee's racially conflicted romantic lover of *Jungle Fever* (1991), is conceived in a different dimension from John

Prentice (Sidney Poitier) of *Guess Who's Coming to Dinner?* (1967), even though in this latter film Hollywood attempted to create a positive portrait of the black male and give a sympathetic hearing to the subject of interracial marriage. Allen's Jews are a slightly more complicated case, since they evolve from Jewish stereotypes within the Jewish comic community. But here too we find resonances beyond *borscht belt* humor, as for example in *Play It Again, Sam* (1972), where the Yiddish *schlemiel* takes lessons in masculinity from the "white" tough-guy Humphrey Bogart. Both are caricatures from the world of popular culture, but the white stereotype is the prevailing trope of mainstream culture while the *schlemiel* is a stereotype from within the minority culture. Allen's use of one stereotype to provide a role model for another affirms the Zangwill parable of assimilation, but preserves the distance between the Jew and Gentile, making it clear that assimilation is a self-conscious act which embodies some risk taking, while promising conspicuous rewards.

My argument throughout the following chapters holds that individual self-fashioning within the ethno-racial community continually asserts itself against social assignment that is imposed from above by the hegemonic class. By which I mean, the cultural aliens of Scorsese, Allen, and Lee bring a skill set and an adaptive potential into a pre-structured, sometimes hostile social world. That world spurs their development in one direction or another, more on the basis of opportunity than through chosen purpose. All three filmmakers construct models of assimilation that fit particular historical circumstances and challenge their protagonists in singular ways. Many are shape-shifters, like the protagonist of Allen's *Zelig* (1983), who feels an irresistible compulsion to transform himself upon contact with every alien environment he encounters. We are told that Zelig is descended from a Yiddish actor who made his reputation playing Puck, the archetype of all chameleons, in *A Midsummer Night's Dream*. Allen's absurdist hero is Puck's spiritual son. Zelig personifies the assimilating ethnic: he is a baseball player when he turns up at the Yankees' spring training camp and a Nazi when he briefly affiliates with Hitler's Third Reich. It is almost as if he had an assimilationist gene, triggered by various circumstances. Although he is sometimes the victim of ethnic slurs, or worse ("Let's just lynch the little Hebe"), he eventually assimilates fully into the hegemonic class, loving and marrying a non-Jewish professional woman. After several false starts, he "performs" whiteness well enough to pass for white. That behavior is typical of most of Allen's protagonists, who consciously leave their Jewishness behind.

The outcome is quite different for the protagonists of Spike Lee. Because of historical disadvantage and continuing racial prejudice, Lee's African American characters find it nearly impossible to imitate the example of Zelig, or any one of several others from Allen's imaginative world.

Hence Malcolm Little, aka Minister Malcolm X, despairs of making common cause with white America and steps back into "black nationalism" buttressed by the ideology of Islam. One of Lee's most tragic characters is Pierre Delacroix of *Bamboozled* (2000). He has fabricated a French name and an almost self-parodic prestige accent to facilitate his career as a television writer-director. At one moment of absolute alienation from his own community, he tells his closest associate, "I don't want to hear about anything black for at least a week." Nor does he lack talent and creative energy. But negotiating the world beyond the racial divide proves impossible, ultimately lethal. As the token black creative artist for a national news and entertainment network, he is effectively denied control of his own productions, which are shaped by the intervention of editors or consultants and the framing apparatus of the advertising industry.

Half a century of ethno-racial filmmaking makes it possible to discern a pattern that is common to the work of these several directors. Guided by their rich experience of a truly multicultural city, they have devoted their careers to dramatizing the assimilative process, never hesitating to remark the pain and violence of intercultural conflict or the powerful undercurrent that sucks the individual back into the world of the tribe. In the films of Scorsese and Allen, issues of ethnic identity are gradually eclipsed, as characters cease to be Italians or Jews, and become instead generic "Americans."

Lee's African Americans remain more resolutely separate, because of resistance and suspicion on both sides of the racial divide. But here too we find some inclination to work within the integrationist model. Both Lee and his characters have begun to imagine a more hybridized selfhood, reflected particularly when this filmmaker ventures to the margins and edges of raciality, shown—for example—in the Puerto Rican heroine of *25th Hour* (2002) or the fictive "white" self of the black detective who infiltrates the Ku Klux Klan in *BlacKkKlansman* (2018).

Ironically, we also see in the work of these three filmmakers that specific minorities may advance themselves without energizing a more general progress, in fact, sometimes at the expense of other marginalized ethnics (East European, Russian, Southeast Asian, Caribbean, and Mexican) who remain seriously disadvantaged and conspicuously unwelcome. But if there is no magic carpet, so also is there no impermeable barrier. What the collective achievement of Scorsese, Allen, and Lee advertises, with vivid imagery that lingers in memory, is the continuing struggle for equity and acceptance in a nation that remains deeply conflicted in its response to ethnicity and race.

ONE

Martin Scorsese

In *Gangster Priest* (2006), the magisterial inquiry into what he subtitles "the Italian American cinema of Martin Scorsese," Robert Casillo emphasizes the filmmaker's determination in his breakthrough film, *Mean Streets*, to "document the Italian American subculture as it then existed in Manhattan's Lower East side," the neighborhood he knew from his childhood and early adolescence with his parents on Elizabeth Street (180). Casillo also does the good service of representing Scorsese as a "third-generation Italian American artist," a vantage point which left him close enough to convey the feel and texture of this world but with enough distance to take the measure of its rapid transformation during the decades after he left his childhood home (56–68).

Considering this longer arc of Scorsese's development, we might want to add the perspective of Fred Gardaphe, who stresses the aspirational dimension of Italian American culture he describes in *From Wiseguys to Wise Men: The Gangster and Italian American Masculinities* (2006). Gardaphe's analysis takes account of the violence of ethnic culture but recognizes the broader horizons of the post–World War II period that allowed New York's Italianate citizens to look beyond family and neighborhood toward career paths closer to the mainstream of American commercial and professional life. His last chapters celebrate "new directions in Italian American-manhood" that call for "redesigning the ethnic male" (171–214). Correctly, he places Scorsese somewhere in the middle of this continuum of development, a director who declines to "romance" the gangster, à la Mario Puzo and Francis Ford Coppola, but who sees Italian males simply as "rough boys," in rather the same fashion as Gay Talese and Michael Cimino. Although the protagonists of *Mean Streets, Raging Bull, GoodFellas*, and *Casino* are not highly evolved specimens of the new American male, Scorsese does represent them as subliminally aware of a world beyond the ghetto, a world where Jake LaMotta can escape the boxing ring into a career as a performance artist and Nicky Santoro can imagine himself as a crime boss in Las Vegas. In addition to accurately reporting on the daily life of Little Italy in *Mean Streets*, Scorsese's more complex purpose is to convey the tension between the security of the ethnic clan and the promise of a richer, but far more risk-ridden world beyond the neighborhood.

In terms of its production, *Mean Streets* is a poster-child example of what the culture critic Mikhail Bakhtin calls a "heteroglossic text": it literally speaks with many tongues. A generation ago, Robert Stam in *Subversive Pleasures* (1989) demonstrated the relevance of Bakhtin to film studies, when he proposed "mass-media heteroglossia" as a valuable phrase to describe the conflicted relationship between the information/entertainment cartels (such as Warner Brothers) and the individual creative voices these institutions invite to speak in their name. As Stam would have it, the motion picture industry is "corporate controlled but pressured by popular desire and dependent upon 'politically unreliable' creative talent to satisfy the inexhaustible need for programming" (220). Which means Scorsese and his creative team had no intention to serve corporate interests but were obliged to create a narrative that fit broadly within the studio's marketing formula, a formula probably no more specific than a decision to depict alienated youth, flirting with violence. Such a picture might tap into the success *of Bonnie and Clyde* (1967) or Columbia Pictures' equally sensational *Easy Rider* (1969), a film that Warner Brothers had helped to distribute overseas. From Warner Brothers' standpoint, the ethnic inflection would seem redundant, but acceptable in light of Coppola's box office triumph with *The Godfather*. In fact, ethnicity might add a competitive touch of "difference." This is the premise from which Stam argues that the cinema offers a forum both to "the voices of hegemony and to the contestatory voices that are muffled or suppressed" (221), always a "plurality of voices that do not fuse into a single consciousness but exist on different registers, generating dialogical dynamism among themselves" (229).

What exactly was this curious body of images that Scorsese and his creative cohorts had placed on the American screen in *Mean Streets*? Its chief protagonist dressed like a gangster but talked like a neurotic seminarian. The actors (Robert De Niro, Harvey Keitel, Amy Robinson) brought with them no high-profile reputations that might cause us to imagine them as *dramatis personae* of a certain stripe. All the action was interwoven into the San Gennaro Festival, a defining ritual of Little Italy, but the characters who mix with the celebrants have no relationship to the Festival or its Catholic pieties. Moreover, the available-light camera work, the abrupt transitions, and the improvised dialogue were seriously at odds with studio precedent. Its shape and substance define the features of what would come to be called "the Independent film."

Mean Streets was also markedly different from ethnic films that had come before. Let one example suffice: in Sidney Lumet's *The Pawn Broker*

(1965), ethnicity is represented as a "problem" (the impact of the Holocaust upon the psychology of an elderly Jew). In *Mean Streets*, ethnicity is not a problem; it is a way of life. This turn toward ethnic subcultures across the spectrum of American awareness has proved central to the creative lives of Scorsese, Allen, and Lee. With active support from a city eager to make film production a vital part of its new, post-industrial economy, they (and others) have imaginatively transformed metropolitan New York into a chronotope of ethnic striving in the late twentieth and early twenty-first centuries. As represented by these filmmakers, the city world is dense, polyvalent, and highly dynamic, not simply in its ever-changing look but, more importantly, dynamic in its representation of the shades and nuances of ethnicity.

SEGMENT 1: FROM THE ETHNIC NEST TO THE DYSTOPIC CITY:
MEAN STREETS (1973) AND *TAXI DRIVER* (1976)

Travis Bickle, the lost soul at the center of *Taxi Driver*, sums up his tragic narrative by admitting, "Loneliness has followed me my whole life—everywhere" (53:10/53:20). As Ellis Cashmore (2009) frames lower Manhattan from Travis' perspective, "cities are terrifying places, teeming with immoral and malevolent fiends who prey on unsuspecting innocents after dark" (77). For some, this estrangement from family, community, and human kinship is the essence of the modern, urban experience, which impels the sons and daughters of the secular city to seek a means of belonging, some way to attach themselves to a social unit beyond the self. In the case of various ethnic cultures, that social network is usually supplied by a sense of shared roots, the memory of a cohesive community that was available and operative in another land or an earlier generation. As early as Upton Sinclair's *The Jungle* (1906), the Lithuanian protagonist Jurgis Rudkus perceives the meat-packing world of Chicago as "a seething cauldron of jealousies and hatreds," without "loyalty or decency anywhere" (70). In his embittered isolation, Jurgis recalls the traditional *veselija*, the village wedding festival of his native land, where neighbors and extended family shared the costs of the feast and enjoyed the social solidarity of the occasion as they danced and drank with the bride and groom. This attraction to an older world and a lost time is what prompts many first-generation immigrants to cling to their ethnic identity. Without completely endorsing this retreat from modernity, Matthew Jacobson (2006) sympathizes with the large number of immigrants who "seize and celebrate the hyphen" as their access to a protective subculture (16).

The Italian community is certainly well acquainted with this trope of cultural yearning. In song, story, and on the screen, we find alienated protagonists who long for a simpler, more ethnically oriented world. One of the classical Italian immigrant narratives is Pietro Di Donato's *Christ in Concrete* (1939): it sets up New York City as "a country of Babel where Christians are beginning to wander about in hungry distress cursing each other in strange tongues" (278). In the "steel stone hives . . . of the New Babylon" (285), only the bonds of family, obliquely supported by residual faith in the Catholic Church, sustain Geremio, his wife Annunziata, and their eldest son Paul against the brutality and cynicism and of the dystopic metropolis. Donato's narrative embraces two generations, which allows us to see the family's increasing estrangement from formal Catholicism and increasing anxiety in confronting a de-sacralized world. Geremio, the *pater familias*, works exhaustively at a low-paying construction job, but he complains little because "the good Christ was crucified" (13), showing the valor with which a Christian should face suffering. Later, his wife and son remember Geremio's "delight in listening to the glorious High Mass" and "the ceremonies dedicated to the Lord Christ up front on the Sacred Altar" (125). Unfortunately, Geremio's faith does not protect him from a fatal accident, which occurs on Good Friday and is represented as a hideously parodic Crucifixion. When the building he is working on collapses, Geremio is impaled on metal rods in a grotesque posture that visually suggests a victim nailed to a cross. Being told that "his blood vessels burst like smashed flower stems" (30), we understand the theme of blood sacrifice that gives a particularly Italian inflection to Di Donato's narrative.

The crucial point is that there is nothing redemptive or restorative in Geremio's blood sacrifice. His widow is unable to collect compensation, the family loses its home, and the favorite son Paul can no longer accept Catholic belief. When Annunziata forces him back to Saint Prisca's Church, "he felt a dread." Alienated from the familiar rituals, "he became acutely alive to the strangeness of the ceremony, the candles and press of Christian faces, the faces and wings of the statues, . . . the convolutions of mass, the torment of incantations, . . . and nausea assaulted his bowels, breast, and brain" (299). Paul crushes the plaster crucifix that spiritually sustains his mother. But mother, son, and family remain united in Annunziata's remembrance of rural Italy and the exciting Tarantella she once danced with her husband during the matrimonial feast in their native village. Like Scorsese in the next generation, Di Donato honors the *via vecchia*, the old path that embodies the folk spirituality of southern Italy.

If it seems strange to imagine the Tarantella as a viable surrogate for the "incantations" of Catholic ceremony, this is from lack of acquaintance with the supremely popular *festas*—village festivals that dominated public streets and squares, quasi-religious rituals that typically paid homage to a local saint, but mixed churchly devotion with dancing, drinking, and music. Discussing them in the context of "Italian folk religiosity," Salvatore Primeggia (2004) sees these emotionally charged street festivals as one of the strongest ties connecting Italian immigrant culture to its old world roots and reinforcing the internal bonds within the ethnic diaspora (15–39). "Seeking to maintain their village customs," says Primeggia, "the Italians who came to America directed much of their religious devotion, fervor, and energy to feasts honoring a particular patron saint or Madonna" (31). Nowhere were these more important than in New York's Little Italy, especially along Mulberry Street, the focal point of devotion to San Gennaro, aka Saint Januarius, the martyred bishop and patron saint of Naples. To a culture that was never remarkably attuned to the Catholic religious hierarchy (particularly the US Catholic hierarchy, which was predominately Irish), the *festas* were an alternative form of worship, built not so much upon theological precept as upon homage to various *santos miraculantes*, wonder-working saints like San Gennaro, whose followers carried his icon through the public streets to advertise his redemptive influence upon the Christian community.

In keeping with Scorsese's sense that *Mean Streets* is "anthropology— that idea of how people live, what they ate, how they dressed" (Smith and Scorsese 1998, 3), the San Gennaro Festival provides the scaffolding that sustains the narrative of *Mean Streets*. Like all rituals of blood, this homage to a beheaded bishop should be restorative and regenerative, all the more so because the myth that inspires the festival celebrates a saint whose blood, according to the legend, liquefies and becomes "fresh" during the days set aside to honor his memory. But in *Mean Streets*, the *festa* fails to fulfill its redemptive function. By the end of the film, the three young protagonists are all drenched with their own blood, but none is cleansed, saved, or renewed by the blood sacrifice of San Gennaro, nor by the Suffering Christ who stands behind him. By virtue of their clan and their neighborhood, they live and move within the ambiance of the Festival, but they are alienated from whatever spiritual influence it might still exert. Charlie Cappa (Harvey Keitel), the most reflective of the lead characters, knows that the Church has failed him and that his salvation must be found "in the streets." But the saint who guards these streets has lost his redemptive efficacy. Represented by his bargain basement icon, as he is carried through the streets of Little Italy, he stares blankly at the crowd with glass eyes that do not comprehend.

Anthropologist Victor Turner's analysis of ritual, what he calls its "liminoid" potential, is helpful here in understanding the way that Scorsese invokes the San Gennaro Festival. Transformed in the 1970s, when the quasi-autonomous ghetto of Little Italy began to dissolve under the pressure of social mobility and a more diverse demographic, the San Gennaro *festa* of *Mean Streets* is a failed ritual, no longer capable of sacralizing the neighborhood the saint spiritually guards. In his work on *Celebration: Studies in Festivity and Ritual* (1982), Victor Turner contrasts the rituals of primal peoples, which exclusively reference the customs and symbols of the tribe, with the more polyvalent rituals of modern urban culture, which open up to a wider range of symbolic reference, as do Rio's Carnival or Pasadena's Rose Parade (11–30). More specifically, he observes that the latter sort of festive occasion is particularly common in the United States, where under the influence of the Puritan tradition "sacredness was interiorized" and "the Word was to be heard, not the icon or the image seen" (13). Given this frame of reference, the national culture made little place for "objects originating in religious celebrations," like "altars and their equipment, sacramentals, vestments, and other religious articles" (13). The only exceptions were "the adornments characteristic of the religious culture of immigrant minority groups now permanently residing in the United States" (13).

Carrying this point another step, Roger Abrams in a further essay on "The Language of Festivals" (1982) remarks how these rival traditions might collide, as the secular begins to erode and displace the sacred. At this tensive intersection point, the procession morphs into a street parade, the religious icons give way to banners and effigies, sacred song dissolves into band music and street dancing: "The techniques of observance remain the same, but their messages are launched into different contexts and therefore come to mean something very different to us. We continue to draw on the same vocabularies . . . by dancing, by moving together in procession or parade, by drawing on objects and actions which are heavily layered with cultural and historical messages" (163). But now they are without the cohesive meaning they had in a particular religious tradition. Hence the liminoid capacity of the ritual is lost: It fails to negotiate the threshold that would allow its devotees to assimilate the new forces, which now pose a challenge.

What we see in *Mean Streets* is that the San Gennaro parade/procession has lost most of its ethnic religiosity, entertaining crowds that have no interest in the saint's miraculous powers and taking on the characteristics of a neighborhood block party. Outsiders turn up from the suburbs, hoping to coax the homeboys out of some part of their drug stash. We also know from information about the production that Scorsese himself came to the scene as an outsider, on cordial terms with neither the city of New York nor the Catholic Church. For reasons of cost and access, the filmmaker did most of the shooting in Los Angeles, turning his camera on the streets of New York only sporadically, catching crucial details of the Festival, only here and there, on an improvised, ad hoc basis. The camera that follows Charlie Cappa down Mulberry Street is as little engaged with San Gennaro as Charlie himself. According to Johnny Boy (Robert De

Niro), the *festa* is an irrelevance, an intrusion upon his personal business, whatever that might be. "I hate that feast with a passion," he says, "you can't move in your own neighborhood." While the camera swoops down from a stone-faced Christ who has lost contact with his flock, Johnny Boy and several companions drive off to settle a grievance with neighborhood rivals (Scorsese 2004b, 27:05/27:15). But the failure of San Gennaro's ritualistic power leaves them open to the convulsive energy of modernism. In the last scene of the film, when Charlie, Johnny Boy, and Teresa are trying to flee the city, they are almost as completely alone as Travis Bickle.

Remarking upon "Screening the Italian-American Male" (2001), Baker and Vitullo scold Scorsese (and others) for "emphasizing a masculinized version of Italian-American identity" (213). They complain that "this image of Italian-Americanness calcified at a time when most Italian-Americans had already moved into middle class suburban spaces and sent their children to learn survival skills at universities rather than through fistfights and gunplay" (213). Mistakenly, say Baker and Vitullo, Scorsese's films "depict Italian-American ethnicity as a timeless identity, characterized by a seemingly stable form of masculinity" (213). But this is precisely what Scorsese doesn't do. In fact, he would surely agree with Siri Johnson's point that "machismo" is a destructive force, because its "rules of masculinity are too rigid for a full human being to emerge from the body of a man" (1994, 95). As much as Baker and Vitullo, Scorsese is aware that many Italian Americans, like himself, for example, become lawyers, paramedics, air traffic controllers, and even film directors. But he turns imaginatively to evoke what remains of the lower Manhattan ghetto because it is a world he vividly remembers from adolescence through early adulthood. And this memory is perhaps the more powerful because his family once moved to the suburbs to escape Little Italy, then was plunged back into that crowded and fretful environment when serious financial reversals forced them out of their suburban home. These facts notwithstanding, Scorsese's model of that ghetto is highly dynamic, always mindful that the world of the *festa* is a world in rapid transition. The gangster culture that is represented not just in *Mean Streets* but also in *Raging Bull* (1980), *GoodFellas* (1990), and *Casino* (1995) is a radically unstable culture, crumbling before our eyes, like the gambling palaces that are blown to rubble in the last moments of *Casino*. What Scorsese catches expertly is the impulse to hold on to the psychic security of the closely knit ethnic unit as its sons and daughters confront the frightening openness of modernity.

At the outset of *Mean Streets*, we can see that the feast of the saint, though it frames the film, has no power over the central characters, nor much relevance to the larger city. The icons are displayed in public space, garishly lit but still unimpressive, with nothing about them to suggest how they might be instruments of personal or social redemption. The lighted arches, which extend over several blocks of the neighborhood, convey a sense of enclosure. Their architecture is intended to turn the street into an analogue of the cathedral nave, suggesting the effort to sacralize these spaces, to insulate Little Italy from whatever sinister forces might impinge upon it from the larger city. Viewed at close range and with the compaction of planes that the telephoto composition achieves, the lights shine vividly and briefly the arches seem like an authentic spiritual canopy (Scorsese 2004b, 03:30/03:50). But later in the film, as if Scorsese intends to cast doubt upon the saint's contemporary relevance, we see the same scene from a much greater distance. Now the canopy has been reduced to a tiny ribbon of light, a slight flicker almost lost in an otherwise dark city, which is simply unaware of Saint Januarius (01:29:25/01:29:35). At no time do the protagonists show any interest in the ceremonies. We first meet Charlie in the parish church, but he is wrestling with his doubts and worried that the sacramental ritual of Penance will not cleanse him of his sins. His cousin Johnny Boy, for whom he feels responsible, is first seen dropping a small bomb into a mailbox, which detonates more or less harmlessly as he hastens away from the scene. Some sense of restraint keeps him from throwing bombs into the midst of the festival, but he later fires a pistol from a rooftop to "wake up the neighborhood." Clearly the explosives represent his resentment of the constrictions that Little Italy imposes upon his ill-defined impulse to escape. Teresa (Amy Robinson), Charlie's neighborhood Italian girlfriend, appears a little later in a scene with Charlie where she deliberately displays her bare breasts in front of a window in full daylight, perhaps to show off her charms to Charlie, but also to deliberately defy the culture's strict sexual code. The camera shoots her from outside the window to underscore her intention to put her unclad body on public display (52:20/52:30). A moment later, Charlie himself chides her for improper behavior (53:15/53:25). Furthermore, much to the distress of her parents, she is resolved to move out of the neighborhood, some place "uptown," where she hopes Charlie can be persuaded move in with her. The sexual revolution, it would seem, has found its way to Mulberry Street.

The figure who speaks for the older generation is Uncle Giovanni (Cesare Danova), a minor underboss of the Mafia and the authority figure of the neighborhood. Effectively, he has replaced Charlie's father, presumably dead, but in any case completely absent from the scene. Giovanni is not a religious man but his office is festooned with Catholic iconography, including an image of the Pope and a colorful poster of *Il Duomo*. For the sake of custom, he listens appreciatively to the festival band when the musicians casually drop into a café while parading through the streets. As the local godfather, he mediates neighborhood disputes, earns a modest income from protection and numbers, and assumes responsibility for training Charlie to play the role he himself now plays. Giovanni fondly remembers the underworld Olympians of the 1940s, like the boss who "looked after the docks" in World War II times (clearly a reference to Lucky Luciano), who was solicited by American Intelligence to be watchful for saboteurs on the waterfront (Scorsese 2004b, 01:03:00/01:05:30). Men like Luciano, he tells Charlie, are utterly unlike the formal political class, bureaucrats and "blackmailers," whom we see as tiny gray shadows on a television set in the background while Giovanni delivers this verbal diatribe. When Charlie asks how the boss controlled the docks, Giovanni answers simply, "he was there." To rule in silence, however, and with seeming effortlessness, assumes a network of extended familial relationships and reliable neighborhood contacts that by the 1970s was beginning to break down. Giovanni may sense he is the last of his kind.

Giovanni's prize possession, the restaurant he plans to let Charlie manage, is itself out of the neighborhood, well-removed from his power base on the Lower East Side. And the younger generation is restless, no longer respectful of his quiet authority. He warns Charlie to stay clear of Johnny Boy, whose behavior is chaotic and unpredictable. He understands the ties of family but insists that "honorable men go with honorable men." Teresa is an even more problematic case. Apparently her parents have asked Giovanni to help them control her. But he despairs of this: "What can I do? Lock her up." Because she is epileptic, he writes her off as "sick in the head," a label that presumably excuses his failure to master her, even though Charlie insists that epilepsy is a remediable ailment, not a mental defect. Giovanni expects eventually to hand over his authority to Charlie, but finds it troubling that his protégé keeps company with the wrong people and doesn't always seem eager to absorb his lessons in leadership.

The plot of *Mean Streets* thus becomes a study in the alienation of what should be the new leadership of the ethnic enclave. Charlie is the heir apparent, but he is tugged away by his affection for Teresa, the rebel whom the ethnic code requires him to reject, since she is clearly not a virgin and lacks wifely docility. In their scene at the beach (for Charlie, a distinctly uncomfortable environment), he insists on his ethnic identity, claiming that his favorite foods are linguini and lasagna and that he prefers "tall buildings" to nature and beach and sun and ocean, all of which he hates. He encourages her to move uptown but won't promise to join her. His favorite hero is St. Francis of Assisi, a son of south Italy, who "had it all down." Teresa quickly pricks that bubble by rejoining, "St. Francis didn't run numbers." Charlie's refusal to acknowledge her criticism suggests his embarrassment at being Giovanni's underling, but he delights in the thought of running his own restaurant and becoming a figure of consequence in the neighborhood (Scorsese 2004b, 00:57:40/01:00:20). Charlie's more serious problem is an even more compromising relationship to Johnny Boy, his cousin. Undertaking to defend him, he agrees to vouch for his debts, which brings him into conflict with the other would-be godfather of the younger generation, Michael (Richard Romanus), a childhood friend who is now something of a rival, as he tries to build a power base independent of Giovanni.

Michael is better focused on his criminal career than Charlie, but not as intelligent or socially competent. His black market entrepreneurship doesn't seem promising: We first see him trying to sell some stolen photographic equipment, but what he takes to be lenses are actually lens adapters, worth less than one tenth the value of a lens. He also gets shortchanged in a drug deal. More seriously, Giovanni regards him as a nuisance and does nothing to advance his interests. The godfather shows pronounced irritation when Michael intrudes upon a conversation between him and Charlie. Angry, Giovanni bursts out, "Can't he see we are talking?" But these missteps sharpen Michael's conflict with Charlie. It's not clear that anyone in the neighborhood will be positioned to replace Giovanni when the aging godfather passes from the scene.

What survives of the old ethnic comradeship is found mostly at Tony's tavern, a bar and strip club in the neighborhood where all the former school chums and little league gangsters gather. Counterpointing the iconography of Catholicism, Tony's place is a shrine to drinking and erotic carousing, whose decor features the image of a naked woman grandly displayed behind the bar. Its sinister red glow gives the whole room the look of Dante's inferno. Here the prodigal sons of Little Italy have full license to share their values, express their prejudices, indulge their appetites, and attempt (not always successfully) to work out their differences (Scorsese 2004b, 07:30/08:30). At no time is their clan sensibility more evident than when they close ranks against "outsiders," particularly ethno-racial outsiders, like blacks and Jews.

These minorities are present as colorful aliens and valued as sexual objects, but otherwise demeaned, sometimes actively abused. The most absolute taboo forbids interpersonal relationships with African Americans. At the private party Tony (David Proval) organizes for one of the neighborhood's returning war veterans, the mere rumor of a woman's allowing an African American to kiss her provokes a moment of wild rage. But Tony employs Diane (Jeannie Bell), a black woman, as an exotic dancer, who performs side by side with an exceptionally pale white woman. So long as she knows her place, avoiding contact with the patrons, she adds to the convivial atmosphere of the bar. Jews are admitted as patrons, but not on equal terms with the homeboys. On one occasion Charlie sees a woman, whom Tony identifies as "a Jew," apparently quarreling with her boyfriend. Charlie intervenes, clearly intending to claim the woman for himself, though she shows no inclination to be claimed. In the fight that ensues, Charlie welcomes the club's regulars to his side as they beat up the woman's companion, presumably another Jew.

Two other Jewish patrons figure in a more tonally complex scene involving Charlie and Johnny Boy. On this occasion, Johnny Boy arrives at the bar escorting Sarah Klein and Heather Weintraub, each giggly creature clinging to one of her escort's arms. He introduces them to Charlie as "bohemians from the Village," but Charlie immediately recognizes the language as code for "Jews." We quickly realize that Johnny Boy is offering one of them (it doesn't seem to matter which) to Charlie as a gesture of sexual hospitality. He has brought her as a gift for which he expects a favor. The logic of this behavior is that Charlie has made himself responsible for Johnny Boy's debts, and now Johnny needs further protection from Michael, since he is in no position to make good what he owes. Though he is clearly angry at his friend's careless ways, Charlie agrees he should not make Johnny Boy "look bad in front of my friends" and accords him the respect of a private conversation, away from the young women and the bar's other patrons. Meanwhile Charlie tells Tony to pour drinks "for the *mazza-Christes*," assuming they won't understand enough of his Sicilian dialect to realize they are being called "Christ-killers." And apparently, they don't (Scorsese 2004b, 12:40/14:30).

In any event, the compact is sealed as Charlie agrees to plead with Michael for greater leniency toward his spendthrift friend. Sarah and Heather thus become marketable exotic objects, sexual commodities appropriate for social exchange.

Charlie is also implicated in the life of Diane, the African American dancer who serves as his forbidden fruit. Their unsettled relationship is an effective measure both of the insistent racial taboos and the emancipatory spirit of modernism. Early in the film, somewhat to Diane's surprise, Charlie bursts into the magic bubble of her performing space to briefly join her in a dance, miming her movements but never letting his hands touch her body, even though her hands begin to reach out toward him (Scorsese 2004b, 08:30/09:40). The pop song on the sound track seems to complicate still further the conflicted emotions of the moment: "I tried to tell you but you really don't want to know." Sensing his transgression, Charlie quickly steps down from the low stage to join his drinking companions, who apparently haven't noticed his delinquency. But the tension between what he genuinely feels and the feelings he can acknowledge is evident in the extended interior monologue that follows. On one swing of the pendulum, he is telling us, "I gotta say that again, she is really good looking." Then, as the pendulum swings back, we hear, "But she is black." Briefly, he lets himself wonder if race really matters, then dismisses Diane from his thoughts to join in the banter with his friends. It's significant, however, that as he sits, a little distractedly, with his cronies, he realizes the conversation he has just had with himself is one he could never have with the guys on the block where he has grown up (Scorsese 2004b, 12:40/14:30).

This theme is picked up later, as Charlie continues to imagine a relationship with Diane. On this occasion he enters her dressing room at the club to propose that she might come to work at the restaurant he soon expects to be managing. Warily, she asks, "Dancing?" supposing she will still be a stripper. But, no, he tells her, she will be a hostess, "showing customers to their seats" and performing other managerial functions. Interested, she agrees to a meeting, provided Charlie will treat her to Chinese food. Apparently, this ethnic demilitarized zone would make it possible for them to meet a little more like professional partners, a little less like master and mistress (Scorsese 2004b, 01:00:40/01:01:50).

The other aspect of this scene worth remarking is Diane's presentation of her own body. When we first see her on stage, she appears to have reddish brown hair, especially as it is accented by the red light of the room. It is also rather curly. But when we are admitted to her dressing room, we learn that the hair we have been looking at is actually a brown wig and that her own hair is much shorter, straighter, and decisively darker. We see that she also has another wig, this one equally full but much darker, that she apparently wears when she is not at the club. Which is to say that, for the sake of the patrons at Tony's, she refashions herself as the classical Creole mulatta, a "whitening" and "Europeanizing" of her body intended to make her more attractive to those she has been hired to entertain. Moreover, when she goes to meet Charlie at the Chinese restaurant, she is still wearing the reddish brown wig, as if she has decided to turn this look into a permanent identity, or at least to seem more ethnically ambiguous when she joins her date/business partner as they meet after hours to dine and talk. Ironically, after going to considerable lengths to draw closer to Diane, Charlie ultimately changes his mind about their meeting. He drives to their agreed-upon tryst point in a cab, but refuses to stop or acknowledge her, preemptively deciding, it would seem, that Giovanni would never tolerate a black hostess in his restaurant and that Charlie himself would be unable to survive the taunts of his ethnic compatriots. Both parties momentarily suspend the racial taboo in the name of social opportunity, or even a shared erotic interest, but the tug of the past is irresistibly strong.

Tony's bar is also the scene for the drastic quarrel between Michael and Johnny Boy that bends *Mean Streets* toward tragedy. This outcome is foreshadowed when Johnny Boy, avoiding the police, lies down on a grave monument in a secluded churchyard (Scorsese 2004b, 01:26:30/01:27:20);

it is made inevitable when he threatens Michael during their last conversation (01:40:30/01:42:20). Charlie is drawn into the closing bloodbath because he is determined to protect Johnny Boy, and Teresa follows in turn out of loyalty to Charlie. It is fitting that these three should flee Manhattan together because all have struggled psychically to escape Little Italy—Johnny Boy by mockery and defiance, Teresa by her search for independent womanhood, and Charlie by thinking thoughts that he is usually too timid or culture-bound to act upon. Michael's pursuit of them is also appropriate, because he has interiorized most completely the archaic values of Little Italy.

Reading the closing scene of *Mean Streets*, it is hard to accept Richard Blake's conclusion that "in keeping with the story of the martyr San Gennaro, Charlie is destined to pass through many ordeals before he finds redemption" (2005, 175). I see no hint of redemption here. Careening around the streets of Brooklyn, Charlie and his friends are far beyond the intercessory powers of the wonder-working saint, even beyond the spiritual ambience that might make this blood bath seem sacrificial. Michael's gunshot attack, which causes a near fatal car crash, is vengeful brutality, nothing more. Scorsese cuts this scene (2004b, 01:47:10/01:50:45) together with the closing ceremonies of the Festival for entirely ironic purposes, so as to let us hear the emcee of the feast urge the guests (in Italian) to drive home "with caution." These words put in place the film's last reference to the failing powers of Naples' patron saint. Yes, all the victims do survive both the gunshots and the crash, but—bloody and tattered—they will never be able to return to the world they've left behind.

Scorsese's next film was *Italianamerican* (1974), a highly personal documentary about his parents that carries him still deeper into the issues of cultural assimilation. But two years later he directed *Taxi Driver*, which turns away from ethnic themes in favor of a more general evocation of Manhattan in one of its darkest decades. In spite of their obvious differences, *Taxi Driver* picks up almost exactly where *Mean Streets* concluded. Stumbling out of their demolished automobile—not together, but singly, in isolation and bewilderment—the three expatriates of Little Italy have lost those protective bonds of kinship that Travis apparently has never enjoyed. In their eagerness to cast off the fetters of tribal identity, they have never looked closely at the dystopic city beyond their ethnic world. And the dark streets of Brooklyn, through which Charlie begins to grope his way, are close cousins of those in the dubious neighborhoods of Manhattan where Travis Bickle (Robert De Niro) prowls restlessly in his cab. Newly returned from a tour of duty in Vietnam, and victimized by the insomnia that is probably related to his war experience, Travis will spend the next weeks and months of his life trying to improvise some shards of a "family," such as the one the protagonists of *Mean Streets* have willingly cast off.

The new voice in *Taxi Driver* is that of Paul Schrader, the brilliant but troubled screenwriter whom Scorsese met through Brian De Palma. Schrader's screenplay furnished the fundamental inspiration for the film, though both Scorsese and star actor Robert De Niro felt deep rapport with their writer's apocalyptic tone. "When I read Paul's script," says Scorsese, "I realized that was the way I felt, that we all have those feelings, so this was a way of embracing and admitting them" (Christie and Thompson 2003, 60). But Schrader was the disturbed Vietnam veteran, the chronic abuser of drugs and alcohol, the man whose failed marriage had cast him adrift on the streets of New York. Though Scorsese himself had issues with drugs and alcohol, what he contributed principally was his feel for the city: "The whole film," he says, "is based on the impressions I have of growing up in New York" (54). As any New Yorker would recall, the 1970s were a difficult decade for the city, which had to contend with rising crime rates, reduced social services, and a rapidly declining industrial base. This sense of decay and ruin is vividly present in Scorsese's evocation of the city after dark. Scorsese says:

> We shot the film during a very hot summer, and there's an atmosphere at night that's like a seeping kind of virus. You can smell it in the air and taste it in your mouth. It reminds me of a scene in *The Ten Commandments*, portraying the killing of the first-born, where a cloud of green smoke seeps along the palace floor and touches the foot of a first-born son, who falls dead. That's almost what it's like: a strange disease creeps along the streets of the city and, while we were shooting the film, we would slide along after it. (Christie and Thompson 2003, 60)

That this plague-ridden city calls a Biblical trope to Scorsese's mind is surely no accident.

It also helped immeasurably that Scorsese's camera crews now had fuller access to the streets, owing to the more film-friendly atmosphere of the city by the mid-1970s and Scorsese's growing prestige as a local filmmaker. These new circumstances of production opened up a vast, sinister urban stage that photographic director Michael Chapman was free to explore with imagination and sensitivity. Travis' cab pushes hesitantly through fog and steam, unidentified street urchins pelt his vehicle with rubbish, water cascades over the windshield but seems not to cleanse. On the soundtrack sirens wail randomly. In every scene, the city is vividly present, not only as background, but almost like another character, instinctively malign and corrupt, always poised to entrap the unwary.

Given the filmmaker's inclination to see Travis in his cab as "an avenging angel floating through the streets of the city" (Christie and Thompson 2003, 54), it's no surprise that some scholars, such as Stanley Corkin (2011), think of *Taxi Driver* as a "vigilante film," like *Death Wish* (1974) and

Martin Scorsese, *Taxi Driver*. The eroticized neon streetscape turn downtown Manhattan into a symbol of corruption and decadence. Travis' cab is his defense against the "filth" of the streets.

Source: This frame-capture is the work of James F. Scott, with technical support from the Instructional Media Center, Saint Louis University.

Marathon Man (1976), which "assert the efficacy and broad social acceptability of personal vigilance" (134). But Scorsese has grave reservations about his protagonist that surely deny him heroic status. He intends that Travis should be "very spiritual, but . . . it's the power of the spirit on the wrong road." According to Scorsese, "it was crucial to Travis Bickle's character that he had experienced life and death around him every second he was in southeast Asia. . . . It's held in him and then it explodes. And although at the end of the film he seems to be in control again, we give the impression that at any second the time bomb might go off again" (Christie and Thompson 2003, 62). Far from being an instrument of divine justice, Travis is a tragic exile, desperately looking for a community to which he might authentically belong.

In his search for community, Travis seeks personal connectedness, not bureaucratic order. Presumably, he found structure in the US Marine Corps and enough authority in the chain of command to keep him minimally functional. But Travis is a desperately isolated man; the most resonant chord in *Taxi Driver* speaks to the theme of alienation. In the in-

terviews with Christie and Thompson cited above, Scorsese remarks that
the first shot he thought of in the film was the camera move that follows
Travis' phone conversation with Betsy (Cybill Shepherd), where she sev-
ers all personal contact with him. The camera slides off the phone booth
and peers down a long hallway that is absolutely empty. Scorsese liked
the shot "because I sensed that it added to the loneliness of the whole
thing" (Christie and Thompson 2003, 54). Travis has just been cut off from
the rich world of the personal voice, and the waste spaces of that long
corridor give no hint of a new beginning (Scorsese 1989, 37:00/38:30).
Travis tells us in one of his many monologues, "I don't believe one should
devote his life to morbid self-attention" (10:10/10:20). But he has no skill
in the forming of interpersonal relationships. We first see him in a tight
close-up as no more than a intense pair of eyes, looking out warily toward
a cityscape that frightens and angers him. The world he sees through his
windshield is a riddle of flashing lights and garish colors, brought to focus
only when he homes in on the slatternly women who parade along the
sidewalks, putting their bodies on display: "All the animals come out at
night—whores, skunk pussy, dopers, fairies . . . Venal! . . . Someday a real
rain will come and wash all this scum off the streets" (05:20/06:30). He
has no contact with his passengers, rarely exchanging words with them,
and is resentful when they stain his cab with their sexual body fluids. At
the cinema he sits in an empty row, speaking to no one, and his attempt
to start a conversation with the cashier impels her to call security. Nor do
his casual contacts with his fellow cabbies lead to any kind of real rapport.

Travis' concept of community is broadly familial. It's not something he
can name, but what he secretly craves is the opportunity to play the social roles of husband, parent, and citizen, roles which collectively would
give him a full-fledged identity as part of the community. Returning
from the swamps of Indo-China with "a clean record" as an American
Marine, he is resolved—he tells his diary—"to become a person." In his
effort to establish a social persona, he projects his desires upon three figures he happens upon entirely by accident while drifting about the city:
Betsy, his imagined bride; Palantine (Leonard Harris), the Senator and
presidential candidate he would serve as a loyal thane; and Iris (Jodie
Foster), the street waif/prostitute, whom he would rescue and treat as
his daughter. In order to fulfill his fantasy, each of these characters must
be wildly distorted, but for a few brief moments they become the stuff of
Travis' dreams. Of course, when the fantasy collapses, Travis lapses into
apocalyptic violence, turning the streets of New York into the scene of a
firefight in the jungles of Vietnam.

Betsy is the first to appear, "an angel," clad entirely in white (the
bridal color), as she appears almost magically out of a bustling midtown
crowd. That she moves in slow motion marks her as slightly surreal. She

is "the most beautiful woman" Travis has ever met, and he immediately senses a deep rapport with this being who stands apart from the filth of the city (Scorsese 1989, 10:25/10:55). But their courtship is doomed from the beginning because he lacks basic social skills and no plausible way to connect to her world. First he stares at her voyeuristically, disturbing her enough that she asks a colleague to make Travis move his cab. Things improve briefly when he seeks her out at Palantine's political headquarters and commits himself, at least nominally, to the Senator's presidential campaign. Though this is obviously a ruse to gain the attention of Betsy, it bears importantly on his evolving relationship to Palantine. Before the courtship of Betsy implodes in the disastrous movie date at the porno house, Travis performs one of his few authentic human gestures. Thoughtfully, he buys Betsy the Kris Kristofferson recording whose lyrics she has used to characterize Travis as "half truth, half fiction, a walking contradiction." She values him more as a puzzle than a partner, but Travis touches a nerve when they meet for coffee and he describes her as "not a happy woman." On this occasion she confesses she has never met anyone quite like him and their relationship briefly flowers (26:00/26:30).

Travis' romantic fantasy unexpectedly brings him into closer touch with Palantine, whom he happens to meet as a passenger in his cab. Recognizing the candidate from the posters and campaign literature at Betsy's workplace, he introduces himself as an ardent supporter of the Senator and claims—falsely, of course—that he has tried to promote Palantine's campaign from the front seat of his cab. Their brief conversation on the political process is one of the most revealing in the film.

In this crucial scene, Palantine speaks for what Max Weber calls "bureaucratic authority," the essence of "modern" political arrangements. Such arrangements assume the operation of assemblies, majority votes, and legislative initiatives. The candidate's catchphrase is "We are the people," but he is sensitive to the lack of immediacy in representative government. Travis, on the other hand, seeks "charismatic authority," which Weber associates with an older, more tribal understanding of community leadership. Impatient with process, Travis grasps at apocalyptic solutions, the Providential rain that, like the Biblical deluge, will "wash all the scum off the streets." Scorsese paces the scene admirably to point up the divide that separates the two speakers. Palantine first remarks that he has "learned more about America from riding in taxi cabs than in all the limos in this country." This populist sentiment appeals to Travis and impels him to announce, with a manic grin, how enthusiastically he supports Palantine's candidacy. Palantine then encourages Travis to tell him what most troubles him about the current state of society, what issues he would like to see addressed. Travis first stalls and defers the question, confessing that, "I don't follow political issues that closely,

Martin Scorsese, *Taxi Driver*. The self-promoting, crowd-pleasing Senator Palantine is first the savior, then the demonized antagonist of the alienated Travis Bickle.

Source: This frame-capture is the work of James F. Scott, with technical support from the Instructional Media Center, Saint Louis University.

sir, I don't know." But Palantine seems open, personal, especially when he calls Travis by name, even though he has read the name off of Travis' ID tag, prominently displayed in the cab. When he asks again, Travis pours out his rage in a verbal tirade that leaves the candidate almost speechless: "He should clean up this city here, because this city here, it's like an open sewer, you know, always full of filth and scum. And sometimes, you know, I can hardly take it. Whoever becomes the President should just really clean it up. You know what I mean? Sometimes I go out and I smell it, it's so bad. And I get headaches, you know. The President should just clean up this whole mess here, should just flush it down the fucking toilet" (28:20/30:20).

For punctuation, Travis sounds the horn furiously at some unseen driver who is apparently reluctant to grant him the absolute right of way. Meanwhile cutaways register the increasingly distraught faces of Palantine and his two assistants, stunned by the outburst they have unwittingly triggered. Finally, after a very long pause, Palantine rejoins with a well-worn political cliché: "Well, . . . it's not going to be easy. We're going to have to make some radical changes." Sadly, these two men do not occupy the same moral universe.

Though he hints at something "radical," Palantine will work patiently through the appropriate channels. Earlier, we have watched his campaign manager worry about the printing on the candidate's campaign buttons. Later, Travis sees Palantine on television. During his interview with a local talk show host, the candidate makes the conventional assurance that "the people are rising to the demands I made on them. The people are beginning to rule" (50:10/50:40). Though Travis still has a huge Palantine campaign poster pasted to the wall of his dingy kitchen, he barely reacts to Palantine's upbeat message and is unmoved by the popular "groundswell" which the candidate claims to feel. Palantine thinks incrementally, looking for a political mandate, standing at a crossroads. Travis demands absolutes, a *dies irae* of cosmic reckoning. Palantine is a negotiator, looking to refine bureaucratic protocols; Travis is a warrior who will take no prisoners. His antagonists are not members of another political party; they are scum, excrement, the stench of a blocked sewer. Travis has no patience with campaigns or elected officials. He wants a godfather, a magical leader, like the fantasy image of Lucky Luciano conjured by Giovanni in *Mean Streets*. The cordial handshake with Palantine that concludes their conversation in Travis' cab conceals a chasm between the two men that cannot be bridged.

Travis' disillusion with Palantine begins as he is estranged from Betsy. When she refuses to see him and later declines to accept his phone calls, he realizes, he tells himself, "how much she is just like the others—cold and distant." Frustrated and angry, he confronts her at Palantine's campaign headquarters, where he tells her, "you're going to die in hell like the rest of them" (39:30/39:50). Before he is evicted from the premises, he strikes a martial arts posture, threatening enough that Palantine's campaign manager promises to summon the police. Exactly when he concludes he has been called to assassinate Palantine is not clear. But suddenly he is admitting to Wizard that he has some "bad ideas in my head." Meanwhile, he is meeting with Easy Andy, who is more than ready to equip him with a small arsenal of lethal weapons (Scorsese 1989, 54:00/56:30). With one of these in his hand, he begins to draw beads on passersby in the streets, as if his violent impulses were fastening upon a set of random urban targets. The next time Palantine is referenced in the film is as the camera is scanning the campaign poster while Travis thinks out loud about "true force" and creating so much havoc that "all the king's men can't put it back together again." Not long thereafter, Travis' fantastic mission as a vigilante gets additional stimulus from his accidental encounter with a would-be robber in a neighborhood quick shop (01:08:30/01:09:40). Armed, and skilled in his use of weapons, he shoots the intruder, perhaps saving the proprietor's life but in any case earning the robbery victim's immense gratitude. Fate seems to confirm that Travis is a latter-day Messiah.

Before his mission can fully declare itself, Travis must mentally process one more chance meeting, this time with Iris, the young prostitute he meets when she climbs into his cab, apparently trying to escape from her pimp, a swaggering lowlife named Sport (Harvey Keitel). Sport is determined to hold on to his property and quickly pulls Iris out of the cab, tossing Travis a crumpled $20 bill. Though the issue seems settled as Travis drives off, the crumpled currency haunts him as an icon of "dirty money," which contaminates his cab as badly as the body fluids that have sickened him since first he took the job. Now it seems he must rescue Iris, since it's clear that Palantine, caught up in speeches and majority votes, will not.

Travis' fatherly relationship to Iris is evident in his refusal to treat her as a sexual object (Scorsese 1989, 01:18:30/01:24:00). He approaches her as if he were a client, paying Sport for time with her, then handing over more cash for access to the room she has ornamented as a pleasure parlor. Once in the room, however, he deflects her sexual advances while chastising her for letting herself be bought and sold. He also reminds her of a lost adolescence—of school, and parties, and teenage fun. He insists on calling her Iris, a flower of early spring, instead of her street name, "Easy," which alludes to her sexual availability. Though they talk at cross-purposes, she agrees to meet for breakfast to continue their conversation (01:24:40/01:29:15). This encounter is cordial enough that she promises to leave Sport and perhaps accompany Travis to an upstate commune. He is determined, on the other hand, to return her to her parents, advising her, *in loco parentis*, that the communes he has seen have not been "clean." Still, he is prepared to give her money to launch her new life, adding that he himself will be "going away for a while," presumably after assassinating Palantine (01:29:20/01:29:30). At this point, there is no suggestion that violence will be required to detach Iris from Sport and her other handlers at the brothel. But with each passing moment, Travis slips deeper into derangement.

Crucial to his delusions is the sense that he is on a mission. Contrary to what we would expect, he makes no effort to conceal himself from Palantine's security detail. In fact, he introduces himself to the head of security, insisting that he is "Henry Krinkle," who wants to be a federal agent. Shortly thereafter, in the midst of a campaign rally for Palantine, he begins to mentally compose a bizarre letter to his parents, telling them of "the sensitive nature of my work for the government," which, of course, "demands the utmost secrecy" (Scorsese 1989, 01:11:30/01:13:00). This meditation in voice-over is accompanied by strong visuals that advertise his now complete alienation from Palantine's campaign. No longer a part of the throngs who gather under the candidate's banner, he is sealed up in his cab, wearing dark glasses and seen through the windshield, where a jagged, ominous shadow frames the image of Travis' face. In the point of view shot that follows, the camera pans the crowd, then glides past the figure of Palantine, who is grotesquely framed. The composition cuts off part of the candidate's face, as if visually beheading him. Caught up in a reverie from which he seems unable to escape, Travis fails to notice the police officer, who sternly warns him "you can't park here," which forces the cabbie to quickly leave the rally. At home he will complete his letter, alluding to his "girlfriend" and to the fact that he is "making lots of money." He is free to divulge that "her name is Betsy," but the confidential nature of his government assignment forbids him to reveal any further details (01:12:20/01/12/50). Significantly, personal success, a fulfilled love life, and the mysterious call to assassinate Palantine are an integral part of his delusional self-image.

Travis' full psychotic break comes in the next scene, where he implicitly acknowledges he has lost Betsy. At the Palantine rally, he has observed her with the candidate's campaign manager, and they obviously are enjoying each other's company, as well as basking in the can-do spirit of Palantine's campaign. What Travis understands as betrayal dislocates everything else in his life that might augur for the recovery of mental balance. This fixation upon a perverse love relationship is also something that makes it easier for him to ultimately change the target of his assassination. When the plot to shoot Palantine goes awry, it now seems natural, almost inevitable, that he would vent his wrath upon Sport and his henchmen at the brothel.

As we watch Travis descend into madness, we are carried through an interesting sequence that culminates in the destruction of his television set. At this stage of events he is no longer following the sound bites of Palantine or any other political figure. Mostly he watches dance programs and soap operas, with their never-ending narratives of personal relationships, failed and otherwise. In the last show we share with him, a straying wife is explaining to her husband why she is attracted to her new lover and ready to disown their marriage (Scorsese 1989, 01:13:25/01:14:30). The distraught male is pleading with her, but she seems unmoved. Amid the tatters of the shabby home space Travis maintains, he watches this scene and becomes increasingly disturbed as the drama progresses. He is holding an unloaded pistol in his hand and squeezes the trigger while the misbehaving heroine is shown in a facial close-up. Finally, when she avows her love for her new partner, he pushes over the set with his foot. This sends it crashing to the floor with sparks flashing from its ruptured tubes and circuits. This self-created ruin is an apt metaphor for the shambles of Travis' mind. But the stage business of the scene also suggests the cause of Travis' breakdown: he is undone by an imagined infidelity.

Before setting out to murder Palantine, Travis burns the bouquet of flowers he had intended for Betsy, but which she refused to accept. Now in their decayed and decomposing state, they are cast into the hellfire he has verbally wished upon his beloved.

Commenting upon the "legitimacy" of the protagonist's "moral outrage," Andrew Swensen (2001) is right to claim that Travis "seethe[s] with an insidious misanthropy and also self-loathing" (280). Surely this disqualifies him from being thought heroic. Nevertheless, he thinks of himself as "God's lonely man." To imagine himself as an avenging angel, he must see himself as "chosen," the agent of a special Providence. This explains, I think, his extraordinary costume and deportment as he attempts to shoot Palantine. Glossing the Schrader script, Scorsese speaks of his screenwriter's "religious background" and the fact that he served "in the Special Forces, in the marines" (Brunette 1999, 61). Travis brings to his mission both the sense of divine appointment and the exact look of a Special Forces operative: "The haircut," says Scorsese, "that's very important at the end—because the Special Forces, before they went out on patrol in North Vietnam, they would shave their hair like that" (61). The metaphor is highly apt: Travis, in his perverse imagination of himself, is God's commando on special assignment, answerable to no political authority, operating beyond conventional boundaries, and bent upon righting wrongs by whatever means are required. Ironically, it is his fantastic appearance that foils the attempted assassination. As Travis advances, against the natural momentum of the crowd, his strange garb and hairstyle make him uniquely conspicuous, quickly alerting Palantine's security team to his presence and putting a federal agent in hot pursuit of him. Thus he is forced to improvise a second target, the less well-guarded precincts of the brothel.

The bloodbath that brings this progression of events to climax is of a piece with the earlier imagery of divine retribution (Scorsese 1989, 01:39:30/01:42:30). Still in his fantastic costume, Travis now undertakes to rescue Iris. Although there's no evidence that she welcomes being "saved," Travis unleashes all his rage upon her captors, dispatching them with every weapon he can hold in his hand or strap to his body. Among this array, Scorsese points out, is "a kind of knife . . . called a K-bar," which "only Special Forces used" (Brunette 1999, 61). Again, Travis is playing the role assigned to him by his credentials as a special class of American warrior. Extraordinary circumstances require extraordinary tactics. Scorsese invites us to see these events as a "blood sacrifice, right?" (60). God's lonely man has at last discharged his mission. "And then the camera," concludes Scorsese, "going back over things is really kind of, like a reexamination of the elements of the sacrifice" (60).

The incongruous epilogue leaves us with a further paradox. Confounding probability, Travis survives his encounter with the dark powers and briefly becomes a small-scale celebrity. A headline describes him as the

"Taxi Driver Hero" and Iris' parents thank him profusely for returning their daughter to her home. We are assured that she is now "back in school" and they are working diligently to make her home life so attractive that "she will never have cause to run away again." He is also encouraged to visit them in Pittsburgh, where he would "find (himself) a most welcome guest in our home" (Scorsese 1989, 01/46/30/01:47:00). Whether this scene is "real" or the product of Travis' delirium is almost irrelevant. In either case, it works no change upon him. He still has no friends beyond the cabstand, and there is no evidence that his social life is any richer than when he was riding the subways or frequenting the porno houses of Lower Manhattan.

In its final moments, *Taxi Driver* comes full circle. Betsy's unexpected reappearance might portend the awakening of old desires, but apparently it doesn't. She has become simply another passenger, whom he transports to a destination with little conversational exchange and no suggestion of emotional resonance. The positive side of their meeting is that Travis no longer craves her, nor shows resentment toward her. We also learn that Palantine has won the presidential nomination and that Travis bears no grudges against him either. In fact, he tells Betsy he hopes Palantine will win, as if totally forgetting that he recently tried to murder him. For the moment, at least, Travis is relaxed, seemingly less stressful, more or less at peace with himself, and no longer at war with the unholy city. And the cab ride with Betsy is to a more suburban destination, quieter and with no hint of the anarchy of Times Square, imagery that at least hints at psychological recovery.

What is troubling about the last scene of the film is the unsteady blur of colored lights through which the phantasmal image of Betsy floats in the rear view mirror. More ominous still is the hint that Travis has once again begun to hallucinate. After Betsy steps out of the cab, clearly leaving it unoccupied, Travis glances once more into the rear view mirror and his attention is riveted on something he thinks he sees in the back seat (Scorsese 1989, 01:50:35/01:50:45). We are allowed no privileged understanding of this event because the cut reveals not a ghostly passenger, but a reflection of Travis' own face. Visible for only an instant, this image is immediately is swallowed up by formless lights and shadows, but the presence hints at demons Travis has been unable to exorcise, even through the horrendous purgation we have just witnessed. Worst of all, Travis is still absolutely alone, having failed utterly to find an ongoing human connection. At the end of *Mean Streets*, Charlie Cappa is gravely injured as well as alienated from the ethnic family that has nurtured him. But even he may be better off than Travis Bickle, driving his cab slowly to nowhere, in touch with no other creature, except perhaps a ghost in the back seat.

SEGMENT 2: YOU CAN'T GO HOME AGAIN:
RAGING BULL (1980) AND *GOODFELLAS* (1990)

After the early fame that came from the success of *Mean Streets* and *Taxi Driver*, Scorsese lost ground professionally with his overly ambitious musical, *New York, New York* (1977), then compounded his difficulties with drug and alcohol issues that brought him close to collapse. Recovery came with his return to ethnic themes, epitomized by the project recommended to him by De Niro, a dramatization of the career of the violent, headstrong Italian American boxer, Jake LaMotta. Loosely adapted from LaMotta's autobiography, first published in 1970, this narrative became—in the hands of De Niro, Mardik Martin, Paul Schrader, and Scorsese himself—the screenplay for *Raging Bull*, another film, like *Mean Streets*, that reflects the tension between the ethnic clan and cosmopolitan America. Here, the plot sets Jake, charged with fierce personal ambition to be the world's greatest boxer, against his Sicilian handlers, who control the boxing profession in New York and manage it as part of their far-flung gangster empire. Though *Raging Bull* is more about boxing than gangsters, it pairs well with Scorsese's most famous "gangster film," *GoodFellas*, another battle royal between unbridled individualism and the power of the familial clan. Both films are slightly elegiac, in that the clan world is beginning to collapse. But we see at the same time its powerful appeal to young men from ethnic neighborhoods, LaMotta in *Raging Bull* and Henry Hill in *GoodFellas*, who relish the camaraderie even while they struggle against the gang's constraints.

When Casillo teases out the implications of Scorsese's status as a "third generation Italian American artist" (2006, 56–68), he sees his subject at a stage of the conflict between the individual and his ancestry that he calls the moment of "ethnic passage," the moment when ethnic artists "move from the periphery to the centre of the majority society, where they no longer feel hyphenated" (64). Confident that they themselves are relatively well assimilated, they now feel free to "remember the Old World origins—the heritage of blood" (58) that might once have embarrassed them. Perceptively, Casillo adds that in Scorsese's case, the moment of ethnic passage coincides very closely with "the ethnic revival of the 1960s and 1970s," which "legitimated ethnic consciousness as never before" (58). Casillo also realizes that Scorsese's acculturation was "formed atypically, of working- and middle-class experiences, dissociated and radically different from each other" (59). As a result, Little Italy and its enclaves in the other boroughs, particularly LaMotta's South Bronx, were available to Scorsese as artistic material, but at enough psychic distance that he could see both the lure of the ethnic nest and the urge to be free of its narrow precincts. The conflicted protagonists of *Raging Bull* and *GoodFellas* yearn

for the connectedness of family and clan yet at the same time chafe bit-
terly at the restraints this connectedness imposes.

The inspiration for *Raging Bull* comes from LaMotta's autobiography
(1970) and the former boxer was used as a "consultant" on the film. But
the plot is the work of Scorsese and his writers and owes very little to the
narrative crafted by LaMotta himself (with help from Joseph Carter and
Peter Savage). Essentially, the Scorsese script picks up certain character
traits LaMotta assigns to himself, among them his guilt, his obsessive
jealousy, and his driving ambition. These are then organized into a fiction film that tightens and redirects the story line, giving more attention
to Scorsese's ethnic concerns. Two changes are particularly consequential:
Raging Bull discards LaMotta's backstory of child abuse at the hands of his
father and the years of reform school that pushed the young man toward
violence and paranoia; the film narrative also assigns to Jake's brother,
Joey, the role of personal advisor and manager, which in LaMotta's own
story was played by his friend Pete Petrella. These adjustments of the
story line incline us to attribute Jake's anger to forces in his immediate
environment, not to his problematic early life. The crucial role of brother
Joey makes the film's concerns more familial, tied not only to an ethnic
neighborhood but to a specific bloodline.

The opening scene of *Raging Bull* (Scorsese 1998, 00:30/02:40) stands
apart from the narrative as a vehicle to roll the credits. But at the same time,
as an autonomous segment, kind of a prologue, it masterfully introduces
the theme of struggle, the struggle of one man against himself, though
he is also hemmed in by a larger world he cannot really see. Filmed in
slow motion in order to further move the action outside the conventions
of realism, the single-take sequence of more than two minutes appears to
show Jake warming up in a boxing ring, but its look is completely surreal.
The dominant image is containment, an enclosed arena from which there
is no exit, in fact, beyond which there is only an impenetrable gray murk
that conceals even the outline of other objects or other paths. The suggestion of a space beyond the ring is conveyed only by occasional flashes of
light, presumably flash bulbs from press cameras, which have the effect
of reducing the lonely figure in the ring to mere spectacle. The extreme
foreground of the image shows three taut strands of rope, photographed
from very close range. These could easily be mistaken for heavy metal
bars. When we turn to Jake, we see him dressed in an animal costume (he
even has a tail), a leopard, a powerful jungle cat, but a creature wrenched
out of its habitat and inserted in an alien environment, much like a zoo
animal that has been captured and caged. He is graceful and strong, but
to what purpose? Without an antagonist to engage, he throws punches
into a void, then steps sideways or backwards to dodge the blows of
phantoms who surround him, or so he seems to imagine. The soundtrack

is the appropriately chosen *"intermezzo"* from Pietro Mascagni's *Cavalleria Rusticana*, a tragic tale of Sicilian village life built around concern for personal honor. In Mascagni's opera, this particular theme is played during an ominously quiet moment just before a fatal explosion of peasant rage. It sets exactly the right tone for the two scenes that immediately follow, which carry us into the real world of Jake's professional life and introduce us to the deeply contradictory images of Jake himself.

The first scene takes place in 1964, after Jake has retired from boxing, and is trying to reinvent himself as a nightclub performer (Scorsese 1998, 02:45/03:50). On this occasion, he cuts a pretty sorry figure. Overweight, stammering, and with a cigar stuffed awkwardly into his mouth, he is the antithesis of the sleek, impressively masculine figure we have just seen in the boxing ring sequence. Nor does he have a good sense of timing or a fluent command of words, the essential talents of a successful performance artist. Even his gestures are mechanical and out of sync with his speech. His would-be comic routine is a muddle of bad rhymes ("Olivier" is incongruously linked to "Sugar-Ray") that sound like a degraded version of Dr. Seuss. At times it's not clear whether he is telling a bad joke or has just lost his train of thought, as when he remembers, without context, the night he took off his robe but had forgotten to put on his boxing shorts. The last shot of the sequence is a tight close-up of Jake's scarred and disfigured nose. It seems pitiful that this is what the world's middleweight champion would turn into.

In stark contrast, we next see the LaMotta of 1941, a trim, muscular athlete who at about the age of twenty was an up-and-coming undefeated contender for the middleweight crown. Ironically, we are about to see this record tarnished by his first loss, though it's difficult to understand how his opponent could by any standards be called the winner. Jake closes the match with a furious barrage of punches that leaves the young black boxer, Jimmy Reeves, sprawled on the canvas and virtually unconscious, magically saved by the tenth-round bell that concludes the match. But the bout is being held in Cleveland, an alien venue for a New York boxer, as his brother reminds him angrily just before the final round begins. We soon learn that the fateful visit to Cleveland was one of Jake's many efforts to escape the authority of his handlers, a small cadre of gang-affiliated Sicilians who exercise almost absolute control over Madison Square Garden and the boxing profession in New York. As his highly theatrical behavior in this scene shows, Jake is convinced he can create his own fan base and subvert the machinations of the promoters, who are chiefly committed to enlarging their profits and only incidentally concerned with fairness to individual boxers. In Cleveland, Jake manages to start a riot in the auditorium, but still loses the fight. This is the first, but by no means the last time that Jake will assert his autonomy only to discover that he has seriously overestimated his ability to construct his personal destiny.

Approached from the vantage point of ethnic psychology, Jake is an immediately recognizable case of the conflict Werner Sollors discerns between ethnicity defined by "consent" and ethnicity defined as "descent" (1986, esp., 1–40). When ethnicity is constructed as descent, the emphasis falls upon "heredity" and "blood." When ethnicity is imagined as "consent," however, the emphasis shifts to individual choices, such as education, job training, or the selection of a marriage partner, anything, says Sollors, that "stresses our ability as mature free agents, as architects of our fates" (6). It is Jake's determination to function as a free agent that alienates him from Tommy Como (Nicholas Colasanto), the underboss of the New York fight game, as well as Salvy (Frank Vincent), Tommy's representative in the neighborhood, and even Joey (Joe Pesci), Tommy's mouthpiece within LaMotta's own family.

These issues are already in the mix during the postmortem on the Jimmy Reeves debacle in Cleveland for which Salvy has apparently taken heavy criticism, plainly visible in the rancor he shows toward Joey as they walk through the South Bronx neighborhood together. Referring to the riot, Joey explains that "everything just went crazy." Salvy's immediate retort is "that would never have happened if Tommy had been over there taking care of him." The answer, Salvy continues, is to "fight in New York," where Tommy knows the rules and probably has some influence with referees and the Boxing Commission. If Jake doesn't learn to follow orders, Salvy predicts, he's never going to "get a title shot" and will "wind up punch drunk." Joey agrees, basically, but insists, "he just wants to do things for himself." Significantly, this conversation takes place on the street in a single-take crane shot (Scorsese 1998, 07:35/08:15) while the characters walk past street vendors, curbside garbage pails, and little clusters of people loitering on the sidewalk. The scene catches the feel of an ethnic neighborhood and the close presence of other people suggests a community, which might sometimes encourage private ambition but is more likely to defer to custom and habit. Salvy stands in front of the LaMottas' apartment until he extracts from Joey the promise to talk to his brother and clarify for him where his interests lie. But the issue remains unresolved, as Jake is completely consumed by his own ambition, resentful because he will never be able to challenge Joe Louis, the heavyweight champion and the fighter generally regarded as the best in the world. Borders and boundaries are not words that Jake is familiar with.

Without moderating his ambition, Jake continues to advance his career, gaining a technical knockout over Sugar Ray Robinson, the most famous middleweight of the postwar generation and undefeated at the time of this fight. At ringside, we hear a sports commentator mention "a shot at the middleweight crown." Meanwhile Jake courts and marries Vikki (Cathy Moriarty), a young woman with bright blond hair, whose look and bearing is far different from that of the ethnic Italian wife Jake has just deserted. (The actress playing the role is of Irish ethnicity.) Vikki relishes her striking good looks and her capacity to attract male attention, showing no inclination to be the self-effacing homebody that the norms of the neighborhood require. Like Teresa in *Mean Streets*, she brings a new sensibility to the neighborhood, a spirit of resistance and rebellion that neither Jake nor the ethnic clan can contain. For the moment, however, she is content with her new suburban home, her backyard swimming pool, and her husband's growing celebrity. Though no shot at the title materializes, we watch Jake pulverize a series of inferior boxers, culminating in his brutal beating of Tony Janero, seemingly the only boxer left in his weight class to fight him. While Jake is frustrated that he is fighting below his skill level, Joey assures him that he is being properly managed and that Jake will fulfill his ambitions "on your own, just the way you wanted to" (Scorsese 1998, 45:30/45:40). This sets the stage for a full-fledged battle between Jake and Tommy Como, a conflict between personal striving and clan power.

The decisive scene comes at the Debonair Club, Tommy Como's private men's club where Joey has been called to sort out a bloody fight between Joey and Salvy that springs from Jake's doubts about Vikki's fidelity. Como first forces Joey and Salvy to shake hands and profess that the quarrel has been settled, allowing both parties to pretend, against all evidence, that their honor has been vindicated. In the later moments of this scene, Como holds back Joey for a moment to make a special point about Jake. Predictably, it's about *rispetto*, the homage Jake owes to his godfather, which Tommy feels is lacking when Jake refuses to take orders from the clan. "He doesn't respect me," charges Tommy, "he doesn't respect anyone." Joey can no longer defend his brother with the evasion that "he just likes to do things his own way." No, says Como, "your brother has become an embarrassment. I'm looking very bad, when I can't deliver a kid from my own neighborhood. . . . Why does he make it so hard on himself?" At this point, what has been left at the level of advice now comes with threats and penalties: "He's not going to get a shot at that title, not without us he isn't. He could beat all the Sugar Ray Robinsons in the world" (Scorsese 1998, 01:02:50/01:07:10). Now we learn that disloyalty has its price. To make sure Jake himself is suitably humiliated (and also to guarantee the clan some quick cash), Como demands that he throw his next fight, in spite of the fact that he is fighting another inferior opponent.

This scene sets up the improbable chain of events that gains LaMotta the middleweight championship belt. He does throw the fight to Billy Fox, though in defiance of Como he refuses to fall to the canvas. This causes the match to look rigged, since it is settled in Fox's favor by the referee, who calls a TKO even though LaMotta looks like he could go on fighting. Furiously scolded by his brother and suspended by the Boxing Commission, Jake's adamant defense is, "I had to fight a bum." The loss pains him so seriously that we find him sobbing out of control in his brother's arms. Shortly thereafter, Joey adds further edge to Jake's rancor, by pretending to demonstrate for his benefit how easy it would be to simply fall down. In real life, this affront to his male self-concept rankled LaMotta so seriously that he couldn't resist alluding to it in his autobiography: "The first round, a couple of belts and I see a glassy look coming over his eyes. Jesus Christ, a couple of jabs and he's going to fall down? . . . I was supposed to be throwing a fight to this guy and it looked like I was going to end up holding him on his feet" (LaMotta 1970, 161).

But precisely this piece of *opera buffa* earns LaMotta his title fight. On screen, the event seems almost magical because we hear nothing of the circumstances surrounding its arrangement. The superscript notes that two years have passed and we might wonder what has delayed the fulfillment of Tommy Como's promise, suspecting only that it has something to do with complications Jake has brought upon himself by his serious misconduct. In reality, it was probably pushed back by the very profitable middleweight rivalry between Tony Zale and Rocky Graziano, which produced three lucrative championship bouts between 1946 and 1948, resulting in the middleweight title changing hands twice. The smart money of the boxing world clearly did well on these fights. It was only after the durable, but seriously ageing Zale (in his mid-30s by 1949) unexpectedly lost the crown to Algerian-born French boxer, Marcel Cerdan, that LaMotta was advanced to fight for the title. Without contextualizing commentary, we also learn that the fight takes place in Detroit, not New York, seemingly outside Tommy Como's sphere of influence, perhaps suggesting that an international bout is not so susceptible to Mafia control. Scorsese's omission of these details invites us to apprehend Jake's good fortune as he himself apprehends it, almost as a gift of the gods. Suddenly, on a particular evening, as if by the wave of a godfather's magic wand, he is at last in the same ring as the champion with a chance to fulfill his lifelong dream. In ten tough rounds he wins the bejeweled middleweight belt.

Somewhat surprisingly, the theme of racial conflict in *Raging Bull* seems less pronounced than we might have expected. But it is there, even if slightly below the surface of events. What's most crucial is that black boxers had emerged in the period after World War II as the most substantial newcomers to the profession. Spurred by the example of Joe Louis, black fighters of the later 1940s began gradually to replace champions of other ethnic extractions (Irish, Jewish, and Italian, among others)

across all weight classifications. Louis had won the heavyweight crown
in 1937 and held it till 1949, giving up the title to Ezzard Charles, another
black heavyweight. We should recall that beating Joe Louis is Jake's most
extravagant fantasy. It may also be relevant that Louis was the iconic figure who inspired Sugar Ray Robinson, the superb black boxer who had
toured with the heavyweight champion during their army years, then
became LaMotta's primary rival in the middleweight class in the postwar
decade. But it can't be accidental that LaMotta is particularly angry about
losses to black fighters: Jimmy Reeves, his opponent in Cleveland, whom
he insults by refusing to leave the ring after his defeat, also doing his up-
most to stir the mostly white pro-LaMotta spectators to a fever pitch; and
Billy Fox, to whom his handlers force him to bow, but not before he lands
several crippling punches to show he is the superior talent. And again, he
stalks around the ring, like an enraged animal, as if mocking the technical
knockout that the referee has just declared.

LaMotta's attitude toward the Latino boxer, Tony Janero, also seems
colored by ethnic stereotypes, this time the stereotype of the Latino: he
is a sissy, a pretty boy, unmanly because there's "no marks on him,"as
Salvy observes (53:35/53:40), Jake's outburst over Janero is rooted in his
obsession with Vikki's fidelity, but it develops into an extended exchange
at the Copacabana between Jake, Tommy, and Salvy, when they all giggle
about Janero's dubious masculinity. In boisterously obscene terms, Jake
remarks that the Latino would make a better bed partner than a fighter
and Tommy laughs with as much gusto as Jake, the only moment in the
film when they share a sentiment in common. Salvy soon becomes the
butt of the same joke, as Jake seems bent on reducing the crony he suspects of seducing his wife to the status of the Latino stereotype. Before the
conversation ends, Jake has vowed to damage Janero's handsome face.
And later, as a Jake brutally assaults the overmatched Latino, Tommy
remarks snidely from ringside, "he ain't pretty no more" (57:50/58:00).

Predictably, LaMotta's most powerful resentment is reserved for Robinson, the only middleweight of that era clearly superior to the Bronx
Bull. They fight six times, twice on screen in Scorsese's film, with Robinson winning all but one. LaMotta's lone victory is slightly indecisive,
since it's awarded by decision and not by a knockout or a TKO. Robinson
is clearly angry about the outcome and we can see his bitter grimace and
the words he exchanges with his handlers and corner men. The second
fight that Scorsese stages is the one which takes from LaMotta the crown
he won two years before from Cerdan. On this occasion Jake is completely
outclassed, absorbing a savage beating that leaves the ropes of the ring
soaked with his blood, which drips to the canvas in a memorable close-
up. He loses by a TKO in the thirteenth round. But LaMotta can't leave the
ring without one desperate effort to taunt the victor. To prove that, unlike

Janero, he could never be "unmanned," especially by an African American, he stumbles in a daze into Robinson's corner and boasts, "I didn't go down, Ray, you didn't take me down" (01:40:10/01:40:30). Robinson's handlers are startled, almost amused, and completely dismissive, but for LaMotta it is an important moment of assertion. The black champion couldn't knock him down.

The Cerdan fight and one successful title defense mark the highpoint of LaMotta's boxing career and the beginning of his effort to get out of the fight game. Rather creatively, he seeks to reinvent himself as an entertainer. Again he is searching for autonomy, a world where he will no longer be answerable to Tommy Como. His first impulse is to flee New York for Miami, where we find him running a nightclub bearing his name and now living in a lush world of palm trees and tropical vegetation, far removed from Madison Square Garden, but also out of touch with his brother, whom he has assaulted while in another jealous rage. Having lost to Robinson, Jake is now "through with fighting," as he tells a Miami reporter, and ready to start a new life in a new city with his well-groomed wife and growing family. At this moment, sitting beside his swimming pool in an upmarket Miami suburb, he seems ready to live out the 1950s version of the American dream.

Unfortunately, Jake lacks the self-mastery that personal autonomy requires. Though he performs his stand-up comedy routine better than we might have anticipated, he drinks to excess, flirts dangerously with underage women, and on one occasion mishandles his relationship with a tableful of political figures who loom large on the local scene. When his behavior gets him into difficulties, as is quickly the case, he has no network to fall back on, not even his brother, the gyroscope that has given Jake what little balance he has had. This is also the moment when Vikki leaves him, taking custody of the children. Jake's downward spiral begins with his arrest for consorting with a fourteen-year-old prostitute, who has presented herself to him as an adult. While the circumstances might encourage leniency, the political culture of Miami owes him nothing and shows no sympathy for the fallen champion. In fact, in his attempt to raise bail money, he breaks up the championship belt, hoping to create extra cash with bits and shards of the jewelry that ornaments this prized icon. Not only does his assault on the belt advertise his poor judgment, it also devalues the professional achievement he has every right to feel proud of. This fury is enacted in Vikki's apartment, visiting collateral damage upon her china and bric-a-brac, so in that sense the act also underscores his rupture with family. His collapse is complete when he fails to make bail and is dragged into solitary confinement by two prison officers who forcibly overcome his resistance. This scene provides the ultimate image of constriction. Far more than the boxing ring or the cramped apartment of the South Bronx from which the young boxer first emerged, Jake's cell space is tiny and dark, frustrating all but the most minimal movements. Alone, despairing, and apparently on the brink of absolute defeat, the former middleweight champion beats his head against the stone cell wall, crying, "I am not an animal, I am not an animal" (Scorsese 1998, 01:53:30/01:56:40). Travis Bickle would have understood his feelings perfectly.

At this point LaMotta begins whatever recovery he achieves. With suitable caution, Ben Nyce calls the last several scenes "the very beginning of the long way back" (2004, 74). Morally compromised and economically insecure, he returns to New York and reconciles, tentatively, with his brother. He is also gainfully employed and free of the gangster clan. The final three scenes build upon each other and extend to Jake some small redemption, both personal and professional. They also give him a halting sense of autonomy (Scorsese 1998, 01:59:00/02:03:40).

First we find Jake performing another nightclub routine, no longer in his own place but at least as his own man. The nightclub is really just a small bar and he shares the stage with an exotic dancer whose best years are behind her. His act is unremarkable, but he wards off a heckler without losing control and then politely supports his female partner. Later, as they leave the premises together, he happens to see his brother Joey and actively seeks him out. Though LaMotta is virtually incapable of expressing affection, he is bent on restoring contact between them and insists on a kiss of peace. Almost fawning, he won't release Joey from his embrace before extracting a promise that they will continue in touch. This prompts a cut to the last scene, which takes us to Barbizon Plaza in New York, a much more elegant venue than the downscale bar where we have just watched him perform. Because of the dress, décor, and the signage out front, this scene seems to return us to the site where the film narrative began, apparently to a later moment in the rehearsal sequence we have already watched. But now the tone is more upbeat, and Jake's delivery is several exponents smoother. No longer muddling through Shakespeare or misremembering irrelevant episodes from his earlier life, he is now performing select bits of the modernist dramatic canon from a bill of fare that includes Rod Serling, Paddy Chayefsky, and—as we are about to discern—Elia Kazan.

The scene we now see Jake rehearse is a climactic moment from Kazan's *On the Waterfront* (1955), where the has-been boxer, Terry Molloy (Marlon Brando), berates his brother for putting the interests of his gangster friends above his responsibilities to his sibling. Critics have had trouble with Scorsese's ending, imagining, mistakenly, that Jake's recitation of Molloy's monologue is self-serving, in that it blames Joey for forcing Jake to throw the fight with Billy Fox, inflicting the worst wound ever dealt to Jake's ego. And of course, the parallelism is unmistakable. In the monologue from *On the Waterfront* that Jake takes over from Molloy, the "up-and-comer" who has become a "down-and-outer" complains that his brother made him throw a fight that gave his opponent a title shot and bought Terry himself "a one way ticket to Palookaville." Deeply dejected and bitter, Terry insists, "You was my brother, Charlie, you should've looked after me. You should've looked after me just a little bit" (02:00:50/02:02:30). Responding to Scorsese's critics, Casillo points out that the parallels between the two scenes are real, but they accentuate differences more than similarities (2006, 262–64). In *On the Waterfront*, respecting orders from his brother, Terry throws a fight that denies him the opportunity to advance his career. In *Raging Bull*, on orders from his brother, Jake throws a fight that gives him his opportunity to become middleweight champion. Moreover, Casillo's instincts about this scene are confirmed in the language of the script. Before he launches into his recitation, Jake introduces the scene by remarking that boxing has been good for him, "but some people [i.e., Terry Molloy] are not that lucky." What this moment of truth actually illustrates is that Joey has taken better care of Jake than he realized at the time. In other words, the scene is entirely in keeping with the theme of familial reconciliation signaled by the fraternal embrace. It expresses gratitude, not resentment.

Jake LaMotta of *Raging Bull* struggles furiously against the Sicilian handlers bent on managing his career, but battles, even more desperately, in his effort to manage himself. His flight from New York to Miami creates an impressive façade, but quickly leads to disgrace, imprisonment, and despair. The measure of redemption that he earns springs from his return to New York, where he confronts his demons and works toward restoring his relationship to his brother. That doesn't necessarily make him morally admirable, but in the gallery of Scorsese's ethnic protagonists, it marks him as relatively autonomous. Jake is the mirror image of Henry Hill (Ray Liotta), the Irish Sicilian protagonist of *GoodFellas*, who works as hard to get into his ethnic family as Jake works to get out. Instead of resisting the influence of Paulie Cicero (Paul Sorvino), the godfather of his neighborhood, Henry does everything in his power to draw close to his adopted "family," even though he eventually betrays them in order to reap the profits of his personal drug dealing. Unlike Jake, he never attempts to restore a meaningful relationship to friends or family. *GoodFellas* ends on a note of perverse nostalgia, with Henry as an anonymous exile in a witness-protection program, angry with the Seattle suburbanites who can't be trusted to make a decent Italianate red sauce.

Lesley Stern in *The Scorsese Connection* (1995) calls *GoodFellas* a "remake" of *Mean Streets*, though quickly adds a set of qualifiers, chiefly related to "the rendition of fantasy." Perceptively, Stern argues that the camera work of *GoodFellas* aligns "Henry's fantasy, of going anywhere, with a camera that can move unhindered through an impossible space" (9). This point is illustrated in the famous steadycam shot that follows Karen (Lorraine Bracco) and Henry into the Copacabana, where they enter from the rear entrance, glide through the kitchen as if on a magic carpet, then emerge in the main auditorium. As the very long long-take continues, they are escorted to a table that is being prepared especially for them (Scorsese 2004a, 31:40/34:00). Because the waiter in charge of seating them is literally carrying "their" table, the cloth covering it spreads and floats like the wings of a giant white butterfly. Impressed by his power to command this level of service at an upscale nightspot, Karen asks, "What do you do?" And Henry's laconic answer, "I'm in construction," at once denies utterly and conveys perfectly what her escort is about in the world. Of course his work has nothing to do with pouring concrete foundations. But his life is about "constructing" a destiny, a magic bubble of power and privilege that he associates with his Mafia family, who have recently become his foster parents. Ultimately, his relationship to Karen—another of a long list of female outliers in Scorsese's films—destroys his relationship to his foster family, but for the moment she and Henry's cronies at the Copacabana are all gathered into the same fantasy, what Ellis Cashmore characterizes as the "American dream gone toxic" (2009, 26–51).

GoodFellas follows the arc of Henry's rise and fall, which conforms closely to the rise and fall of the American Mafia. "*GoodFellas*," says Scorsese, "is like a history of postwar American consumer culture, the evolution of a cultural style" (Smith and Scorsese 1998, 2). But, "the naivete and romanticism of the Fifties," he continues, "corrupts and degenerates . . . I guess I admire the purity of the early times . . . but I'm part of the decadence of what happened in the Seventies and Eighties" (2). Particularizing a little further, Scorsese adds, "there's a breakdown of discipline, of whatever moral code those guys had in the Fifties and Sixties. I think now with drugs being the big money, . . . the Mafia is nothing" (3). *GoodFellas* commits itself to dramatizing this loss of credibility, the process by which the godfather culture lost its authority over the ethnic thanes who once were its willing servants. These broader social transitions tie in with Henry's personal life in that he first experiences the gusto of "belonging," then watches this magic kingdom of easy money collapse under the weight of its own corruption.

The rising arc of Henry's underworld career is rendered in images of family and brotherhood. Tony Bennett's "Rags to Riches," a mainstream pop tune of the 1950s, leads us into this sequence, not only marking the time line of events but also linking Henry's personal assent to the broader upward mobility of the American middle class. We first see Paulie Cicero's cabstand as a POV shot, which has Henry peering through the slats of Venetian blinds to the world he longs to join, but is cut off from by what seem like bars on the window (Scorsese 2004a, 08:00/08:10). His home is a prison, crowded, dull, and sometimes violent, since his rage-ridden Irish father beats him regularly with a fierce-looking strap. Paulie's world, on the other hand, is full of laughter, tasty-looking food, and well-tailored men wearing expensive jewelry and handing out lots of cash. Henry gains admission because his Sicilian mother has family from the same village as the Ciceros. Once admitted to Paulie's premises, Henry quickly makes himself part of the family—running errands, making sandwiches on social occasions, even holding an umbrella over Paulie's head as he discharges his godfatherly obligations. "I was part of something," he says proudly in voice-over, "I belonged." Soon he is meeting, through Paulie, the two characters who will become his closest colleagues, Jimmy Conway (Robert De Niro) and Tommy DeVito (Joe Pesci), partners in crime, inseparable social friends, and almost brotherly in their day-to-day dealings with one another. Henry's initiation into the family is fulfilled when he is arrested and gives up nothing at the police interrogation (14:00/15:20). Upon his release, he is warmly embraced by Jimmy, who praises him for his unflinching adherence to the clan's code of silence. When he returns to the cabstand, Paulie and an assortment of his henchmen greet him affectionately and applaud his behavior. This test of fire bonds him to his Mafia family.

Henry's secure place in the crime community is confirmed in a scene that quickly follows, at the Bamboo Lounge, another Cicero property, where the "goodfellas" gather to socialize (Scorsese 2004a, 16:40/19:40). While the camera strolls casually among the patrons, Henry introduces them as personal acquaintances that greet him in both English and Italian as he turns toward their several tables. He calls them by their nicknames: Frankie the Wop, Freddy No Nose, and Jimmy Two Times, who obliges the camera by performing the speech tick that earned him his name: "Think I'll go out and get a paper, get the paper." Soon the camera settles upon Henry's table, large enough to accommodate at least a dozen people and laden with an array of fine foods. Now we hear Henry scoff at the drudges who "worked shitty jobs and took the subway to work every day." The Bamboo Lounge is also the site where crime capers are planned, like the Air France robbery that nets Jimmy, Tommy, and Henry their first big score. The only discordant note is a tensive moment between Tommy and Henry, where Tommy imagines for a moment that Henry is laughing at him, not with him (19:50/21:10). Suddenly there is a crisis, but it's quickly resolved when Henry turns the incident into another joke. Considering that Tommy is a short-tempered and violent man, this is an expert read of a situation that might have turned deadly. Not only does

Henry show how completely he fits into the group, he also understands his close associates well enough to manage their dangerous moods.

Henry's courtship of Karen seems to further consolidate his success, though his marriage to an ethnic outsider will eventually undermine his relationship to Paulie. From the outset, Karen's Jewishness sets her apart from Henry's world, not so much because of religion as because of class. Henry must cover the crucifix around his neck when she introduces him to her mother as "half Jewish," but their differences are more apparent in the scene where he joins her at her country club. He is astonished that the members sign tabs instead of handing over cash, and the décor is utterly unlike that of the Bamboo Lounge. White is the all-pervasive color and beach umbrellas are the most conspicuous stage props. But the chemistry between them drives the relationship forward and both make whatever adjustments are required.

In his analysis of the gradual weakening of ethnic bonds, Werner Sollors makes much of romantic love as an almost universal solvent. "A marital union," he says, "or a love relationship across boundaries that are considered significant, . . . is what constitutes melting pot love" (1986, 72). Sollors works this point through a wide variety of ethnic cultures (Indian/Settler; Gentile/Jew; Catholic/Protestant, etc.) to arrive at his well-documented conclusion: "By yoking love and marriage, betrothals were removed from the controls of descent . . . and opened to the forces of consent" (111). According to this paradigm, the family of blood must yield its authority, however reluctantly, to the personal choices of its sons and daughters, thereby jeopardizing ethnic integrity. Even though most may still shun "intermarriage" or "out-marriage," the impregnable barrier has been breached. Scorsese repeatedly uses this formula as a plot device that empowers the female rebel (Teresa in *Mean Streets*, Vikki in *Raging Bull*, Ginger in *Casino*) to challenge the ethnic code by virtue of her romantic involvement with the male protagonist. This is Karen's role in *GoodFellas*.

Here, more than in any of his earlier films, Scorsese makes his female protagonist a shaping force in the outcome of events, not only giving her a narrative voice to explain herself, but also granting her a consequential level of agency in the dramatic action. Ironically, Karen enters Henry's life only because of Tommy, who uses the prospect of a double date to lure one of his girlfriends into a romantic relationship she would otherwise have avoided. And Henry's first date with Karen is a full-fledged disaster. But Henry is drawn to her sparkling eyes, which he thinks resemble Liz Taylor's, and their courtship goes forward, even though Henry realizes she will be difficult to keep under control.

Their courtship is lyrical, but already turbulent. They begin to associate seriously after Karen calls him out in front of his friends. She is also aware of his ties to dangerous people, but acknowledges, "he was an exciting guy." Besides, she enjoys the trips to the Copa on Henry's arm and the aura of celebrity that surrounds him. When her mother complains that Henry is "not Jewish," Karen orders her out of her life. The crowning event is the moment when Henry avenges her honor by fiercely beating a would-be suitor from the neighborhood who has sexually molested her. On this occasion, Henry uses his gun to pistol-whip the culprit and threaten his two buddies who seem about to intervene. Then he hands over the gun (bloody from its use in the beating) to Karen, which provokes a revealing interior monologue: "I know there are women, like my friends, who would have gotten out of there the moment their boyfriend gave them a gun to hide. But I didn't. I gotta admit the truth: it turned me on" (41:10/41:25). With this thought the bargain is sealed, and Scorsese cuts directly to the couple's wedding.

Henry's marriage to Karen (Scorsese 2004a, 41:30/44:20) is one of those resonant ritualistic moments that always loom large in Scorsese's films. It is nominally a Jewish wedding, though the guest list includes so many of Henry's Sicilian associates that they really define the event. Karen's parents are nowhere to be seen, and Henry's blood family is represented in one relatively brief shot. In Sellors' language, this is an event when the "ethnicity of consent" takes priority over anything connected with bloodlines. Appropriately, the scene begins with a tight close-up of the crushing of the wine glass, which in Jewish ritual signifies both the fragility of all relationships (such as the destruction of the Temple that created the diaspora) but also, in more mystical texts, the separation of the soul at birth from a complementary part of itself. The implication of this latter doctrine is that, if one finds the right partner, marriage will be that magical moment when the soul finds its complement. And we might discern a further meaning from the context of this film, since the shattered glass harks back to the violence upon which the relationship of Karen and Henry is founded.

Beyond the ceremonial wine glass, there is little else in the iconography or the behavior of the celebrants that reflects the culture of Judaism. During the brief moment when the couple stands before the rabbi, Henry wears a white yarmulke, but this has vanished by the time he begins dancing with his wife. The music (seemingly non-diegetic) is entirely secular, a medley of 1950s pop songs, concluding with "my life, my love, that is my dream." Most of the guests are seated at the "Italian table" and we quickly notice lots of the same faces first seen in the Bamboo Lounge, when Henry was introducing his mob-related cohorts. Their tribute to the newlyweds is not formally part of the ceremony, but it soon turns into a ritual of its own, as a huge procession of well-wishers (chiefly Paulie's nephews and cousins) queues up and begins to come forward, each bearing identical gifts. All plant the same mandatory kiss on Karen's cheek and place the same envelopes full of cash in her hands. Karen's interior monologue expresses amusement and admiration in about equal portion: "It was like we had two families. The first time I was introduced to all of them at once, it was crazy" (Scorsese 2004a, 42:20/42:35). What she remembers is that all had wives and daughters named Maria, and Paulie had innumerable relatives named Peter and Paul. On this festive day, Karen's bewilderment at the ways of ethnic Sicilians is offset by her fascination with her husband, but the dark side of her marginalized relationship to Henry's world will soon reveal itself.

The first off-key note is sounded at Micky Conway's "Hostess Party" (45:40/47:50), where Karen first mingles with the Mafia wives. Amid a profusion of creams, nail polish, and other cosmetics, we get a glimpse of their private lives, the gossip that floats from child rearing, to relationships, to travel experiences. Karen is surprised to learn that to visit Miami is to "wake up in Jew heaven" and genuinely shocked when told that the Sicilian wives beat their children with belts and broom handles. Her overall impression, gathered as she watches a woman having her face painted blue, was that they all "had bad skin and wore too much make-up." But she quickly decides that, in spite their hopelessly bad taste, they are reliable friends with strong communitarian impulses. This revised impression is offered in conjunction with upbeat images of birthdays, christenings, and visits to Vegas or the Caribbean. "We were very close," she says, "and being together made everything seem very normal. None of it seemed like crime, it was more like Henry was enterprising" (48:30/48:50). Her lingering anxiety comes from the fact that the "risks" of the job might send her husband to prison. But Henry, secure in his unshakeable self-confidence, assures her that only idiots go to jail: "Do you know who goes to jail, Karen? Nigger stick-up men, who fall asleep in their getaway cars" (Scorsese 2004a, 48:10/48:20). For a few bedazzled moments, Karen doesn't see the storm clouds gathering.

One thing that Karen fails to confront is the flagrant sexual infidelity of this culture. Henry says straightforwardly in his voice-over monologue that "Saturday night was for the wives, but Friday night at the Copa was for the girlfriends." We eventually are privy to a scene which reveals that these "family men," who participate in each others anniversaries and carry around each other's babies, all have mistresses for whom they provide food, lodging, and relatively pricy entertainment. Henry's Friday night wife is a woman named Janice Rossi, a character much like the wives at the hostess party in her dress, speech, and dubious taste. Having moved into the new apartment Henry has made available to her, she schedules her own version of Mickey Conway's hostess party to show off her living quarters. Predictably, the apartment is garish and littered with gaudy ornaments. All this transpires while the singer on the music track croons, "Pretend you don't see her, my heart." But unlike the other wives who never seem to raise this issue, Karen is enraged to find she is sharing her husband with Janice Rossi. Far from pretending not to see, Karen expels her husband from their home, publicly curses Janice over the apartment intercom, and complains incessantly to Paulie that she has been shamefully betrayed. Fearing the larger repercussions of this incident, Paulie orders Henry to return to his wife. Though the problem appears to be resolved, this is the moment when the crime syndicate begins to self-destruct. One substantial factor in this turn of events is Karen's joining her husband in a private drug-dealing business that has no ties with Paulie. In fact, Henry even persuades two of Paulie's most trusted lieutenants, Jimmy and Tommy, to join him in the improvised drug ring he now runs in deliberate defiance of his mentor.

Other circumstances also come into play. Tommy's behavior becomes increasingly erratic, as he commits two senseless murders, one of them a so-called "made-man," a major breach of gangster protocol. Tommy and Henry are sent to prison for battering a man who didn't pay a debt, normally not something that would raise a great stir, but in this case the victim has a sister who worked for the FBI. Even Paulie is briefly incarcerated. Henry also notices the increased level of casual violence among comrades of long standing. "Guys would get into an argument over nothin' and before you knew it, someone would be dead" (Scorsese 2004a, 01:00:30/01:00:40). But the real change is in the structure of the gang world itself, where new players are encroaching upon the old guard, and the drug trade is becoming the new cash cow of illicit enterprise. Karen and Henry catch this wave, moving drugs from a hub in Pittsburgh, so as to escape the close surveillance of Paulie, who has warned his energetic protégé about taking things into his own hands. What we also notice at this time is that Henry himself is becoming an addict, and his own habit takes a toll on both his income and judgment. Always headstrong, but sharp-witted and well organized, he now drifts toward paranoia.

At this point of the narrative, we have scenes that are mirror images of earlier scenes, similar in their setting or occasion, but darker and with hints of impending catastrophe. After everyone is out of prison, Paulie hosts a special dinner for Henry and Karen, characterized by the usual array of appetizing meats and sauces that the camera seems more than ready to follow to the table (Scorsese 2004a, 01:27:00/01:28:05). It resembles earlier food feasts, but the occasion isn't quite as frictionless as we might suppose. In one of the most poignant moments of the film, Paulie escorts Henry into his private garden (enveloped in greenery and graced by an icon of the Virgin Mary) to insist that Henry must cease to build a drug empire of his own. The tone is stern but fatherly, as if Paulie were addressing a prodigal son. He forgives the drug dealing Henry did to support his family while he was in prison, but demands that he now rejoin the clan. He also makes clear that Henry is his favorite lieutenant, his judgment superior to both Tommy's and Jimmy's, both of whom are prone to anger and careless behavior. This is their last cordial meeting, almost a last supper. The elderly Cicero, rather incongruously, has innumerable nephews and cousins, but no children or grandchildren. Clearly, Paulie would love to welcome the wayward Henry back into the family. But Henry pledges his loyalty while doubling down on his own reckless entrepreneurial adventures.

The other parallel scene is the second huge airline robbery, this time a theft from Lufthansa instead of Air France (Scorsese 2004a, 01:33:05/01:33:20). But as the first daring robbery launched several crime careers, this one will destroy many of them. As the Air France robbery was marked by cooperation and a willingness to share the spoils, the Lufthansa heist is marked by suspicion, resentment, and greed. Ultimately, it will take the lives of almost all the goodfellas who once gathered cordially at the Bamboo Lounge or were guests at Karen's wedding. Scorsese accentuates this sense of empires falling by weaving together the ruinous outcome of the Lufthansa robbery with the mob-style execution of Tommy and the impending prosecution that causes Henry to betray Paulie and seek refuge in the witness protection program.

At first glance, the airport robbery seems to succeed beyond the most extravagant expectations. The reporting media estimate the take at between two and five million dollars. Even that turns out to be a little low. Getting the news while he showers, Henry screams in ecstasy, jumping and pounding the walls. "This should have been the heist of a lifetime," he tells us, "six million in cash. More than enough to go around" (Scorsese 2004a, 01:38:00/01:38:10).

Inevitably, the hugely profitable robbery is followed by a raucous Christmas party, at which the thieves gather to celebrate their success. The mood is first upbeat with hugging, toasting, and backslapping. But as guests arrive, we find that several have already violated Jimmy Conway's prime directive, namely that no one should spend any of the loot before the trail of the robbery has had ample time to grow cold. One of the robbers has just bought a new car; another is showing off his wife in a $20,000 white mink coat. Jimmy is so angered by this affront that he actually strips her of the coat, while ordering her and her husband out into a New York winter's night. But the problems don't stop there. Maury, the low-level lieutenant who set up the robbery, seeks an advance for his services before the event takes place, then later pesters Jimmy doggedly for a quick hand-over of the cash. Worried and also crudely selfish, Jimmy is reluctant to share he money at all. When the Air France robbery succeeded, there was a relatively extended scene in which Paulie was given his "tribute," as everyone dutifully paid homage to the godfather. After Lufthansa, Henry Hill as narrator tells us that Paulie received his cut, but the only distribution we see is clandestine. Avoiding Maury, Jimmy retreats to a back room at the bar to give Henry his cut and Henry hides the cash in his jacket pocket before returning to mingle with the guests. A series of murders then follows: the couple who came in their new car; the culprit who had bought his wife the mink coat; even Maury who dies a particularly grim death and whose wife frantically begs Henry to intervene.

These scenes of corpses turning up in parked cars and meat lockers are intercut with the drug-induced breakdown of Henry, who is now being closely watched by federal helicopters. The man who was so confident of his organizational skill is at this point so distracted that he doesn't grasp his own complete incoherence. On his last day before capture, he is committed to selling a sack full of guns, closing a drug deal, and cooking his disabled brother a special Sicilian dinner that must be meticulously prepared. Dodging helicopters while racing about the city, Henry barely avoids a serious car crash. In the midst of these events, he is also calling home to remind his brother to stir the red sauce. In the end, he is undone by a wiretap that gives the FBI all the information necessary to mount felony charges against him.

The real climax, however, comes with the death of Tommy, who is murdered because he killed Billy Batts, himself an unsavory character but a ranking officer in the Gambino crime family. In what Henry describes as "real greaseball shit," Batts has special status because, on ethno-racial grounds, his behavior can only be challenged by another "made-man," meaning another Sicilian, who can trace his ancestry back to the homeland and has officially been admitted to the Mafia's highest circle of power. Practically speaking, Henry explains, a made-man can never be dealt with violently except after a "sit-down" with a godfather who must authorize the violence. Tommy, of course, is a brutal man whose behavior no one would be likely to defend. We watch him casually murder "Spider," the young flunky who waits tables while the gangsters play cards. But the killing of Batts is more ambiguous. Tommy is responding to a series of taunts that are surely intended to start a fight. He is certainly guilty of homicide, but to say the least there are extenuating circumstances that bear upon this crime. Tommy dies at the hands of his Sicilian brothers not because of the grave magnitude of his crime, but because of the ethno-racial rigidity of the crime empire.

This code holds implications for other behavior in the film. The crime empire is racist to its core, as evidenced by its uniformly hostile treatment of African Americans. They are all-purpose scapegoats. The driver who arranges for Tommy and Henry to highjack his truck feigns surprise that it is missing, then rushes back into the diner he just left to shout, "Would you believe it, a couple of niggers just stole my truck." Henry, of course, sneers at black lawbreakers, too stupid or lazy to evade the police. During the Friday-night-is-for-girlfriends scene, Tommy scolds his date for suggesting that Sammy Davis Jr. might be thought attractive. Even when couched in abstract and hypothetical language, the comment is unacceptable, as Tommy warns her. When she suggests she was imagining how, perhaps, a woman from Sweden might feel, Tommy insists this is a topic that must be avoided, since it could be misunderstood as an openness to interracial relationships. In the one instance where an African American is included in the Lufthansa theft, he is the first to be murdered when the project begins to unravel, even though he has nothing to do with buying fur coats or expensive automobiles. Ironically, the Mafia's ethno-racial xenophobia extends to Irishmen and half-Irishmen, like Jimmy and Henry. They both know they must conceal Tommy's "crime" from Paulie, since—with their defective racial credentials—they would have no right to advise or negotiate on Tommy's behalf.

Tommy's murder (and the grotesque ruse that sets it up) draws together all the threads of disaster, dissolving whatever bonds of friendship once united the closely knit partners. Henry and Jimmy were both witnesses to the murder and helped Tommy bury the body. They join him in reburying the decomposing corpse when the improvised burial site becomes part of a new housing development that will soon be excavated. When Tommy seems slated to become a made-man, both stand ready to celebrate his good fortune and share vicariously in his rise up the ladder of criminal achievement. They don't discern that this supposed promotion is a device to lure him to his death until they hear of his execution by way of a phone call Jimmy has arranged. Receiving the call, Jimmy becomes completely unhinged, first banging the phone against the cage of the phone booth, then violently kicking the phone booth until it falls over. Thereafter, he gives himself over to uncontrolled weeping, the only time in the film where he shows positive emotion. Henry is less obviously disconsolate, but he too is hurt and angered by the duplicity of the "brotherhood" that both have served dutifully. The shot to the face that kills Tommy mortally wounds the crime empire.

In Scorsese's reading of the American gangster world, the 1970s mark the end of an era. In the interview from *Film Comment* cited earlier, Scorsese speaks of a "breakdown of discipline, of whatever moral code those guys had in the Fifties and Sixties" (Smith and Scorsese 1998, 3). By the end of the 1970s, he continues, "the Mafia is nothing. They'll always be around, there'll always be an organized crime idea. But in terms of the old, almost romantic image typified by the Godfather films, that's gone" (3). As this arc is reflected in *GoodFellas*, "the film's first section represents a kind of idealized underworld with its own warmth and honor-among-thieves code. This gradually falls away, reflected in the characters of Tommy and Jimmy" (3). After Henry has turned states' evidence and ratted out all his old friends, the lengthy parade of characters being handcuffed and led off to prison puts in high relief this sense of an empire falling. Henry survives in a safe place, but all he has to show for his life is "my birth certificate and my arrest record." Like Jake LaMotta, he has felt the explosive individualism that resists all codes and constraints in its zeal to make its own mark upon the world. But unlike LaMotta, Henry has had no success in finding a repurposed life beyond the ethnic clan. Even the lavish wealth that is the usual measure of personal success has eluded him, like the fortune in heroin that his frightened wife flushes down the toilet. Like *Raging Bull*, and *Mean Streets* before it, *GoodFellas* is another map of the roads out of Little Italy, which in Scorsese's rendering are inevitably marked by closures, detours, and unreliable signage. Though his imagination of these events is perhaps too skeptical (where are the successful lawyers and neuro-surgeons?), it is congruent with the demographics of this period, which show an Italian-Sicilian community that is increasingly dispersed, no longer a society of specific nooks and crannies. This accelerated diffusion of ethnic culture is evident in the last of Scorsese's "gangster films," *Casino* (1995), to which we will turn in segment 4.

SEGMENT 3: THE IRISH INTERLUDE: *GANGS OF NEW YORK* (2001) AND *THE DEPARTED* (2006)

Broadening the investigation of ethnicity that had marked the "Sicilian phase" of his career, Scorsese reaches out in the new millennium to imagine the new-world Irish, who comprise the first powerful wave of ethnic undesirables to crash upon American shores in the middle of the nineteenth century. Impoverished, uneducated, and largely without marketable skills, they were immediately shunted into an underclass that drew scorn and blame from the Anglo-Nordic majority who controlled the levers of power. Their history represents in paradigmatic terms the struggle to assimilate that would be repeated through most of the next century in the similar striving of economic and political refugees from south and east Europe, as well as in the complex internal migration of African Americans from the rural to the urban world. The Irish provide Scorsese's template of the conflict between tribal values and civic loyalties that repeatedly shows itself in the performance of immigrant culture. Scorsese's analysis adheres closely to Karen Brodkin's formula, whereby "cultural capital" gradually offsets "ethno-racial taint."

In a richly comic scene early on in *Gangs of New York*, a renegade Irishman, who has betrayed his ethnic identity by joining Bill Cutting's (Daniel Day-Lewis) fiercely anti-immigrant Federation of American Natives, is
confronted by an awkward moment with Boss Tweed's (Jim Broadbent)
pet bird, which he keeps apparently as kind of an office ornament. Clearly
McGloin (Gary Lewis) has never imagined a bird as anything other than
a prospective target, or a snack for lunch, and begins to tease the creature
by twisting and twirling its cage. At once excusing and sneering at his inept crony, Bill remarks to Tweed, "Don't mind him, he *used to be an Irishman*" (Scorsese 2003, Disc 1, 18:45/18:55, emphasis added). The phrase
sums up the universe of ethnicity as Scorsese understands it: For the Irish,
as well as for the Italians and the Jews, ethnicity is a kind of affliction,
which might be remediated, but always with the threat of a relapse, or a
wound that will leave a telltale scar.

Though Scorsese is best attuned to his material when he is working
with the various offshoots of Little Italy, he undertakes in *Gangs of New
York* to paint the new world Irish on a broad historical canvas covering the
crucial period from 1848 through 1863. For better and worse, by the turn
of the new millennium, Scorsese's status as a celebrity auteur allowed him
to command production budgets comparable to those available to more
commercially oriented Hollywood directors, like Oliver Stone or even
Stephen Spielberg. Hence even a big budget costume drama, like *Gangs*, is
not out of reach, though the wider array of creative opportunities brings
with it a larger set of risks. Working from a massive set, which he built at
Cine City in Rome, he refurbishes the classical Hollywood history film,
but converts it into a vehicle to examine a marginalized subculture, rather
than adhere to the more typical narrative of national identity. Obviously
a work of imagination, and not a documentary on immigration, or a saga
meticulously respectful of fact, *Gangs* effectively engages the issue of assimilation and works through it precisely from the standpoint of ethno-
racial self-fashioning in conflict with ethno-racial assignment. Though
Leonardo DiCaprio remains a rather improbable Irishman and a few
details of the plot are wildly improbable (a one-eyed man who throws
knives and hatchets with deadly accuracy?), the film is powerful and
persuasive, in spite of a number of faults.

Without conscious intention, *Gangs of New York* follows the argument
threaded through Noel Ignatiev's *How the Irish Became White* (1995).
According to Ignatiev, and in keeping with Scorsese's filmic paradigm,
the Irish between the 1840s and the 1870s transformed themselves from
"white Negroes," a racially ambiguous people not clearly different
from black slaves (34–59), into citizens of "the White Republic," by no
means equal to what Ignatiev calls "the Protestant Ascendency," but
eligible for work, empowered to own property, and ready to participate

in politics (148–76). Imagining the world of the Irish immigrant during the two decades leading up to the American Civil War, Scorsese's film accurately apprehends how the Irish created a niche for themselves in New York City, in spite of the unwelcoming stance of the official culture and the furious resistance of nativist vigilantes who are immediately above them in social rank.

Numerous scholars and critics have noticed historical inconsistencies in *Gangs*, among them the anachronism of a public hanging in the 1860s, the misdating of the fire that destroyed Barnum's museum and menagerie, the fabrication of a naval assault upon Lower Manhattan, and—perhaps more seriously—the exaggeration of the number of Chinese in New York during the Civil War period (see DiGirolamo 2004, 123–41). Bryan Palmer (2003) brings most of these issues together under the rubric of the "Asbury/Scorsese myth-making" that serves to heighten the theatrical energy of the film, often at the expense of historical fact (329). But Palmer's more valuable insight, I think, lies in his recognition of Scorsese as "the unconscious Brecht of our times" (320). Though I'm not sure why the Brechtian strain is called "unconscious" (Scorsese is quite well informed about modern literature), the director handles his historical material in a decisively Brechtian manner, selectively placing and managing it, so as to convey a sociopolitical theme. That's why, as Palmer notes, the film projects a solid grasp of "the wider worlds of class and state formation" (321). More specifically, Palmer's analysis sheds light on the rapid transformation of New York's underclass and how the reach for power by the huge mass of new immigrants changed "relations of reciprocity with other structures of order" (331). In effect, Palmer credits Scorsese with successfully dramatizing how the despised Irish attached themselves to "the rising bourgeoisie of the capitalist nation" (335). But what unfolded, he concludes, was a "deformed working class insurrection" that fell short of its full potential (335).

While Palmer's essentially Marxist analysis prioritizes class, the ethnic factor is everywhere evident, since all of Scorsese's lead characters are unmistakably Irish (in their roles, of course, not their true ethnicity), an identity that advantages and disadvantages them at the same time. The film charts the fate of three Irishmen, all of them members of a Catholic gang whom the aggressively white Federation is determined to disperse and drive from the public streets. Given the circumstances of the time, their adaptive strategies reveal almost the full range of risk and opportunity that the challenge of assimilation entails. In the strivings of McGloin, Monk McGinn (Brendan Gleeson), and Amsterdam Vallon (Leonardo DiCaprio), we see a set of options, all seriously limited, that are played out against a background of brutal hostility and fast-paced historical change. As is typical of Scorsese, the assimilative efforts largely fail, but still cast

a glow of possibility across an otherwise dark and forbidding social landscape. The film begins with a near-massacre of the much-resented Irish
ethnics and ends in their finding new leadership and exacting revenge.
But their vengeance is a distraction from the energy they might have invested in building the cultural capital necessary for more authentic social
advancement. Amsterdam acknowledges this point in the last scene, but
only after it is too late to change the outcome of events.

Gangs of New York opens in the mid-1840s, when harsh conditions
in Ireland have pushed a huge wave of economic refugees toward the
United States, so many that Bill Cutting's Federation thinks them a dire
threat to American values, of which he and his band of violent patriots
are the self-appointed guardians. The Irish are organized under Priest
Vallon (Liam Neeson), himself a stern and violent man, who has no truck
with civics-book clichés or sentimental pieties. Politics is power, a turf
war with determined enemies who must be made to give ground. When
he accidentally cuts himself shaving, foreshadowing the stab wounds that
will soon take his life, he advises his young son, "the blood stays on the
blade." His prayers before the combat invoke a warrior faith: "St. Michael,
the Archangel, defend us in battle . . ." To underscore this point, he carries a giant metal cross, obviously a religious icon, but just as clearly an
instrument that might be used as a powerful bludgeon. The Irish forces,
unified by their Catholicism, assemble from living quarters that fulfill all
the English stereotypes of Celtic barbarism. They are dark, subterranean,
illumined by torchlight, virtually devoid of furniture or ornament. It is as
if the Irish rise from an almost demonic underworld, persuaded of their
own righteousness but unlikely to win sympathy or support from anyone
beyond their tribe (Scorsese 2003, Disc 1, 02:00/14:30).

While both sides take casualties, the Irish are soundly beaten—their
leader killed and their forces demoralized. But the camera carefully sorts
out the figures whom Scorsese will follow. McGloin, the traitor who later
makes common cause with the Federation, is shown preparing for combat, but never actively fighting for Priest Vallon. The boy, who will soon
name himself Amsterdam, is excluded from battle because of his age, but
later, after his father falls, seizes a knife and tries to engage his enemies.
Monk McGinn is the most effective of the warriors, kicking the door
open to launch the attack on the Federation and repeatedly clubbing his
way through rival warriors, still very much in the fray when Vallon dies
and the Irish accept defeat. McGinn and Amsterdam will later partner as
Scorsese frames his narrative of resistance.

Of these three characters, McGloin is the least admirable, accepting a
flunky role in Cutting's organization in return for reasonably tolerant
treatment and some sense of pseudo-power. Most notably, because he
now keeps company with the Federation of American Natives, he is al-

lowed to act "white," particularly when abusing the African Americans who attempt to celebrate Lincoln's Emancipation Proclamation. Crudely imitating Cutting, he proves his ethno-racial acceptability by assaulting his racial inferiors. Later, he takes the ultimate step of excoriating the Irish, even their Bishop, for having let "niggers in the church" (Scorsese 2003, Disc 2, 39:10/39:50). Beyond that, McGloin dresses well, laughs heartily, and stands as close as possible to Cutting in public places, shouting and cheering on his behalf. But he is treated like a house servant and soon will be humiliated in a fight with Amsterdam, who fifteen years later returns as an adult to contest Bill Cutting's authority and eventually overcome the Federation. As Bill's legions begin to lose power, McGloin is completely marginalized, dying meaninglessly in New York's anti-conscription riots of 1863. This is the fate of traitors, who lack conviction in any direction whatsoever.

McGinn is a far more interesting figure, who enters importantly into the political dialectic of *Gangs* as the only Irish character to attempt formal politics. Unlike McGloin, he completely shuns Cutting, but gains a modicum of autonomy as a property owner and an independent proprietor. Self-segregated among the ghettoized Irish, he serves his fellow ethnics as a barber. Aloof from the daily strife of the Five Points district, he stands above the jobless vagrants and pickpockets, including an array of blacks and Asians, that Cutting's gang polices and controls. His barbershop is built upon high ground, and as the narrative resumes after a fifteen-year hiatus, we first see him almost towering above the people scurrying about the muddy, crowded streets. He is a subaltern and without public power, yet relatively self-sufficient and eligible for power when the appropriate moment arises.

McGinn interacts with Amsterdam, looking down suspiciously when he first spies him on the streets, later reminding him of his Irishness and scolding him when he seems to have partnered with Bill Cutting. On one occasion, he lectures him at some length on the folly of bringing old-world grudges to nineteenth-century New York, a message Amsterdam largely fails to hear. But when Amsterdam looks for an ally with enough stature to credibly represent the Irish in the political arena, McGinn is the figure to whom he turns.

This is a moment in history when the macro-forces of the culture suddenly favor the upstart Irish. They are now much more welcome than in the 1840s because the males among them are potential conscripts for Lincoln's army as it struggles with the Confederacy. They will be fed regularly, and presumably be paid, even as they are sent to places they've never heard of ("Where's Tennessee?" asks one) to die for a cause they don't understand. Furthermore, as they are recruited for Lincoln's army, there is no doubt of their racial status—they are "white" soldiers, whatever Bill Cutting's

Federation of American Natives might think of them. Though the Irish
have no interest in the nation and only an opportunistic commitment to the
war, they sense their new circumstances and, on Amsterdam's initiative,
push to share power with other white gangs of the Five Points. All parties to these hostile encounters implicitly confirm the cynical wisdom Boss
Tweed imparts to his friends in uptown Manhattan, "you can always hire
half of the poor to kill the other half." But the film treats McGinn with considerably more sympathy, when on the recommendation of Amsterdam
and with Boss Tweed's endorsement, he runs for sheriff and wins an office
with some real political power.

Naturally, McGinn's transformation from street fighter to officer of the
law requires a serious makeover. First amused by the sober, well-dressed
image of himself he finds on the campaign poster, he quickly becomes
the proper, socially concerned ethnic this image connotes. Soon he's
wearing a plaid jacket, a bow tie, and a top hat, representing himself as
"the chosen voice of a new testament in a new world." He is now "Walter
McGinn," a highly credible candidate for sheriff. Instead of responding to
the ethnic slurs of his political rival, he reminds his constituency that "the
first war to win is not down in Dixie but right here in the Five Points."
After his landslide victory, achieved with the help of Boss Tweed, the
camera reflects McGinn's enhanced social status by shooting him from
a low angle, which causes him to tower over Bill Cutting, who has come
to challenge him to a duel. Fittingly, McGinn refuses to duel and instead
invites the champion of native-born Americans to "resolve our grievances
the democratic way." But the narrative has a tragic outcome. McGinn's
gesture toward civics-book virtue costs him his life. Enraged that he has
been vanquished by the system he purports to defend, Cutting buries a
knife in the back of the "Irish bog bastard," then offers to "burn him and
see if his ashes turn green" (Scorsese 2003, Disc 2, 44:30/50:00). In spite
of his dedicated effort to assimilate to the majority culture, even in death
McGinn will be not quite white.

McGinn's personal misfortune notwithstanding, his funeral is a huge
public event in the Five Points community, creating an image of the
Irish strikingly different from the one in the opening scene. Scorsese
self-consciously makes the two scenes parallel because they both begin
with the dramatic opening of a door, which brings the Irish forward into
public space. But the earlier scene of combat opens upon a bleak, snow-
covered landscape dominated by armed enemies. The funeral scene
pulls us through the church door toward a huge crowd of mourners
who have gathered to pay homage to their martyred sheriff (Scorsese
2003, Disc 2, 51:15/53:00).

We can see, moreover, how much the Irish themselves have changed
since the 1840s, both in how they look and the company they keep. No

Martin Scorsese, *Gangs of New York*. Sheriff Monk McGinn's well-attended funeral marks the beginning of Irish political assertion in New York City.
Source: This frame-capture is the work of James F. Scott, with technical support from the Instructional Media Center, Saint Louis University.

longer a rag-tag, cave-dwelling mob under the inspiration of an old-world priest, the Irish now march in an orderly procession that includes several carriages, a set of well-dressed dignitaries, and an array of mourners stretching for several city blocks. Earlier, when McGinn had appealed to them for support against Cutting, they seemed bewildered and reluctant to be involved, unaware that they could be a political force. But their behavior at the funeral is much more unified and committed. They emerge from a well-kept church and parade through a civilized neighborhood, a built environment with a coal yard and a tailor shop that suggest gainful employment and a certain level of affluence. The change is not lost on Boss Tweed, the chief political power broker of the era, who marches with them in the funeral procession, a few respectful steps behind Amsterdam, his new political ally. Already Tweed has broken with Cutting, who accepts his own marginalization when he tells Tweed that the future he seeks to build by assimilating the Irish is "not our future," a line spoken as he turns his back and dramatically walks away from his onetime friend and ally (Scorsese 2003, Disc 1, 01:12:40/01:12:55). It's from this newfound power base of Irish immigrant culture that Amsterdam momentarily steps out of the funeral procession to propose the combat in which Cutting will die. And significantly, at this moment Cutting stands completely alone, first flanked by McGloin in a two-shot, but utterly isolated as the camera tightens its composition to a one-shot in a slow, heavily charged zoom.

Amsterdam himself is the film's most complex character and central to Scorsese's analysis of ethnicity. Like many protagonists of Scorsese's earlier films (Charlie in *Mean Streets*, Jake in *Raging Bull*), he embodies all the contradictions and cross-purposes of upward mobility in conflict with the ethnic self. While his name is evidence of his deracination (we never learn how he got it), its oblique reference to the New York Dutch makes him a hybrid creature, not quite part of any community. It also is the disguise that allows him to join the ranks of Bill Cutting, presumably for purposes of vengeance, though at one moment he is tempted to accept respectful subalterncy in the Cutting clan. Eventually he will break with Cutting to bond with McGinn, and even Tweed, but he remains incompletely political, in no way attached to the axis of national power and always more loyal to the clan than the civic culture of New York.

The narrative in *Gangs* positions Amsterdam somewhere between McGloin and McGinn. He is also connected romantically with Jenny Everdeane (Cameron Diaz), an accomplished thief and former lover of Bill Cutting. Like McGloin, Amsterdam is invited into Cutting's organization, provided he does the leader's bidding. Like McGinn, he holds his tongue and keeps his own counsel, concealing his origins and cultivating an aura of independence. Like Jenny, he operates outside the civic order but shares with her a gift for mimicry that helps both of them succeed. They also share an ambiguous relationship to Cutting: she has carried (though aborted) Cutting's child; he saves Cutting's life by killing the Irish assassin who threatens it. Their erotic relationship complicates the ethnic paradigm but advances both toward assimilation, through partnership in another environment, where new beginnings are possible and "Irishness" might not be quite so unwelcome. According to Jenny's plan, they will escape to San Francisco, that western frontier which Frederick Jackson Turner believed turned ethnics into Americans. But this solution is shot through with irony: they fail to escape from the Five Points and, more importantly, they leave no progeny, an issue of consequence both in the real world and within the conventions of Hollywood costume drama.

The decisive point is that Jenny helps Amsterdam distance himself from Cutting and fiercely reassert his ethnicity. As Cutting's subaltern, Amsterdam has inserted himself into the New York world at the intermediate level of power, unofficially the second in command to Cutting and, through Cutting, affiliated with Tweed. Real power in the city belongs to the bankers and brokers of uptown Manhattan, who visit the Five Points very irregularly, only to satisfy themselves that lesser figures like Tweed are keeping the lower orders under control, by whatever means might be necessary. On one occasion Tweed organizes a public hanging, choosing his victims almost at random, in keeping with the principle that "the appearance of law must be upheld, especially when the law is being broken"

(Scorsese 2003, Disc 1, 22:05/22:25). Cutting's Federation serves Tweed's interests by adding vigilante muscle to the local police forces, which spend as much time fighting each other as they do enforcing the law. Amsterdam quickly discerns that he can advance himself in the community by associating with the Federation, which not only gives him modest social status but encourages his entrepreneurial skills. "We all worked for the butcher," says Amsterdam, "even Tweed, and even me, my father's son" (Disc 1, 01:10:01/01:10:50). When the Cutting clan has difficulty staging a prize fight that promises profit from bets and paid admissions, Amsterdam rescues the event by moving it out into New York harbor, beyond the conflicted jurisdiction of both the municipal police force and the metropolitan police force, one of which has not been appropriately bribed. This ingenuity earns Cutting's respect, and even provokes P. T. Barnum, the ultimate entrepreneurial adventurer, to cite Amsterdam as Cutting's public-spirited "young associate" who has made the profitable entertainment possible. At this moment Amsterdam meditates in a voice-over, "It's funny being took under the wings of the dragon, it's warmer than you think" (Disc 1, 01:11:30/01:12:40).

During this period Amsterdam is part of the Cutting coalition that manages local affairs and maintains the ethno-racial hierarchy, particularly with reference to African Americans and Chinese. When the city celebrates Lincoln's Emancipation Proclamation, Cutting's clan is quick to make sure that local blacks realize this legal fiction will not alter their status as underlings. Without the slightest provocation, McGloin attacks one of the dark-skinned celebrants, mercilessly beating him for assuming there might be something to celebrate. At the Chinese Pagoda, which Cutting seems to effectively control, the Asian women play geisha roles, donning colorful dancing costumes and doubling as prostitutes who are available to the white patrons, including figures like Tweed who routinely patronizes the establishment to enjoy the entertainment and casually conduct business with Cutting. The exotic Asians are welcomed as sexual commodities, but fall victim to constant sneers and slurs. Though they seem at moments to have some autonomy, Cutting is their master, insulting them at will and driving their "heathen music" off the stage when he chooses to proclaim "a night for Americans," full of flags, fireworks, and patriotic fanfare (Scorsese 2003, Disc 2, 09:00/14:30).

Nor are the Irish exempted from these ethno-racial insults, particularly when Cutting chooses to discourse upon racial mongrelization. At one moment we are watching a black male dancer, who seems to be awkwardly imitating Irish step-dancing. This prompts Cutting to remark on how the "rhythms of the Dark Continent might be thrown into the kettle with an Irish shindig." In a perverse rendering of the melting pot metaphor, the captain of the Federation finds amusement in "a jig doing a jig" (Scorsese 2003, Disc 1, 01:20:50/01:21:15). Cutting's unrelenting racism, and his determination to comprehend Irish culture as "non-white," makes it impossible for him to think of the Irish as prospective citizens. When Tweed tells him "that's the building of our nation, Americans aborning," as they watch Irish immigrants stepping off boats in New York harbor, Cutting's rejoinder is unsparingly rigid and racist: "I see no Americans, only trespassers, . . . Irish Harps who will do a job for a nickel that a nigger will do for a dime, and what a white man used to get a quarter for." In other words, as racial mongrels they undercut "white work." And in keeping with Babb's understanding of the "biosocial," Cutting's contempt for the Irish elides their genetics with their religion, their music, and their general social deportment. That's why he insists so furiously, "if I had the guns I'd shoot every one of them before they set foot on American soil," spitting at Tweed's feet as he concludes.

Amsterdam's only intervention during Cutting's angry exchange with Tweed is to say, very discreetly, almost too softly to be heard, "Bill's got mixed feelings as regards to the Irish." He then he walks away from Tweed in Cutting's company, with Cutting's arm draped over his shoulder (Scorsese 2003, Disc 1, 01:12:45/01:14:10).

Though he may not explicitly denigrate the Irish, Amsterdam joins Cutting in lampooning the national civic culture, at no time more obviously than when Lincoln is publically ridiculed for his stand against slavery. This is one of the most telling scenes of the film, since it plays off the vibrant energies of the ethnic gangs against an abstract civic culture which denizens of the Five Points find almost unintelligible. On this occasion, the Five Points Mission, a collection of clueless Evangelical Christians, treats local theater-goers to a stage play version of *Uncle Tom's Cabin*. The core image is one of Lincoln, suspended over the stage by ropes, like a giant puppet, asking the crowd to "stand united" in the name of the Union. Though he is supposed to appear god-like, he is weak and laughable, dangling helplessly in space while he mouths moral platitudes. When he touches upon race, inviting "dear Topsy" to "cradle Uncle Tom's head," the crowd becomes abusive, throwing vegetables at the stage and causing the Lincoln figure to gyrate wildly, broadly miming the death spasms of a man being hanged. Amsterdam joins Cutting in disparaging Lincoln, both shouting "down with the Union" as they hurl trash at the stage (Scorsese 2003, Disc 1, 01:15:15/01:18:45).

At this point the play is interrupted by the skirmish in which a would-be assassin attempts to shoot Cutting, but instead is shot by Amsterdam in Cutting's defense. This turn of events immediately makes national politics irrelevant, bringing us back to local issues of the Five Points. Cutting soon kills the wounded assassin, but not before cursing him as a "mother-whoring Irish nigger" (01:17:45/01:17:55), which ties the action in the

Martin Scorsese, *Gangs of New York*. The Lincoln Republicans bring the Anti-Slavery movement to New York City. The ethnic Irish, and others, respond with rioting and disruption.

Source: This frame-capture is the work of James F. Scott, with technical support from the Instructional Media Center, Saint Louis University.

theater to the abstract concerns the play purports to address. The last glimpse we have of Lincoln is another shot of a figure suspended amid billowy clouds and entangled in a web of ropes that make purposeful movement impossible. More decisively than at any other moment, Amsterdam is here identified with Cutting, at odds with his own ethnicity, and alienated from the national movement represented by Lincoln, from which the Irish will ultimately benefit. Not surprisingly, the scene causes Amsterdam to be throttled and physically shaken by a fiercely angry McGinn, who might possibly have been implicated in the assassination plot.

Thereafter, Amsterdam begins the process of separating himself from the Federation, hatching his own assassination plot, attaching himself to McGinn, and building a relationship to Jenny, a complicating figure in the political discourse of *Gangs*. Formerly Cutting's mistress, Jenny now prospers as an accomplished thief who gains entrance to affluent uptown homes by miming the good manners and soft voice of a well-behaved Irish servant girl. Her distancing of herself from Cutting prefigures the break Amsterdam himself will soon make.

In the romantic company of Jenny, now his constant companion, Amsterdam recovers his Irish ethnicity. After he is brutally assaulted by Cutting, she nurses him back to health, at the same time reconnecting him to McGinn. Significantly, these scenes are enacted in the same subterranean premises where we saw Amsterdam as a child. Here he is given his father's razor and recalls that "the blood stays on the blade" (Scorsese 2003, Disc 2, 28:00/28:10). His internal monologue invokes his Irish comrades' "common home across the sea," though the premises are also a charnel house, where we see piles of skulls behind Jenny as she ministers to her lover. Quite improbably, Jenny and Amsterdam even seem to embrace Catholicism, invoking the Virgin Mary, joining cohorts in a rebuilt church, and kneeling to pray for the murdered Johnny, who has paid with his life for his presumed disloyalty to Cutting. "Our faith is the weapon most feared by our enemies," says Amsterdam in an internal monologue, and "the past" is now made sacred as that place where "our fathers have shown the way." When Amsterdam resurfaces from months of subterranean hiding, he is the self-appointed leader of the "15,000 Irish a week" who are debarking from boats in New York harbor. Aware of his newfound power, he announces to followers, "we're not a gang, we're an army." And he is aware that "the earth turns," even if "we don't feel it" (Scorsese 2003, Disc 2, 41:00/42:50).

Though Jenny is essentially unpolitical, she assists Amsterdam in approaching Tweed to promote McGinn's candidacy for sheriff. This act brings her and Amsterdam to the threshold of political engagement. Significantly, however, both pull back from this threshold to pursue their romantic relationship and settle personal grudges against Cutting. In terms of mimicry, Amsterdam has managed to simulate "whiteness," modeling his behavior upon Cutting's and making himself the leader of an ethnic clan, much like the Federation, except for the fact that it is less obsessively racist and admits at least one African American to its inner circle. But its totem, "The Dead Rabbits," advertises its anachronism and its detachment from concerns with national identity. Amsterdam never breaks through to the point that he can think of himself as a "citizen." The larger world remains unknown to him, just as it does to Jenny, even while she makes plans for both of them to start a new life in San Francisco. And as a couple they remain childless, cut off from the future. From the standpoint of metaphor, the scars from Jenny's abortion are the decisive visual marker of a dead end.

These themes come to completion in the closing scene where Amsterdam is avenged upon Cutting, but at the expense of the fullest potential in himself (Scorsese 2003, Disc 2, 00:58:30/01:08:30). Loyal to the Dead Rabbits, he launches his clan war against the Federation at the same moment when the larger city is caught up in the brutal anti-conscription riots that will eventually be put down by intervention of the military. The imagery of this scene is full of contradictions and dislocations, visual as well as thematic. The action of the rival gangs waging their battle is cut together with the more generalized rioting, so that the cross-purposes of the several groups is underlined in the editing and composition. At one moment the Dead Rabbits and the Federation pause in wonderment, as they watch an elephant, newly released from Barnum's animal menagerie by the erupting mayhem, casually stroll along one of the streets of the Five Points. Moments later, artillery shells fired into downtown New York from ships in the harbor burst amid the battling clans, randomly cutting down fighters from both groups. And again, there is a kind of amazement in this encounter with the national narrative. To the Dead Rabbits and the Federation, the Civil War is simply a confusing interruption, a distraction from the overriding question of which clan will prevail.

Meanwhile, we are shown that the more consequential political process is continuing, virtually unrecognized by Amsterdam and Cutting. Tweed surveys the carnage wrought by the brutal suppression of the draft riots, which after four days has left whole streets populated by corpses awaiting burial. His comment is "get down to the docks and make sure everyone coming off the boats is given hot soup and bread—we're burying a lot of votes here tonight" (Scorsese 2003, Disc 2, 01:09:45/01:10:05). Recognizing that lots of his constituents have died at the hands of the New York militia, he wants assurance that their number will be immediately replenished by Irish immigrants who are just coming ashore. They will be primed to vote for Tammany Hall by the next election.

In commenting on these scenes from his own work, Scorsese remarks the complexity of Amsterdam and the factors that impact his destiny (2003, Disc 2, "Special Features"). After his break with Bill Cutting, says Scorsese, his protagonist must rethink completely who he is, effectively "be reborn." Amsterdam finds a way, the director continues, "a way that is within the American system, which is politics," an apparent reference to his compact with McGinn and Tweed. "But that's cut short," so Amsterdam is "forced back into a primal state" where he represents nothing more forward-looking than the values of the clan and loyalty to his dead father. This makes him and Jenny "almost antique . . . makes them obsolete." In his closing monologue, delivered in voice-over, Amsterdam himself seems aware of his irrelevance. As he is burying the razor that symbolizes the clan warfare for which he has lived and died, he speaks of "our great city . . . born of blood and tribulation." Yet he adds, "for those of us who lived and died in those furious days it was like everything we knew was mightily swept away." Then as we enter upon a series of dissolves which morphs the smoldering ruins of 1863 into the skyline of modern New York, Amsterdam concludes, while he and Jenny are dissolved out of the scene, "whatever they did to build the city up again, for the rest of time, it would be like we was never there" (Disc 2, 01:11:10/01:12:00). Hence the closing theme song, U2's "The Hands That Built America," has a somewhat ironic ring. Contemporary New York City has come after them, but not really out of them. The hands that built America were other hands than those of Amsterdam and Jenny.

Scorsese is a master storyteller of the assimilative process that falls short of its goal. Charlie Cappa dreams of an uptown apartment that he never moves into; Jake LaMotta flees to Miami but is drawn back to ethnic New York; Ace Rothstein makes it to the top of the world in free-wheeling Las Vegas, only to watch the Tangiers crumble, reducing his own strivings to glare and dust. Like these other Scorsese protagonists, Amsterdam advances to the threshold of full emancipation but stumbles before taking the last step. The pattern repeats itself in *The Departed*, as Scorsese returns to the social history of the Irish, this time in a more contemporary context. Though the ethnic protagonists of this drama seem to have escaped the coils of family and neighborhood, the lure of the tribe is ultimately too powerful and they succumb to violence rooted in an archaic past.

By situating *The Departed* in Boston rather than New York, Scorsese evokes a world that the Irish virtually dominate through their sheer numbers and the degree to which they control the instruments of power. A full century has passed and their gift for political discourse (already anticipated in *Gangs*, with the easygoing fluency of McGinn) has advanced them to positions of genuine authority: the police force, even its most elite unit, overflows with Irish surnames—Queenan, Sullivan, Dignam, Costigan, Barrigan. But somehow they are still haunted by vestiges of the ethnic clan. Family, neighborhood, acquaintanceship, church, and school count for more than professional résumés or bureaucratic formalities. Moreover, patronage and political corruption are a way of life. That's why Irish gangsters fraternize so cordially with lawmen, and police special forces find it relatively easy to insert themselves into criminal gangs. Though the action of the film centers upon bringing down the Irish crime boss, Frank Costello, the outcome of events is so chaotic as to suggest the civic order may not be susceptible to repair.

Loosely based on the Chinese thriller *Infernal Affairs*, *The Departed* gets its Irish pedigree by borrowing selectively from the career of Whitey Bulger, a Bostonian Irish mobster from the 1970s and 1980s, who combined the brutality of a violent criminal with the social service impulses of an old-fashioned political boss. As Dick Lehr and Girard O'Neill recount in *Black Mass: The Irish Mob, the FBI, and a Devil's Deal* (2000), Bulger used his younger brother, a state Congressman, to secure protection from the FBI in return for occasionally performing as an informant. When Scorsese assimilates this narrative into *The Departed*, Bulger morphs into Frank

Costello (Jack Nicholson), a witty, likeable, but absolutely savage man. His brother is erased from the script but Costello's status as informant is retained to complicate the already labyrinthine relationships within the special-forces unit of the Boston police force. Like Bulger, Costello is depicted as a character who can publicly project himself as Robin Hood, but who is secretly implicated in murder, drug dealing, and other criminal schemes. The plot revolves around his efforts to maintain his power by recruiting two young disciples to ward off the police and sustain his authority in a community that is undergoing rapid change.

In *The Irish Way* (2012), James Barrett describes in careful detail how the Irish appropriated political power, not always at the highest levels of authority, but particularly within the immigrant community that looked to the Irish for orientation and leadership (see esp. 195–238). This was because their native fluency in English "gave Irish politicians a vital advantage over most other groups" (200). But the Hibernian oligarchs used their power with some generosity, allowing Italians, Jews, Poles, and others to make modest advances so long as they were respectful of local Irish bosses. There was a rough-hewn democracy in this system—a fully articulated network of community relationships organized around "the Catholic Church, the Democratic party, the police and fire departments, the unions, the social athletic clubs and the street gangs, and other vital bonding institutions" (201). Among these other "bonding institutions," none were more important than the saloon and the vaudeville theater, the first, a public space that functioned as a political club, the second, a source of innumerable ethnic stereotypes that furnished serviceable images of inner-city culture. This was the social base that produced at least two generations of Irish power brokers, including Timothy Sullivan and Francis Murphy in New York, the Daley dynasty in Chicago, and James Michael Curley, the four-term mayor of Boston, who also served as governor and in the national Congress.

The influence of these political bosses was based on their control of patronage, the power to hire and fire public employees. Which meant, as a grateful Italian immigrant once said, "If ya needed a job, ya went over and saw some Irishman" (Barrett 2012, 200).

The darker side of the system was its tie to organized crime. The saloon might double as a house of prostitution or a site of illegal gaming. It could also serve as a command center for fixing prize fights or collecting protection money. Even Mayor Curley, in spite of his unfailing success at the polls, had to ward off two felony indictments in the course of his career. Scorsese's Frank Costello is the sinister child of this culture in its waning moments, as it has drifted more deeply into criminality and responds in near panic to real and imagined threats. As is clear from *The Departed*, the other new circumstance is the faltering influence of the Church, once closely allied with the political establishment, but increasingly margin-alized after the turbulence of the 1960s. In *Catholic Boston* (1985), James O'Toole notes "a new period of estrangement between the religious and political realms" that set in after 1970 (61). Catholicism gives the protago-nists of *The Departed* a common language, but it no longer provides a set of real beliefs or a viable code.

In the first scene we meet Costello, whose ironic voice-over guides us through the events we are observing. Riot and discord spill out from every corner of the screen. Though he seems to be losing control of his kingdom, Costello doesn't intend to let inhospitable circumstances determine his fate: "I don't want to be a product of my environment. I want my environment to be a product of me." The imagery tells us it is the early 1970s, shortly after Massachusetts' Racial Imbalance Act (1965) mandated that black students be bused into white neighborhoods of Boston to attend previously all-white schools. This thrust against white privilege generated a powerful backlash from local political leaders like Louise Day Hicks, who raged against black "agitators" who were disrupt-ing the social landscape. In the scene unfolding before us, street fights are cut together with defense lines of blue-clad, helmeted police officers on hand to guard black students against hostile crowds. A young black male peers tentatively through the broken window of a school bus, while a brief cut catches a black leader chastising white citizens for the "hate in your heart." The would-be students are challenged by a phalanx of angry white protestors of the stripe Hicks regularly turned out during these years to intimidate racial intruders. Costello resents this power shift in the culture, though his tone is cool and cynical: "If there's one thing I have against the black chappies, it's this: nobody gives it to you; you've got to take it" (Scorsese 2006, 00:35/01:40). Clearly, he is rankled by the sense of entitlement that the black community has gleaned from affirma-tive action. He wants this restless minority to earn power, presumably by street-fighting and mayhem, the way he imagines the Irish did it two or three generations back, and as he himself is doing it now.

Besides, Costello's more immediate enemies are the "Knights of Co-lumbus, the real head-breakers, real Guineas" (01:50/01:05), namely the Italians, who have moved into the neighborhood in greater num-bers and pose a more serious threat to his authority. In this moment of challenge, we find him looking for disciples and allies who belong to the upcoming generation.

The next scene, where Costello recruits Colin Sullivan (Matt Damon), is a brilliant compression of well-performed ethnic politics. Costello finds Sullivan, a boy about ten years old, in a quick shop where he has come to collect protection money from a client who has not paid his dues in a timely way. The crime boss is seen only in silhouette, a dark shadow that lurks in front of the camera as an almost ghostly presence. "This won't happen again, Mr. C.," the client assures Costello, after receiving a reprimand that veils a threat. But to provide the carrot as well as the stick, Costello puts cash in the hand of the proprietor's daughter, encouraging her to "go buy some make-up." His real target, however, is Colin, a smart, shy child, who is frightened but fascinated by the powerful gangster, a little like the young Henry Hill. Unsurprisingly, they are connected through the neighborhood: "You're Johnny Sullivan's boy, aren't you? Live with your grandmother?" When the boy acknowledges the connection, he is given a big bag of groceries for the family, topped off with a couple of action comics for himself. "Do well in school?" When Colin's answer is positive, it's followed by an invitation: "If you're ever interested in a little extra money, come 'round and see me." Clearly that does interest Colin (Scorsese 2006, 01:50/03:40).

The next scene is of young Colin in altar service, sucking in the smell of burning incense from a thurible that swings immediately in front of his face. At this point he seems a dutiful child of the Catholic Church. The priest is reciting the funeral liturgy for a deceased member of the parish, but these ceremonial words are drowned out by a voice-over from Costello, which draws us into the scene that follows. Now Colin is a few years older and the scene is someone's garage. The abrupt shift to a completely secular location sets the stage for Costello's preachments against Catholic authority: "Church wants you in your place—kneel, stand; kneel, stand. If you go in for that sort of thing, I don't know what to do for you. A man makes his own way." Later we find Costello openly insulting a local churchman and claiming he has had a love affair with a woman who is now a nun (Scorsese 2006, 03:40/05:00).

But Costello comes from a Catholic world that he shares with Colin. Earlier, in an interior monologue, he had spoken rather wistfully of Catholicism, as of something once valuable, now lost: "Years ago, we had the Church. That was only a way of saying we had each other." In other words, it was the ethnic tie, not the doctrine and discipline of Catholicism, that made the Church important to the community. In the scene with Colin, the boy and the man connect through their Catholic childhood. This is ironically confirmed when Costello announces his credo, "*non serviam*," which Colin immediately identifies as "James Joyce." Both realize, of course, that Stephen Daedalus, Joyce's protagonist in *Portrait of the Artist,* is paraphrasing Milton's Satan, who rises from a fiery lake to proclaim, "Better to reign in hell than to serve in heaven." In *Portrait,* Stephen cites Lucifer as his exemplar, resolving to turn away from church, family, and nation: "I will not serve in that which I no longer believe, whether it call itself my home, my fatherland, or my church." Costello and Colin thus partner as renegade Catholics brought together under the banner of Lucifer, by another renegade Irish Catholic, James Joyce. Colin evidently accepts Costello's assurance: "When you want to be something you can be it, something they don't tell you in the Church." This scene ends with a close-up of Colin's face, which dissolves directly to a close-up of a mature Colin, now a cadet at the Police Academy. But the voice of Costello lingers on the soundtrack as he pronounces the newly minted police officer, "My boy." Costello has succeeded in putting his "boy" in the elite special forces of the Boston police. Together they will "reign in hell" (Scorsese 2006, 03:10/05:00).

The second subaltern Costello recruits is Billy Costigan (Leonardo DiCaprio), whose path into the gangster's inner circle is even more labyrinthine than that of Colin. In fact, Costigan's relationship to family, gang, and police bureaucracy is bewildering in its intricacy. The son of an airport baggage handler, Billy is the nephew of Jack Costigan, a well-connected crime boss who once was in the same gang as Costello. Most members of the Costigan family have criminal connections. But young Costigan is determined to be a police detective, to the amazement of almost everyone. When he enters Costello's gang it is as a police mole working undercover for the special-forces unit.

Scorsese plays Sullivan and Costigan against each other as diametric opposites of Boston's Irish world, each with its own stereotype from vaudeville, stage, and screen. Sullivan is the convivial Irishman—radiant smile, outgoing disposition, charm, and confidence in the presence of women. Costigan is the conflicted, self-destructive Irishman—introverted, self-conscious, and prone to violent outbursts. Sullivan's motivation is straightforward: he is greedy and craves status. The condo he buys has a balcony that looks out on the golden dome of the state Capitol. From first sight of it he is mesmerized by its elegance. Serving Costello is the easiest way to get rich. Costigan's motives are much more oblique. He joins Costello as an undercover agent only because the police academy will accept him in no other capacity, and he never considers how easily he could perform as a double agent, serving Costello while pretending to serve the police. Why he is determined to become a police officer is never completely clear, though it's partly to spite his extended family, which he feels has disrespected and abused his mother. Whatever the full spectrum of his motives, his insistence upon going his own way entangles him in a hopelessly dense web of familial and ethnic relationships.

These disruptive tendencies surface conspicuously when Costigan is interviewed for the special-forces unit. Sullivan slides smoothly through this process, even though he is Costello's hand-picked henchman. Costigan, on the other hand, is subjected to brutal questioning by Queenan (Martin Sheen) and Dignam (Mark Wahlberg), who apparently have already decided he is the wrong kind of Irishman. "Do you know what we do here?" asks Queenan, but in spite of Costigan's positive answer, Dignam insists, "You have no idea." Instead, he wants to invoke Costigan's "family tree," which includes "your Uncle Jackie," a well-known local thug and another family member who tried to sell stolen guns to a federal agent. Costigan's rejoinder, "What's this got to do with me?" carries no weight, even when he adds that one of his relatives was a priest. Soon we learn Costigan is suspect for reasons other than the family's criminal connections. "You grew up on the North Shore," Dignam charges, a relatively posh suburb where Costigan spent time with his mother: "What's a lace curtain mother-fucker like you doin' in the staties?" Dignam insists he speaks with two different accents, the street slang of the projects and the pretentious middle-class inflections of the North Shore. Sullivan was praised for his intelligence and his ambition. Costigan is told, "You scored 1400 on your SATs. You're an astronaut, not a statie." Queenan is less fierce than Dignam but warns Costigan against "self-deception." Apparently Costigan's illegible acculturation (which is admittedly complex) disqualifies him for membership in the special-forces unit. He is accepted only when he agrees to operate as a police mole in the Costello gang (Scorsese 2006, 09:10/11:50).

What's interesting is that Costigan encounters a mirror image of Dignam's response as he goes back to his extended family and apprentices himself to the gang. When they meet at the hospital where Billy's mother is dying, his Uncle Edward asks, "What's this I hear about you becoming a cop?" After Queenan has performed an elaborate ruse to create Billy's undercover identity (it includes an incarceration for assault at the state penitentiary), he still has difficulty convincing his cousin Sean (Kevin Corrigan) of his criminal credentials: "I'm not a cop, I'm your cousin." Though we see him in his prison cell pumping iron while other prisoners are resting, he still seems to lack the full-spectrum tough guy image (on two occasions he is mocked because his favorite drink is cranberry juice, a vestige, no doubt, of the North Shore years). It takes two brutal fights to establish his credentials as a genuine thug. Throughout this extended moment, however, Costello maintains personal contact with his favorite underling. The condolence wreath the crime boss sends Costigan at his mother's passing is the most elegant floral display at her sparsely attended burial service. Unlike Billy's immediate kin, Costello appreciates his closeness to his mother. Finally, Costello approaches him, but the ordeal is not yet over. In a harrowing interrogation, Costello's principal enforcer breaks the cast on his injured arm, and then Costello himself beats Costigan's vulnerable limb with the heel of a heavy work shoe. In the midst of this trial by fire, Costigan shrieks in pain, "I am not a cop" (Scorsese 2006, 35:50/36:10). The price this society exacts for cultural ambivalence is frightening.

Once these force fields are in place, Scorsese organizes the narrative to emphasize how much the warring factions have in common as
disharmonious elements of a single ethnic community. Costello and
his henchmen are so well known to the special-forces unit that, in the
information briefings, they are treated almost like drunken uncles who
misbehave at Christmas parties. There are chuckles all around the table
when the mother of one of Costello's most brutal enforcers is introduced
as "straight out of *Going My Way*." In one memorable moment of ethnic
solidarity, Dignam and Queenan happen upon Costello somewhere along
the street and they share a joke at the expense of a Chinese gang. Costello
has just outwitted the police team while carrying through a massive theft
of micro-processers that he apparently then sells to the Chinese. But instead of actually turning over millions of dollars worth of militarily sensitive hardware, Costello passes off to his clients several crates of worthless
knock-offs, much to the amusement of Dignam and Queenan. Scamming
the Chinese touches both racial and patriotic chords, which resonate as
powerfully for the cops as for the robbers. Costello's smoothly executed
double-cross of the racial aliens so pleases Dignam and Queenan that it
almost compensates for the fact that Costello, assisted by Sullivan, has
made laughing stocks of the special-forces unit with his embarrassingly
easy backdoor escape. The police have looked inept but the Irish community, with Costello at its helm, has stood tall against the demonic "other."

The blurring of boundaries continues as Costigan and Sullivan make
repeated moves and counter-moves against each other, both coordinating
their behavior with the police unit one serves and the other pretends to
serve. Moreover, both men enjoy a romantic relationship with the same
woman, Madolyn (Vera Farmiga), who works for the police department
herself as a psychiatrist. Because they share her as a confidante, we gain full
access to their thoughts about their respective jobs. Ironically, the disloyal
officer, Sullivan, is completely comfortable in his role, praised and valued
by his peers. In his first exchange with Madolyn, he makes clear to her that
he is not a "policeman." He is a special investigator. He also persuades
her that secrecy is crucial to his sensitive law-enforcement mission, hence
not something she would ever be allowed to ask questions about. Their
courtship is a model of middle-class protocol, from a casual flirtation in
the elevator, to dinner at an expensive French restaurant, to an invitation
to move into his posh condo overlooking the Capitol, which she accepts
without hesitation. This sexual conquest impresses his boss, because it
proves he "isn't a homo" and adds to his "immaculate record." The aura of
masculine bravado is also evident in the police intramural with the fire department, where Sullivan leads the taunting of the vanquished firefighters
who lose the tug-of-war match. The crowning irony is that when the unit

finally discerns there is a mole in its midst, Sullivan, with his "immaculate record," is put in charge of the inquiry to ferret out the traitor.

Costigan, on the other hand, is relentlessly abused by his fellow officers, as if he could never be a worthy member of the force. There is an altercation every time he meets with his handlers, and on one occasion he and Dignam actually come to blows, with a reference to Costigan's "lace curtain" family life again serving as the flashpoint. He is never tough enough to satisfy the unit, though we see him take severe beatings and also remain mute while he witnesses the violent reprisals of Costello's enforcers. Perhaps taking her cue from the department, Madolyn is similarly condescending in her first meeting with Costigan as a patient. When she asks about his feelings, he makes no overt reply, but the question touches off a quick montage of disturbingly contradictory images: family album pictures that are tender and positive; a sequence where a disobedient underling is shot, and his premises torched; Costigan pleading with Queenan and Dignam to extract him from the undercover world before he is found out and murdered. Unsatisfied with his narrative, Madolyn's first thought is to deny him medication, surmising that she's dealing with a junkie who is trying to feed his drug habit. Moments later, she softens and pursues him, understanding that she might have misjudged. The positive transformation of their relationship becomes one of the small upbeat elements in an otherwise very bleak narrative.

Madolyn ultimately becomes the moral center of the film, a relatively neutral observer who parses the behavior of her rival lovers and gradually recognizes Costigan's superior worth. In spite of seeming intimacy, Sullivan and Madolyn are not really close: the comfortable transparency of their relationship is largely a mirage. In one crucial scene, they are separated by glass walls, fully visible to each other in wholesome daylight, but in separate worlds (Scorsese 2006, 01:11:00/01:13:00). Sullivan's voice escapes Madolyn's hearing, as he discusses her with Costello in crude and demeaning terms. The relationship with Costigan, in marked contrast, is tentative, but genuine. He blunders into her life confusedly, first confronting her fiercely in their therapy session, later turning up at her apartment, apologizing for his intrusion. In this second scene, both are framed in doorways, archetypes of liminal space. Costigan says almost nothing, but the agitation of his fingers, spastically tapping the doorframe, speaks silently of powerful, largely positive emotions. Sullivan takes no interest in a picture of Madolyn as a child, as if to say he is unconcerned with any world besides the present. Finding the same picture, Costigan studies it carefully, clearly eager to know who she is. Madolyn encourages him to make love to her, because "your vulnerability is really freaking me out" (01:19:20/01:22:40). Though they never form a coherent partnership,

Costigan entrusts her with the tapes that certify his identity and clear him of culpable involvement with Costello.

Nothing, however, can ward off the Celtic bloodbath that concludes *The Departed*. Queenan dies while trying to protect Costigan, and Sullivan murders Costello, in what is officially a shooting in the line of duty, but in reality is an act to assure that Costello cannot expose his protégé's true character. Costigan is murdered by another inside man that Costello has planted on the police force. Dignam is fired for insubordinate behavior toward Sullivan, but returns to murder him, just when it seems the corrupt police officer has fully succeeded in his massive deception. Ironically, Costello has already foreseen the tragic inevitability of this outcome. In an early voice-over, he cynically provides the collective obituary of all these problematic Irishmen: "They told us we could be either cops or criminals. I say, when you're looking at a loaded gun, what's the difference?" (Scorsese 2006, 04:45/05:00). Costigan ultimately stands recognizably above all others, as he is given a hero's burial and posthumously awarded the Bronze Star. But we are left with a sense of tremendous waste, made inevitable by the inability or the unwillingness of any of these men to separate themselves psychologically from the ethnic clan.

In *Scorsese's Men* (2004), one of the most ambitious monographs devoted to this director, Mark Nicholls reads the filmmaker's entire creative output as a "melancholy momentum" resulting from tension between the individual and the "mob." Here the word "mob" is understood by Nicholls not as the Sicilian Mafia, or its Irish equivalent, but in Freudian terms as the horde that doggedly resists the self-pleasuring of the individual, driving him toward conformity and the defeat of his private impulses (2004, xv–xvi). Simply put, Scorsese's protagonists are "melancholy" because the object of their desire is beyond what the mob allows them to strive for. This is a powerful formula that yields valuable readings of several films central to the Scorsese canon. What's missing is the conspicuously ethnic character of this "mob" and the special pressure these ethnic factors exert. In treating *Gangs of New York*, for example, Nicholls never mentions that the characters are Irish or that the conflict is deeply embedded in ethnic history. Surely he is correct in assigning a significant place in the film to the son's relationship to his father—Bill Cutting's father, who died in what his son regards as the founding of America, and Amsterdam's father, who died seeking a place for the Irish in the new land. But Nicholls is wrong in saying the film presents "no alternative point of desire to challenge obedience to the father" (153). The problem is that the "alternative point of desire" lies outside the web of ethnic obligations, which pose more serious barriers to personal growth than the simple constraints of neighborhood or family.

This formula also holds true for Costigan in *The Departed*. Like Amsterdam in *Gangs* (both roles are enfleshed in celluloid by the same actor), Costigan arrives at the threshold of psychic independence, but pulls back, entrapped by real and imagined constraints imposed by his mother, his peers, and several authority figures who insist upon his obligations to them. He lives and dies trying to prove that a "lace-curtain" Irishman from the North Shore can be as tough as a shanty Irish street kid without surrendering to the criminal enticements of Costello and his gangster cronies. Couldn't he be a stock broker? A tax accountant? A software engineer? His relationship to Madolyn (like Amsterdam's romantic commitment to Jenny) suggests the possibility of a new beginning, but he is gunned down before finding a role model upon which to pattern his assimilated, post-ethnic identity.

SEGMENT 4: ETHNICITY REIMAGINED: *CASINO* (1995) AND *THE WOLF OF WALL STREET* (2013)

GoodFellas is the capstone to what some critics call "Scorsese's Italian-American trilogy," a designation that ties it closely to *Mean Streets* and *Raging Bull*. This naming instinct is a correct one, since the three films clearly belong together, even though they were not conceived as a unit. But there is also something to be said for thinking of Scorsese's work among the Italians as a tetralogy, which invites us to understand *Casino* as another of his ethnic films, now set on a far frontier of American culture, where the sons of Jerusalem and Palermo make one final effort to build a home. The film's chief protagonist is a smooth-talking, high-performing Jew named Ace Rothstein (Robert De Niro), who for at least two decades has loaned his odds-making expertise to the Mafia, which values him as an expert consultant in their far-flung gaming empire, although he is expected to take orders from the Italianate hierarchy of crime bosses, represented (badly!) in Las Vegas by Nicky Santoro (Joe Pesci). Ace is rewarded for his good service to the mob with an opportunity to manage the Tangiers Casino, one of the flagship gambling palaces the New York and Chicago families had built in Vegas during the 1960s, when their criminal enterprise moved west. He is fully aware that this is his chance for a new beginning, quite literally a new frontier. Speaking of Ace, Scorsese says, "This is the only place where he can use his expertise in a legitimate way, and so become part of the American WASP community" (Brunette 1999, 224). His elegant gaming parlor, he says in an early voice-over, is "a kind of morality car wash . . . [that] does for us what Lourdes does for hunchbacks and cripples" (Scorsese 2005, 05:35/05:50).

He has come west to be cleansed of his ethnic taint, to found a family, and establish himself as a legitimate businessman. On this trajectory, *Casino* is another failed escape from the ethnic nest, an opportunity to transcend ethnicity that falls short of its mark.

The companion theme in this film is Scorsese's critique of greed, the corrosive power of unbridled individualism. Always mindful of the ways in which ethnic cultures mime the priorities of the hegemonic class, Scorsese represents Ace and Nicky as corrupted by the same obsession with wealth and power that takes down Henry Hill in *GoodFellas* and, some twenty years later, will take down Jordan Belfort in *The Wolf of Wall Street* (2013). What's remarkable is that the latter film makes no mention of Belfort's Jewishness, even though the "real life" figure on whom the character was based is in fact Jewish. It is as if by the second decade of the twenty-first century Scorsese had decided that class more than ethnicity has become the crucial variable in the calculation of American behavior. *Casino* is Janus-like in its two directional glance, looking back at the myth of the frontier, particularly as an agent of assimilation, but also looking ahead to a post-modernist world, where all sense of ethnicity has been overwhelmed by the universal impulse of greed. Respecting *Casino*, Scorsese says, "What interested me was the idea of excess, no limits" (Brunette 1999, 223). The same impulse drives *The Wolf of Wall Street*.

Casino is another cooperative endeavor between Scorsese and Nicholas Pileggi, with roughly the same division of labor. "He hadn't finished the book yet," Scorsese told Richard Schickel, "so we worked on the script together for about six months, in a hotel, and we ordered transcripts and whatever other interviews we could get" (Schickel 2011, 209). Pileggi researched the facts and background of the Mafia's extended embroilment in Vegas, while Scorsese consolidated the material, found its dramatic center, and added the accents of his personal style. Speaking of the director in a recent interview, Pileggi says: "He has a total vision of the film. It's all in his head. When we sit down, he already knows where he's going with this. I'm in a sense a facilitator. I provide the data and he and I together begin to block out the scenes" (Konow and Pileggi 2014). In this case, as Pileggi would have it, the center was the tension-ridden triangle built around Ace, "the master gambler," Nicky, "the Mafia muscle man who was there to keep everybody in place," and Ginger (Sharon Stone), Ace's exciting but unstable girlfriend/wife, whose ill-advised love affair with Nicky brings everything down. The new figure on Scorsese's creative team is Robert Richardson, whose action-oriented camera work (which he perfected in a long-term relationship with Oliver Stone) coheres well with the expectations of the gangster genre as well as with the editing craft of Thelma Schoonmacher, who has worked on every Scorsese film since *Raging Bull*.

Though every inch a "gangster film" in its violence and its fascination with organized crime, *Casino* is also a hybridized Western. It springs up from what Neil Campbell calls *The Rhizomatic West* (2008), a term he summons from botanical science to describe a culture of profuse but haphazard growths, related off-shoots that lack a discernible tap root (see particularly 151–82). While the "classical" Western requires period décor and a relatively predictable cast of characters, Scorsese's "rhizomatic" variant propels us into a west of sleek late-model cars, high-rise pleasure palaces, and garish neon signage. Nonetheless, the film adheres to several fundamental tropes of the genre, chiefly the myths of settlement and progress, community building, wilderness, and civilization, upon which it works a series of ironic turns. It also includes the ethnic under class, here a Jew and a Sicilian, in a schematic that devalues the melting pot and its potential for assimilation and healing. But the ultimate irony is reserved for the city itself, the dystopic Las Vegas, not the magical blending of freedom and order, which Frederick Jackson Turner (and John Ford) once foresaw in the American west; rather, a ghastly Babylon destined to collapse into the dust from which it was born. Like the Western template to which it refers, *Casino* is a meditation upon violence, but a profoundly negative meditation, which questions the tenaciously held belief that violence is potentially redemptive and, as such, an essential instrument of civilization.

In his much quoted essay on "The Significance of the Frontier in American History"(1893), Frederick Jackson Turner argues that the west is the birthplace of the authentic American, the pioneer who has shaken off the encrustations of Europe and the urbanized east to become the democratic, self-fashioning representative of a new society. "From the time the mountains rose between the pioneer and the seaboard," he says, "a new order of Americanism arose." As further frontiers declared themselves across major rivers and more westerly mountain ranges, the same process repeated itself in one generation after another, until this phenomenon of continually moving borders had given "the American intellect . . . its striking characteristics." This uniquely American disposition included, says Turner, "that restless, nervous energy, that dominant individualism, and withal that buoyancy and exuberance which comes with freedom." Moreover, these newly minted Americans "were of non-English stock" (F. Turner 1893).

Although ethnic history is not Turner's forte, he knows the demographics of the colonial period well enough to realize that "the frontier promoted the formation of a composite nationality" (F. Turner). He continues, "the coast was preponderantly English, but the later tides of continental immigration flowed across to the free lands." The lands west of the Alleghenies and in the Ohio valley were settled by "free indentured servants, or redemptioners, who at the expiration of their time of service passed to the frontier." Quoting Governor Spotswood of Virginia in 1717, Turner notes that "the inhabitants of our frontiers are composed generally of such as have been transported hither as servants, and, being out of their time, settle themselves where land is to be taken up . . . that will produce the necessities of life with little labor." Knowing these formerly indentured servants to be chiefly Scots-Irish in their ethnicity, Turner concludes that "in the crucible of the frontier the immigrants were Americanized, liberated, and fused into a mixed race, English in neither nationality nor characteristics." Fifteen years before Zangwill had coined the term, Turner had already produced a western version of "the melting pot." The "democracy born of free land" would fuse the best traits of "English and non-English stock."

Scorsese may or may not have read Turner (he probably did), but he is a lifelong devotee of the Western (especially the films of John Ford), as is clear from his short documentary *4 Westerns: A Personal Journey* (1995), which shows his deep indebtedness to the genre, particularly its dark side. Referencing the career of Ford, Scorsese emphasizes the gradual transformation of the genre from the patriotic, national-identity narratives of *Stagecoach* (1939) and the Cavalry trilogy (1947–1951) to the skeptical, alienated saga of *The Searchers* (1956), the story of "a drifter doomed to wander between the winds" (Scorsese 1995, 03:55/04:05). In the later 1950s, and even more obviously in the sixties and seventies, says Scorsese, the Western acquired a still more skeptical outlook, rendering the "frontier" as a world that had given way "to greed, vengeance, megalomania, and violence" (05:55/06:05). To this point, he quotes the rage-ridden protagonist of *The Naked Spur* (1953), a bounty hunter, who tells his disillusioned lady friend, "it's the money, that's all I want, that's all I ever cared about" (06:30/06:45). This turn of the genre, concludes Scorsese, looks forward to the ultimate revisionist Western, Clint Eastwood's *Unforgiven* (1991), where three bounty hunters hold center stage, as they sally forth to avenge the grievances of a cadre of prostitutes. No longer is the west a wilderness awaiting the benign touch that will transform it into a garden. In Eastwood's narrative, the farmstead is deserted for the sake of quick cash, and the would-be settler abandons his two children to resume his career as a gunslinger. Nor is there any sense of legitimate authority in Big Whiskey, the site of the huge blood bath that concludes the film: justice is simply the will of the stronger. *Casino* picks up at the point where this de-mythologizing of the west is complete and absolute.

With respect to the ethnic theme, Turner thought the west was the ideal place for a "mixed race" culture to establish itself, because here the racialized "other" (meaning, primarily, the Irish, and marginally, the Mexicans) would have time and opportunity to be guided to civility by a leadership community that would remain largely English. But the English would gain from this assimilative endeavor, since the ethnic underlings were strong in "that masterful grasp of material things" required by frontier conditions. Turner's template of the assimilative process is less nuanced than the one Glazer and Moynihan would develop three-quarters of a century later in *Beyond the Melting Pot*, but it is essentially a similar concept: the master class will teach the underclasses how to behave. And the underlings themselves will cooperate with each other, each looking to the tier immediately above it for models of behavior that will promote a progression toward civility.

In *Casino*, Scorsese looks at the same ethnic stratification, but with greatly less optimism. Indeed, the orderly escalator of progress, which invites each disadvantaged minority to occupy the niche just vacated by the minority immediately above it, is inevitably subverted in Scorsese by forces at work in both the social system and the individual psyche. Nowhere is this fracture of progress more apparent than in Las Vegas, where Ace Rothstein and Nicky Santoro carry their respective aspirations into the New West, only to find that the Turnerian frontier is not really as open as they imagined. The fact that they belong to what Karen Brodkin names as the "off-white races" (1998, 1–24) and Matthew Jacobson calls "whiteness of a different color" (1998, 13–38) denies them access to the higher levels of power. Even the well-tested formula of "working toward whiteness," which David Roediger lays out in his book of that name, fails the well-disciplined Rothstein in his struggle with the cowboy princes of the desert. Though they themselves are little more than a parody of what Turner and Ford had imagined as the new master class, they salvage enough of the exclusions of the WASP establishment to close ranks against Jews and Sicilians. Remarkably, what brings down Rothstein is not his criminal behavior, his ill-conceived marriage, nor even his toxic alliance with Nicky Santoro. What defeats him is his failure to respect the nepotistic relationships that dominate Nevada's back-scratching politics.

This theme comes to focus in a set of scenes where Rothstein is denied his gaming license entirely through political chicanery. The problem begins when he fires an incompetent underling who has failed on several occasions and finally allows the house to be cheated through the rigging of several slot machines. Ace dismisses the underling's threat, "You might regret this, Mr. Rothstein," but soon finds that the cashiered employee has relatives in high places. Ace's colleague Philip Green warns him, "You can't just fire him. Webb [the County Commissioner] is his brother-in-law." But Ace's rejoinder shows he will not give ground: "Everybody out here in cowboy boots is somebody's brother-in-law." Green's rejoinder to this remark is even more ominous, "This is his state" (Scorsese 2005, 01:09:20/01:10:40).

Inevitably, Ace receives a visit from Commissioner Webb (L. Q. Jones), who makes a plea for his humiliated brother-in-law (Scorsese 2005, 01:20:40/01:23:45). Delighted that "money is rolling in" to the Tangiers casino, he has come only to "smooth over a fracas" and courteously requests a small "personal favor," which of course is a non-negotiable demand. The imagery of this scene puts the characters in completely separate worlds: Webb's string tie, blue jeans, and cowboy hat make him a true son of Nevada; Ace's pale blue suit and matching silk tie look like they were shipped in from Chicago or New York. The décor of the office speaks well of Ace's status and power, while behind him a spacious interior window reveals the productive energy of the casino itself. But sophistication and even wealth count for little against the bonds of blood for which Webb speaks. Conceding that his hapless brother-in-law is "useless as teats on a boar," Webb suggests that perhaps he could simply be moved "further down the trough," making clear that the conversation has nothing to do with administrative competence, just palm-greasing. When that ploy doesn't produce a workable outcome, the Commissioner is ready to deliver his final verdict: "Your people will never understand the way it works out here. You're all just our guests. You're not at home." If there were any doubt that the phrase "your people" is an ethnic slur, the ambiguity is quickly resolved when Webb later tells one of his cronies, "We've got to kick a kike's ass out of town" (01:31:50/01:32:05).

Prior to his fall from grace, Ace has made every effort to simulate the behavior of the "model minority" Moynihan and Glazer celebrate. Though he is not well educated in formal terms, his expertise in betting and handicapping is unrivaled, a talent that makes him immensely valuable to the casino culture, the "Golden Jew," in Nicky's memorable phrase. He also seeks, in the best Turnerian mode, to found a family and put down roots in the community. Ginger, his Irish wife, is the mother of a blond daughter on whom he dotes. And his home, however chaotic his life there, speaks architecturally of solid suburban affluence. He seems ideally poised to translate his work ethic and his professional skills into success and social advancement. In spite of these seeming advantages, however, his undoing is made inevitable, not only by his lack of a proper bloodline, but by close ties to his gangster friend, Nicky.

A brutal thug sent west by the mob, to keep Ace safe, but also to keep him under surveillance, Nicky is first heard from as a faceless voice-over, who interrupts Ace's narrative with commentary of his own. "It should have been perfect," Nicky says, celebrating his partnership with Ace: "He had me, Nicky Santoro, watching his ass and he had Ginger, the woman he loved, on his arm." Both he and Ace know they are implicated in a criminal conspiracy, but Nicky's rhetoric keeps the facts of their behavior in very low relief. As he would have it, corpses are "packages" that sometimes turn up at awkward moments, but all problems are solved by "holes in the desert" which need only to be dug in a timely way (Scorsese 2005, 04:15/04:45). Though Ace is less violent than Nicky, he too deals in expansive euphemisms. While the camera shows visuals of Nicky mercilessly beating someone who has defied him, Ace's voice-over speaks in almost lyrical terms of what a good team they make: "With my innovations and [Nicky's] dedication to his job, I soon had the best operation of the Strip" (54:10/54:25). Leaving unmentioned several murders and innumerable physical assaults, Ace reminds us that Nicky proudly supports little league baseball and regularly fixes breakfast for his son. Although Ace takes a wife, fathers a child, furnishes a home, and seeks to put down roots in the community, he remains always outside the law. Nicky is an even more improbable homesteader. His restaurant is a front for his loan shark business and his living quarters is a place to hide stolen property. Even his wife is part of the criminal enterprise, most conspicuously when her superabundant hair is used to smuggle stolen jewels into the country.

Ace is proud of what he has made of himself in Vegas and relishes his standing in the business community. When he is given a plaque for public service, he thanks his benefactors with a trace of ironic amusement: "Anywhere else I'd be arrested for what I'm doing. Here they're giving me awards." He doesn't welcome Nicky's arrival, but cordially invites him and his wife to the elegant Rothstein home, where they meet Ace's wife, Ginger, and seem to become a close-knit social group. Ace helps Nicky get his son into school and soon we see the youngest Santoro standing beside a nun in a Catholic classroom, making a speech about George Washington. As they take a driving tour of the city, Ace tries to strike a note of caution without expressing any doubt that Nicky will prove a trusted friend. "You've got to be careful," he warns, "I've got a licensed place." Actually, the license is in the name of Philip Greene (Kevin Pollak), the mob's squeaky-clean front man, but at the moment this fact seems to make no difference. Yet Nicky sees Ace's reach for respectability simply as a failure of nerve. He imagines himself as beyond the control of his midwestern bosses and tough enough to defy any challenge to his power that the local culture could mount. Soon he is beating and threatening his way to the top rung of his fast-growing gangster empire. Of his many transgressions, the most egregious is the assassination of Greene's silent partner, who has begun to insert herself into the affairs of the casino. Suddenly, the Tangiers is under federal scrutiny, and Rothstein's name turns up repeatedly in the news coverage of Nicky. Nor can Ace rein him in.

Nicky's attitude toward Ace, and his refusal to honor the advice of his more cerebral colleague, is founded upon ethnic stereotypes of the Jews: that they not only have a magical gift for finance, but more pointedly, that they are sissies, given to effeminate behavior, lisping in high-pitched voices, and often inclined toward homosexuality. In reams of anti-Semitic literature, particularly in hyper-nationalist tracts of the early twentieth century, the "Eternal Jew" emasculated whatever state he settled in because of his irremediable weakness and cowardice, his female softness and pliability. Even positive representations of Jewish culture, ably summarized in *Jewish Masculinities* (Baader, Gillerman, and Lerner 2012), acknowledged its "feminine spirit" and absence of "military swagger." In some anti-Semitic screeds, these character traits were linked to the practice of circumcision, thought to be a kind of castration, which permanently stigmatized *The Jew's Body* (see Gilman 1991, esp. 60–103). In her contribution to *Immigrants in the Far West* (2015), Karen Wilson notes the particular difficulties of frontier Jews, whose familial culture made headway slowly against the "temporary, chaotic, and dangerous" bent of western cities (205). What all agree was the "softness" of Jewish masculinity is construed by Nicky as weakness. His avoidance of violence (far from absolute) is interpreted as a lack of manly spirit.

This is powerfully dramatized in a scene that takes place in Ace's home, when the two men are under pressure from both the federal authorities and the local power elite. Nicky intrudes upon a conversation between Ace and his banker to complain that the banker has mishandled some of Nicky's funds. When the banker disavows these claims, Nicky threatens to "crack your head open in front of everyone at the bank." The banker looks to Ace for support or defense, but receives neither, and Ace's look suggests an anxiety level just short of panic. His guest then flees in terror. When Ace protests that Nicky has put both of them at risk, Nicky's response is, "Where are your balls?" Thereafter, the scene becomes an escalating confrontation between the manly Sicilian and the effete Jew, who feigns the deportment of an East Coast gentleman: "Look at you," says Nicky, "walking around looking like John Barrymore." In this scene, Ace is not fully dressed and wears a pink bathrobe, which Nicky singles out for particular scorn. In Nicky's eyes, this man commands no authority, even though the appointments of Ace's home (table-top sculptures of galloping stallions and powerful-looking hawks) suggest a decisive effort to create a masculine (and western) ambience. While Ace argues that he is simply trying to protect the assets of the Tangiers from legal scrutiny, Nicky sees only weakness in his refusal to respond violently to those who encroach upon their desert empire. "I'm what counts out here," says Nicky in a later scene, where the two men continue this quarrel, "not your country clubs, not your TV show." Without him, Nicky concludes his tirade, "every wise guy out here will take a piece of your Jew ass" (Scorsese 2005, 01:33:30/01:37:30).

Nicky's doubts about Ace's manliness also motivate his disastrous love affair with Ginger, which does more than irreparably violate his friendship with Ace. It also brings down the wrath of the Mafia bosses and sets in motion the events that ultimately drive the mob out of Vegas. As Nicky understands things, however, Ace deserves to be betrayed because he fails to take charge of his wife in the same way he fails to protect his property. His timidity and effeminacy are his undoing

Though Nicky's encroachment upon Ace's marriage is somewhat hesitant (it's advanced in part by Ginger herself), the issue first surfaces in the scene at Ace's home, where Nicky charges that his friend's weakness invites "disrespect" (the inevitable *rispetto!*) from all his acquaintances, including his own wife. This reveals Nicky's close contact with Ginger and causes Ace to warn him about overstepping the bounds of friendship. But Nicky remembers that Ace has summoned him and his violent buddies to beat up Ginger's lover (and drug supplier), while Ace himself declines to soil his hands on the lover or discipline Ginger herself. From that point on, the tragic events move forward, with Nicky escorting Ginger to numerous romantic appointments in a construction trailer, while Ace sits alone in his elegantly appointed home. This assault upon hearth and family culminates in the scene where another of Ginger's trysts with Nicky requires that she tie Ace's daughter to the bed, so that she can escape her babysitting chores for another night of drinking and carousing. In imagery that reflects Scorsese's inversion of tropes from the classical Western, the home yields to the saloon and the gaming parlor, as the wild world overcomes the tame.

This turn of events in *Casino* is of a piece with Scorsese's broader effort to portray Las Vegas as the ultimate dystopic city, the site of a civilization gone wrong, the diametric opposite of what a confident, optimistic John Ford, and his like-minded contemporaries, once imagined for the American west. In *My Darling Clementine* (1947), the saloon with its upstairs brothel loses ground to the school and the church. In George Stevens' *Shane* (1953), settler families go grocery shopping on premises once given over to drinking and gambling. Female shoppers carefully study the vacuum seals of canning jars that will enable them to preserve fresh vegetables. In some instances, as in *San Antonio* (1940), the dance hall girl, with the right male encouragement, turns into a respectable married woman, stepping away from her unladylike past. Everywhere in the classical Western the world is becoming more peaceful, more refined, more hospitable to family life. In Hawks' *Red River* (1948), even the cattle, which had once stampeded, now quietly lie down on the public streets of Abilene, as if gentled by the civilized environment of this well-kept, orderly town. In *Casino*, on the other hand, the institutions that were supposed to be obsolesced by the advance of the settler culture have actually become more powerful. Given an elegant home and financial security, Ginger reverts to promiscuity and drug taking, cutting short her life with a drug overdose. Violence is ubiquitous, sometimes turning tools into near lethal weapons. A cattle prod brings down a patron at one of the gaming tables, another is threatened with an electric saw, then mutilated with a hammer, and a third has his head crushed in a vise. Roulette wheels, baccarat tables, playing cards, dice throws, and slot machines marginalize all other visuals, rivaled only by images of copious drinking, sexual indulgence, and physical assault. The saloon/gaming house/brothel—negative archetype of the early west in Ford, Hawks, and Stevens—has displaced all positive images of community. The "Strip" has become the world, advancing its claims unmercifully against the civilizing power of the school, the church, and the grocery.

Some critics have charged that in *Casino*, "Scorsese repeats himself," producing little more than "gaudiness and inflation" (Nyce 2004, 139). But the décor is more than just celluloid eye-candy. Casillo is more accurate when he recounts how the film "painstakingly focuses on organized crime in its most intimate relation not only to the social order but to the state, which, by supporting casino gambling, has condoned an event allied secretly with the mob" (2006, 329). He then details exactly how organized crime insinuated itself into all the nooks and crannies of the state's political bureaucracy (329–41). Various scholars have filled out the more detailed back story of the city and state: the chronic scarcity of water, the relative failure of homesteading, the gradual shift of the economy toward gaming and tourism, the increasing prominence of pawn shops, loan sharking, and the sex trade. All the while, law and government are bent to accommodate these economic expediencies. Historian David Littlejohn in *The Real Las Vegas* (1999) charges that today's corporate criminals have left things much "as they were when mobsters and their agents, instead of publicly traded corporations called most of the shots" (258; see also 147–66, 243–58). This is the substance of Ace's last monologue, which complains of the "junk bonds" that built the post-Mafia city and that, though the Strip now looks like Disneyland, it's still the place where "Mommy and Daddy drop the house payment at the poker slots" (Scorsese 2005, 02:50:20/02:51:35).

The stage business of the film continually reminds us of the way formal political processes shade over into criminal practice. Commissioner Webb, pursuing his personal grudge against Ace, appears in his cowboy costume at every step of the hearings, as if he were supervising the behavior of public officials who are in no sense under his jurisdiction. More crucially, a dubious character known only as "the Senator" (Dick Smothers) is shown frequenting the Tangiers and consorting with prostitutes whom the management makes available to him. But later when he presides over the session that decides the question of Ace's license, he acknowledges no relationship to Ace or the Tangiers. Nor is there even a pretense to due process at the hearing. Ace has brought mountains of data upon which to build his defense, but the Senator waves it aside with a preemptive motion that denies Ace's application without a word of public debate.

Two powerful images from *Casino* linger in memory, each underscoring the failure to transform the wilderness into a garden. The first is the desert—barren, empty, utterly forsaken. In a memorable single take that is held for at least forty-five seconds (Scorsese 2005, 04:10/04:55), the camera swoops over the land, showing it to be not simply vacant, but dry, infertile, clearly incapable of sustaining life. What we see of the city within the context of this landscape is a tiny pool of light enveloped by a vast darkness, a tiny glow that cannot possibly illumine the larger environment. The electrical energy of the city is lost in the immense waste of the desert. This barren landscape is the site of Ace's last confrontation with Nicky and ends with Ace virtually enveloped by a great cloud of dust. The second image is of demolition. The montage that goes with Ace's elegiac monologue shows the glittering cityscape of the 1960s being dynamited to make place for whatever will follow. Walls crumble and explosions rock the sound track, while perfectly serviceable structures topple amid clouds of fire, smoke, and debris. Though new buildings replace them, the feeling that this sequence leaves is of radical transience and instability, a world that has no foundation and may at any moment collapse. As if to confirm this subjective impression, a contemporary historian notes that 200,000 people turned out to watch strategically placed dynamite charges bring down the Dunes Hotel, once the flagship of the Strip. "Extravagant demolitions," says Mike Davis, "have become Las Vegas' version of civic festivals" (1998, 53).

Contrary to the ideology of Turner and Ford, the west of Scorsese promises no hope, no redemption, squandering its resources on waste production while sacrificing its moral authority to a culture of bribes and deal making. Even Ace and Nicky came west with a sense of possibility, the conviction that the future could be other than the past. This is the expectation that crumbles to dust with the fall of the Tangiers in the closing scenes of *Casino*. In questioning the progress myth, Scorsese enlarges his critique of ethnic gangsters to express doubt as to the future of the nation itself. When Richard Schickel seems to defend the Vegas world by noting, "That's America's family playground," Scorsese's retort is fierce: "It's America's playground. Yes. What does that say about our values?" (Schickel 2011, 205). Scorsese sums up the wrong-headedness of those values through what he calls "the complete embrace of excess" (208). Massive self-indulgence, represented in images of drugs, alcohol, and frenetic sexuality, is the link that connects *Casino* with *The Wolf of Wall Street*.

Hal Rothman, in *Neon Metropolis* (2002), introduces Las Vegas as "the first city of the new century, the one that owes its allegiance to the shape

---

of the new universe, to the signs and symbols of a culture of entertainment" (31). As he explains, the economy generates no tangible goods, but earns massive profits from gaming, tourism, and their various offshoots. Vegas shows the way into the new millennium because here the service sector has completely superseded industry and manufacturing. This makes it strangely similar to contemporary New York City, in what John Mollenkopf calls its "post-industrial transformation," the radical restructuring of the 1980s that brought about "a massive and irreversible shift of employment away from the manufacture and distribution of goods toward services" in a context of "basic changes in global capitalism." In New York as well as Las Vegas, these included "the globalization of economic competition, the increasing importance of finance relative to production, [and] the globalization and centralization of financial markets" (see Mollenkopf 1992, 44–68). Furthermore, the Las Vegas gaming industry, with its culture of odds making, risk taking, and even the rigging of outcomes, bears a striking family resemblance to the empire of clepto-capitalism that Jordan Belfort and his cohorts built on Long Island during the free-wheeling 1980s. Like Ace Rothstein presiding over the success of the Tangiers, Jordan makes a fortune in penny stocks, after his bid for a legitimate career on Wall Street collapses in the stock market's mini-crash of 1987.

The narrative for Scorsese's *Wolf* derives from two memoirs Belfort himself wrote, *The Wolf of Wall Street* (2007) and *Catching the Wolf of Wall Street* (2009). Unlike the production of *Casino*, however, *The Wolf* involved no direct collaboration between the memoirist and the film director on the script. Scorsese did employ Jordan Belfort, however, to coach Leonardo DiCaprio in the role he would play and gave him a small part in the picture, as the fictive Belfort's public relations director in the last phase of the wolf's career. But Scorsese chose Terrence Winter, fresh from his striking success as one of the major writers for *The Sopranos* (1999–2007), to create the screenplay. His script mines the memoirs for vivid detail and intense conversational exchanges, yet injects fierce irony into the personal redemption narrative that Belfort himself puts forward. Although Belfort insists that his life story "serves as a cautionary tale," Scorsese and Winter clearly doubt the author's claim that his crime career gives warning "to any person who's considering taking a God-given gift and misusing it [or] to anyone who decides to go to the dark side of the force and live a life of unbridled hedonism" (Belfort 2007, 11). In place of the repentant sinner that we find in the last chapter of *Catching the Wolf of Wall Street*, the rehabilitated criminal who has proven "the leopard can definitely change its spots" (Belfort 2009, 468), we see the same consummate con artist, now self-exiled to New Zealand, beginning another up-by-the-bootstraps scheme to hoodwink a new audience into signing up for what promises to be a grandiose self-help project. What does carry over to the film, however, is Belfort's "God-given gift" for persuasive talk. "If you want to talk about *speaking*," he tells Tommy, his prison buddy, "that's something I can do, I'm a really *great* speaker, I promise you. You put me in front of a room, and I'll make people cry" (Belfort 2009, 463). Scorsese's Belfort shows no sign of regret or repentance, beyond regretting that he was caught and punished. In fact, the film's abrupt juxtaposition of the criminal and the "reformed" entrepreneur who has replaced him drastically blurs the distinction between the criminal and the entrepreneurial world.

More blurring occurs when Scorsese erases virtually all references to Belfort's Jewishness, presumably to make his characters more generically "American." The memoirs, on the other hand, are saturated with whispered asides about the Jews confronting the WASPs in a battle for primacy in New York's real estate and financial communities. Belfort calls himself "a lowly Jew," or a "savage Jew," living in a neighborhood that shuns "anyone who wasn't a blue-blooded WASP bastard" (2007, 47). The bluebloods, as he sees them, seclude themselves in covenanted enclaves, private gated communities, which are their "last bastions against the invading *shtetl* hordes" (47). Jordan has recruited many of his Strattonite colleagues from among "the most savage young Jews anywhere on Long Island: the towns of Jericho and Syosset" (108). Jordan's partner Danny Porush (who becomes Donny Azoff in the film) is also Jewish, but hides his ethnicity, as best he can, with "WASPy" glasses, even though he has 20/20 vision. Another of Belfort's lieutenants is Todd Garrett, one of the "very wacky Jews [who] had fled from Lefrack City in the early 1970s" (199). He has strayed so far from the ethnic stereotype as to turn himself into a marshal arts expert, collect a Slovenian girlfriend, and somehow "end up looking . . . much like Fu Man Chu" (202). These ethnic signifiers are fully in place when Belfort's team visits Geneva in their effort to set up an intricate money-laundering scheme with the aid of an unscrupulous Swiss banker. Though Monsieur Sauret politely disowns "Adolf Hitler and the despicable Nazis," Belfort has not forgotten that in the World War II era "virtually every country in Europe . . . denied millions of Jews safe-haven within their borders" (143). "How very ironic it was," concludes Belfort, "that Switzerland had been so quick to accept Jewish money yet so reluctant to accept Jewish souls" (143). Though Belfort in no way resembles the stateless refugees of the early 1940s, he feels that his Jewishness still marks him as a man apart and that his money is more welcome in Switzerland than he or his business associates.

Writing in *Haaritz*, a journal of Jewish cultural life, Malina Saval thanks Scorsese and his colleagues for "downplaying the Jewishness of their scumbag heroes" and attributes this reticence to Scorsese's determination to avoid being judged "politically incorrect" (2013). But this explanation is a bit puzzling, since the film's principal supporting actor, Jonah Hill, the Donny Azoff figure, is well known as a Jewish performer. Besides, Scorsese has made a career of representing ethnics straight-forwardly, even at the risk of sliding over into stereotypes. It seems more plausible to assume that he is self-consciously making a statement about a further stage of assimilation, one in which the process is effectively complete, except perhaps for a few lingering cultural imprints. These include a tendency to think in terms of the insider/outsider binary as well as the habit of falling back upon family and neighborhood as guarantors of loyalty and trust.

The only conversation about ethnicity in The *Wolf of Wall Street* marginalizes ancestral roots and promotes self-assignment as the defining feature of ethnic status. On their first dinner date, Jordan (Leonardo DiCaprio) assumes that his new girlfriend, Naomi Lapaglia (Margot Robbie), has to be Italian, on the evidence of her unmistakable surname and her childhood in Bay Ridge, Brooklyn, at that time a heavily Italian neighborhood. But her answer reframes the discussion. She's Italian, "on my father's side," she says, "but I'm also Dutch, English, and German," adding, with a confident grin, "I'm a mutt." But she is a high-achieving mutt, impeccably well groomed, always wrapped in designer dresses, and equipped with enough managerial skills to launch and develop her own business. Yes, she admits to Jordan, she comes "from *Saturday Night Fever* territory," but unlike that film's protagonist, Tony Manero, from a full decade earlier, Naomi doesn't feel constrained or compromised by her lack of pedigree and identifies with the Anglo-Nordic roots of her mother's family. Her personal template is Aunt Emma (Joanna Lumley), who lives in London and carries a UK passport. Jordan is sufficiently impressed by what Naomi has made of herself to rechristen her as "the Duchess of Bay Ridge" (Scorsese 2014, 55:20/57:20). In Belfort's postmodern New York, the characters are the sum total of their cultural assets, not the victims of a problematic ethnicity.

While deliberately effacing ethnic references, Scorsese employs the same insider/outsider binary that he has used many times in representing the ambitions of his favorite ethnics, the Italians, the Irish, and the Jews. When he is apprenticing to Mark Hanna (Matthew McConaughey) and momentarily has a true Wall Street address, he is awkwardly aware of how badly he fits into the life world of the "masters of the universe." He arrives by bus instead of taxi (much less a private limousine) and immediately recognizes that his "cheap blue suit and clodhopper shoes" don't give him the same look as his better-tailored peers. Humbled, he more or less accepts the verdict of a particularly unpleasant colleague, who dubs him "lower than pond scum." He is also amazed by the sense of entitlement that Hanna exudes, as he drowns himself in martinis, casually uses drugs at the lunch table, and openly acknowledges that stock trading amounts to an ongoing swindle. "We don't build anything," Hanna tells him, implying that financial services are largely smoke and mirrors. Like young Henry Hill, enthralled by the expensive rings and watches sported by gangsters who stop by Paulie's cab stand, Jordan is mesmerized by the aura of wealth and power that emanates from figures like Hanna. With the sharp economic downturn of 1987, Jordan finds himself terminated almost before he begins, but he learns from his unscrupulous mentor that everything is a function of commissions and the capacity of the broker to trap the client into an endless cycle of reinvestment. These are the lessons he applies with a vengeance when he puts together his ragtag army of penny-stock swindlers at his corporate headquarters.

As in Scorsese's ethnic films, we again have a decisive sense of place. "Outsider" connotes a geography as well as a state of mind. On the morning of his first visit to the drab precincts from which near-worthless penny stocks are sold, Jordan shares with his wife his surprise that there are stockbrokers doing business from Long Island. Later, when he invents his own company to palm off these previously unmarketable stocks, he gives his firm the fantasy identity of Stratton Oakmont, with "roots stretching back to the Mayflower" and a fine-sounding Anglo-Nordic name "chiseled into Plymouth Rock" (Scorsese 2014, 32:10/33:30). In reality, Jordan's work force does business out of a refurbished warehouse but their telephone discourse represents them as a cadre of fiscal professionals worthy to keep company with Wall Street's executive elite. Nonetheless, throughout the film they worry that they are still unwelcome in the "WASP strongholds," such as the exclusive country club that Jordan stumbles into after he has overdosed on a particularly potent cache of Quaaludes.

Striking a stance of self-defense against WASP hegemony, Belfort's cohort creates an ethos that combines crony capitalism with vestiges of ethnocentrism. The buddy principle, heavily laced with drugs, alcohol, and testosterone, is never far from the epicenter of action. But the ties that bind also include what Jennifer Thompson, in *Jewish on Their Own Terms* (2014), calls "the kinship obligations of Jews," the persuasion that "ethnic familialism" is their best refuge against the "universalist individualism" of the majority culture (123). As she surveys Jews living on the periphery of Jewish culture, Thompson draws heavily on the concept of "*mispoche*," literally "family," but a term that "reaches beyond the nuclear family to a broader kinship network" (126). Amid the "competing responses to modernity," she finds a place for "symbolic ethnicity," which "entails belonging to an ethnic community but emphasizes the individuals' choice to do so" (170–73). Woven into these conflicted and often contradictory accounts of contemporary Jewry, we also find the figure of the "*ger toshav*," literally, the "resident alien," who is a gentile living among Jewish people, happy to be part of the Jewish world (see 163–76). Although Thompson is writing about Jews in interethnic marriages who cling to remnants of a "Jewish life," the social improvisations she describes closely resemble those of Scorsese's characters in *The Wolf of Wall Street*.

Nowhere is this more apparent than in the chaotic mix of family, extended family, neighborhood, and professional comradeship that plays out in the formation and performance of Stratton Oakmont. Jordan's primary partner, Donny Azoff, feels connected to Jordan because they both live in the same apartment complex. He brings with him his wife, Hildy (MacKenzie Meehan), who also happens to be Donny's cousin. Jordan's chief security officer is his father, Mad Max (Rob Reiner), who has a furious temper but a level head and who, more than anyone else, is probably responsible for keeping the firm afloat longer than ever seemed likely. Jordan's wife, Naomi, is responsible for recruiting Emma, her beloved British aunt, who brings with her a British passport and an anarchistic sensibility that fits perfectly with the ethos of the firm. She is crucial to sheltering the massive amounts of cash that Stratton Oakmont exports and deposits in a Swiss bank. Steve Madden (Jake Hoffman), the shoe designer at the center of the firm's IPO scam, is a friend of Donny, like family, it seems, because "I grew up with this guy." Brad (Jon Bernthal), the drug dealer who furnishes Jordan with a template of the perfect salesman, is a friend from Jordan's adolescence. Brad's wife, Chantalle (Katarina Cas), is the most efficient smuggler among Stratton's league of moral miscreants, carrying millions of dollars taped to her body across the Atlantic. Even the Swiss banker, Monsieur Seuret (Jean Dujardin), their overseas partner in crime, was a law school buddy of Nicky ("Rug Rat") Kostkoft (P. J. Byrne), Stratton Oakmont's third in command, and the most likely to be sober at any given moment. One or more of these characters is implicated in each over-heated expansion of Jordan's quest for wealth, power, and high-gloss celebrity. But his jerrybuilt pseudo-family is inherently unstable, hence both vulnerable and in constant need of stimulation.

From the moment Jordan renames his non-descript firm as "Stratton Oakmont," its *modus operandi* is orgiastic and obsessive in its telephone salesmanship but also given to wild parties that take their inspiration from the frat-brat excesses of *Animal House* (1978). Like every charismatic leader, Jordan is blessed with spellbinding rhetorical fluency, the capacity to virtually hypnotize the underlings he has hired, gathering them into a shared delusion of profit, power, and pleasure. Jordan achieves perfect pitch at every level of demagoguery, augmenting his verbal firestorms with marching bands, dancing girls, and what seems like half the prostitutes in Manhattan. His most passionate exhortations are often interrupted by shouts from the ecstatic subalterns, "Wolfie, Wolfie, Wolfie!"

Jordan's manic spirit captivates his whole workforce, from the woman who shaves her head for the prize that pays for her breast implants to the zany games that include pitching dwarfs at a dartboard set up for this particular ceremonial occasion. Anyone not caught up in the mayhem is subjected to brutal hazing, like the nerd who tries to clean his goldfish bowl during a corporate pep rally. Donny deals personally with this would be joy-spoiler, dramatically swallowing his pet goldfish, then urging his cohorts to pelt him with trash and drive him from the premises. These over-the-top corporate love feasts are the pep pills that take the place of secure relationships and serious commitments, the bonds of fellowship that hold together Jordan's pseudo-family.

"Family," somewhat fancifully constructed, is at the center of Jordan's empire building. It replaces the ethnic clans of *GoodFellas* and *Casino* with a covenant of true believers who push kinship beyond its elastic limits. Nor does it hurt that there's a generous cash flow; it truly seems like everyone is getting rich. But their comradeship lacks the empathy and in-depth loyalty of kinship, which creates the vulnerability of Stratton Oakmont. Scorsese's analysis of their fall reflects his thinking about corporate relationships in postmodern America, where ethnicity has lost its once potent leverage and corporate spirit—no matter how extravagantly articulated—doesn't quite compensate for the loss.

One instance of this vulnerability is the effort to turn Steve Madden, one of Donny's buddies from high school, into a tool of Stratton Oakmont, when the firm makes its first move to market an "Initial Public Offering." These initiatives, known in wonk-speak as IPOs, invite investors to bid on stocks never before marketed, which makes them highly volatile, at least in the first days of their availability. Though IPOs are fully legal, this particular venture is both illegal and dishonest. Donny and Jordan own 85 percent of the stock, which constitutes a substantial conflict of interest. Beyond that, the stock is probably worthless, being pushed onto the market only as part of a "pump and dump" strategy, which enlists the firm's sales force to artificially inflate the stock in early trading so that it can then be abruptly sold off, before the public realizes it is overvalued. Donny's childhood chum, who designs women's footwear, seems completely oblivious to the scheme, and apparently is not cut in on the quick profits. But he is introduced at the corporate rally as Donny's lifelong friend, with deep ties to the firm's directors.

The pep rally that follows is a showpiece of Jordan's public relations mastery and DiCaprio's theatrical flair. When Madden first appears on screen, Donny is holding him in an affectionate headlock, feigning intimacy but implicitly coercive. Madden's blue jeans and baseball cap look tacky beside Jordan's well-pressed $5,000 suit, even though Jordan presents him as "the hottest person in women's footwear," an entrepreneurial genius of the first magnitude. Madden performs awkwardly, but Jordan embraces him cordially and exhorts his loyal thanes "to ram Steve Madden's stock down your clients' throats" insisting that "they buy or die." What follows is improvised theater at its best, with DiCaprio pulling out all the stops in his frenzied enthusiasm for the stock that Stratton Oakmont is marketing. According to Jordan, Madden is an artist who appears only once every decade, a peer of such super-stars of design as Armani, Versace, and Coco Chanel. But he will not have the recognition he deserves until Stratton Oakmont's sales force takes to the telephones on his behalf. Making this pitch, Jordan dances, grimaces, gyrates, and turns the microphone into a baseball bat that he uses to simulate an out-of-the-park swing. His crowning gesture involves stripping off his "$40,000 watch" and flinging it out over the outstretched arms and fingers of his audience. This piece of personal jewelry, captured in slow motion as it floats over a rapturous crowd, is the perfect icon for the promise of great wealth that hovers just a few inches out of reach. Significantly, this symbol of ultimate achievement is a timepiece, connecting the wealth they all seek with the mandate to do everything in a timely way. It creates the exact context for Jordan's insistence that "there is no nobility in poverty," that aggressive salesmanship is the solution to every problem: "Are you behind on your credit card bill? Good, pick up the phone! Is your landlord ready to evict you? Good, pick up the phone! Does your girlfriend think you're a worthless loser? Good, pick up the phone and start dialing!" At once ranting and exhorting, Jordan is a stern, but loving parent, a beloved mentor. While he insults them and sets them against each other, he hugs several members of his team one by one, mingling with staff and assuring them, "you are my killers, my warriors." They need only to "speak the words I have taught you" to seize the treasure within their grasp. "I want you to deal with your problems," he says in closing, "by becoming rich." Spurred by Jordan's rhetoric, the phone brigade pushes up the stock value from $4.50 per share to $18 per share in one afternoon. If Donny's self-congratulatory account can be trusted, he personally earned $22 million dollars in three hours (Scorsese 2014, 01:19:00/01:26:05).

Ultimately, however, the scheme collapses because Madden sabotages it, selling short his own holdings in anticipation of what Jordan, Donny, and a few other insiders are preparing to do. Though Donny expresses righteous fury over "betrayal" at the hands of a trusted friend, Madden does Stratton Oakmont no worse than they had planned for him.

The same problematic reveals itself in the stratagem to store illicit cash in a Swiss bank account. This is a much larger operation that requires a more robust support network of friends and family. Though the scheme gets off to an admirable start, personal rivalries and dubious loyalties lead to its unraveling.

Naomi's Aunt Emma is the key figure in this transaction, and she plays her role flawlessly. She is introduced to the narrative early on as Naomi's favorite relative, effectively a surrogate mother, and she is warmly embraced by both Naomi and Jordan when she makes a surprise appearance at their wedding. When Jordan needs someone with a European passport to open a proxy account in Switzerland under his name, Aunt Emma becomes his inevitable collaborator. He calls on her in London, cultivates her friendship in a scene that looks like a courtship, and assures her of legal immunities he couldn't possibly guarantee (in fact, she's toward the top of list of names he eventually surrenders to the FBI). Nonetheless they are greatly like-minded, as is quite clear when she announces, "Risk is what keeps us young." Properly, the covenant is sealed on the basis of familial bonds. Emma will take charge of the money laundering if Jordan will promise to "take care of my favorite niece" (Scorsese 2014, 01:45:30/01:46:00). The bargain struck, Emma recruits a small cadre of her UK relatives as couriers of the funds Jordan is trying to move out of Manhattan. Posing as a solid, unremarkable British family on holiday in Europe, Emma and her kinfolk have no difficulty wheeling millions of dollars in cash past customs officials, the money hidden in plain sight in their carry-on luggage. The scheme goes awry only because Emma dies suddenly of a heart attack, which leads in a complicated way to incriminating disclosures.

Problems also arise with other links in the chain. Jordan's arrangement with Emma makes no provision for the cash Donny needs to move out of the country, which requires widening the smugglers' network. In this case, the bonds of kinship are stretched too thin to bear the load. Jordan appeals to Brad, whose wife Chantalle also carries a European passport. Though without enthusiasm for the task, Chantalle successfully transports millions in cash, and the project appears to succeed, in spite of the friction between Brad and Donny. Unfortunately, Chantalle involves herself in a love affair with Monsieur Seuret, the banker, which causes Stratton Oakmont's secrets to circulate beyond the family. When Seuret is arrested in Florida as an unrelated money-laundering schemes misfires, Seuret gives evidence that undermines Jordan's criminal enterprise.

The other factors in the demise of Stratton Oakmont are the towering egotism of Belfort himself and the furious class rivalry he feels for his FBI antagonist, Patrick Denham (Kyle Chandler). Here Scorsese works with what in earlier films would probably have been an ethnic rivalry, but which he now frames as a conflict of class. Jordan displays all the gaudy excess of the *nouveau riche*, but Denham is the poor-but-proud public servant who is offended by Jordan's crude assertion of power and privilege. Their war to the death is evident in their first meeting, as each feels out the other in a memorable encounter on the deck of Jordan's 170-foot yacht (Scorsese 2014, 01:29:00/01:37:35).

Jordan intends to dominate his adversaries, flaunting his affluence and perhaps hoping to strike a deal with the FBI agents investigating him. He looks down on them from the high angle vantage point of the deck of his yacht as they find their way from the street and up the steep stairway. His broad smile and cheery greeting display an easy-going cordiality that is pure showmanship. Before they begin their conversation, he offers a drink and a lunch, then introducing them to two bikini-clad women who offer to "help" in unnamed ways. Denham politely declines whatever is being offered and is careful to reveal no part of his game plan. When Jordan chides him for having to ride the subway, Denham shows no rancor, though big shots, like Jordan, clearly annoy him. Well-schooled in his own role, he feigns bewilderment about Jordan's case, noting that it was "just dumped on my desk." This prompts Jordan to extol the virtues of hard-working Americans, "the people who built this country," whom he regrets are so seriously underpaid. The stage is thus set for Jordan to propose a bribe, sufficiently well disguised so that it could not be legally actionable. But Denham calls him for his proposal, which instantly turns the conversation sour. Jordan now orders the two agents off his boat, and Denham retaliates by promising to impound it on some indefinite further occasion. As the two federal officers find their way back to the street, Jordan pelts them with live lobsters to punctuate his anger over their insults to his hospitality. It's no surprise that Denham leaves with a determination to bring Jordan down.

As his house of cards begins to collapse, Jordan has a chance to escape almost unscathed through a plea bargain engineered by his father, eager to save Jordan from himself. But instead of resigning and turning over the leadership to Donny, as had been agreed, Jordan is seduced by his own rhetoric, reversing his course in the middle of his resignation speech and vowing to fight on in the name of the can-do spirit he has made the Stratton Oakmont credo. When Denham hears "the fish is back in the water," he tightens the noose that good police work has already looped around Jordan's neck. The demise of Stratton Oakmont visually recalls the breakup of the gangster cultures at the end of *GoodFellas* and *Casino*. Despite a momentary show of defiance, Jordan, like Henry Hill, betrays his close comrades, incriminating them in return for leniency to himself. As the FBI strike force overwhelms the firm's offices, various subalterns are seized and handcuffed, while Donny Azoff frantically pounds the delete key of his laptop for the sake of whatever damage control might still be possible.

The conclusion of *The Wolf of Wall Street* is ambiguous and problematic. Its epilogue dramatizes the rehabilitation of Jordon Belfort, the reformed criminal who has paid his debt to society and now is ready to use his great gifts for lawful purposes (Scorsese 2014, 02:51:00/02:52:55). We find he has reinvented himself as a motivational speaker, now living in Auckland, New Zealand, and training a sales force that no longer works for him, but continues to work from the script he wrote for his compatriots at Stratton Oakmont. As the CEO of Straight Line, a service industry devoted to wealth creation, he is building another empire of words, manufacturing nothing and actually generating nothing other than need, anxiety, and expectation. Ironically, he still takes his inspiration from Brad, the neighborhood drug dealer, who was the only member of Jordan's first inner circle that could solve the riddle of "Sell me this pen." Brad, incidentally, persisted in criminality, did jail time for money laundering, lived at a hyper-intense pace, and died at thirty-five of cardiac arrest. But when Jordan poses Brad's challenge to the eager acolytes of Auckland, he is looking upon faces full of uncertainty and yearning, hopeful they will hear the magic words that will turn them into millionaires. As if to mime the movement of Jordan's can-do spirit, the camera rides out over the crowd, just as it did on an earlier occasion when he was addressing his staff on Long Island. Moreover, there is another figure in this scene, the figure of Jordan Belfort himself, the reformed felon of real life now residing in Australia. Unnamed in the scene (but acknowledged in the credits), the real Jordan Belfort introduces the fictive Jordan Belfort, representing "himself," we might say, as "my good friend and the world's greatest sales trainer" (Scorsese 2014, 02:51:15/02:52:00). This bit of reflexivity might simply be an insider joke, something like Alfred Hitchcock boarding a bus in one of his own films. But it hints at a darker meaning. Real people, it would seem, now create avatars of themselves, so that their image multiplies itself indefinitely, reaching people far beyond any circle of contacts that a human character could possibly engage. Jordan Belfort has not only started a new career; he has made himself into a movie, available in multiple languages and showing on screens worldwide. At once confident and casual, he, like the film he now stars in, is the face and voice of the America's postindustrial economy. Significantly, *The Wolf of Wall Street* has turned out to be Scorsese's highest grossing film.

Shortly after the release of *The Wolf of Wall Street*, Scorsese told a reporter for *Variety*, "the film came out of frustration over the unregulated financial world" (McNary 2014). And the film's topicality is undeniable. But the director gets closer to his deeper concerns in a more robust interview, where he speaks of characters who "had no real model for leading a decent life, because this is what they learned from the world around them." Thinking in these terms, he elides "Jordan, Jake LaMotta, Tommy," in fact, the whole motley array of deeply flawed males from *Raging Bull* through *GoodFellas* and *Casino* to *The Wolf of Wall Street*. They are "not someone else," he insists, they are "you and me. I think it's a matter of facing and recognizing—acknowledging that part of us, which is part of our common humanity" ("Martin Scorsese: *Wolf of Wall Street Interview*" 2013, 00:30/01:50).

What has occurred in the evolution Scorsese's career is simply a shift of emphasis. Whether he is among the clans of Little Italy, or examining the polyvalent cultures of Bay Ridge and Long Island, or casting a side-long glance at what remains of the ethnic Irish in Boston or New York, his ongoing concern is with nature and nurture, the ways in which the close acculturation of family, neighborhood, and workplace shapes and decisively modifies our genetic inheritance, our "common humanity." If Scorsese has decided to put less emphasis on ethnic themes in the last phase of his long career, it is only after he has honed valuable tools of analysis from his careful look at the remnants of Italy, Sicily, Ireland, and even Jerusalem in New York and elsewhere. This same analytical perspective has apparently persuaded him that his favorite American ethnics have now morphed their particular identity into the complex hybridity of contemporary America.

TWO

Woody Allen

Woody Allen's enmeshment in ethnic culture as well as his relationship to the film industry is both more complicated and more long-standing than Martin Scorsese's. As early as 1966, while Scorsese was just finishing his master's program at NYU, Allen was already writing and starring in "Jewish" plays, like *Don't Drink the Water*, which wrings a good share of laughs from a stereotypical Jewish couple clattering around in the Soviet Union and accidentally embroiling themselves in Cold War pratfalls. His earliest pieces for the *New Yorker*, such as "Hassidic Tales," are already rich in Jewish caricature. Here we meet Rabbi Chaim Yisroel, "on his way to celebrate the sacred Jewish holiday commemorating God's reneging on every promise" and "Rabbi Yekel of Zans, who had the best diction in the world until a Gentile stole his resonant underwear" (Allen 1966, 63–69). Allen's more sophisticated work of a few years later continues the comic rendering of Jewish culture with portraits of Sandor Needleman, the klutzy Jewish intellectual of "Remembering Needleman," who has authored *A Systematic Reevaluation of Nothingness* and who gets investigated by HUAC for preaching that the true "model society [is] an ant farm" (Allen 1975, 3–8). In another *New Yorker* story from the early 1970s, "The Kugelmass Episode," Allen inserts a "bald Jew" into *Madame Bovary*, and Flaubert's *femme fatale* becomes Kugelmass' escape from his controlling Jewish wife and her cousin Hamish (1975, 41–55). Though their time-traveling romance starts well, it begins to sour as Kugelmass reveals his stereotypical Jewish stinginess, complaining that Emma's "hotel tab . . . reads like the defense budget" (53). Still earlier, Allen had established himself as a stand-up comic, always writing his own material, and bringing ethnic humor to avant garde Manhattan venues, like The Blue Angel, where he launched his career in 1960.

Allen also built his filmmaking career upon a secure foundation, entering the Manhattan market place at the right time and with enough leverage to achieve relative autonomy. Unlike Scorsese, he was offered the director's chair after having already made a considerable reputation

113

as an actor and a writer. Though he was discouraged by the way his writing was mishandled in early ventures like *What's New Pussycat* (1965) and *Casino Royale* (1967), these experiences persuaded him to insist on a level of control over his productions that Scorsese was rarely able to count on, at least not before the success of *Taxi Driver* in 1976. By the early 1970s, Allen had gathered about him a small cadre of close associates, including Charles Joffe and Jack Rollins, his producers, Ralph Rosenblum, his editor, Marshall Brickman, his principal writing collaborator, as well as Louise Lasser and Diane Keaton, his favorite female stars. From the outset of his career, Allen was in sync with his creative talent, while Joffe and Rollins negotiated contracts with United Artists (UA), a distributorship doing business out of New York instead of Los Angeles, that gave the director full creative authority over the "final cut" of a Woody Allen film.

Allen's most recent biographer, Daniel Evanier, confirms the esteem which UA executives, particularly Arthur Krim, felt for their young actor/ director:

> What endeared him to these men was not only his talent but also his integrity. He always kept his word to them, and he was not disdainful of their commercial concerns. And there was another, perhaps unspoken factor. Woody was the first to put his Jewishness on screen so forthrightly. Jewish Hollywood, with its many refugees from Hitler—from Billy Wilder to Arthur Preminger and dozens more—with its years of concealing the identities of Jewish stars, embraced him, the first Jewish star of the seventies, from the start. Allen was, indeed family, and not least to the cultivated Jewish figures who ran United Artists. (2015, 172–73)

Woody Allen's emergence as an ethnic filmmaker also coincides with the more public expression of the Jewish presence in New York City. In 1973, Abraham Beame became the first Jewish mayor of the five boroughs. Four years later, the city elected another Jewish mayor, Edward Koch, who would preside over New York for the next twelve years, creating the powerful "Koch coalition," as John Mollenkopf describes it, which spurred forward the city's transition to a post-industrial economy. That new economy made a respectful place for the entertainment industry, including film and television (Drier, Mollenkopf, and Swanstrom 1994, esp. 100–128). Mayor Koch received an on-screen credit for his "cooperation" in the production of *Manhattan*. The 1970s find us barely on the threshold of that recovery, but already Allen is emotionally invested in the city and prepared to populate it with Jewish characters different from those we had previously seen on American screens. His attitude toward Jewishness is much like the one Eric Goldstein formulates as he describes "Jews in multicultural America": they remain conscious of their own ethnicity but want it understood that they are "part of a pluralist, rather than an exclusivist social order" (2006, 213).

SEGMENT 1: JEWISH IN NEW YORK
ANNIE HALL (1977) AND *MANHATTAN* (1979)

Both *Annie Hall* and *Manhattan* are affectionate portraits of New York City, lovingly photographed by Gordon Willis, who represents its urban substance much differently than Michael Chapman had shown it in Scorsese's *Taxi Driver* fewer than five years earlier. Everyone remembers the magnificent visual evocation of New York that opens *Manhattan*, but *Annie Hall* has similarly fine visual moments, like Annie and Alvy strolling along an urban beachfront while a bloodred sun sets over the quiet water. Allen also imagines the city as reasonably benign toward ethnic minorities, at least as far as upwardly mobile Jews from Brooklyn and Queens are concerned. In fact, both films concentrate on rapidly assimilating Jewish protagonists who realize they have easier access to the corridors of power than their fathers had had, though they remain more tentative and hesitant in navigating the intimate spaces of love and romance. Both Alvy Singer (Woody Allen) of *Annie Hall* and Isaac Davis (Woody Allen) of *Manhattan* are self-conscious of their Jewishness, but each is eager to claim New York as his home, interpreting its cosmopolitanism as supporting the well-worn Yiddish proverb, *Staat macht frei*: The city creates freedom.

In *Jews and the American Soul* (2004), Andrew Heinze maintains that Jewish culture, from colonial times onward, but particularly in the twentieth century, contributed markedly to "the psychodynamics of American life." From the time of Freud's 1909 visit to the United States, which three years later was reprised, discussed, and brought to national attention in *McClure's Magazine*, "new interpretations of the human psyche, and Jewish newcomers who specialized in interpreting the psyche, gained greater and greater importance in American life" (11). The centrality of Jewish contributions to psychology, psychiatry, and psychotherapy became more evident in the decades after World War II, when a remarkable number of Jewish intellectuals including Theodor Reik, Wilhelm Reich, Erik Erickson, Erich Fromm, and Abraham Maslow joined others within and beyond the Jewish community in the "creation of American humanism" (Heinze 2004, 261–90). Some, like Fromm and Maslow, were explicitly anchored in New York, Fromm at the Institute for Social Research and Maslow at the New York Psychoanalytic Institute. The common thread that held together these diverse strands of inquiry, says Heinze, was that "as Jews [they were] sensitive to the destructiveness of fascism, aware of their outsider status, cognizant, as only immigrants could be, of the fluidity of personal identity and deeply influenced by a Jewish concept of human relatedness" (261–62).

By a complex process of osmosis, this mix of attitudes would soon impact American literature, giving a Jewish inflection to the literary voices of the rising generation, notably writers like Budd Schulberg, Saul Bellow, Philip Roth, and Allen Ginsberg. Appropriately, Heinze puts Woody Allen on this list of Jewish artists who take their cue from the thinking of social psychology, especially its "strong preoccupation with *relatedness*" (2004, 275, italics in original). He insists that the "expressive style of postwar Jewish writers achieved its most enduring visual statement in Woody Allen's cinema and its most enduring aural monument in Allen Ginsberg's poetry" (265). Applauding "Allen's innovative use of the Freudian confessional as a comedic device," Heinze singles out *Annie Hall* as a film predicated upon relatedness and "unafraid of publicizing the angst within" (266). Like this cohort of Jewish writers who gave "brilliant, almost baroque expression to the central image of the age, the image of the trapped individual seeking catharsis through emotional, sexual, and verbal liberation," Allen too is to be found at that "grand junction where literature met psychology in the postwar decades" (267).

Allen himself knew that *Annie Hall* was a departure from wildly farcical films, like *Bananas* (1971) and *Sleeper* (1973), which had won him quick fame in the early 1970s. "I think *Annie* may be a mild turning point," he told Gary Arnold in 1977. "I'm used to looking for laughs in the dailies. Here there weren't nearly as many laughs to go by. I had to trust to the relationships." Going further in this vein, Allen suggests that "the contemporary playing area for comedy has shifted. Chaplin and Keaton operated in a very physical world where people worked and struggled to cope with tangible objects and frustrations. I think the conflicts are interior now. They're psychological conflicts, and it's difficult to find a vocabulary to express those inner states" (Kapsis 2016, 44). In search of this new vocabulary, Allen was persuaded, almost inevitably, to examine his own ethnicity and how that affected his "relatedness" to his own social world.

In his career as a stand-up comic, Allen had woven multiple Jewish stereotypes into the fabric of his routines, including a memorable encounter with a moose, where the skinny, weak-eyed Allen persona attempts to stand tall as an avatar of heroic masculinity. He shoots a moose, as he assures us confidently, then brings his trophy back to Manhattan. But we quickly sense this overreach will end badly, because the Jewish schlemiel looks incongruous when attempting to live "the strenuous life" that Rough Rider Teddy Roosevelt had once recommended to his Anglo-Nordic blood brothers. And, yes, the rest of the routine mocks the heroic premise. Stunned but by no means dead, the trophy moose awakens to signal an illegal U-turn from the fender to which he's been tied. The rest of the skit is a series of challenges to the authority of the great white hunter, with the moose getting the better of every exchange. As a narrative sidebar, Allen adds an anecdote about a Jewish couple that inadvertently integrates the notoriously anti-Semitic

New York Athletic Club when they are stuffed and mounted as trophies after being mistaken for the moose. Allen's early films are also marked by farcical treatments of Jewishness. Fielding Melish of *Bananas* (1971) and Miles Monroe of *Sleeper* (1973) are both fragile Jews forced toward revolutionary heroics for which they are utterly unsuited. Both films also find time to joke about Jewish custom and practice. One critic has even chastised Allen for "dragging in bearded Hasidic Jews whenever he wants an easy laugh" (Pinsker 2006, 10). But *Annie Hall* calls up the Jewish life world much differently, interrogating the stereotypes Allen had previously used as his comic signature.

Allen was aware that *Annie Hall* would be an "ethnic film," and he embeds a coy homage to Francis Coppola in an early scene (1977, 07:15/08:50). While waiting in front of the Beekmann cinema for Annie (Diane Keaton), Alvy is greeted by an enthusiastic, conspicuously Italian admirer, who salutes him boisterously as a Manhattan celebrity and asks for his autograph. Before the episode concludes, others who belong to this cohort gather round Alvy, summoned by the cry, "Hey, over here, Alvy Singer." Finally escaping his hero-worshipping fan club, he complains to Annie of his encounter with "the cast of *The Godfather*." The scene is wonderfully good comedy, but has no relationship to the film, except as an insider joke in which Coppola seems to welcome Woody Allen into the pantheon of ethnic filmmakers. And perhaps it is not completely accidental that Gordon Willis, director of photography for *The Godfather*, was Allen's personal choice to serve as director of photography for both *Annie Hall* and *Manhattan*.

Exactly what change takes place in the rendering of the ethnic Jew between *Sleeper* and *Annie Hall* can be illustrated by a scene in *Annie*, where Alvy meets his first wife, the obviously Jewish Allison Portchnik (Carol Kane). Having spent thirty seconds getting acquainted with her, he confidently frames her Jewishness as caricature: "New York Jewish left-wing liberal intellectual, Central Park West, Brandeis University, and socialist summer camps." Alvy's profile of Allison must contain a grain of truth since she is working for Adlai Stevenson, whose campaign to deny a second term to the popular President Eisenhower was the left-liberal lost cause of 1956. But Allison responds to Alvy's cheap shot with a pitch-perfect rejoinder: "That's wonderful—I enjoy being reduced to a cultural stereotype" (Allen 1977, 13:50/15:50). The exchange reminds us that, though stereotypes are half-true, they ignore the full density of the human person. What Allen's creative strategy implies is that we can now expect the ethnic stereotype to resist the erasure of her complexity. Allison's ironic response foreshadows Annie's resistance to the same pigeonholing that later characterizes Alvy's reductionist behavior toward the one woman he truly loves.

One of Allen's most perceptive recent critics recognizes the director's deep indebtedness to the thinking about psychological "relatedness" that Heinze details carefully in *Jews and the American Soul*. In representing *Annie Hall* as an encounter between "the anhedonist and the singer," Mary Nichols explains precisely why Alvy and Annie cannot achieve a lasting relationship, in spite of their deep affection and their strenuous efforts to establish themselves as a loving couple (1998, 33–48). Noting that Allen "originally intended to name this movie 'Anhedonia' (34), Nichols traces the concept back to Freud, who speaks at length in *Civilization and Its Discontents* (1930) about persons who cannot accept "the program of becoming happy, which the pleasure principle imposes on us" (Nichols 1998, 34). The inkhorn term "anhedonia" was actually coined by Abraham Myerson, a Jewish psychiatrist of the 1910s and 1920s, who used it expansively in *When Life Loses Its Zest* (1925) to frame a discussion of clinical depression. Myerson's study of this phenomenon also convinced him that Jews were peculiarly susceptible to manic-depressive behavior and that we could "step into any clinic for nervous diseases in any large city in Europe or America" and find that "the Jew is unduly represented amongst the patients." But Myerson and his intellectual progeny argued forcefully that these disorders were rarely organic, rather that they were a function of anti-Semitism and the problematic of the Jew's having to adapt to an often hostile environment (see Heinze 2004, 117–18; 149–57). This ethnically inflected analysis of anhedonia figures crucially in the dramatic logic of *Annie Hall*.

As Nichols explains, the other psychoanalytical text essential to understanding *Annie Hall* is Ernest Becker's *The Denial of Death* (1973), a seminal work of contemporary times that Allen explicitly incorporates into his film. Along with Marcel Ophuls' *The Sorrow and the Pity* (1969), an iconic text for the study of the Holocaust, Becker's *Denial of Death* is the companion piece that Alvy insists Annie must read in order to appreciate her lover's mental formation and outlook on life. Though she resists this draconian demand upon her time and her nervous system, the book is remarkably prescient in contextualizing anhedonia and in summing up how the Olympians of modern psychology—Freud, Kierkegaard, Fromm, Maslow, Otto Rank, Norman Brown, among others—positioned themselves *vis-à-vis* the inevitability of death.

In characterizing "the terror of death," Becker argues that all anxieties, all phobias, together with chronic depression are all disguises and displacements of the "basic fear that influences all others," the fear of one's inevitable mortality (1973, 11–24). "Recasting some basic psychoanalytic ideas," Becker examines the vulnerability of the human body and how its fragility terrifies us: "Who wants to face up to the creatures we are, clawing and gasping for breath in a universe beyond our ken?" (27). Hence the neurosis of anal-fixation: "Excreting is the curse that threatens madness because it shows man his abject finitude, his physicalness, the likely un- reality of his hopes and dreams" (33). Unsurprisingly these fears declare themselves powerfully in the dawning consciousness of the child, who apprehends his dependency and vulnerability even though he cannot yet express his feelings in language. While the child shudders in the presence of these terrors, however, he also "comes to know something about the power relations of the world" (19), that the cat catches and kills the mouse, that the hawk pulls the fish from the stream, that the family butchers and cooks the chicken. This experience of surrogate power, especially parental power, propels the child toward the "vital lie" of character, whereby we compensate for our own frailty by putting on the armor of the civilization that created us (47–65). "Each child grounds himself in some power that transcends him. Usually it is some combination of his parents, his social group, and the symbols of society and nation" (89).

But Becker, like Allen, who follows in his footsteps, is not persuaded that the symbolic order of culture truly reconciles us to what Kierkegaard called "fear and trembling and the sickness unto death." Our accultura- tion reveals too many fracture points through which the abyss is visible. Young Alvy Singer, who has just learned that the universe is destined to expand chaotically at some final moment, sees no purpose in doing his homework. Nor can his mother console him with the assurance that "Brooklyn is not expanding" (Allen 1977, 02:35/03:15). His anxiety goes deeper than family or neighborhood. He is similarly unimpressed by the advice of a family therapist, Dr. Flicker, apparently called in to support the frustrated parent. The therapist enjoins Alvy to live in the present, to take pleasure from the world immediately about him and not let his mind drift toward the far future. No cosmic chaos is in the immediate offing. If Becker were to intervene in this counseling session, he would be likely to say: This "is living for the day. . . . Its aim is to deny one's lack of control over events, his powerlessness, his vagueness as a person in a mechani- cal world spinning into decay and death" (1973, 84). If parental scolding and personal therapy are not sufficient to seal us off from our creaturely anxieties, what further armor of civilization might we put on?

Although Becker's analysis has no specifically ethnic inflections, the prospect of moving in that direction is there at every turn. Building upon Freud's examination of the "death instinct," Becker turns to Otto Rank for the further point that "the death fear of the ego is lessened by the killing, the sacrifice of the other; through the death of the other, one buys oneself free from the penalty of dying, of being killed" (Becker 1973, 99). Hence the scapegoating impulse that surfaces in virtually all psychoanalytical accounts of demagogic political behavior. Drawing particularly upon Er- ich Fromm, Becker indicts the "the mystique of the group" for its "blind obedience, illusion, and communal sadism," its compulsion "to draw sharp lines between those who are like me and belong to me and those who are outsiders and aliens" (134). Fearful of our own impotence, we seek to "keep [ourselves] tucked into a larger source of power," caught "in the prison of the motherly, racial-national-religious fixation" (134). These points resonate powerfully with *Annie Hall*, particularly Alvy's troubled sense of his Jewishness as he moves romantically into the world of his conspicuously Anglo-Nordic love friend.

With its emphasis on immediacy and improvisation, *Annie Hall* resists reduction to an analytical formula, but clearly it is sensitive to the issue of "marginality," the awareness of borders, especially the permeability of those borders and the way this permeability threatens to destabilize the individual whose life world and social status is in flux. Largely because of his professional talent, Alvy, when he first introduces himself to us, has advanced spectacularly in his show business career, leaving behind a bleak Jewish childhood of loveless parents, hyper-strict teachers, schoolmates who he "thought were idiots," and empty religious rituals that have provided no discernible spiritual nurture (Allen 1977, 03:55/06:00). We don't know all the details of his acculturation, but we know he has formed and dissolved two marriages, both with Jewish women, which presumably means he has lived his life of intimacy largely in a Jewish world. The film handles these relationships through cinematic shorthand, but what we learn is revealing. He admits to undervaluing his first wife, Allison, and attributes the failed relationship to his general immaturity. We get only one glimpse of his life with Robin (Janet Margolin), his second spouse, but we see enough to understand Alvy's impatience with intellectual and academic Jewry (20:10/21:50). Alvy takes Robin herself to be overly cerebral (he would rather watch basketball than swoon over book titles) and clearly resents the time she gives to chatting up prospective editors, publishers, and authors of arcane scholarly monographs. His send-up of New York's Jewish literati is caught in imagining a new journal, "Dysentery," which he says sprung up from the merger of *Dissent* and *Commentary*, easily the two best known journals of Jewish opinion publishing in New York City. This personal history suffices to explain his alienation from the Jewish community and his inclination to insert himself into WASP culture, epitomized by his friend Rob (Tony Roberts) and, of course, Annie.

It's worth remembering that Annie and Alvy meet at a private tennis club, most of which had been segregated by race and ethnicity until the civil rights movement of the mid-1960s. With respect to Jews, American custom built upon German and European precedent, which from the nineteenth century onward disparaged "the Jewish body" as "diseased" or "degenerate," unfit for military service or for serious athletic competition (see Gilman 1991, esp. 38–59). In the next century, the latter fixation led to the widespread practice in German-speaking lands of insisting that gymnastic and athletic facilities be *Juden frei*. Most memorably, the Hitler regime strove doggedly to prevent Jewish athletes from competing in the Berlin Olympics of 1936. But these precedents of racial exclusion were largely honored in the United States as well. Notoriously, in 1959, the black diplomat and Nobel prize winner Ralph Bunche was denied membership in New York's West Side Tennis Club, an institution that also excluded Jews on "racial" grounds. The incident was consequential enough to persuade the *Jewish Telegraphic Agency*, a social advocacy journal, to complain editorially about the "tight bars against Jews and Negroes" that characterized most of the city's private sports centers (Jewish Telegraphic Agency 1959). The New York Athletic Club, for instance, (which figures in Allen's comic routine about the Jewish moose) was similarly guilty of excluding Jews from membership until the later 1960s. Though Alvy is certainly no civil rights crusader, he would be numbered among the first generation of Jews who integrated the private athletic clubs of New York City.

Annie is not anti-Semitic (it seems she would have felt very comfortable among the flower children of Woodstock), but she is not in the least cosmopolitan. Her dysfunctional relationship to urban space is caught in her comic drive home from the tennis club, as she barely avoids several traffic catastrophes, zigging and zagging from lane to lane with the chaotic gusto of Chaplin or Keaton. Her unfamiliarity with the ways of a truly international city helps explain the problems that inevitably surface in her relationship to Alvy. In their first extended conversation, as Annie invites him to her apartment for a drink, Alvy asks, "Did you grow up in a Norman Rockwell painting?" This is said not so much in sarcasm as in genuine astonishment. When she mentions a present from her "Grammy," he rejoins with "my grandma never gave me presents. She was too busy being raped by Cossacks." However guileless and genuinely talented Annie might be, her 1950s' slang and seeming obliviousness to cultural practices unknown in Chippewa Falls mark her as unmistakably rural, which accounts for her wonderful innocence, but also her naiveté. When she blurts out, without forewarning or context, "you're what Grammy would call a real Jew," Alvy is completely bewildered, mystified by what his new friend might mean. It doesn't help when she adds, "Grammy hates Jews. She thinks they just make money" (Allen 1977, 27:45/33:20). Alvy is hypersensitive to being identified as a Jew. He would like to be securely an "American," a "New Yorker," the cultural insider his professional success should entitle him to be. Earlier, he has suspected that the music store clerk who alerted him to a sale on Wagner (pronounced in a self-consciously Germanized way) was taunting him about his Jewishness. And, on another occasion, he translates the apparently innocent phrase, which he heard at the tennis club, "Did'ju eat yet," into an accusatory, anti-Semitic slur: "Did Jew eat yet," which Rob finds ridiculous. When Annie orders her pastrami sandwich on white bread instead of rye, then compounds the affront to Jewry by adding mayonnaise to the order, Alvy rolls his eyes but makes no comment. His discomfort with his Jewishness complicates and eventually damages his relationship to Annie.

Without intending to dampen his lover's zest for life, Alvy urges Annie to read *The Denial of Death* and join him at a screening of Marcel Ophuls' *The Sorrow and the Pity*. This second agenda item is particularly relevant, since it speaks directly to the question of Jewish marginality. Produced in 1969 after considerable controversy, this four-and-a-half-hour documentary on France's complicity in the Holocaust made its American debut at the New York Film Festival of 1971, then experienced a fifteen-month run in New York City, finding a highly appreciative audience that few realized existed. Ophuls saw his film as a rebuke to "the myth of the heroic Gaullist resistance" to the Nazi occupation of WWII, a widely circulated patriotic cliché of the 1950s and beyond (see Wilhelm 1999, 5). Exhaustively gathering the testimony of politicians, bureaucrats, shopkeepers, soldiers, and everyday people, Ophuls tells a dark tale of fear, collaboration, opportunism, and moral ambiguity, which discredits the narrative of those Frenchmen who had been seduced by Gaullist propaganda and encouraged to forget what it was really like in France between 1940 and 1944. Considering how crucially the Holocaust figures in Allen's understanding of twentieth-century politics it can hardly surprise us that Alvy Singer wants his WASPish sweetheart to grasp the implications of this narrative.

Ophuls' "Chronicle of a French City under the Occupation" is much more than a polemic against right-wing political chauvinism. It makes a powerful statement about national identity and the problematic of "belonging." We hear from Marius Klein, for example, a self-serving French shopkeeper, who explains matter-of-factly how he paid for an ad in a local newspaper insisting that he was a Roman Catholic, under no circumstances to be confused with a Jew, in spite of a German name that could easily be Jewish. And also from Madame Solange, once the proprietress of a beauty salon, who now denies that she helped identify Jews and report them to the local authorities for deportation. More chilling still is the archival footage that shows how Jews were forced to wear yellow stars, so as to make sure no one mistook them for "Frenchmen," which they could legitimately claim to be until May 29, 1942. Suddenly, as if by sorcery, "Jews" were separated from "Frenchmen" and given an entirely new identity as criminal aliens. Could that happen in New York? Probably not, given the degree to which Jewish immigrant culture had by the 1970s assimilated to the American mainstream. But when Alvy visits

Annie in Chippewa Falls during Easter Week and, under the cold stare of "Grammy" (Helen Ludlam), imagines himself transformed into an Orthodox Hasidic Jew (Allen 1977, 45:40/48:50), we sense the fear Alvy experiences among people very much like certain Vichyites from *The Sorrow and the Pity.* In this context, his impulse to warn Annie about the darker side of human nature becomes understandable, if not fully defensible. Even in the Hall family, as we become acquainted with Annie's psychotic brother, the sentimental worldview of Norman Rockwell threatens to morph into the ominous pitchfork image of "American Gothic."

Two consequences flow from Alvy's insecurity and his sense of victimization. He clings to New York as his refuge from a larger anti-Semitic world, and he demeans Annie as a way of protecting himself. The joke that he borrows from Groucho Marx, namely, "I wouldn't belong to a club that would have someone like me for a member," reflects both his discomfort with his Jewishness and his lack of confidence he can find another "club" to join. In the middle chapters of *The Denial of Death,* Becker worries about the more sinister aspects of group dynamics, man's susceptibility to the "psychic cement that lock[s] people into mutual and mindless interdependence: the magnetic powers of the leader, reciprocated by the guilty delegation of everyone's will to him" (1973, 132–33). Still, Becker realizes the necessity of "transference," the life-affirming urge that the human creature also feels to transcend the fragility of selfhood, to find a "second world, a world of humanly created meaning, a new reality that he can live, dramatize, nourish himself in" (188). For Alvy, estranged from his Judaic heritage, which once might have provided a religious destiny for its children, this transcendent world of "humanly created meaning" is New York City, almost a Jewish city, as he tells Rob while defending it against critics unsympathetic to its fiscal problems of the 1970s and unwilling to invest or assist in its needed rehabilitation. Becker maintains that "cultural illusion is a necessary ideology of self-justification, a heroic dimension that is life itself to the symbolic animal" (188). Which explains Alvy's intense polemic on behalf of New York, his determination to persuade Rob he should be doing Shakespeare in Central Park instead of yearning for California. It also underlies his obsession with "rescuing" Annie from Los Angeles, the conflict that ultimately ends their relationship.

Alvy's deteriorating relationship to Annie, which constitutes the last two thirds of the film, flows directly from his own insecurity and his compulsion to control her. As he imagines his motives, Alvy intends to "guide" her toward maturity, to educate her into an appreciation of New York, to build her career as a singer out of the materials and according to the blueprints he himself has drawn. Christopher Knight is correct in representing the film as "Galatea's triumph over Pygmalion," Annie's successful effort to resist the "subtle and not so subtle ways that men impose meaning upon women" (2004, 213). What Knight perhaps doesn't sufficiently emphasize is the degree to which Alvy's power over Annie is bound up with the city of New York, the ethnic space that anchors his self-concept. This point figures importantly in the film's resolution: Alvy loses Annie, much to his personal grief, but consoles himself with the thought that his influence eventually brings her back to New York. Obviously this is not a victory for Alvy. But it is a victory for the larger value system that Alvy in some sense embodies.

From this standpoint, the representation of Los Angeles has relevance beyond its value as a site for comic stage business. As we see California through Alvy's eyes, this city is a fun house mirror, a surreal universe where reindeer pull sleighs across green lawns, jokes are funny only when supported by a laugh track, and beguiled sun worshippers go about in space suits that magically assure them they will never grow old. Perhaps more to the point, Los Angeles is a city utterly without a cultural past, where one can drive down a palm-lined boulevard and see in the suburban architecture "French, next to Spanish, next to Tudor, next to Japanese." The women are synthetic figures, "like the women in *Playboy*, except they can move their arms and legs." In this dystopic metropolis, everything is unnaturally clean "because they don't throw their garbage away. They make it into television shows" (Allen 1977, 01:11:45/01:12:50). At the "fabulous Christmas party," to which Rob has secured an invitation for Annie and Alvy, we meet a guest who plans to turn "a notion into a concept and later into an idea." Another is on the phone to his therapist because he has "forgotten his mantra." One prides himself on owning a house inhabited consecutively by Nelson Eddy, Legs Diamond, and Trigger, one of several incarnations of Roy Rogers' horse. Rob identifies a woman he admires by referencing her underwear. In this sexualized environment, the host of the party, Tony Lacy (Paul Simon), invites Annie to move in with him for six weeks while she cuts a record album he will market. She suspects that he has in mind a further agenda, which as we learn later he does. When New York enters into the conversations of this sun-drenched world, it is always yoked to bad weather, crime-ridden streets, and the unwelcome stress of noise and crowds (01:14:55/01:18:05).

At this moment Annie is inclined to become a Los Angeline: "I go to parties, meet people, and play tennis." Alvy finds her response to California incomprehensible: "If she likes that life style, let her live there." This precipitates their breakup, which includes Annie's request that Alvy take back all "those books on death and dying." Though she tries to give back *The Denial of Death*—"a great weight off my back"—Alvy secretively stores it among the things she takes with her, which in a complicated way actually foreshadows the film's conclusion (Allen 1977, 01:19:05/01:19:35).

Later, he makes one final effort to retrieve her from the Pacific coast, this one more disastrous than the first, ending with harsh words and a traffic accident that lands him in jail. Unrelenting, he returns to New York and writes a wish-fulfilling play, which climaxes when Annie surrenders to him, admitting she should never have strayed beyond the reach of his manly authority. At this self-delusive moment, Alvy still needs Annie's weakness to certify his own strength.

But the film does not end on this false note. The closing sequence, a memory montage accompanied by Annie singing "Old Times" in a New York venue, shows Alvy in a more mature mood, more comfortable in his own skin, and at last prepared, albeit reluctantly, to let Annie live her own life. He has not succeeded in making her his permanent romantic partner but he has somehow been instrumental in bringing her back to New York, which she once had pronounced a "dying city," dirty and decaying, like the Venice of Thomas Mann's famous novella. Now her return from Los Angeles augurs a change of mind. Moreover, what Alvy calls his "personal triumph" is her newfound appreciation of *The Sorrow and the Pity*, a film she is introducing to her new male friend when Alvy accidentally meets her at the cinema. In embracing New York, she seems also to have achieved a new level of understanding, a new sensitivity to suffering, loss, and pain. Alvy is probably right in thinking that her spiritual growth owes considerably to his influence, the contribution of his Jewishness to her mature sensibility. With no expectation that their relationship might resume, Alvy is still able to acknowledge, "what a terrific person she was and how much fun it was just knowing her" (Allen 1977, 01:29:00/01:31:10).

Allen did well to call his film *Annie Hall*, because it really is Annie's story, a female *bildungsroman* filtered through the mind of a male narrator. Although Alvy's voice-over monologue might seem to give him the last word, his remarks are counterpointed by Annie's voice, performing the lyrics of Jacob Loeb's "Seems Like Old Times." In words that inevitably become a commentary on Alvy, and images that recall highlights of their time together, she tells us she still feels "the thrill it was the day I found you." Furthermore, her voice is now confident, controlled, in no way resembling that of the insecure woman who was afraid to let Alvy hear her sing in public. At this conclusive moment, Annie is also the voice of New York City, performing the lyrics of a Jewish composer, whose melody now becomes the music of Manhattan itself, as it expands beyond the site of her performance to resonate in urban space, wafting over streets and sidewalks, as if audible to any passerby who might want to hear. Having met for lunch on very cordial terms, the two former lovers kiss affectionately on the street corner by the café, and then exit the film frame in opposite directions. But the camera lingers on the carefully composed street scene, as though Annie were now addressing her song to Manhattan: "Seems like old times, being here with you." We hear Alvy still muttering about "relationships that are totally irrational and crazy and absurd," but in reality he and Annie have found a new kind of belonging, sharing the experience of the modern city (Allen 1977, 01:29:10/01:31:00). He has coaxed her from the world of Norman Rockwell and helped her find her way out of Los Angeles; she has taught him to accept her personal autonomy and respect her career as a professional singer. At the same time, both have found a cultural identity as New Yorkers, which is more substantial than their individual goals or strivings.

Searching for a countervailing power to compensate for the fear of mortality he has conjured up in such harrowing terms, Ernest Becker concludes *The Denial of Death* by hoping for "a new birth bringing new adaptations, new creative solutions to our problems, a new openness in dealing with stale perceptions about reality," in fact, "a continual transformation of reality" achieved through the agency of "an evolutionary creature making his own peculiar responses to a world that continue(s) to transcend him" (1973, 277). In the last scene of the film, Annie and Alvy, having linked themselves to the larger life world of a vibrant modern city, seem within reach of this "new birth." What they have, as they go their separate ways, is not the Earthly Paradise of Los Angeles, nor the transcendent faith of the Chosen People, but it is a kind of modernist "salvation" that Allen will explore in films of the next four decades.

After his painstaking, but largely failing effort to imitate Ingmar Bergman in *Interiors* (1978), Allen returned to the streets and sites of his favorite American city in *Manhattan* (1979), picking up threads he had left dangling in *Annie Hall*. Again, the male protagonist is Jewish, a young writer and media artist much like Allen himself. Far less self-conscious of his ethnic roots than Alvy Singer, Isaac Davis represents the Jewish culture of New York almost at its vanishing point, the place where Jewishness becomes indistinguishable from the mainstream sensibility of the city. Isaac blends in effortlessly with his Anglo friends, rarely refers to his Jewish parents, and only his vengeful ex-wife characterizes him as a "paranoid Jew." We do notice, of course, that he frequents museums and galleries associated with Jewish philanthropy and should remind ourselves that New York City has a Jewish population larger than that of Tel Aviv. Which is to say, as does Cheryl Greenberg, that American Jewry struggles "to balance Jewish identity with a commitment to full engagement with the larger world" (2013, 44). *Manhattan* is another love letter to the city, but now composed by Isaac Davis (Allen), who—despite his Jewish genes—sees nothing incongruous about representing himself as the voice of the metropolitan world. With musical support from the powerful chords of George Gershwin, another American son of Palestine,

Isaac tells us, "New York was his town, and it always would be." What better guide could we find to lead us through this drama of "relatedness," which yields no answers to the riddle of human sociality, and certainly no creedal admonitions, but still is rich in the psychological nuances that Heinze associates with the Jewish psychoanalytical tradition?

Jewish identity in a secular, pluralist culture is currently a subject much debated among Jewish and other social thinkers. Introducing the topic in *Race, Color, Identity* (2013), Sander Gilman is careful to point out that "being Jewish [is] not about genetics" (xv), but the twenty-one contributors to this anthology have widely different understandings of what Jewish identity might be. Historicizing the concept of a Jewish race, Ivan Kalmar finds Jewishness defined "by virtue of its association with religion" (2013, 325), whereas Fran Markowitz, in an earlier chapter of the same anthology, names "blood, race, soul, and suffering" as "key metaphors for delineating, discriminating against, and unifying the Jews" (2013, 276). What is beyond question is the point Calvin Goldschneider makes in *Religion or Ethnicity: Jewish Identities in Evolution* (2009): "As generational distance from immigrant origins has increased . . . the ethnic distinctiveness of American Jews has faded. Jews have become thoroughly and indistinguishably American" (267–68). Meditating upon this context in *Modernity, Culture, and "the Jew,"* Zygmunt Bauman warily concludes, "one may say that identity production, much like the rest of industry, has been deregulated and privatized, with the state ever more declaring it is not its business and not its responsibility and leaving it to the putative wisdom of market forces. Without clear institutional anchorage and guarantees, concerns with identity are fraught with anxiety, rebounding as aggression. Collective identities can be born—and survive, however briefly—only through acts of self-assertion" (1998, 154). Unsatisfied with naming himself "a Jew," Isaac decides he will instead shout out his identity as a "New Yorker."

This comes in the opening montage, as Isaac experiments with the voice he will use to narrate the novel, or memoir, he is now composing. In synch with imagery that reveals a glorified Manhattan, Isaac introduces himself confidently, as a personification of the city. But we can see that his identity is unstable, shifting, really fabricated in order to fulfill a strategic purpose. It changes moment by moment in his search for the right tone to strike with the world. "He adored New York," we are told, a metropolitan wonderland that "pulsated to the great tunes of George Gershwin." It was full of "beautiful women and street smart guys who seemed to know all the angles." But suddenly the star-struck booster is displaced by a moralistic scold, who finds the city to be a "metaphor for the decay of contemporary culture," a world "desensitized by drugs, loud music, television, crime, garbage." Sure that he now sounds too "preachy" or too angry, Isaac crafts a further persona "as tough and romantic as the city he loved." Presumably, this confident, streetwise *mensch* and *macher* can handle the decay and the garbage, along with other desensitizing experiences of the urban world. His mental and physical prowess also make him a superior romantic partner, for "behind his horn-rimmed glasses was the coiled sexual power of a jungle cat." Aware of these spur-of-the-moment revisions, we are not surprised that the jungle cat is not much in evidence when we meet Isaac having drinks with his friends at Elaine's, a fashionable nightspot on the Upper East Side. Tellingly, Isaac's persona makes no mention of his Jewishness, except perhaps indirectly through his identification with Gershwin (Allen 1979, 00:20/02:15).

Sander Lee does right to say that in both *Annie Hall* and *Manhattan*, "the city of New York itself is a character," because "for Allen, it is the only place where life may be faced honestly" (1997, 57). We can easily take that point one step further, particularly in *Manhattan*, to say that the city is a fully embodied character, whose geography and architecture not only envelop the action but also stage and motivate the action. Because of the close cooperation between Allen and his DP Gordon Willis, the various sites of the film interlock admirably with the inconsistent, uncertain, and often duplicitous behavior of the five leading characters, including Isaac himself. *Manhattan* is, *par excellence*, a drama of relationships, the tangled web of pleas, promises, hopes, betrayals, hesitancies, and changes of mind, which the fast-paced life of the modern city makes almost inevitable. The opening montage projects a heroic New York of iconic sites like the spiral interior of the Guggenheim, the vibrancy of Yankee Stadium, and the fireworks over Central Park.

But we also see wet wash hanging from a limp clothesline at the rear of a shabby tenement, the claustrophobic space of an urban tunnel, and a shot of a work crew excavating a broken sewer or gas line. Peter Bailey is on the mark when he asserts that the film's "sumptuously gratifying visual experience finds nothing resembling an answering moral perfection in the characters" (2001, 48). But often the well-crafted image provides exactly the right décor to express the intricate emotional force fields of a particular moment, even a moment of deceit, exploitation, or evasion.

Allen's moral stance is complex, situational. As Christopher Knight concludes, the film's "ethic does not reduce itself to any one voice," certainly not "to Isaac's remarks about decaying values" (2006, 147). Allen's protagonist is immersed in, actually corrupted by the desensitizing forces he sees as contaminating the contemporary world. Isaac despises television, but has grown rich as a television writer. After quitting this job in a spasm of moral indignation, he quickly confesses to his friend Yale (Michael Murphy) that he has just made the mistake of his life, which may drive him into a smaller apartment and compromise his upscale lifestyle.

Woody Allen, *Manhattan*. Allen's romanticized iconography of New York's architectural gems speaks implicitly of the upscale lives of the characters who inhabit his fictional world.
Source: This frame-capture is the work of James F. Scott, with technical support from the Instructional Media Center, Saint Louis University.

Is Isaac's response to the world in any way Jewish? He rarely mentions his parents, remembering his mother only as a "castrating Zionist" and dismissing his father's Judaic spirituality as little more than a wish to have a seat "farther forward" at the synagogue, "closer to the action." He brings up Jewish themes only once in conversation with his friends, when he spiritedly recommends that the neo-Nazis planning to march in New Jersey should be met with baseball bats. But Monica Osborne remains convinced that Allen's "process of ethical and moral interrogation" is fundamentally Judaic (2013, 520). "Built into the very structure of Judaism and its beginnings in Torah," she says, "the impulse to question pronounces itself, and in the impulse we discover the beginnings of the ethical: the acknowledgement that there is always another way, another question in response to each question" (524). This insistently interrogative habit is basic to Isaac's sensibility, which doesn't make him the film's moral authority, but does make him the film's moral provocateur. In the space of ninety-five minutes, he and his confidantes raise questions about marriage, love, sexuality, friendship, fidelity, parenting, career, wealth, and the human concern for honesty and responsibility that such questions generate. The "answers" we hear are tentative, improvised, never with the slightest accent of finality. Allen's penchant for cutting away from a scene while it seems still in progress supports this absence of closure.

The narrative strategy of the film is to move the characters through a broad range of urban environments, public and private, neutral and biased, casual and formal, giving them an appropriate theater to stage their feelings and intentions. Allen conjures up a postmodernist maze of romantic misalliances that involve a man unsettled by a messy divorce, a married couple on the verge of a breakup, a teenage woman forced to show maturity beyond her years, and a talented but deeply neurotic professional woman whose mantra is, "I'm beautiful, I'm bright, and I deserve better." From this *ménage a cinque* (or perhaps *sept,* if we count Isaac's ex-wife and her new lesbian partner) comes Allen's directorial effort to make sense of the kaleidoscopic shifts and turns of human striving that the helter-skelter of urban living enables, perhaps encourages. The streets and sidewalks of New York, which themselves express the pace and flux of contemporary life, convey Allen's characters to social spaces that reveal their status, their aspirations, and their anxieties.

Urban spaces figure powerfully in *Manhattan* from it first moments. In the opening scene at Elaine's, where Isaac, Tracy (Mariel Hemingway), Yale, and Emily (Anne Byrne) are gathered for drinks and good-natured banter, Isaac announces that life's chief virtue is "courage," but then proves himself cowardly, as he confesses he would not risk his own life to save the life of another. Immediately we know we are in a world where principle and practice are not closely partnered. The point of the scene, however, is to give Emily and Yale, an apparently rock-solid married couple, the chance to meet and evaluate Tracy, Isaac's lovely new girlfriend, about whom he is embarrassed because she is a high school student about twenty-five years his junior. Tracy passes whatever test has been informally set up, as Yale pronounces her "gorgeous" and Emily calls her "a bright girl." The scene suggests intimacy and cordiality, in the tight composition of the foursome leaning toward each other with good eye contact and multiple close-ups of smiling, jovial people (Allen 1979, 04:00/06:40).

But the scene is in sharp contrast to the one that immediately follows as the two couples leave Elaine's to embark on foot to their next destination. Now they are no longer really together, since Mary and Tracy have dropped behind for some girl talk while Yale has pulled away to have a private conversation with Isaac. On the street, the décor, lighting, and spatial deployment of the actors are totally different: the faces are shadowed, sometimes totally obscured, except for a few glints of light reflected from Isaac's glasses. When we do catch a legible image of Yale, he is looking furtively over his shoulder to be sure his wife cannot overhear what is said. The low-key chiaroscuro lighting gives the scene the look of a confessional. We learn that Yale craves privacy because he is informing Isaac that he has launched a love affair with Mary Wilkie (Diane Keaton), a journalist he met in a professional setting but with whom he has become intimate. Suddenly all the markers have shifted and it is Yale who is asking for advice, looking for validation. Feeling close to both partners in the marriage, Isaac is reluctant to make judgments, except to say that he's "stunned," having "always thought for sure you and Emily had one of the best marriages." His negative body language indicates disapproval, but the scene concludes with Isaac's caveat, "you shouldn't ask me about relationships." His two failed marriages evidently disqualify him as a family therapist (Allen 1979, 06:40/08:35).

Another street scene that immediately follows shows Isaac in a much less favorable light, as we see him surprise his ex-wife, Jill (Meryl Streep), on the sidewalk, darting out from behind a concrete slab to accuse her of defaming him in a tell-all book about their marriage (Allen 1979, 09:40/10:50). Here he seems aggressive, almost predatory, though he may have a point about her profiting at his expense from the scandal she herself has created. He also mistreats his young girlfriend Tracy, now in the indoor space of his swanky, split-level apartment. These plush surroundings speak insistently of his power as the scene opens with Isaac good-naturedly scolding his young friend, while descending the long spiral staircase that joins the two levels of his home. Essentially he uses his proprietary authority to keep Tracy from spending the night, even though she announces, "I think I'm in love with you." He clearly relishes her sexual favors, but insists she doesn't want her to get "hung up with one person at your age." Throughout the scene, Tracy is confined to one corner of the couch, bathed in a small pool of light to the far left of the screen, while Isaac moves freely through the ample spaces of the downstairs, making pronouncements from afar. He finally sits down with her, but quickly takes her by the hand to move her from the couch and insist that she leave. Although the scene has a friendly and quasi-romantic tone, the low-key lighting gives it an ambiguous edge and the entire site is a citadel of male wealth and power. Isaac's personal space is sacrosanct. While it could be argued that he is safeguarding the reputation of an inexperienced young woman, it's clear that Isaac's own interests are paramount, not Tracy's (10:55/12:55).

City space is also crucial in negotiating the complicated love triangle that later develops as Isaac loses interest in Tracy and transfers his affection to Mary, a more age-appropriate partner but in all other ways the antithesis of Isaac. It's significant, for example, that their romance springs from an accidental meeting at a fundraising event on behalf of the Equal Rights Amendment. This leads to a shared cab ride, a meal at an all-night diner, and an extended dog-walking episode that carries us deep

Woody Allen, *Manhattan*. Largely unlike the protagonists of Lee and Scorsese, Allen's ethnics belong to a relatively affluent Jewish community well assimilated into the higher echelons of New York society.

Source: This frame-capture is the work of James F. Scott, with technical support from the Instructional Media Center, Saint Louis University.

into the early hours of the morning. Secluded in romantic darkness, they evidently convince each other that they have more in common than they actually do. To the strains of "Someone to Watch over Me," they perambulate around the quiet city, closing out their stroll by sitting on a bench looking out on the majestic Queens Bridge at 59th Street and sharing the dream of "a great city, a knock-out." Quite possibly, the iconic image of the bridge promotes the illusion that they might be joined romantically by their shared loyalty to a world-class city (Allen 1979, 24:00/29:25).

Further spatial metaphors at first confirm this impression, but then undermine it. Yale continues his adulterous relationship with Mary, though his effort to schedule time with her complicates his relations with his wife. We see him and Mary rushing frantically about, ultimate careening off to an afternoon encounter in a nearby hotel. When Mary tries to see him on the weekend, he declines in deference to his marital responsibilities, which impels Mary to turn decisively toward Isaac for the affection she craves. Their courtship begins auspiciously on "a beautiful day for a walk" in Central Park, which Mary proposes to Isaac. But a sudden thunderstorm overtakes them, and they must dash for shelter at the Hayden

Planetarium. The imagery of this scene is particularly revealing, interfacing seamlessly with Mary's worrisome self-revelations about her anxieties and fixations (Allen 1979, 37:35/40:20).

Allen effectively weaves the virtual landscapes of outer space into the representation of the soon-to-be lovers who slowly walk among dry, craggy worlds, where no human creature could survive. A massive pockmarked sphere looms ominously in the foreground, as Mary speaks of her guilty relationship with Yale and then of her broken marriage, which left her stifled and frustrated. She is as scarred as the frozen moon that dominates the frame. The lighting is low, shrouding every corner of the frame, showing the characters only as rim-lit silhouettes, sometimes lost in complete darkness. The technical effects are brilliant, but the tone of the scene portends disaster. The last astronomical image is of Saturn, another vast frozen world, rendered pictorially so that the dark band of its rings bisects the frame, creating a sinister black barrier between Isaac and the woman who wants him as a romantic partner. Their differences briefly declare themselves as Mary, with little motivation, begins to name the moons of Saturn, challenging Isaac to match her in a game of moon-naming. This is when Isaac tells her, "Nothing worth knowing can be known with the mind" and she rejoins with, "Where would we be without rational thought?" In spite of these unpromising omens, and the reservations Isaac himself expresses, their relationship goes forward (Allen 1979, 37:30/38:55).

All the interpersonal relations of *Manhattan* are disfigured by evasions and rationalizations, moments when narcissism and self-interest overwhelm justice, fairness, and honesty. Yale deceives Emily shamefully, while pretending to love her, and Isaac abruptly abandons Tracy, even though he realizes he is hurting her badly. Mary opportunistically encourages both of her lovers, yet repeatedly expresses regret that she behaves as she does. Emily might seem to stand on the moral high ground, with her interest in childbearing and mothering, but she refuses to see her husband's philandering or to look closely at the excuses he gives for not founding a family. When Mary deserts Isaac to commit more seriously to Yale, Isaac's anger provokes an explosive confrontation with his closest male friend. Their exchange and its outcome drive the film to its conclusion and also sum up Allen's effort to articulate an ethical norm.

Isaac's last conversation with Yale takes place in an anatomy classroom on the campus where Yale teaches. It's a private conversation, but with a quiet audience of four human skeletons and several shelves of human remains. Though the dialogue is driven by Isaac's personal sense of betrayal, the symbolic décor introduces a broader sense of humanity and invites us to see these events *sub specie aeternitatis*. When Isaac, challenging Yale, charges that "you're too easy on yourself, you're not honest with yourself," he is flanked in a two-shot by a skeleton, which seems to summon earlier generations of humanity to this indictment of his false friend. The same composition reinforces his insistence upon "some kind of personal integrity" that we can look back on with satisfaction as we go to the grave. This is a very different world from *Everyman*, but it shares with the Christian morality play of late medieval times the belief that "good deeds" are the only efficacious grave goods. Isaac's query, "What are future generations going to say about us?" also echoes the anonymous playwright's admonition, "Everyman, look to thy ending." That point is punctuated by the last image of the scene, a shot of the silent skeleton, which gives death the last word (Allen 1979, 01:18:55/01:21:20).

The issues here arise from, but do not reduce to Isaac's private grievances. In a classroom where, according to the chalkboard, the "Anthropology Club" will soon be meeting, Allen makes an effort to sketch out a few moral markers with a claim to universality, the chief of which is honesty. To avoid oversimplifying, we should remember Yale's remark about Isaac's "self-righteousness," but also recall that the posture of self-righteousness does not exclude the possibility that one might still be right.

Manhattan closes ambivalently with another street scene, enacted in liminal space, literally a threshold. After Isaac confesses to Emily that he mistreated Tracy, he dashes to her apartment in a desperate effort to reclaim her. Arriving short of breath, he stands in the doorway of her residence, looking through a further doorway, as Tracy readies herself for a six-month stay in London that has long been on her agenda. While a mirror image shows the doorman depositing her luggage on the sidewalk, Isaac makes a futile effort to dissuade her from going, admitting his mistake and affirming his love. Wisely, she refuses to change her plans but suggests that their love should be able to survive six months of absence. To his skepticism she responds, "You have to have a little faith in people." The final comment on their relationship is the perplexed, hesitantly smiling look on Isaac's face as he digests her comment on the prospective durability of human relationships. At this point we cut back to images of the New York skyline, as dusk settles upon its sturdy architectural majesty. But these durable facades of Manhattan give no hint of the chaotic energy of its streets. These raw forces have shaped all of the film's protagonists and will continue to transform them in ways no one can possibly foresee (Allen 1979, 01:28:20/01:33:30).

SEGMENT 2: THE ECLIPSE OF JUDAISM:
RADIO DAYS (1987) AND *CRIMES AND MISDEMEANORS* (1989)

In the decade following his breakthrough success with *Annie Hall* and *Manhattan*, Allen continued to use New York as the focal point of his filmmaking and imagine this city as the stage on which to present Jewish ethnicity in the late twentieth century. By the end of the 1970s, he had severed his partnership with United Artists and followed his friend and colleague Arthur Krim to the newly minted production company Orion Pictures, another filmmaking corporation headquartered in New York City that was committing itself to the creation of independent, slightly off-beat product. Fortunately, Allen was able to take much of his production team with him, including executive producers Joffe and Rollins as well as his new editor Susan Morse. As Allen began to do nearly all of his own writing, he terminated his fruitful relationship with Marshall Brickman, while Carlo di Palma and Sven Nykvist replaced Gordon Willis as his directors of photography on *Radio Days* and *Crimes and Misdemeanors*, respectively, with no loss of quality in the visual design. Meanwhile, Mia Farrow, Julie Kavner, and Diane Wiest joined Diane Keaton and Allen himself as the leading theatrical talents of the production team. The films of this period make clear Allen's conviction that "Jewishness" should not be equated with Judaism in any formal sense of its religious expression. His characters define their ethnicity in completely secular terms, although the last scene of *Crimes and Misdemeanors* suggests the ongoing quest for an ethical norm, grounded in psychology, that might reinvigorate the Jewish conscience.

In quite different ways, both *Radio Days* and *Crimes and Misdemeanors* remark the irrelevance of Judaic theology and ritual. Allen's parents kept a kosher house, celebrated their son's bar mitzvah, and made sure he spent eight years in Hebrew school. But he insists in a 1976 interview that he "hated every second of it" (Kapsis 2016, 38). As he tells Ken Kelly in the same conversation, his lawgivers are Kafka, Camus, and Sartre, not the Talmud and the Torah. Allen identifies with the victimized Jews of *The Sorrow and the Pity*, not the Jews who look forward to a more prominent seat in the synagogue during the High Holidays. He doesn't think of himself as a "Jewish filmmaker," but allows that "certain subjects, like Jewishness are unusually vivid; they have a disproportionate resonance" (Kapsis 2016, 66). Monica Osborne makes a valuable effort to show that Allen's commitment to a dialectic of endless questions relates him to Jewish theologian/philosophers like Emmanuel Levinas, though she exaggerates a bit (albeit tongue-in-cheek) in calling Allen the "Hollywood Rabbi" (2013, 520–38). In his own voice, Allen pleads for "an impulse toward humanitarianism that has got to arise in each person non coercively" and "an enormous restructuring of thinking in terms of religion, philosophy." But as a way to achieve this utopic future, he can only recommend "psychoanalysis rather than politics" (Kapsis 2016, 30–31), and nothing that would express itself as doctrine or creed.

At first glance *Radio Days* might seem to be only incidentally related to Jewishness, its focal point being the broadcast industry of the early

1940s. But it situates us in a small Jewish neighborhood in Queens, mostly within the life world of one multigenerational Jewish family living near Rockaway Beach. This setting invites Allen to examine the power of radio as an assimilative force, its capacity to transvalue the urban sensibility and to create what Judith Smith calls "visions of belonging." These are media-generated simulations of "the ordinary family" and its routines, heightened and idealized in a manner resembling the popular illustrations of Norman Rockwell, and always assuming "that white middle-class Main Street could fully represent Americanness" (J. Smith 2004, 1–37). What *Radio Days* reveals through its comic wit and careful stagecraft is how these synthetic images incongruously insert themselves into the everyday world of the ethnic family, hybridizing its real-life experience in disruptive and transformative ways. Fascinating, deceitful, and inspirational at one and the same time, Manhattan's electronic fictions powerfully affect the ethnic boroughs on the other side of the East River, remodeling Jewishness and other ethnic identities into a more mainstream "Americanism."

Describing "the religion of *Radio Days*," Maurice Yacowar observes that in this film the medium of radio functions as "a kind of secular religion," presenting its audience with "an idealized world, populated by gods and goddesses, providing moral guidance, offering spiritual consolation and uplift, and—most importantly—forming a bond of emotional and imaginative support among its nation of congregants" (Yacowar 2006, 250). This comment is strikingly apt, but we should add that Yacowar's "nation of congregants" is not really a national audience, at least not in terms of the imaginative life of the film. *Radio Days* is narrated from the perspective of a Jewish child, Joey Green (Seth Green), now grown to adulthood, who recalls his boyhood in Rockaway, in the borough of Queens, where he lives in a large Jewish household that is virtually addicted to radio. They absorb its syndicated broadcasts as delusion and diversion, but also as instruments of aspiration and sources of a surrogate life beyond the ethnic ghetto. Joey is most deeply affected by radio culture, drinking in its music, identifying with its superheroes, and taking inspiration from its wartime patriotism. On the arm of his adventurous Aunt Bea (Diane Wiest), he also completes the pilgrimage from Rockaway to Manhattan, where together they worship the new gods of the air at the Radio City Music Hall. In this modernist temple, Joey discovers the magic of the movies, foreshadowing the career in filmmaking we realize he will pursue as an adult.

Early studies of the impact of radio upon American audiences offer insight into the imaginative life of *Radio Days*. The scholars who worked for Paul Lazerfeld at the Office of Radio Research in the early 1940s were particularly interested in what people learned from radio and how they learned it. Fixated upon print culture as the norm by which the communicative content of radio should be judged, Lazerfeld's team assumed that news programs and informed commentary on current events would be valued as the most consequential avenues of learning. To their surprise, however, the listening audiences of that decade were far more interested in musical shows, like *Your Hit Parade,* and soap operas, like *The Romance of Helen Trent,* or even gangster programs, like *Gang Busters,* professing that these also were sources of inspiration and knowledge (see Douglas 1999, 136–58). What the research team missed was the primary appeal of radio—the color and texture of the human voice. That voice was particularly appealing when music encouraged it toward song or as it entered into a dramatic relationship with the ensemble of voices that fleshed out a narrative. Several of these early radio scholars, particularly John Peatman and Herta Herzog, gradually apprehended this point, as is reflected in the last volume of *Radio Research: 1942–43.* In "Radio and Popular Music," Peatman concludes that pop tunes of the times may provide "emotional satisfaction that comes through identification with an environment which is harmonious" (Lazerfeld and Stanton 1944, 392). Taking a second look at radio drama, Herzog in "What Do We Really Know about Daytime Serial Listeners?" decided that many of them looked to these shows for personal guidance. One housewife told her neighbor she could "listen to *Aunt Jenny* to learn good English" or "learn refinement from *Our Gal Sunday."* Another woman that Herzog interviewed found a template for good behavior in *The Romance of Helen Trent:* "When Helen Trent has serious trouble she takes it calmly. So you think you'd better be like her and not get upset" (Lazerfeld and Stanton 1944, 28). Without quite approving of the counsel that radio drama imparts, Herzog feels compelled to say that "a large proportion of the listeners take these programs seriously and seek to apply what they hear in them to their own personal lives" (32). In spite of the concessions made on the strength of this empirical data, the scholars of the radio research project struggle to convey the visceral power of radio as well as it is articulated in the several interlocking narratives of *Radio Days.* These testify to the power of radio as a formative agency in the lives of young and old, Jew and gentile, especially those who hunger for a world larger than the borough of their birth.

When we first see ten-year-old Joey, he is wearing his Masked Avenger goggles, signifying that this is the lens through which the protagonist will see the world. His perspective clearly disadvantages traditional Jewish wisdom. Unlike the unpredictable Jehovah of Hebrew Scripture, who intervenes a bit haphazardly into human affairs, the Masked Avenger is a high-energy vigilante, who soars across the skies of Manhattan crying out, "Beware evil-doers wherever you are." Small wonder that Joey wants to join this dedicated wonder-worker by buying a Masked Avenger Ring, even though his loyalty to the electronic super-hero pushes him into a war-to-the-death conflict with Rabbi Baumel (Kenneth Mars).

Like any dutiful Jewish child of the 1940s, Joey and his friends from the neighborhood Hebrew school are asked to seek donations to support the founding of a Jewish state in Palestine, sought after as a secure homeland for refugees from the war and Nazi persecution. But Joey subverts the rabbi's mission, pretending to collect funds for Palestine but actually gleaning money to buy a Masked Avenger ring. Though comic, Joey's priorities are an implicit vote for secular humanism over Hebraic orthodoxy. Rather than the Talmud and Torah, Joey takes his inspiration from the media-generated Providence figure who guards the immediate neighborhood, unmindful of the Jewish heritage or the plight of European Jewry. When Joey's scheme is found out, he gets a beating from his parents and a rebuke from Rabbi Baumel on the evils of radio, which produces only "false dreams, lazy habits," or "stories of foolishness and violence," instead of the "discipline" that the value system of Judaism would surely supply. It doesn't help when Joey obliquely endorses the Rabbi Baumel's admonition by quoting the Lone Ranger: "You speak truth, my faithful Indian companion." Already we see the unlikelihood that this child will grow up to be a loyal son of Zion (Allen 1987, 12:30/14:00).

Though Joey's parents have sent him to Hebrew school, the family as a whole is not markedly religious. They do try to observe Jewish fasting laws, particularly during the High Holidays, though on one occasion Uncle Abe (Josh Mostel) is guilty of a conspicuous infraction. This flows from the family's ongoing squabbles with their near neighbors about everything from excessive noise to eavesdropping on a multiple-party telephone line. In this instance, Abe confronts the rogue family from next door, which has deserted Judaism for the more this-worldly promises of the Communist Party. Dramatizing their apostasy, they are not only playing their radio boisterously on Yom Kippur, instead of giving their time to quiet meditation, but also making a public display of their breach of fasting laws. As a stalwart champion of orthodoxy, Abe barges into their yard and chastises them for disrespecting Jewish custom. Unfortunately, he is seduced by their food feast and drawn into their gastronomic orgy. Not only does he overeat to the point of nausea, he returns to his own family to announce that religion is the opium of the people and that the future lies with the Communist Party. Again, radio is the disruptive force, no longer through the magical power of the Masked Avenger, but by the more material inducements of consumerism, which shows no inclination toward fasting and self-denial.

Not maliciously hostile to traditional custom and practice, radio culture is most likely to reveal its power through surprise and unsettlement. The film opens with the havoc worked upon the Needlemans when thieves break into their house. But even a neighborhood burglary is mediated by syndicated broadcasting. While making off with the silverware, the robbers pause in their plundering to answer an insistent phone ring, which turns out to be a call from the quiz show, "Guess That Tune." Ironically, they win the jackpot, but the Needlemans receive the prizes the thieves cannot claim for themselves. This results in a theater-of-the-absurd event the next morning, when the Needlemans are unexpectedly treated to the delivery of a vast assortment of housewares, including a cook stove, a washer, several upholstered chairs, and a wine basket. This is not the manna that fed the Chosen People in the desert, as God guided them to the Promised Land. It's a conglomeration of unsolicited commodities that may or may not satisfy a true need. But its appearance is equally magical, the work of a capricious sky god who performs random acts, answerable to no logic. The same absence of logic governs the fate of Mr. Zipsky (Joel Eidelberg), who seems to go mad to the lyrics of a popular nonsense tune of the early 1940s, "Mairzy Doats." While poor Zipsky gyrates through the streets of Rockaway, crazily swinging a meat cleaver dangerously close to every passerby, the musical track intones, "Mairzy doats and dozy doats and liddle lamzy divey. A kiddley divey too, wooden shoe." This is the only explanation we get of Zipsky's behavior (Allen 1987, 37:40/38:10).

For all the raw energy radio culture might release into their lives, nearly all the characters see it as a positive force. Joey's mother, Tess (Julie Kavner), uses radio to escape the humdrum routine of her daily life. She treasures the fantasy life of the elegant Manhattan couple, Irene and Roger, who broadcast their sophisticated breakfast-table conversation to households across the East River, while eating an elegant morning meal in their upmarket, glass brick Manhattan condo. Joey's mother enters vicariously into this affluent, well-bred world while she herself washes the breakfast dishes in the family's grubby kitchen in Queens. No harm seems done, however, as she remains her earthy, well-grounded self, the one who advises her more romantic sister against aiming unreasonably high, and the one who takes the risk of bearing a Jewish child in 1943, amid the horrors of the Holocaust in Europe.

Cousin Ruthie (Joy Newman) is a more specialized case, utterly captivated by the explosive music of Carmen Miranda. "To this day," says Joey, "there are certain songs that, no matter where I am, the minute I hear them I get instant memory flashes." Ruthie's iconic song is Miranda's show-stopping tune of 1940, "The South American Way." Hearing it, she is virtually transported out of her body by its passionate samba beat). "She loved it," says Joey, but "loving" hardly does justice to her enthusiasm for the Brazilian starlet, who launched her radio career singing on the "Royal Gelatin Hour," broadcast from the Radio City Music

Hall (Allen 1987, 36:20/37:35). And Miranda, with her fruit-infested hats and vibrant body language, was about as far removed from the culture of ethnic Jewry as the Masked Avenger. Yet somehow the pulsating rhythm of "The South American Way" takes complete control of Ruthie, normally a quiet, well-behaved, unremarkable young Jewish matron. The fervor of Miranda's music seems to make her entranced protégé utterly forget the immediate surroundings, as if she had been magically propelled into the streets of Rio at Carnival time. Not only does Ruthie know the lyrics from memory, she has conjured up at least part of Miranda's costume, swirling about the room in a bright red blouse with a loud floral pattern, while using a pink bath towel, elaborately wrapped around her head, as a surrogate for one of Miranda's signature hats. What's more, the spell that grips Cousin Ruthie is powerful enough to draw in two other members of the family. First they watch in amazement as she mimes both Miranda's voice and body gesture, but soon they have joined the chorus, echoing the "eihy-eihy" refrain that the orchestral ensemble picked up when Miranda herself performed this number. The supreme incongruity of this event in a Jewish household of the 1940s lends emphasis to what John Peatman concluded from his radio research, namely, that studying the impact of popular music might hold a key to "increased understanding of many people's needs, their hopes and their frustrations" (Lazerfeld and Stanton 1944, 391).

The most musical member of Joey's family is his Aunt Bea, who, he says, "listened almost exclusively to music," which is why his childhood was full of "the most wonderful songs" (Allen 1987, 34:05/34:15). Bea responds to music of romantic titilation and its seeming promise of love and marriage. Though neither material nor ethnic considerations are ever mentioned, she relishes dating partners who take her from Queens to Manhattan and suitors who are better groomed and softer spoken than the self-important Mr. Manulis (Andrew Clarl), a stereotype of the pushy Jewish *ganze macher*. She is thrilled to hear that the faddish conga line holds the key to meeting the perfect partner and coaxes several members of the family into rehearsing its gyrations in the crowded precincts of their home. Much like Joey himself, precociously aware of a world that is too confined for his spirit, Bea values radio as an instrument of emancipation and advancement into a more affluent and pluralistic environment.

Though the conga line fails as an instrument of romantic adventure, Bea's search for a wider world transfers much of her social life to Manhattan, to the delight of Joey, who accompanies her on two occasions. When we next see Bea in male company, she is with Chester, a much more attractive prospect who escorts her to the Radio City Music Hall. Though, like all of her romances, this one fails to mature into a marriage, the moment is perfect, as she and Chester ascend the grand staircase of Radio

City to the tune of "If You Are but a Dream." Ultimately, the scene holds more meaning for Joey than Bea, but this moment is hers. For a few brief seconds, the threesome looks like a family, well dressed and upwardly mobile, with the ascent of the staircase as the iconic gesture that represents both Bea and Joey rising in the social world. The music is perfectly in sync with the mood, though the ironic bite is deep:

> If you are but a dream / I hope I never waken.
> It's more than I could bear / to find that I'm forsaken.

(Allen 1987, 38:10/40:10)

For Bea, this is indeed a fantasy, which she does not succeed in making real. For Joey, on the other hand, the surrogate Woody Allen figure, the scene is prescient of what we take to be his future career as writer and filmmaker.

Though Bea will remain unmarried and unable to escape the cultural constriction of the family home, she enjoys one more moment of triumph in Manhattan when she wins first prize on one of popular quiz shows, where she is unexpectedly a contestant. On this occasion, she's on the arm of Sy (Richard Portnow), another romantic prospect who is, according to his personal narrative, about to break up with his wife. This never comes to pass, but it's another one of those magical moments, again enjoyed in the company of Joey, who seems part of a family that is being founded. Bea's success in the quiz show is a moment of masterful self-assertion based on expertise she has gleaned from long years of subjection to the family's steady diet of fish. Because they can't afford the better cuts of meat, the household reluctantly turns to Uncle Abe, a dedicated fisherman, who daily throws a line in the bay and comes home each evening with a large bag of fish to be cleaned, cooked, and served. Fish are an embarrassment to the family, almost a humiliation. On one occasion Aunt Ceal won't answer the doorbell because "my hands smell like fish." But as the adult persona of little Joey explains in voice-over, "Years of living in the same house with Uncle Abe had turned us all into ichthyologists" (Allen 1987, 01:09:30/01:09:40). When Bea is selected as a contestant, she chooses "fish" as her category and wins fifty silver dollars. The money treats Sy and Joey to a tasty dinner (fishless, we surmise) in a supper club ballroom beautifully appointed and caressed by Carlo di Palma's camera work. Ultimately, Bea never quite emancipates herself from Rockaway, but she is instrumental in whetting Joey's appetite for the richer culture of Manhattan.

The second woman who is infatuated with radio and uses it as a vehicle of self-advancement is Sally White (Mia Farrow), not Jewish and not of the family, but a resident of nearby Canarsie, another lower-middle-class neighborhood, largely Italian. She herself may or may not be of Italian ancestry, but her narrative furnishes a template of ethnic self-betterment. As Joey recounts her story, Sally is almost mythic, "one of the radio legends of the time." Quick-witted and intensely ambitious, she is, according to Joey, "one of those characters who always seemed to be around when things were happening" (Allen 1987, 40:20/40:30). Unlike Bea, she puts career above romance, determined to get on the radio. Her early efforts are not promising, as we find her caught up in a sleazy love affair with Roger (David Warrilow), the male partner of the celebrity breakfast couple that enthralled Joey's mother. Roger, of course, has promised to launch Sally's radio career, but Irene's discovery of her husband's infidelity cuts short this prospect of quickly ascending the professional ladder. What we don't realize at the time, however, is that Sally has intuitively mastered the format of the celebrity talk show, which she will one day use as the template for her own program, *The Gay White Way*.

Naturally, Sally's path to radio celebrity is not smooth and requires one extremely significant adjustment. The mismanagement of her love life costs the ingénue her first job and the next one puts her life at risk, as she accidentally witnesses a gangland murder and briefly becomes an assassin's target. But she is rescued, almost magically, by the gangster's mother who remembers her as a girl "in pigtails" who used to run around the old neighborhood in Canarsie. Thereafter, Sally's resourcefulness and persistence carry her forward. She burnishes her credentials as a performer by volunteering to sing at USO events and even tries her hand at a tuneful laxative commercial. But Sally's breakthrough to stardom comes when she takes diction lessons and alters the high-pitched, dialectal accent of her personal voice. The next time we hear her she is the hostess of her own talk show, sponsored by Lady Lydia's Facial Cream. She now speaks with a voice as mellifluous as those of Irene and Roger, from whom she has learned the rules of the game. Very much like the breakfast couple who delighted Joey's mother, Sally now banters knowingly about the beautiful people of Broadway and Hollywood, wondering out loud about Clark Gable's new girlfriend and coyly asking, "Didn't Rita Hayworth look stunning last night at the Copacabana?" (Allen 1987, 01:04:10/01:04:20). Sally's rise to fame is the analogue that complements the story of Joey himself, who will also creatively improvise his way into a career in media.

Not surprisingly, the character most shaped by the radio experience is Joey, the quick-witted child of the Jewish family, who feels the impact of the medium from the earliest moments of his conscious life. It estranges him from his Jewishness, attaches him to the themes of World War II, and enthralls him with the electrical culture, from the serial exploits of the

Masked Avenger, to the elegant lights of the Radio City Music Hall, to the silver screen of cinema, with which he immediately falls in love.

The moral watchfulness of the Masked Avenger bears fruit in Joey's determination to guard the American coast against the Nazi menace, as he and his neighborhood friends patrol the streets and scan the skies. The Avenger has warned that the German high command was "working on rockets" that might reach American shores. But another American patriot, G-man Biff Baxter, thinks the greater threat is posed by Nazi U-boats, which are "sneaking around the coasts of America." Biff's on-air crusade against seafaring "axis rats" sets up the scene where Joey imagines he has sighted a German submarine off Rockaway Beach, "just like Biff Baxter described it." The scene is clearly a fantasy and even the youthful Joey realizes he can't share this experience because only Biff Baxter would believe him. But the mature narrator uses this moment as a segue to suggest Joey's growing awareness of a conflicted, cosmopolitan world. Alone on the beach, after the departure of his friends, Joey—suddenly equipped with the discernment of an adult—describes how: "I just stood there for a long time looking out at the Atlantic. My mind was thinking about life, women, and a million different things" (Allen 1987, 01:50:00/01:50:50). At that moment, the enemy submarine emerges from the depths of the sea. This monster from the underworld, of course, has no literal reality. But the threatening spaces of an expansive, turbulent, essentially unknowable world are painfully real to the sensitive child staring out at the empty ocean.

Joey's closest thing to an epiphany of his future in media occurs during his visit to Radio City with Bea and Chester. He recalls the scene as his "most vivid memory connected with an old radio song." The song is the early Frank Sinatra hit, "If You Are but a Dream." Entering this sacred space dedicated to the new media, Joey feels that "it was like entering heaven." The décor of the grandiose atrium supports this impression: the tall ceiling and internal columns are reminiscent of a cathedral and the awestruck youngster moves forward toward a massive mural of parting clouds that reveal the infinite space of the open sky. The sense of opportunity is confirmed in the ascent of the grand stairway, accomplished while the lyrics of Sinatra's song indicate that the youthful protagonist might "see my dream come true." That dream then achieves concrete form when a theater door opens, giving Joey a full view of the silver screen at the climactic moment when two Hollywood lovers lock themselves together in a prolonged romantic kiss. Joey's romance is not tied to the larger-than-life celluloid heroine, as Bea's had been associated with her male suitor. The boy's love is for the medium itself, the motion picture, to which he has been led by his creative infatuation with

radio. Indeed, the "old radio song" anticipates and sums up the career
expectations of Joey's adult persona:

> If you're a fantasy / then I'm content to be
> In love with lovely you . . .

> (Allen 1987, 38:15/40:15)

Note that in this altered context, "fantasy" carries none of the negative
connotations it holds when applied to the unsatisfied romantic longing
of Bea. Motion pictures are surely nothing "but a dream," a rectangle full
of two-dimensional shadows masquerading as a peopled world. Understood as a career track, however, motion pictures are a multibillion-dollar
industry in which one may be gainfully employed for a lifetime, as young
Joey, we know, will be.

Radio Days abounds in characters who yearn for a richer and more exciting world, even if it is achieved at the expense of their ethnic identity.
There is humor but also a hint of anger in Joey's father's remark to his
wife that they never cross over to Manhattan because "the Stork Club
doesn't admit Jews or Coloreds." When Joey asks his parents why he has
to study but his parents do not, his mom tells him it's "because our lives
are already ruined." Bea extracts from pop music enough inspiration to
orchestrate a series of romantic adventures and inserts herself into Manhattan culture at least long enough to win first prize in the quiz show. Our
last glimpse of her conjures up another romantic daydream, as she listens
wistfully to a radio voice singing, "You'd Be So Nice to Come Home To."
But the irony of failed romantic expectations is softened by the fact that
in her extended family Bea actually has found a "home." Besides, she is
the catalyst who propels her nephew toward a life much more expansive
than the sparse world of Rockaway. Sally painstakingly rebuilds her voice
to the point that no trace of her Brooklyn vowels can be heard in her con-
secration of show business celebrities on *The Gay White Way*. In the final
scene of the film, we find her ringing in the 1944 New Year "at the King
Cole Room in midtown Manhattan" with the media elite of the city. She
herself has a date with the Masked Avenger (Wallace Shawn). She feels
so secure in her new social identity that she can allude playfully to her
earlier years as a cigarette girl, remarking to her escort, "I used to work
here." Later, she takes her well-dressed comrades away from bright lights
and multicolored balloons up to the roof of this elegant nightclub, the site
of a shabby sexual encounter with Roger, her first role model of success
in radio. When someone asks how she happens to be so familiar with this
chilly world of deep shadows and industrial clutter, she replies evasively,
"I was up there once when my circumstances were quite different" (Allen 1987, 01:17:00/01:21:20). As a measure of how far Sally has traveled

socially by mastering the rhetoric of radio, we see her buy a package of Lucky Strike cigarettes from another cigarette girl, toward whom she smiles broadly while tipping generously. There but for the grace of diction lessons goes she.

Radio works its most profound effect upon Joey, as Peter Bailey discerns when he calls the film "a dramatization of the genesis of its maker's artistic life" (2001, 65). Joey is the film's primary example of learning from radio and using radio as a vehicle of self-fashioning. For the most part, Allen restricts himself to the boyish perspective of Joey, rarely allowing his own adult persona to take control of the narrative. But one conspicuous exception to this design is provided by the story of Polly Phelps, the eight-year-old child who falls down a well and becomes the subject of a rescue effort covered live by a radio news team. Unlike virtually every other episode of the film, this set of events does not in any perceptible way flow from the mind of Joey. In fact, we experience it as an extended news bulletin, which is overheard on the radio while Joey is being rather brutally spanked by his father and Bea is leading her conga line. The scene comes closer than any other in the film to suggesting Allen's own editorial intervention, as it speaks on behalf of the instructional impact of radio.

Allen structures this climactic scene to illustrate the power of radio as public discourse. We watch the news bulletin catch the attention of Joey's family, quieting the gusto of Bea's conga line and interrupting the beating Joey is receiving from his father. As radio listeners, we are "live on the spot" in rural Pennsylvania where rescue crews make a desperate effort to retrieve Polly Phelps, who has fallen down a well. The scene is fully visualized even though the conventions of realism ask us to imagine we are "hearing" the scene as a radio report. We do hear live voices from the site, a confused collage of instructions, warnings, and distress. The reporter whose voice presides over the events sounds reassuring, but it's clear that no one can foresee the outcome. Allen then constructs a montage to show several sets of listeners—a woman dining alone in a cafeteria, a small klatch of people sharing drinks in a neighborhood bar, a family similar to Joey's crowding closer to their radio. Gradually, they give up attending to their immediate surroundings and involve themselves in the drama of Polly's rescue. Most significantly, when the camera takes us back to Joey's family, his father has ceased to beat him and now embraces him warmly, as if to shield his son from the threat that has overtaken Polly Phelps. When the rescue effort turns tragic, the reporter is clearly discomfited, conveying deep personal emotion, even though mediated by microphone: "Oh God, this is terrible. . . . The little girl is dead." When he signs off with the line, "I'm sure all Americans share the grief of the Phelps family," we have every reason to believe this is no less than completely true (Allen 1987, 01:15:30/01:16:10). For this extended moment, the logic of events has made serious listeners out of the casual assortment of people who happen to be tuned to this station. Moreover, Allen has used the event to confer dignity upon the electronic media and upon the career track that will make him famous.

The Jewish conscience plays a very small role in *Radio Days*, dismissively reduced to the indignant sputtering of Rabbi Baumel. The moral compass is set by the Masked Avenger, the god and guide of ten year olds. Otherwise, we are left to imagine that the media culture will benignly affect the social order through the buoyancy of song and the bracing honesty of on-the-spot reportage. The question of a Jewish ethic enters much more powerfully into *Crimes and Misdemeanors*, Allen's last film of the 1980s. In what most critics regard as a true masterpiece, Allen inquires seriously into the impact of secularism upon the faith community of Judaism, as a new generation of American Jews assimilates successfully and rises dramatically in the professional world. *Radio Days* expresses the pull of modernity against traditional Judaic values; *Crimes and Misdemeanors* represents the yearnings of conscience in the absence, or extreme attenuation of the Judaic tradition.

In this latter film, moral disruption is associated primarily with Judah Rosenthal (Martin Landau), a renowned ophthalmologist, who has risen to the heights of his profession but must wrestle with the temptation to deal violently with his former lover, a woman who threatens his marriage and his career. After much soul-searching, Judah hires out her murder, turning the film into an extended meditation upon crime and punishment as well as the objective status of ethical norms. Though Judah is the only explicit criminal in the story, Allen draws all his major characters into an exploration of moral grounding, creating a chorus of voices that turn *Crimes and Misdemeanors* into a testament regarding the Jewish conscience in a post-Judeo-Christian world. The Holocaust theme also darkens the narrative, giving Judah's moral dilemma a larger cultural resonance that engages Judaic theology and its modernist derivations.

Judah Rosenthal is a classical role model of high performance and civilized behavior. Like Isaac Davis of *Manhattan*, he has fully assimilated to mainstream New York culture, but far surpasses Isaac in wealth and status. When we first meet Judah, he is being honored at a banquet that celebrates completion of the new Ophthalmology Wing of the hospital where he is a respected physician. We are told in a hero-worshipping run-up to his formal speech that Judah is a great fundraiser for the hospital, but more importantly, that he is a valued friend as well as a dedicated husband and father. He is also a deeply civilized man, who can direct you to the "best hotel in Paris, or Athens" or perhaps help you find "the best recording of a particular Mozart symphony" (Allen 1989, 1:25/2:30).

Woody Allen, *Crimes and Misdemeanors*. Judah's crime springs from the deep-seated respect in Jewish culture for the sanctity of the Jewish home, his suburban refuge.
Source: This frame-capture is the work of James F. Scott, with technical support from the Instructional Media Center, Saint Louis University.

At the podium himself, Judah speaks in modest terms, crediting the hospital's success to the "community" and to the "answered prayers" of those who share his vision of a caring partnership between the hospital and the city. He convincingly strikes the pose of a profoundly moral man who was taught in childhood to understand that "the eyes of God" are always upon us, "unimaginably penetrating," compelling us to take responsibility for our deeds. A moment later, he wonders aloud if his decision to specialize in ophthalmology had something to do with thinking that he himself must gather into his own being the unimaginably penetrating eyes of God (Allen 1989, 4:20 / 5:15). This reference is reinforced by an image (apparently a memory from childhood) of a menorah at the center of what is probably a Hanukkah liturgy. In Judaic ritual, this icon not only represents enlightenment and the dispersal of God's wisdom among men, but more explicitly, its seven bright candles, according to Scripture, stand for "the Eyes of the Lord ranging over the whole earth" (Zechariah 4:10). Everything in Judah's spiritual formation urges him to believe he is under divine scrutiny, indeed that he is compelled by God to be ever watchful of himself.

But between the two segments of this scene, Allen intercuts a discordant narrative. We learn that Judah has been indulging himself in a love affair with a somewhat neurotic woman who now threatens to confront his wife, revealing that "your husband and I are more than friends" and insisting that this special relationship must "be confronted in some fashion" (Allen 1989, 2:35/4:20). Judah quickly burns the letter he has managed to intercept, but this is only the beginning of Dolores' (Anjelica Huston) efforts to make her lover acknowledge her. Her increasingly shrill demands for a face-to-face conversation with Miriam (Claire Bloom) drive Judah to arrange Dolores' murder, through the devices of his gangster brother Jack (Jerry Orbach). This fateful decision induces guilt, summons memories, prompts consultation, and brings Judah to the brink of confessing to murder. At the same time, Judah's moral dilemma touches by analogy the subplot of the film, which has filmmaker Cliff Stern (Allen) undertaking to make a documentary about philosopher and Holocaust survivor Louis Levy (Martin Bergmann). Levy's voice is heard as a series of on-camera voice bites where he reflects upon God, love, forgiveness, and relatedness, together with their bearing upon moral responsibility. Ultimately, the film gives us a full spectrum of moral reflections, including—in addition to Judah's own—those of a rabbi, an artist, and a philosopher. Allen's narrative casts doubt on the relevance of theological orthodoxy but looks more favorably on elements in the Jewish tradition that might survive the moral nihilism of Judah's blatantly irreligious Aunt May (Anna Berger).

Pressed relentlessly by Dolores, Judah first seeks advice from his friend Ben (Sam Waterson), whose failing eyesight has made him one of Judah's patients. Ben is a very open and generous-minded rabbi, a spiritual cousin of the rabbi in *Broadway Danny Rose* (1984), who taught Danny "to accept, to forgive, and to love." In his conversation with Ben, Judah admits fault for his miscreant love affair, confessing that "I instigated it, I caused it," seeking "pleasure, adventure, and lust." Without scolding his friend, Ben speaks to Judah about "a moral structure" in the universe that gives "real meaning" to our lives. In light of his moral obligations, says Ben, Judah must "confess to wrong and hope for understanding" from his wife Miriam. In spite of Judah's skepticism, Ben foresees the possibility of forgiveness and of rebuilding his relationship to his wife. Judah is less confident of his wife's willingness to forgive (Allen 1989, 14:50/17:50). Desperate enough to explore more dangerous options, Judah now turns to his brother Jack, a rather sinister character with clear ties to the underworld. Though they are not fond of each other (Jack looks conspicuously ill at ease when visiting Judah's elegant home, where he knows he is not really welcome), he is willing to help his brother get "the dirty work done." Realizing that Jack is planning to have Dolores murdered, Judah is shocked and pulls back in horror: "She's not an insect, I can't just step on her." Jack remains convinced there is no other way (32:40/36:40).

The implicit debate between Jack and Ben is extended in a scene where Judah yields to the sinister counsel of his brother. But we hear the rival voices as Judah's interior monologue, which he conducts late at night while a fierce electrical storm is in progress. Having fully internalized the advice of his good and bad angels, Judah now overhears his own mind, as he prowls the dark corridors of his homestead. Rabbi Ben speaks first, reminding him of the healing power of "forgiveness" and the hope provided by faith in a "higher power." Yet nothing in the visual décor suggests hopefulness. What's left of a nurturing hearth fire is smoldering down to angry orange ashes, while lightning flashes in the darkness, illumining the set with a sinister brightness. Ben claims that Judah too believes in a moral order and "a spark of that notion" will persuade him to confess his adultery and be forgiven by Miriam. But Judah answers bluntly, "Miriam won't forgive me. . . . She'll be broken, humiliated in front of her friends." He also worries that Dolores might accuse him of mishandling hospital funds. While thunder continues to rumble in the background, Judah remarks that "God is a luxury I can't afford," prompting Ben to reply, "now you sound like your brother Jack." As indeed he does! Clearly becoming more cynical with each passing moment, Judah concludes, "Jack lives in the real world, you live in the Kingdom of God." Firmly committed to Jack's violent solution, Judah resolves, "I will not be destroyed by this woman" (Allen 1989, 40:10/43:40).

Though he has resigned himself to Dolores' murder, Judah is deeply shaken as he confronts the *fait accompli*. When Jack greets him with the news, he blurts out, "May God have mercy on us." A moment later, he confesses to his family, without explanation, "I have done a terrible thing." His most powerful guilt feelings, however, are triggered by his visit to the dead woman's apartment, where he has come to pick up several personal, perhaps incriminating objects. For one memorable moment, he stares into the victim's eyes (composed as a powerful close-up), not seeing the proverbial "windows of the soul," but the blank stare of death. That is followed by a sudden flashback to childhood, when his father warns him that the eyes of God see all: "Listen to me, Judah, there is nothing that escapes his sight." Will the empty stare of a dead lover now haunt Judah in the same way that the all-seeing divinity of the menorah promised his father that "the wicked will be punished for all eternity"? (Allen 1989, 55:20/58:50).

This question is held in suspension through the remainder of the film, as Judah grapples with sleepless nights, heavy drinking, and the thought he might turn himself in to the police. But at the same time Allen introduces an alternative narrative in the form of a subplot, featuring Cliff

Stern, the marginalized documentary filmmaker who is undertaking to make a program about the worldview of philosopher and Holocaust survivor Professor Louis Levy. Levy provides an oppositional voice in a very literal sense, because the actor who performs this role, Martin Bergmann, actually is a philosophy professor at Columbia University whom Allen permitted to script his own lines and thus to enact himself as a Jewish philosopher and public intellectual (see Evanier 2015, 273–79). Much in the same way that the thinking of Ernest Becker had inserted itself into *Annie Hall*, through Allen's references to *The Denial of Death*, Bergmann implicates himself in *Crimes and Misdemeanors* by drawing heavily from the reflections on love and human values that he analyzed in *The Anatomy of Loving* (1987). Another of those celebrated Jewish psychologists we find remembered in *Jews and the American Soul*, Bergmann preaches a post-theological humanism that effectively counterpoints the moral nihilism of Judah's Aunt May and his cynical brother Jack.

Levy enters the story as a robust voice, speaking of life and death, from the standpoint of Jewish psychoanalytical humanism. He is brought to the screen in a series of on-camera excerpts that Cliff plays for his friend and colleague Halley Reed (Mia Farrow), while trying both to court her and to interest her in his prospective video production. Though Levy lacks the status of a "character," he is the film's most effective spokesman on behalf of a moral order, which he defines in psychological rather than theological terms. What gives him authority in the film is that he stands both inside and outside the narrative. As a segment of Cliff's unfinished video documentary, Levy is a diegetic voice, limited and culture-bound, speaking on camera to Cliff and Halley, as they listen to and evaluate his comments. But he returns at the end of the film as a non-diegetic voice, no longer speaking audibly to the characters on screen, but directly to the theater audience. In this new context, he is now Allen's voice, the editorial voice of *Crimes and Misdemeanors*.

Sharing with Halley one of his interviews with the philosophy professor, Cliff represents him as "a man who wrote a very interesting book on human relationships" (pretty clearly, *The Anatomy of Loving*) that introduces a new term into the consideration of moral structures, the term "love." In his first on-camera excerpt, Levy speaks of the relative incapacity of Judaic culture to define and describe a God of love. According to Levy, "the unique thing that happened to the early Israelites was that they conceived of a God that cares. He cares but he also demands that you behave morally" (Allen 1989, 26:05/26:25). Though not directly involved in mediating Judah's conflicted feelings about moral responsibility, Levy is an implicit ally of Rabbi Ben, declining to affirm the theology of a benevolent God, but insisting that the human capacity to love might project a moral order in an otherwise indifferent universe. Unfortunately, he has no opportunity to advise Judah, else the film's outcome might have been significantly different from what it is.

In crude fact, Judah ignores Ben's counsel, orders Dolores' murder, and continues to deceive his wife as well as ignore the promptings of his conscience. During this extended moment, he searches for guidance in his Judaic upbringing, which carries him back to the world of his piously Orthodox father. After a meeting with Jack, in which he describes looking into the "black void" of the murdered woman's eyes, we see him in the black void of an urban tunnel, which includes a cut to the memory of a liturgy featuring the menorah (Allen 1989, 01:08:40/01:09:00). But the image prompts no enlightenment, even though the religious iconography is vivid.

Significantly, the soundtrack does not convey the sound of the liturgy: we hear only the drone of tires or other traffic noises and, like Judah, continue to "see" only the impenetrable darkness of the tunnel. Second by second, Judah is carried into deeper blackness. Judah's last chance at liturgical redemption is lost in the following scene, as he remembers a Seder service he experienced in his childhood home (Allen 1989,

Woody Allen, *Crimes and Misdemeanors*. In Judaic culture, the menorah is a symbol of the ever-watchful Providence in which Judah can no longer bring himself to believe.
Source: This frame-capture is the work of James F. Scott, with technical support from the Instructional Media Center, Saint Louis University.

01:09:05/01:13:25). In this most important recollection of his childhood faith, Judah does hear the call to leave Egypt's secular kingdom and begin the arduous trek to the Promised Land. But he also hears discordant voices, as the celebrant himself claims most of the ritual is "mumbo-jumbo" and his cynical Aunt May overtly challenges the myth of the Chosen People. Expressing a widespread Jewish sentiment of the 1940s and beyond, she wonders how religious orthodoxy can look at the Holocaust and still believe in a God that cares for his people. Witnessing the Seder service from the liminal space of a doorway, Judah sees his aunt get the better of the argument, even though his father doggedly insists that misdeeds of every sort will be divinely punished. The burden of guilt brings Judah close to defeat and despair. In his last meeting with Jack, the composition frames him as completely entrapped. Their rendezvous is at a small urban park, but what is featured in the décor is an environment of wrought-iron fences, suggesting a prison or a cage. Either metaphor is equally relevant. At this point, somewhat incongruously, Jack offers Judah the same advice that came from Rabbi Ben: "The time to confess was to Miriam, about your mistress. Not about this. This is murder." Deeply shaken, Judah drives past Dolores' apartment for the last time, muttering to himself that "without God the world is a cesspool" (01:20:10/01:21:15).

Which brings the discussion back to the closing scenes of *Crimes and Misdemeanors*, when the principal characters have all come together to celebrate the wedding of Ben's daughter Sharon. Several months have passed and Judah, much to his own surprise, seems to have magically recovered his well-being and poise. The other surprise, perhaps even greater, is that Professor Levy, whose hard-won wisdom seemed so comforting, has inexplicably committed suicide, leaving Cliff utterly devastated and Halley completely bewildered. Though Levy's self-destructive act remains deeply puzzling, the interview excerpt Cliff plays for Halley immediately after his death explains more than either realizes: "We must remember . . . we need a great deal of love in order to persuade us to stay in life. Once we get that love it usually lasts us, but the universe is a pretty cold place. It's we who must invest it with our feelings and under certain conditions we feel that it just isn't worth it" (Allen 1989, 01:15:25/01:15:55). In Levy's case, we cannot know what "conditions" made his life no longer worth living, though we might suspect that chronic loneliness and the absence of family would loom large. What his remarks advance powerfully is the thought that loving is most crucial of human relationships, but also the one fraught with the most difficulty, requiring ongoing and complex emotional investment.

These concerns supply context to the last scene, which has found critics sharply divided respecting the film's resolution. The plot and the subplot finally converge, because Judah virtually confesses his crime to Cliff, though he is careful to disguise its details as fiction, proposing them simply as the plot of "a great murder story" that Cliff might want to make into a film. For Judah, the special "twist" to the tale is that the murderer goes "scot-free," at first feeling "deep hidden guilt" and "only an inch away from confessing the whole thing to the police," but eventually recovering his equilibrium and going "back to his protected world of wealth and privilege." Cliff, on the other hand, wants the guilty man to confess, à la Dostoevsky's Raskolnikov, and thus assert through art the "moral structure" that Judah's father and Rabbi Ben take to be built into the architecture of the cosmos. Judah responds by calling Cliff's script of crime and punishment a "Hollywood ending," emotionally satisfying, but dishonest because it fabricates a moral order that is in no sense real (Allen 1989, 01:27:05/01:41:00).

Allen's most recent biographer says the film testifies to "the death of all meaningful religious belief," which it surely does (Evanier 2015, 272). But Mary Nichols maintains that the film attests to "insight supportive of moral responsibility" (1998, 164). Mark Roche makes a still stronger claim that in the "most comprehensive reading, *Crimes and Misdemeanors* remains moral" (Silet 2006, 279). This critic is convinced that Judah's supposed psychic recovery from his guilty act is hollow and deeply ironic, indicating the persistence of bite from a guilty conscience. Why else would he feel compelled to confess his crime to Cliff, even if behind the screen that he is simply proposing the plot of a murder mystery? The other relevant data point is the shadowy, underlit composition of the close-up where Judah makes the revelation, as well as the grimace of his facial mask as he speaks. The look of the scene contrasts decisively with the bright buoyant look of the wider shots depicting the wedding of Ben's daughter, which are full of color and music. Roche sees Judah as tragically aware that he has betrayed his own best self, having "internalized much of modernity, its consumerist greed, its external standards of success, and its moral bankruptcy" (279). I think a fuller and more attentive look at Levy's place in Allen's design strengthens Roche's reading of the film.

As Levy would understand it (in terms of Martin Bergmann's relational psychology), Judah's moral shortcomings betoken a limitation of Judaism itself, its incapacity to project a loving divinity. Like much of modernist Judaic thinking about the godhead, Levy/Bergmann apprehends "God" as a social construct that personifies the transpersonal ideals of the community. This means in practice that the attributes of God reveal the limits of the moral imagination of a particular culture. Speaking of the Israelites, Levy praises them for projecting a God "that cares." But he immediately alludes to a paradox: "One of the first things that God asks is to ask that Abraham sacrifice his only son, his beloved son to him. In other words, in spite of these efforts, we have not succeeded to create an entirely loving image of God. This was beyond our capacity to imagine" (Allen 1989, 26:25/26:50). As the real-life incarnation of Levy enlarges this point in *The Anatomy of Loving*, the Israelites constructed powerful taboos to shield themselves from human sexuality, with the result that, in spite of their enmeshment in the sensuous culture of the Middle East, they had no concept of Eros, who "has no known Semitic prehistory" (Bergmann 1987, 33). For this reason, "the reader of the Bible is more likely to become acquainted with the destructive aspects of lust than the healing power of love" (87). The most sensuous scriptural text, "The Song of Songs," is disembodied as allegory. To the detriment of Judaic theology, says Bergmann, it was left to the Greeks, and most explicitly to Plato, to integrate Eros into the emergent rationality and sublimating potential of the ego, thus liberating sexuality from its purely physical expression and joining it to the higher powers of mind and spirit. Because Judah's moral paradigm does not include forgiveness, he is unable to imagine a loving wife who might forgive an adulterous husband.

Some of this complex analysis of love comes to expression in Levy's comments on the phenomenon that psychologists call "transference." This process commits the lover to "refinding" something he darkly remembers from his personal past: "If we fall in love, . . . we are seeking to refind all or some of the people to whom we were attached as children. On the other hand, we ask our beloved to correct all of the wrongs that those parents or siblings inflicted on us. So love contains in it a contradiction—the attempt to return to the past and the attempt to undo the past" (Allen 1989, 45:00/45:45). The intricacy and awkwardness of this process explain the impulse to experiment with multiple love partners as well as the imperfect satisfaction with the one contracted to in marriage. In the case of Judah's sexual psychology, it's interesting that he has no memory of his mother, or any female siblings, only a patriarchal father whose principles consist entirely of thou shalt nots.

These broader contours of Bergmann's thinking explain why Levy's voice is appropriate to sum up the import of *Crimes and Misdemeanors*. Much as in *Annie Hall*, the closing montage reprises a memorable set of images from the film, recontextualizing them, so that they now signify differently than they did when we first saw them. This summative strategy, in effect, allows Woody Allen to direct the film about crime and punishment that Judah invited Cliff Stern to undertake. While Judah is not explicitly punished, he doesn't exactly go "scot-free." We define ourselves, says Levy, "by the choices we make, in fact we are the sum total of all our choices." The image joined to this comment shows Judah, secretive and alone, receiving the news of Dolores' murder with a deep grimace. Judah realizes he has made some bad choices and it's unlikely he will shake off all his guilt. "Events unfold so unpredictably, so unfairly,"

Levy continues, "human happiness doesn't seem to have been included in the design of creation." Here the scene is of an unsuspecting Dolores making her way home on the night she will be murdered. Again, Judah is implicitly indicted. But the tragic tone is alleviated by positive images as well: the shot of Sharon and her prospective husband advancing under the huppah to declare their wedding vows comes as Levy proposes, "it is only we, with our capacity to love, that give meaning to an indifferent universe." Finally, as the irrepressibly optimistic Ben dances lovingly with his daughter, Levy brings closure with a sober, but fundamentally optimistic message: "human beings seem to have the ability to keep trying and even to find joy in simple things like their family, their work, and from the hope that future generations might understand more." *Crimes and Misdemeanors* concludes with an act of faith, but it's a faith that owes nothing to religious orthodoxy (Allen 1989, 01:39:40/01:41:00).

SEGMENT 3: PORTRAITS OF THE (JEWISH) ARTIST: *STARDUST MEMORIES* (1980) AND *DECONSTRUCTING HARRY* (1997)

The alienated artist is one of the most conspicuous figures in the landscape of Western European and American modernism. As early as the 1930s, the young and highly perceptive critic Edmund Wilson in *Axel's Castle* (1931) identified the reclusive protagonist of Villiers de L'Isle-Adam's novel as the character who best personified a distinctly new literary type. Deliberately isolated from the industrial/technical culture that had emerged around him, particularly the culture of commodities and material objects, the contemporary artist, as Wilson saw him, had deliberately distanced himself from the larger community and taken refuge in the private fortress of his own mind. Wilson saw this profile fulfilled in writers like Marcel Proust, T. S. Eliot, and perhaps above all James Joyce, whose signature novel, *A Portrait of the Artist as a Young Man* (1916), became the touchstone of this new sensibility. Its aloof protagonist, Stephen Daedalus, resolves to turn his back on family, church, and nation to fulfill the mission of the artist, the self-imposed obligation to "forge in the smithy of my soul the uncreated conscience of my race" (Joyce 1993, 218). Joyce's fiction brought into being a new generation of writers and artists bent on following in the footsteps of young Stephen.

Though this culture figure was not explicitly ethnic (Proust was a Jew, but Eliot prided himself on being an Englishman, expatriating from the United States to Britain). Joyce, however, spoke for the Irish, who were still the colonized minority culture of Great Britain in the first decades of the past century. Would he be the voice of the colonized Dubliners? By no means! Far from being a typical Irish patriot, Joyce and his surrogate Stephen Daedalus were at least as seriously at odds with the parochial culture of the Irish as they were with the imperial culture of the United Kingdom. When Joyce's aesthetic persona migrated across the Atlantic to incubate in the souls of American Irishmen like Eugene O'Neil, the ambiguous attitude toward ethnicity persisted. The deeply alienated poet Edmund Tyrone of O'Neil's *Long Day's Journey into Night* (1956), trapped in a fogbound summerhouse with a father whom he despises, is as much estranged from family and tribe as Stephen is when he explains his aesthetic theories to his uncomprehending university classmates in Dublin. The African American Ralph Ellison drew water from the same stream when he created the protagonist of *Invisible Man* (1952). This underground exile from both the white and the black worlds of 1930s New York finds little in either community to call him away from his subterranean haunts. Jewish ethnicity as well provides its share of alienated artists, from Nathaniel West's disillusioned Hollywood set designer in *The Day of the Locust* (1939) to Allen Ginsberg's tormented artist persona at the center of "Howl" (1956).

In *The American Jewish Novel* (2007), Philippe Codde complicates the portrait of the Jewish artist by remarking how the "Jewish Renaissance" in mid-twentieth-century American literature (the emergence of Saul Bellow, Bernard Malamud, and Edward Wallant, among others) was energized by the Holocaust narratives that began to emerge in the 1950s as well as by the philosophical writings of Sartre and Camus, whose dark sense of human destiny was entirely consonant with the ongoing revelations of Nazi atrocities against the Jews. Hence Codde finds Jewish fiction of the next several decades inflected by existentialist themes, proposing that "we stand in a cold, sad, unfeeling cosmos, unaided by any purposeful power beyond our own resources" (56). These same sentiments (from substantially the same sources of inspiration) dominate the imaginative universe of Woody Allen, though in his early work he literalizes Camus' concept of the "absurd" to the point that it elides with the slapstick chaos of the Marx brothers. His portraits of the Jewish artist, most vividly drawn in *Stardust Memories* and *Deconstructing Harry*, mark the new departure of what might be called his "middle period," a time of outreach and experiment with films of a more complex tonality. This issue figures not simply in flagship productions, like *Manhattan* and *Crimes and Misdemeanors*, but also in the more limited successes, where the management of tone is not quite secure.

One pattern very much in evidence when we look at how the artist is personified in modernist texts is the revolt of the creative individual, the epitome of private genius, against assembly line products, the kitschy consumer commodities that replicate themselves endlessly, like prepackaged salads or turkey sandwiches. Nowhere is this pattern more insistently at play than in cinema, perhaps the most popular of public arts and thus the one most susceptible to homogenization at the hands of profit-oriented producers eager to design this year's model of a comedy or a thriller along the lines of last year's most successful expression of the same genre conventions. While the artist demands, as Ezra Pound would have it, that we "make it new," the studio (or the cohort of independent backers who now assume most of the financial risks of film production) seeks instead an easily recognizable variant upon a proven "great grosser." How many times will the Jedi Knights brandish their light sabers? How many times will Batman return to rescue Gotham City? In the case of *Stardust Memories*, how will Sandy Bates gain permission to break with the formulas of slapstick comedy that have brought him fame and enriched the coffers of his producers, but which now bore him and urge him toward radically new departures?

Allen's template for his first *extempore* portrait of the alienated artist is a film from two decades earlier, Federico Fellini's hyper-energetic masterpiece *8½* (1962). When he made the film, Fellini was confronting the phenomenon of European coproduction, which had the national film industries of Germany, France, and Italy pooling their resources so as to share stars and find broad pan-continental markets for their product. Fellini chafed under the pressure of this business model, since he had emerged as a first magnitude director on the strength of films like *La Strada* (1954) and *I Vitelloni* (1953), which were grounded in the culture of rural Italy, parochial and idiosyncratic. The hero of *8½*, Guido Anselmi, whose career closely tracks with Fellini's own, is suddenly confronted with projects that bear no resemblance to his prior work or his real interests, like the crazy science fiction film he is asked to direct about a frantic escape from the planet Earth, after a nuclear exchange has apparently rendered Europe uninhabitable. Like Sandy (Woody Allen) in *Stardust Memories*, Guido is trying to make the plot into a vehicle to carry his personal emotions, but finding that the genre conventions won't accommodate the nuances of feeling he seeks to communicate.

Mark Siegal (1985) treats Allen's film as a "parody" of Fellini, arguing that it "parodies the self-indulgence of the artist who thinks his personal feelings are important in and of themselves" (80). Three decades later we might see the work as more complex than parody, though the attention to parodic elements does explain the amount of visual quotation from Fellini, which sometimes distracts us from the forward movement of Allen's own film. Siegal seems on firmer footing when he notes that "parody can be a tool to stretch artistic forms" (77). In Allen's case, the forms he seeks to stretch are the conventions of romantic comedy, which he had already challenged in both *Annie Hall* and *Manhattan*. Like those films, and many that would follow, *Stardust Memories* proposes a more open structure that refuses to honor the "happy-ever-aftering" formula, which was the staple of the genre throughout the studio era. *Stardust Memories* achieves distinction as a transitional film, which repurposes the conventions of romantic comedy and points the way toward several much more persuasive portraits of the artist that Allen was to make in the 1990s, including *Deconstructing Harry*.

Stardust Memories is, in some sense, a "Jewish film," though it addresses the circumstances of the Jewish artist very obliquely, always with much more than Jewishness in the mix of things that cause Sandy's frustration. We are aware of his Jewish upbringing because of the riot he started at his Hebrew school by refusing to be the sacrificial victim in a pageant celebrating the patriarch Abraham. We also note that one of the women currently among his romantic interests has spent time in Israel, though her ethnic identity never comes up directly in the film. His most visible connection to the Jewish world is through his sister (Anne De Salvo), who turns up midway through the film, bringing the exuberant confusion of the Jewish household (not unlike the family of *Radio Days*) into the cultural environment of modernism. Together Sandy and his favorite sibling remember their childhood home as a place where mom and dad were "always screaming, always fighting" to a point where "one time the police had to come." She is now in a dysfunctional marriage herself, estranged from her children and surrounded by a menagerie of characters, who seem to accidentally reproduce the chaotic familial environment of their childhood. When Sandy himself looks for moral guidance, he isn't sure whether he needs "a good analyst, a good rabbi, or an interplanetary genius" (Allen 1980, 35:30/38:00). Perhaps he needs all three, but the point is moot since he pays little attention to any counsel whatsoever. The secret Jew lurking somewhere inside of him is embodied in Sidney Finkelstein, a primal monster, who in a scene from one of Sandy's earlier films, gets loose to kill his schoolteacher, his brother, his ex-wife, and his mother, leaving their corpses scattered about in the snow as he goes his wrathful way. It's not accidental that two of these casualties are members of Sandy's blood family, exemplars of his Jewish heritage.

This heritage is only one component of a larger "past" that has become a burden and an encumbrance. Allen's film is built upon the theme of escape—a new beginning salvaged from the ruins of his personal life and from his determination to take his career in another direction. The two strands intertwine, as Sandy discovers he will require a new romantic partner to successfully define for himself a new set of artistic objectives. Allen's ambitious narrative technique, characterized chiefly by a bewildering array of flashbacks and film excerpts, is intended to transform romantic comedy into a vehicle that will carry significantly heavier thematic freight at the expense of conventional closure.

For Celestino Delegto, in "The Narrator and the Narrative" (1994), *Stardust Memories* illustrates Allen's development from "comedian comedy" to "classical narrative," which means "a move away from the self-conscious authoritarian author, who obliges the spectator to be constantly aware [of him], toward his inclusion in a narrative of which he is only a part, in a film which includes him and encompasses his intention within a wider frame" (40). In effect, this means his increasing detachment from borscht belt stand-up routines and their New York comedy club derivatives and his experimentation with more complex narrative devices. These carry us to what Michael Dunne calls the "Metaleptical Highjinx" (1991) of *Stardust Memories*, whose hallmark is "the mingling of two distinct diegetic levels" (115). In Allen's "metafiction," the real and the fantastic, the fictive and the experiential, the past and the present blur and interpenetrate each other so confusedly that all sense of borders and boundaries is lost. Though Allen is not yet the master of this mode, its imaginative potential is already in evidence as he tells the story of Sandy's creative emancipation in a bold cinematic language he is learning to speak. Gordon Willis's expert low-light photography adds the right darkening of individual scenes to match the nonlinear narrative that would otherwise be out of keeping with the genre.

Like Fellini's *8½*, *Stardust Memories* opens with an image of entrapment, a rail carriage with sealed windows and locked doors, populated by characters who are almost like zombies, frozen in their seats, paralytic in their manner, and seemingly unable to speak. Sandy's effort to escape his confinement by pulling levers and scratching on window glass points to a level of desperation suggestive of an imminent mental breakdown. His plight is made worse by the sight of another train on the adjacent track that is full of happy convivial people, sharing wine, laughing, and talking to each other as the train pulls out of the station. We surmise that this is Sandy's private nightmare but soon discover it is actually a scene from a new film he is proposing to make, while his producers and financial sponsors shake their heads in dismay and despair. "Absolutely terrible" is the consensus verdict, while someone mutters that the film "was supposed to be a comedy." His sponsors can't understand why he would give up "the gift of laughter." As we begin to acquaint ourselves with Sandy Bates, we learn that he has already won fame as a comic, who could probably turn a profit for the investors simply by creating near clones of the films he has acted in and directed for the past decade. But the problem, says Sandy, is that he doesn't "feel funny anymore," especially in a world of grave social and political unrest (Allen 1980, 00:25/04:10). Sandy's disquietude is underscored by the poster-sized image on the wall of his condo that shows the horrific public execution of a suspected Viet Cong guerilla. Complicating his situation is the fact that his admirers are expecting him to appear at the Stardust Hotel film festival devoted to his comic works, the *oeuvre* that has brought him fame but which now stifles the further development of his creative gift.

Sandy's prospect of escaping this impasse depends, most basically, on his ability to sort out his romantic misadventures, which are tied closely to his past and present performances as a lover and a director. In the simplest terms, he must choose between two women, one who—broadly speaking—represents excitement, mystery, and above all unpredictability, and another who stands for coherence, stability, and long-term potential. That's a choice Sandy finds difficult, even though his more rational self realizes the stable Isobel would be the more reliable partner. Sandy's dilemma is further complicated by the fact that the mystery woman of his fantasies is really two different women. One is the stunningly beautiful Dorrie (Charlotte Rampling), a phantom from his past, and the other is Daisy (Jessica Harper), a woman whom he has just met at the festival and immediately finds fascinating.

The first to appear is Dorrie, his former lover, now only a phantom presence but powerful in spite of her purely ethereal status. She inserts herself into the narrative as a rescuer, a ghostly voice that materializes into a living creature when the camera tracks left to reveal her as present in a scene she could not possibly be part of (Allen 1980, 09:45/11:00). Her fantasy intervention calms one of Sandy's more serious anxiety attacks, proposing to feed him a special dish, saving him from an in-house cook who seems only to be able to set the stove afire. Soon we learn that Dorrie was once his favorite female co-star, explaining why she is so frequently on screen after Sandy takes up residence at the Stardust Hotel, the festival site. Thereafter, she will frequently revisit his life at various moments of crisis, masquerading as his savior but frequently displaying her dark side, which results from bipolar disorder. Ominously, in one of their first phantasmal conversations, Dorrie confesses she has gone off her lithium medication, though Sandy pleads with her to reconsider this decision.

Dorrie's antithesis is Isobel (Marie Christine Barrault), a well-balanced, down-to-earth French woman who is now at the center of Sandy's romantic life and whom he also looks to for mentoring. She is going through a divorce and comes to the relationship with two young children. She joins Sandy at the festival on his invitation, but the complicating circumstance of her children causes him to have second thoughts about their partnership. The third woman in Sandy's life is the enigmatic Daisy, who reminds him of Dorrie, though the two women do not in any obvious way resemble each other. Somehow Isobel must win a two-front war, battling one antagonist who is a phantom, capable of shape shifting into different figures and personae as occasion might dictate. For Sandy, the worst outcome of the Stardust Festival is that it unlocks his erotic memories of Dorrie.

When Sandy first meets this ghostly femme fatale, she seems an icon of coherence and good sense, quietly reading at the beach while she waits to recite her few lines of dialogue in a film that he is directing. He is struck by her poise and exceptional good looks as well as her apparent indifference to the bustle of the production process, ongoing throughout the scene. Approaching her as an off-screen voice, Sandy confesses, "I've been looking at you all morning," romantically smitten by her "really strange quality." There should be alarm bells ringing when Dorrie mentions being "fascinating but troubled" and known to "fake my way through most situations." Gordon Willis' unfailingly good composition also emphasizes distance and separation: we (like Sandy) see his would be lady friend through the elaborate scaffolding of what is probably a light tower. Even after he sits down with her, their faces are kept apart by two rectangular metal grids that deny them full-fledged closeness. It might also bode ill for their future that she is reading Schopenhauer, not the happiest spirit among the Olympians of philosophy. Impervious to these discordant notes, Sandy acknowledges, "I'm fatally attracted to you." He speaks much more accurately than he realizes (Allen 1980, 22:20/22:50).

Their courtship is then represented in a series of scenes that dissolve the boundary between film and life. Dorrie is his lover and his co-star, but it's sometimes not obvious whether they are on camera or off. In close-up we see them quarreling and Dorrie slaps his face. But the ensuing shot of the clapboard tells us this was just a bad take in the staging of a lovers' quarrel. Soon they exchange a long kiss in close-up while standing in front of a rotating carousel. But a moment later the camera pulls back to the point we can see the light stands and the huge Klieg light in the left foreground. What we thought was a personal romantic moment is actually an excerpt from one of Sandy's films. In the scene that follows there is no confirming evidence whether we are dealing with life or art. As a romantic couple, they are enjoying some good wine and the prospect of a quiet dinner at home. They hug, touch, and good-naturedly amuse each other. Suddenly a pigeon flies into the room setting off an anxiety storm in Sandy, while Dorrie giggles and tries to settle him down. Bent on thwarting the "pigeon from hell," Sandy attacks him with a massive fire extinguisher, spraying everything in sight and surely doing more damage to the living quarters than the bird of ill omen. Is this a scene from "real life" or an outtake from a movie? The set resembles what we know to be Sandy's quarters, but the giant poster of Groucho Marx suggests the world slapstick comedy. Whichever is the case, this moment is a kind of epiphany. We can see that the precariously situated Dorrie is both the center of Sandy's life and the center of his art. His human character is indistinguishable from his starring role in his own comic movies. Small wonder that he has trouble moving on (Allen 1980, 22:50/27:00).

Allen effectively plays off Dorrie against Isobel, as Sandy struggles to decide how his midlife crisis will resolve itself. Although he lavishes affection on Isobel, even insisting that she move in with him, he is unprepared to cope with her children, in spite of his determination to be a supportive foster parent. This issue comes to sharp focus in a scene where Sandy and Isobel take the kids to get something to eat, and one of the children is exceptionally restless. While Isobel tries to get control of her offspring, Sandy gazes through the window into a fantasy scene of a beach drenched with sunlight, a setting similar to the scene of his first meeting with Dorrie. Here it prompts recollection of one of their most tender moments together, the occasion when she takes charge of celebrating his birthday.

In this scene, Dorrie is first imagined as a mother figure, ministering to Sandy the child and offering the unbounded love he evidently never received from his flesh-and-blood parent. Its symbol, incongruously, is an elephant, impossibly out of place on the beach, but answering to the wish young Sandy is said to have repeatedly expressed to his mother. In a split-second transition, Sandy the boy is replaced by Sandy the man, and Dorrie is now his lover, as the scene (absent the elephant) morphs from fantasy to memory. She is still the hyper-generous gift giver, doling out presents with both hands. These include a flute and an elegant watch, both of which are tied closely to Sandy's personal past. But the most exceptional of her gifts is a copy of Alan Watts' *The Way of Zen*, which preaches what the California guru of the 1950s thought to be the deepest wisdom of the East. Sandy correctly interprets its meaning as a "way of telling me I'm not at peace." At this moment Dorrie, improbably representing coherence and calm, clearly has priority over the frazzled Isobel and her hyperactive children (Allen 1980, 54:50/56:05).

Eventually we see Dorrie in a less positive light, as she experiences a near mental breakdown and confesses to having been sexually abused by her father. Sandy doesn't dispute his friend's comment that she was normal only two days a month. By this stage of the film, however, Sandy has begun to transfer his affection to a third woman, Daisy, whom he has met at the Festival and who reminds him of his lost love. Sandy and Daisy are first together as a threesome, but Daisy notices that Sandy's eyes are fixated upon her. When she later asks him why she "reminds [him] of an old girlfriend," he tells her she has the same "lost quality" that made Dorrie virtually irresistible. From an overheard phone conversation, Sandy also learns that Daisy has had a lesbian relationship with her friend in Israel and that she is subject to eating binges and sleep disorders, both now encroaching upon her. But this doesn't deter him from an extended flirtation with his new lady friend, creating the possibility that he may yet find a way to completely ruin his life.

Sandy's attempt to create private time with Daisy ushers in the zaniest moments of his weekend at the Stardust Hotel, episodes intended as metaphors of the dislocation and aberration Daisy would bring into his life. These begin when he contrives a way to detach himself from Isobel and escort Daisy to a screening of DeSica's *Bicycle Thief*. Thereafter we find them, in rapid-fire sequence, escaping to the countryside in Sandy's automobile, experiencing an on-the-road breakdown, wandering aimlessly in search of assistance, and accidentally stumbling into a cadre of science fiction fans who await the landing of a troupe of space aliens. The loose plotting and helter-skelter action (as well as the conspicuous visual quotations from *8½*) disrupt the cohesion of Allen's narrative, but these episodes allow Sandy to worry over why "people can't love" and invite Daisy to run off with him. They also supply the last Jewish references in the film, as Sandy's sister appears, stepping out of the confused swarm of autograph hounds and favor seekers to plead with Sandy, "You've got to help me, my life's a mess." Overwhelmed as he clearly is, Sandy sees his Jewish family as simply another set of encumbrances from which he must desperately flee (Allen 1980, 00:57:30/01:06:40).

In a magical universe, the celebrity director might successfully elope with Daisy, as is suggested when he is suddenly morphed into a magician and manages to levitate Daisy's body, defying gravity while raucous circus music plays in the background. But the bubble is burst as one of his fans remarks, "this is exactly like one of your satires, it's like we are all characters in a film." Effectively, the chaotic events of the sci-fi episode foreshadow the disaster that would result from an effort to create a serious relationship with his new friend. At its conclusion, the scene shifts from the misadventures of Sandy and Daisy to a series of jump-cut, choker-tight facial close-ups of Dorrie, plaintively asking, "Are you in love with anyone?" but immediately confessing "I can't feel anything" (Allen 1980, 01:02:40/01:08:20). Whatever their differences, Daisy and Dorrie convey Sandy to the same dead end of his creative life.

At this moment, Allen turns the film toward resolution, though a few loose threads continue to dangle. The space aliens advise him to go back to Isobel, pronouncing Dorrie "a basket case" and commending the French housewife as "someone you can depend on." Their recommendations for his art are more ambivalent, but they include "funnier jokes" and continued respect for the muse of comedy. As Sandy tries to translate this counsel into practical behavior, he follows Isobel to the train station announcing he has found a new ending for his film. What he now plans returns us to the railway journey of the first scene, but the details of the new narrative are quite different. Again we are on board a train, he says, but this time he is traveling with Isobel and her two children, just as, in fact, they are now poised to do. "But it's not as terrible as I originally thought it was," he continues, "because we like each other and we have some laughs, and there is a lot of closeness." As before, there are "many sad people" on the train, and the travelers have "no idea where it's headed." But that doesn't matter because Sandy has the comfort of human companionship. His new leading lady is Isobel. His film, he tells her, "is based on you, and you're very warm and very giving, and you love me." When Isobel, suddenly his self-appointed film critic, complains that the plot is "sentimental," Sandy counters with, "So what, it's good sentimental." He admits to being "ridiculous" and "floundering around," but assures her that the scene (just as we are observing it) will play well if they seal it with an intense romantic kiss. As they do—clinging tightly to each other while the train pulls out of the station and Isobel's children look on approvingly (Allen 1980, 01:19:55/01:22:20).

Now as this image is overlaid by unexpected applause from an unseen audience, we realize we are watching a film in the screening room of the Stardust Hotel, which miraculously concludes the retrospective festival by exhibiting a film that Sandy has not yet made. The surreal turn of the plot underscores Allen's most important thematic concern: The life-affirming, community-building modality of comedy is legitimate, in spite of the pronouncements of Schopenhauer, and its conventions are elastic enough to digest most of what happens in real life. Moliere knew that, as did Shakespeare, Mozart, and Shaw. Moreover, since we are on the interior stage of Sandy Bates' own mind, it should not be startling to find that his audience now includes figures from the director's memory bank, including Dorrie, Daisy, and Isobel. Dorrie remains the character we have come to know well—self-absorbed and introverted, muttering to herself about private griefs that have nothing to do with Sandy. Daisy, on the other hand, seems quite different. No longer a would-be lover, subtly encouraging Sandy's impulse to court her, she leaves the auditorium in the company of Isobel, congratulating her rival on how well she has played her part as Sandy's new co-star and praising the English of the French-speaking Isobel, who continues to apologize for her oral performance in a language other than French. The outcome bodes well for Sandy in the realm of both life and art. Isobel will become both his partner and his muse, permanently replacing the unstable Dorrie and providing Sandy with an appropriate escort into his newfound artistic domain. Here there will be "some laughs," as the space aliens have advised in reminding him that he's a comedian, and "lots of closeness," in keeping with the spirit of romantic comedy. After the auditorium has emptied, Sandy returns briefly to gaze at an empty screen, suggesting a future that is open to possibility. He still doesn't know where the train "is headed," but he has resolved to enjoy the ride.

After completing *Stardust Memories*, which was a calamity at the box office and not well received by critics, Allen did not return to his portrait-of-the-artist theme for more than a decade. By the middle 1990s, he had directed near-masterpieces like *Radio Days* and *Crimes and Misdemeanors*, but also had to survive a first magnitude scandal when he broke up a twelve-year relationship with Mia Farrow and chose a new wife in Soon-Yi Previn, Farrow's adopted daughter. Though neither party emerged from these events unscathed, Allen perhaps incurred the worst of the blame, since Farrow leveled charges of child abuse against her long-term lover. The events undoubtedly darkened his imagination (at least temporarily), though did not impair his performance as a filmmaker. When he returned to the image of the alienated artist in *Husbands and Wives* (1992) and *Bullets over Broadway* (1994), he brought to the portraiture a surer hand than he had shown in *Stardust Memories*. But his most complex film of this period, and also his most Jewish, is *Deconstructing Harry*, which, as Allen noted in his interview with *Positif* (1998), is the direct descendant of *Stardust*, "where you got to know the protagonist through his films" (Kapsis 2016, 153). Like the film to which it looks back, *Deconstructing Harry* is a nonlinear collage of memories, imaginings, and dramatized excerpts from the writings of Allen's protagonist, the novelist Harry Block.

The plot of *Deconstructing Harry* is deceptively simple. Its celebrity protagonist is to receive an award from Adair College for his contributions to comedic literature. The complicating circumstance is that he is presently experiencing writer's block, which fills him with anxiety. The spine of the film is his journey to receive the prize, together with a brief prologue in which he seeks out a few guests to accompany him. Because Harry is largely bereft of friends and family, his efforts to recruit a personal audience prove more problematic than we might have expected. The journey quickly expands into an all-encompassing pilgrimage, summoning the real and the fantastic, the living and the dead, zigzagging wildly and cross-referencing every nook and cranny of Harry's life and mind. In the compressed time frame of about two days, we meet his three wives and his most recent girlfriend, his father and his son, as well as the fictional surrogates of several of these characters, who have emanated from the real-life figures they represent.

Remarkably sophisticated in its narrative technique, the film also introduces a new Allen persona, more jaded and more cynical than Isaac Davis, Cliff Stern, or Sandy Bates. In "Woody Allen After the Fall" (2003), Rubin-Dorsky charges that the rupture of Allen's romantic partnership with Mia Farrow occasioned "the withdrawal of the Woody figure," who had been the "moral center" of Allen's films, and with that, the disappearance of "the person on whom the audience could rely, in the midst of uncertainty and confusion, to articulate the ethical issues and problems, if not actually solve them" (2). Christopher Knight also asserts that "something did happen in the period of the Farrow/Allen breakup that had consequences for the later films" (2013, 75). What emerges, Knight says, is a stance toward the world he calls Allen's "late style," not mellow and generous, such as, say, the Faulkner voice of *The Reivers,* but angry, hostile, and unforgiving, like the voice Edward Said describes in challenging "the notion that aging entails a discernible movement in the direction of reconciliation" (Knight 2013, 73). Whatever the reason for this shift of tone, the result is a much more negative image of the Jewish artist and a much more dyspeptic view of the Jewish family that produced him.

In ethnic and cultural terms, Harry Block (Allen) is what Adam Chalom (citing rabbinical literature) calls an *"apicoros,"* a figure that Judaic Orthodoxy disowns as a "heretic who is both familiar with and scornful of rabbinic wisdom and knowledge" (2009, 286). According to the paradigm of "secular Jewishness" that Chalom constructs, these unrepentant apostates from *Yiddishkeit* are the least worthy members of the Jewish community, because they not only ignore diet and ritual but actively preach against the doctrine and practice of Jewish belief. Historically, they might be recognized by their allegiance to socialism and anarchism, which were actively endorsed as alternatives to Observant Jewishness in the early twentieth century, but in the post–World War II period these types blur into a less well-defined group that "understands Jewish and human history through scientific and academic study rather than through traditional wisdom, and . . . sees ethics as a function of personal and social consequences rather than the keeping of commandments" (289). For Chalom, "Secular Humanistic Judaism is both philosophic and cultural, both ethnic and universally human." It is "a non-theistic religion that combines a humanistic philosophy of life" with principles that "affirm the value of reason, individuality, and freedom" (292), often with relatively little attention to symbol, diet, and ritual. This latter comprehension of Jewishness would clearly include Isaac, Cliff, and Sandy (as it would Primo Levi, and perhaps even the ethically challenged Judah Rosenthal of *Crimes and Misdemeanors*) as Secular Humanist Jews, but would have more difficulty assimilating Harry Block, since he knowingly and opportunistically repudiates the ethical imperatives that are at the core of Jewish tradition. He has assumed a purely spectatorial view of humankind, which turns his fellow creatures into mere raw material for his writing.

This reductionist mentality is dangerous, as we learn from an early scene. Harry's narratives belong to the genre of black comedy, which takes the most problematic features of contemporary life, in this case largely Jewish life, and exploits their ludic potential. Like Lester, the self-important television producer in *Crimes and Misdemeanors,* who thinks that *Oedipus Rex* is basically "funny" because of its extreme incongruity, Harry sees everything about him as a source of dark laughter. On this occasion he celebrates a flagrant infidelity, which involves betraying his wife by making love to her sister in their own home and virtually in the company of friends and family. Stumbling upon the lovers, the blind grandmother of the family "observes" their lovemaking, but only by ear, wildly misinterpreting what she overhears. In reliably theater-of-the-absurd fashion, she imagines their sexually induced moans and cries to be inspired by food preparation: "You must really like onions!" To his appreciative readers, Harry is a mirthful wordsmith, with a wicked wit that transforms scenes of deceit and betrayal into "inspired comic flights." Naturally, this is how Harry himself thinks of his work: He is not debasing or slandering an intimate friend; he is crafting a well-wrought urn, reshaping a flesh-and-blood creature into an *object d'art,* outside of time, space, and moral relationships. But to the distraught Lucy (Judy Davis), Harry's sexual partner in this quirky misadventure, he is a "black magician," an evil alchemist who "take(s) everyone's suffering and turn(s) it into literary gold." Carelessly indulging his creative urge, Harry destroys Lucy's marriage, drastically damages her relationship to her sister Jane (Amy Irving), and brings his former lover to the threshold of suicide or murder. Not so much malevolent as simply indifferent to human consequence, Harry stands at the furthest remove from Jewish humanism, a virtual narcissist who recognizes no interests other than his own (Allen 1998, 06:20/11:45).

This issue of the ethical imperatives of Jewishness is complicated in the new century by the fact that Jewish American literature is now sometimes expected to define Jewish ethnicity and expand the moral ambience of the Judaic tradition. In "People of the (Secular) Book," Julian Levinson looks closely at anthologies of Jewish American writing as contributors to "the making of Jewish identity in postwar America," arguing that this practice "preserves the traditional image of the Jews as 'people of the book,' while broadening the definition of 'the book'" (2009, 131). He is particularly interested in *Jewish American Literature: A Norton Anthology* (2001) as a seminal document that embeds the wisdom of Jewish tradition within the more secular context of contemporary American letters. Capitalizing on the ambiguity of the Yiddish word *veltlekh* (literally, "worldly"), which can mean both "cosmopolitan" and "materialistic," Levinson maintains that "a Jewish literary culture, including pronounced secular currents," should claim its place as part of "a vibrant pluralistic society in which multiple ethnic identities and cultures can maintain themselves" (141–42). In this modernist paradigm, Clifford Odets, Tillie Olsen, and Saul Bellow become a vital extension of Jewish tradition, not because of a mysterious

"Jewish temperament or Jewish sensibility," but because of a deep-seated moral idealism "linked to the Jewish past" (142–44). Regrettably, Harry—with his amoral and corrosively ironic worldview—does not meet this standard of what in some circles is now expected of the "Jewish writer."

Of course, Harry does not always write about Jews. One of his most revealing stories deals with Mel (Robin Williams), an actor who strangely goes out-of-focus when subjected to exceptional stress. According to the premise of the story, the only way Mel can be part of the film production, or even avoid this "softness" in the company of his own family, is for everyone interacting with him to wear special glasses designed to sharpen his image. In one of Harry's therapy sessions, his analyst interprets the latent content of this narrative as Harry's determination to make the entire world modify its vision in order to see Harry in the way he would like to be seen. This narcissistic mindset is the key to Harry's creative energy. His gift is the problematic ability to transform his friends, family, and professional associates into fun-house-mirror images of themselves. Inevitably, such distortions play havoc upon the world of contemporary Jewishness that some of his less sympathetic readers expect him to accurately describe.

The Jewish subject in Harry's work is brought into the film through the protagonist's interaction with two characters in particular, his second wife Joan (Kirstie Alley), who is also the fictional character, Helen (Demi Moore), and Harry's sister Doris (Caroline Aaron), from whom he is seriously estranged because of her marriage to an ardent Zionist and her own deeply conservative feelings about faith and family. We first meet Joan as a real-life figure, fighting with her ex-husband over his request for an exception to their contractual child custody arrangements. Harry wants to take his son Hilly (Eric Lloyd) to the awards ceremony, but Joan is adamant in her refusal. Clearly she resents any contact between Harry and his child, charging immediately that she wants to keep her son permanently away from his "pill-popping, alcoholic, beaver-banging excuse for a father" (Allen 1998, 23:00/25:20). We sense that there's much more in this encounter than incidental friction over one small (and perhaps not unreasonable) request. For Harry, this shouting match that spreads out over a public street triggers a memory of their courtship and marriage that he has represented in his writing as the experience of the fictional couple, Helen (Demi Moore) and Paul (Stanley Tucci) Epstein.

In flight from an early marriage, which was itself the escape from an unhappy home, Harry (Paul) finds in his therapist, Joan (Helen), a woman he instantly connects with and quickly marries. In spite of the professional irregularities of their first coming together, Harry imagines himself in a "perfect marriage"—interactive, loving, and sexually robust. But this blissful state evaporates with the birth of their son, Hilliard (Eric

Lloyd), who becomes a source of strife between them for the rest of the film. According to Harry, the process of birthing and mothering causes Joan to "suddenly become Jewish with a vengeance," apparently drawn back toward clan and tribe by the act of founding a family. When we see Joan impersonated by Helen, we see a woman who has been flexible and open, particularly in her sexuality, become more and more insistent about her Jewishness, demanding that Hilliard (whom she now calls Hillel) be circumcised and bodily shaped into a Jewish child. She also begins to pray in Hebrew and builds a small candle shrine as a meditative object, her focal point of worship in a Jewish home. Helen now dresses differently as well, abandoning the modernist, professional look of her secular identity for a wardrobe of floor-length skirts and a shawl to cover her hair. She is also hyper-aware of heritage and tradition: "I see my father's face in Hillel," she says, while her husband protests that they "didn't name him after a rabbi." Their marriage ends, so far as we can tell, when Helen meets an Israeli and enters into a relationship with him (Allen 1998, 25:20/28:45). Later we learn that the fictional personality of Helen owes much to Harry's remembrance of his sister Doris, whom he visits en route to the awards ceremony. Their meeting clarifies Harry's (and presumably Allen's) refusal to perform as a "Jewish American artist," even if the burden is no heavier than the stripped-down tradition of Secular Jewish Humanism.

The scene with sister Doris and her husband Burt (Eric Bogosian) begins on a cordial note and an exchange of pleasantries, but quickly deteriorates into a sharp-edged exchange between the two siblings, as Hilly and Burt seclude themselves on sun porch, separated off by immense panels of glass. Harry remembers his sister as "a wonderfully sweet kid that got me through my childhood," but regrets that she "married a zealot" and gave in to "superstition." She speaks of returning to her roots and respecting "tradition," a concept Harry dismisses as "the illusion of permanence." He finds Jewishness, like Catholicism, or any other faith community, to be "clubby, exclusionist," inclined to see certain members of the human race as more important than others. Doris largely confirms this point, noting that the Jews are "my people," hence deserving of her more serious care and concern. According to Harry, the whole human family should be her "people," though he himself seems rarely given to a generous embrace of his fellow creatures. In Doris' eyes, Harry is a "self-hating Jew," though Harry rejoins with, "I may hate myself but it's not 'cause I'm a Jew" (Allen 1998, 53:10/56:10).

What seems to decide the argument, as Doris understands it, is Harry's own performance as a writer: "Look at how he talks about them (the Jews) in his stories." Here we cut to an excerpt from the story of Dolly (Shifra Lerer) and Max Pinkus (Hy Anzell), arriving *in medias res* at a Star Wars–themed bar mitzvah, which masterfully presents what Calvin Goldscheider calls "the continuities and transformations" of contemporary Jewish life in the United States (2009, 267). Even though Goldscheider feels that "communal institutions . . . and family networks are the core elements sustaining communal continuity," he recognizes that "the ethnic distinctiveness of American Jews has faded," often leaving behind "only symbolic religion and symbolic ethnicity" (268–69). This asymmetrical hybridity is evident at young Donald's bar mitzvah. Conspicuous signage in the banquet hall prays that "the force be with" the young man at the center of this "traditional" initiation rite. The initiate himself carries a green light sabre, as Princess Leia wheels up a cake decorated with stars, clearly from the firmament of Lucasfilm, Ltd. and not the House of David. Searching about for tradition, we find it in the white yarmulkes worn by virtually all the male guests as well as in the occasional "*mazel tov*" offered in ceremonial greeting. But the residue of historical Judaism is overwhelmed by the Darth Vader masks that decorate almost every table and by the Storm Troopers of the Empire who deliver hors d'oeuvres to the guests.

Judaism is also spoofed in the "dark secret" that Max Pinkus carries in his soul. In spite of the sunny disposition he displays at the bar mitzvah ceremony, it is rumored that he once committed an act of cannibalism. He answers this accusation, however, with an appeal to the fashionable stance of Jewish multiculturalism: "Some bury, some burn. I ate." This comic caricature of the Observant Jew compels Burt to join the fray in support of his wife, declaring that Harry's characters are "like something out of *Der Stürmer*" and proof that he "is not a Jewish man" (Allen 1998, 01:01:10/01:02:50). Burt seems not to understand satiric intent and faults Harry for lacking the ethnic loyalty he apparently thinks is required of a "Jewish man." As a couple, Doris and Burt are a template of Jewishness in transition, particularly in the insecurity they feel in trying to hold on to what they may think is slipping away. Like Goldscheider, they hunger "to construct new forms of Jewish cultural uniqueness that redefine the collective identity of Jews" (2009, 269). But they are uneasy in the presence of "the institutional contexts [that] may also expose Jewish Americans to new networks and alternative values not ethnically or religiously Jewish" (274). Harry has been schooled too well in the dogma of the autonomous artist to honor even the minimal demand that the Jewish artist create sympathetic and morally admirable characters.

To further relativize Harry's relationship to his sister and further complicate his narrative, Allen introduces another fantasy character, Fertile Imagination, who shows us a scene not included in Harry's visit with Doris and her family. This exchange between Doris and her husband apparently takes place shortly after Harry and his companions have departed on their journey to Adair College. Suddenly becoming an advocate of her sibling, Doris represents Harry not as Jew hating, but "just lost," a man who "could never accept the fact that there are some things you can't know." What she had angrily dismissed as "sarcasm and cynicism" now becomes an inability to fully function in the face of profound doubt. "I'd like to hug him again," she tells her husband, "like I did when we were kids. When I was upset, he was a real comfort." This epiphany suggests that Harry's imagination is potentially more generous than he allows it to be. Perhaps for purposes of his art or perhaps more for his personal comfort, he has chosen to think of his sister as more hostile than she actually is (Allen 1998, 01:10:15/01:10:55).

Peter Bailey contextualizes these tonalities quite effectively, while accurately remarking the distance that separates Allen himself from the persona of Harry Block. Unlike Harry, Allen refuses to treat art as a form of secular salvation. Linking *Harry* to *Stardust Memories* (and also to *Interiors*), Bailey points out that "the fallibility of human memory necessarily adulterates the Grecian Urn perfection that art is supposed to be able to achieve; it is one of [Allen's] central and most consistently dramatized aesthetic axioms that the creations of imperfect beings must necessarily be correspondingly imperfect" (2001, 242). Bailey maintains that "the movie constitutes no reversal of Allen's consistently articulated position on the meaninglessness of literary reputation, on the fraudulence of the Modernist credo that art confers upon the artist the only form of immortality available to humanity" (243). Allen himself confirms, but qualifies this point, when he tells Ciment and Garbarz, "I've always had the feeling that, for me, artistic creation was a savior. If I didn't have it, I don't see what else I could have done. But it was never a solace to me . . . because, when it comes to ponderings about the meaning of life and existential anguish, art never brings any answers—it's never brought me personally any answers" (Kapsis 2016, 153–54).

In *Deconstructing Harry*, art does nothing to redeem the protagonist or the Jewish ethnicity he personifies. As Allen says of his central character, "you can see his life is a total disaster: he's self-destructive, he makes everyone who's close to him suffer, he lives in a state of personal excess, he's addicted to barbiturates; he's a sex addict. That's what happens . . . when he can't keep on transforming reality according to his desires" (Kapsis 2016, 152). But art does "save" Harry in a more literal sense, as in the opening scene of the film, when Lucy is actually attempting to shoot him, but is distracted from this task by the wit and charm of his zany story about Harvey Stern's encounter with Death, an awkward case of cosmic mistaken identity. More generally, Harry's passion for the written word and his delight in the imaginary universe of his characters has probably saved him from complete dissipation or suicide. He may not have written positively about contemporary Jewishness, but he has written memorably and with absolute personal absorption.

Throughout the journey that is supposed to crown his career with a prestigious award, we have premonitions of a gathering storm that will end in calamity. The first omen of disaster is the difficulty he has in finding anyone in his immediate circle willing to join him on the Adair campus. His girlfriend Fay Sexton (Elizabeth Shue), for whom he has betrayed two other women, declines his invitation because she is about to marry his childhood friend, Larry. He craves the company of his son Hilly, but has to resort to kidnapping to whisk him away from his mother, who is furious at the thought of the boy having private time with his apostate father. Richard (Bob Balaban), the one personal friend he recruits to accompany him, is at best a casual acquaintance, who turns up unexpectedly right before Harry leaves home. And this arrangement proves disastrous, because Richard dies of cardiac arrest just as they arrive at their destination.

Ironically, the character who proves most dependable and supportive is the black prostitute Cookie (Hazelle Goodman), who is the only African American actor to play a major role in an Allen film. In spite of her dubious profession and appalling costume (abbreviated high-gloss pink shorts), Cookie supplies Harry with the best advice he receives and steadies him through the first few of the catastrophes that begin to rain down soon after his arrival at Adair. Like Mel, whom we met earlier as one of Harry's characters, his creator also experiences a moment of "softness," becoming a blob and a blur as stress overtakes him. Without help from special lenses, Cookie talks him back into sharp focus before his handlers arrive to convey him to the ceremony. Unfortunately, not even she can save him from what awaits, as Adair's guest of honor must cope with a corpse, a kidnap victim, a raging ex-wife, and an assortment of bewildered academics, who can't get their heads around what's found its way to their campus.

The metaphor that dominates the awards ceremony is a descent into hell, fashioned as a postmodern reconfiguration of Dante's *Inferno*. Here Harry characterizes himself as a lost soul searching for the appropriate level of damnation, eventually debating with the Devil the question of which of them is the worse sinner. In spite of his self-hatred and recklessness, Harry self-servingly imagines the scene as a mission to rescue Fay, whom he envisions as having been carried off by the diabolic Larry (Billy Crystal), the friend who has just "stolen" his one true love. The infernal interval also allows Harry to skewer some of his favorite targets, by assigning "serial killers and lawyers who appear on television" to the sixth level of damnation and bury the NRA two circles deeper. More substantially, these moments record his final encounter with his father, on whom he seems to have based Max Pinkus, the cannibal and wife murderer. Astonishingly, he now forgives him and secures his release from the infernal regions. It's the only moment in the film when Harry appears in a positive moral light. Meanwhile, he is abruptly returned to the real world when Joan arrives to accuse him of kidnapping their son and stands by as he is summarily dragged off to jail. Now in the crowning irony of the film, it is Fay and Larry who put up his bail and rescue him from the Inferno of his own self-indulgence and self-deception (Allen 1998, 01:19:00/01:24:30).

For all its negativity, *Deconstructing Harry* concludes on a positive note, conjuring a fantasy of reconciliation that lets the frustrated novelist resume his writing (Allen 1998, 01:29:20/01:32:15). After the awards ceremony is canceled and Harry returns to his "sewer of an apartment" in apparent disgrace, he absentmindedly picks up the autographed baseball that Fay had given him as a birthday present at a moment when she seemed to be turning into the one love of his life. The memento calls up a benign feeling for Fay, whom he has reluctantly forgiven for marrying his best friend. And the baseball holds talismanic powers. It implies forgiveness toward Fay and Larry, perhaps even the recognition that Larry will prove a more satisfactory marriage partner than Harry himself, in spite of his protestations that he loves her immeasurably. We must also recall that the iconic baseball represents the achievements of the 1951 New York Giants, who came from behind in the last of the ninth inning to win the National League pennant, defeating the Brooklyn Dodgers, who had once led them by thirteen games. Delighting in Fay's gift at the time it was given, Harry remarks that it was the only true miracle he had ever directly experienced and the only occasion he had ever imagined there might be a God and a Providential design in the universe. Everything Allen holds dear about luck and magic comes into play at this moment: Harry's spontaneous joy in remembering Fay earns him the fantasy ceremony that sends him back to his typewriter.

This elaborate fantasy also reconfigures his relationship to his imaginative creations, for the most part making them more positive and coherent than they seemed when we were previously introduced to them. Harvey Stern, who once was in danger of being carried off by Death, now is in the company of a woman he had relished in the days before he was mistaken for Mendel Birnbaum; Jane and Ken, who couldn't get along with each other while they were thrust together in Harry's novel, stand side by side as they applaud the guest of honor at the ceremony; Helen and Paul are also agreeably together, though their marriage had gone less smoothly when they were Harry's creatures; even the Pinkus family, which was formed after several acts of murder and cannibalism, appears to be happy and well adjusted, none the worse for the unpleasantness that is buried somewhere in their fictive past; Mel too appears, as a surrogate of Harry himself: he is still out of focus, but not seriously uncomfortable. Even the band that plays for the ceremony is indebted to Harry's imagination, as we see them wearing Darth Vader helmets borrowed from Donald's *Star Wars* bar mitzvah. What Allen offers here, in his sweeping symphonic coda, is a tribute to the plasticity of the imagination, the virtual life that may beget innumerable forms of further life. He confesses that he can "only function in art" but that his imaginary family has "given me some of the happiest moments of my life." The collective gratitude felt by these creatures for their creator empowers him to continue, and he returns to his typewriter while the musical track plays, "If they asked me, I could write a book." Implicitly, that's exactly what they have asked for (Allen 1998, 01:29:10/01:32:55).

Deconstructing Harry is one of Allen's most carefully wrought films, even if it is not the best of the best. True to the mystique of "deconstructionist" criticism, as we know it from Jacques Derrida and others, this film puts us in touch with a text rich in ambiguity, advancing contradictory strands of discourse, which intertwine with each other in dauntingly complex ways. It is a kaleidoscope of fragments, cleverly deployed to both reveal and conceal the American a social landscape at the end of the twentieth century, as it is refracted through the prism of Harry Block's psyche. This landscape includes the American Jewish community and Jewish Secular Humanism, which the film in a certain sense "deconstructs." In keeping with its logic of binaries, which locates meaning in the space between opposing terms, Jewishness is both present and absent, affirmed and denied, apprehended both honestly and fantastically. Taken from the perspective of Doris and Burt, Harry might be a "self-hating Jew." But Harry too is correct in his realization that the venom poisoning his life is not primarily ethnic, though it might be familial. *Deconstructing Harry* is not intended to be Allen's last word on his Jewishness or the status of American Jews in the new millennium. But it may mark a turning point, at which the filmmaker looks beyond Jewishness, beyond New York, even beyond the United States for the inspiration that drives his imagination in the next decade.

SEGMENT 4: BEYOND JEWISHNESS: *BLUE JASMINE* (2013) AND *CAFÉ SOCIETY* (2016)

In the new century, Allen took his filmmaking in a substantially new direction, marked chiefly by the loosening of his ties to New York City, which for three decades had been both nerve center of his productions and the stage set for his films. The complication of his relationship to Tri-Star and later the Orion corporation resulted in the departure of producer Robert Greenhut, who had been part of the Allen team since 1976, and shortly thereafter he also lost the services of Susan Morse, his editor of long standing, and Carlo Di Palma, his director of photography. A further rupture of his production arrangements came in 2001, when he broke with Jean Doumanian, his personal friend and the head of production at Sweetland Films, which had been his chief financial backer since 1993. In this instance, Allen sued Sweetland for a fuller share of the profits from several films that were barely profitable, and the legal wrangling caused him to break with his New York financers. Thereafter he began to explore European production in conjunction with Dreamworks, the BBC, and later, the Sony Corporation and Amazon. The goal, apparently successful, was to cut costs (see Evanier 2015, 323–27).

Allen's international initiatives brought a new cultural mix to his films, first marked in *Match Point* (2005), which like two other productions of the next decade was set in London. During this period he also produced films in Paris, Rome, and Barcelona, polishing his reputation in Spain so successfully that there is now a Woody Allen sculpture sited on one of the boulevards of Oviedo, chief site of the action in *Vicky Christina Barcelona* (2008). Meanwhile, his controversial marriage to Soon-Yi Previn further distanced him from his well-charted New York world. In this new environment, Allen becomes increasingly less attentive to Jewish characters and Jewish themes.

The international perspective brought with it a surge of creative energy that has impelled scholars and critics to look for a paradigm to describe the films of Allen's "European Cycle." This cycle, says Richard Blake, the critic who coined the term, shows Allen in the most unhopeful mood of his career, reporting upon "a pointless universe [that] has darkened to its bleakest degree ever" (2013, 539). Robert Polhemus (2013), in his contribution to the same edited volume, speaks more positively, recognizing "a remarkable string of intellectually challenging, original films that include some of his finest work." But he sees the films of this period as a struggle to hold by a "comic faith," which is "what some witty, creative people can have—or try to have—instead of God and/or eternal bliss" (116–17). Scholar/critic John Macready finds his way into Allen's late style by gathering his films under the rubric of Allen's "exilic period," characterized by an effort "to open a new creative space in his cinema, [a space] produced by an inherent tension in the exilic experience itself—a tension between being and becoming, leaving and returning, despair and hope" (2013, 95–96).

This last formulation seems best designed to describe the dramatic action in two of Allen's most recent films, *Blue Jasmine* and *Café Society*. These situate his protagonists back in the United States, but have them shuttling awkwardly between New York and California, unsure of where to set their roots, if they have roots to set. Here, Allen's interest in recognizably

Jewish characters gives way to more generic outliers, who are "othered" by class, gender, status, and circumstance more than by ethnicity.

From the 1970s onward, Allen's films have reflected the increasing assimilation of the Jewish community into the mainstream culture of upper-middle-class New York. Beyond the intense self-consciousness of his Jewish protagonists, his New York films offer few clear markers that would separate New York Jews from rank-and-file New Yorkers. Marie Wilkie and Isaac Davis of *Manhattan* are ultimately incompatible, but not for reasons of ethnicity. Allen's change of venue in the new millennium further reduced the salience of Jewish concerns. Perhaps most importantly, the director has largely ceased to act in his own films, obviating the need to write parts for someone who had made his reputation as a "Jewish character." These circumstances freed him to investigate gender and class in *Blue Jasmine* before looking back to study Jewishness in a broader historical context in *Café Society*. In the latter film, the story of Bobby Dorfmann is imagined as a costume drama, dating from the late 1930s, a time when Jews were much less fully assimilated and much more likely to confront ethno-racial barriers or have to acknowledge their shabbier immigrant origins. The other significant difference between *Café Society* and earlier films like *Annie Hall* or *Manhattan* is the narrative structure. During the 1980s, Allen's narrator is typically an on-screen protagonist, interpreting the action from an implicitly Jewish perspective. But in *Café Society*, the narrator's persona is more ambiguous, the detached observer more than the invested participant in the action.

One consequence of Allen's vacating the role of leading man is to open up a more central place for women, especially for strong and accomplished actors, such as Melanie Griffith, Scarlett Johansson, and Penelope Cruz. The list includes Cate Blanchett, who takes center stage for a timely examination of gender-inflected themes in *Blue Jasmine*. Jasmine is another of Allen's exiles, reluctantly transplanted from New York to San Francisco in the wake of a failed marriage, premature widowhood, and a financial meltdown. Sympathetic in spite of her narcissism and delusion, Jasmine exemplifies, according to Joanna Rapf, Allen's ability to "give voice to female desire" and to "explore issues with which women struggle in late twentieth-century and early twenty-first century America" (2013, 274). Her personal catastrophe owes as much to the structural disadvantages of her female gender as to self-indulgence and misguided romantic choice.

Pretty good evidence suggests that Allen allowed Blanchett to build her own character within the broad framework that his script demands. Blanchett is a theater director in her own right, partnered with her husband in the management of the Sydney Theatre Company, Sydney, Australia. She is also an actor of great range and talent, having impersonated stage characters as various as Sophocles' Electra and David Mamet's accusatory heroine from *Oleana*. She also starred in Liv Ulmann's production of *Streetcar Named Desire*, whose heroine, Blanche DuBois, is a spiritual cousin of Jasmine. Her film credits are equally impressive, from the rugged frontier mother of *The Missing* (2003) to the reticent lesbian lover of *Carol* (2015).

Several interviews Blanchett gave shortly after the film's release make clear her great respect for Allen's creative gift but also suggest how she found in the film a place for her own sense of its distraught heroine. Relishing Allen's benign neglect of the specifics of her performance, Blanchett admired his script as a schematic, a blueprint, which left the actor free to translate her character into a full-bodied human presence. "Ninety-seven percent of his direction is in the writing," she tells *Variety*, "all those clues, and there are so many of them in a part like this, they're all in the writing. There's an incredible rhythm to the way he writes, and you have to be quite sure about changing a word because you break that rhythm" (Khatchatourian 2014). This homage to Allen notwithstanding, it's clear that Blanchett took full command of her character and articulated Jasmine very much as a character she herself had imagined. "Jasmine is a woman without any agency, without any autonomy," she tells Ella Alexander, in a wide-ranging interview with *Vogue* magazine (2013). "She has given that away to her husband, and that's what makes her current today, even in this post-feminist world." Jasmine arouses our sympathy, Blanchett insists, because she represents a calculated disempowerment far more typical of the modern woman than some are inclined to admit: "There are a lot of women out there who have given their power away to their husbands, to their brothers, to their fathers and the only way that they can see a way of getting themselves out, or reinventing themselves, is to attach themselves to another man. It's very sad" (Alexander 2013).

Speaking on another occasion to Robert Siegel for National Public Radio, Blanchett celebrated "the level of craftsmanship" in Allen's script, but felt that Allen's careful plotting set her own creative juices flowing: "What I hope I brought out in Woody's screenplay," she says, "is that Jasmine is utterly constructed" from the shining surfaces of her jewelry to her elegant home and the network of social relationships that defines her. Blanchett was fascinated by Jasmine's back story, the narrative of a woman "estranged from her biological beginnings" and persuaded to invent herself moment by moment, with no sense whatsoever of an authentic selfhood (Siegel 2014).

Building upon small hints in Allen's text, Blanchett presents the physical image of Jasmine as a collection of costumes and body parts tentatively assembled and always threatening to disintegrate. "She never had a sense of self," Blanchett says in a further interview. "The gaping chasm in her is only vaguely covered by her Chanel jacket, her logo this, and her quaffed that" (Karger 2014). Attentive to grooming, costume, and body language, Blanchett convincingly charts Jasmine's breakdown through her smeared mascara, frazzled hair, and quivering, increasingly distracted speech, all of which are in evidence when we contrast Jasmine's New York persona with "the bits she'd held onto" in her recycled San Francisco identity. But in spite of this elaborate artifice, Blanchett concludes, she sought to make the heroine "fragile and human." Allen admired what Blanchett did with the role and credits her with giving Jasmine a human dimension he probably couldn't have called forth himself: "I wasn't trying to make people like her. I think her humanity comes across because of Cate. . . . Cate is so full of humanity and complexity that you see her suffering, and you feel for her. A character like that is to be pitied. . . . Cate was able to infuse her character with a tender dimension" (Kleinmann 2013). Working in tandem, Allen and Blanchett convey a full-bodied sense of the downwardly mobile woman and the sparse proletarian world into which she falls.

In "White Woods and Blue Jasmine: Woody Allen Rewrites *Streetcar Named Desire*" (2015), Verna Foster provides one of the most careful and detailed readings Allen's film has yet received. Her insight into Jasmine's insecurity and emotional fragility is pitch perfect, as is her sense of the active revulsion Allen's heroine feels in the presence of the underclass, particularly of rude, sexually assertive males of that class. Jasmine is as viscerally uncomfortable in the presence of Ginger's (Susan Taylor) fiancé, Chili (Bobby Canavale), as was Blanche under the hostile stare of Stanley Kowalski. But this analysis falls short of understanding the contemporaneity of Jasmine. Unlike Blanche, who is a sad ghost that drifted away from Scarlett O'Hara's plantation, Jasmine is completely a creature of our time, a product of the same culture that created Jordan Belfort and the wolves of Wall Street. While Blanche is as much an anachronism as Amanda Wingfield, dreaming of her jonquil bouquets and the crowd of suitors who gathered round her at Blue Mountain, Jasmine is in most ways a perfectly modern woman, in no sense trapped in a time warp, or even seriously alienated from the modern city. When she meets Dwight (Peter Sarsgaard), the up-and-coming entrepreneur who is beginning to lay the groundwork for a political career, she knows exactly how to persuade him they would make perfect romantic partners, a power couple ready to move about in the most high-end company. Jasmine instinctively grasps that with a more robust bank account, she could mingle confidently at a celebrity fundraiser or host a wine and cheese party for a select group of her prospective husband's friends. While Blanche is a phantom from a world that died at Appomattox, Jasmine is a passenger who fell from a sleek, high-speed train that seemed to be carrying her to the Emerald City of free market capitalism.

Jasmine's tragic place in the schematic of social modernism is obliquely reflected in Katherine Newman's *Falling from Grace: Downward Mobility in the Age of Affluence* (1999), which devotes a full chapter to "middle class women in trouble" (202–28). Usually the victims of a disadvantageous divorce (in Jasmine's case, her husband's incarceration and suicide), these "once-secure women find themselves sliding right out of the middle class" (202). Though they have invested most of their lives in honing the social skills that advance their husbands, when their high-earning spouses "no longer contribute to household support, the 'female-headed' families left behind are pushed into downward mobility" (202). The death spiral is made more precipitous by the fact that these recently affluent women cannot immediately forget their earlier habits. When the self-exiled Jasmine turns up at her sister's door in San Francisco, she wildly over tips her cab driver, causing him to almost burst with unexpected glee. Later, we find that, to the utter amazement of Ginger, Jasmine has flown first-class across the continent, though she confesses to being "completely broke." The problem is that her connubial house of cards collapsed so quickly she has not fully adjusted to her new circumstances. As Jasmine puts it, "one minute you're hosting women, the next you're measuring their shoe size."

This last remark reflects Jasmine's experience as she attempts to re-enter the work force. Already when she is babbling about her life to the woman she meets on the plane, she realizes she was seriously imprudent in "leaving college before I got a degree." Now she seeks a chance to do "something substantial," scorning the suggestion that she might train as a nurse, or go to work as a receptionist. She thinks her prospective career path might involve mastering computers but realizes further education will require an upfront capital investment that she lacks the resources to make. Frustrated by the economic barriers that loom at every turn, she first scorns the thought of handling phone calls and appointments in a dental office, but soon yields to circumstance and goes to work for Dr. Flicker (Michael Stuhlbarg). Unfortunately, he first scolds her for trying to study on the job, then presses her for sexual favors that cannot be denied without explicit physical resistance. Leaving Dr. Flicker sprawled on the floor of his office, Jasmine hurries away from her first adventure in building a professional dossier. While Jasmine stumbles into her post-marital life, Ginger loyally supports her with bed and board, even though the two women have never been close and Jasmine feels she deserves more than her proletarian sibling can provide. Issues of class, gender, and cultural expectation have to be negotiated in the intimate space of family dynamics.

Though Allen has created a dramatic narrative and not a social science treatise, his analysis closely coheres with Newman's argument in *Falling from Grace*, respecting two points particularly. First, Jasmine's circumstances illustrate how the failed marriage narrative of economic calamity (as opposed, say, to loss incurred in a major economic downturn) radically personalizes abstract questions of investment, the job market, and corporate practice, rendering these issues as "forces internal to the family, cultural concepts of what the family should be—of how men and women should treat each other, of what parents owe their children and what adults can expect of their own parents" (Newman 1999, 205). In Jasmine's case, her shattered marriage alienates her completely from her son and the effort to form a new bond with her sister ultimately fails as well. Newman's second point remarks the paradox that the fallen princesses of the upper middle class often have more difficulty attaching themselves to a helpful network of friends and extended family than do refugees from failed blue collar marriages. "Middle class women," says Newman, "find themselves lacking the built-in support systems which poor women have had to maintain throughout their domestic lives. People adapt to foreseeable crisis situations; when crises are not part of the repertoire of daily experience, they are caught unaware and unprepared" (1999, 221). These judgments accurately characterize the shunning and humiliation that drive Jasmine out of New York and the difficulty she experiences in accepting the safety net that Ginger is temporarily willing to drape about her after she lands in San Francisco.

Though Allen's plotting is fundamentally linear, *Blue Jasmine* calls upon multiple flashbacks to convey the breakdown of the relationship between the two sisters, in fact, the breakdown of the nuclear family that nourished them as children. In conversational exchange we learn that both children were adopted, that their adoptive parents died young, and that the two siblings grew up knowing they were not related by blood. As Jasmine remembers these years, Ginger was always "so wild" while she was "little Miss Perfect." Even Ginger seems willing to acknowledge that Jasmine got "the good genes." Unsurprisingly, their paths went "in totally different directions." Soon both are married, Jasmine to a very wealthy investment broker, Ginger to a builder whom Jasmine sees as "just a handyman." That they have settled at opposite ends of the continent is a fitting symbol of their estrangement.

In one memorable flashback, Ginger and Augie (Andrew Dice Clay) visit Jasmine and Hal (Alec Baldwin) in New York, giving the Manhattan power couple the perfect opportunity to showcase their spectacular home, strategically exclude their poor relations from their social world, and, tragically, convey these ill-informed innocents to financial ruin. By sheer chance, Augie and Ginger have won $200,000 in the lottery and their news is that Augie will invest it in starting his own business. Instead of leaving well enough alone, Jasmine joins her hubristic husband to persuade Augie, against his better judgment, to hand over his winnings to Hal, who will invest the money in one of his projects and make Ginger and Augie rich beyond their wildest dreams. One segment of this sequence profoundly compromises Jasmine as a moral agent. While soaking in the abundant suds of her luxurious bathtub, Jasmine is given an expensive gold bracelet by her husband, obviously intended as her reward for coaxing a $200,000 investment from a couple who really have no discretionary capital to put at risk. Jasmine's giggly insistence that Hal promise to "help them make money" clearly has no credibility in the harem-like atmosphere of this setting. At this stage, Jasmine perhaps does not realize that her husband is a fraud and a criminal, but knowledgeably or not, she colludes in appropriating the lottery prize, which later is lost when Hal's business practices are exposed and prosecuted. Without fully understanding her culpability, Jasmine explodes her sister's hope of economic security, wrecks her marriage, and probably ruins her husband's life. That Ginger is still willing to befriend her sister, after this experience, is a remarkable tribute to her basic decency and to the family bond (Allen 2013, 13:00/19:30).

The spine of the film is the relationship between the two sisters, and the coping mechanisms they design to withstand the adversity visited upon both of them by the collapse of Jasmine's marriage and her husband's business empire. The task is to stabilize Jasmine's life without compromising Ginger's hard-won self-respect and modest financial security. The problematic of the sisters' relationship invites Allen to explore status, class, and gender as marginalizing forces that put both women at serious disadvantage in seeking to better their lives.

Inevitably, both women toy with new romantic relationships, again adhering to Newman's point that downwardly mobile women frequently hoped "to find white knights who would pull them out of the quagmire" (1999, 217), where divorce or widowhood had mired them. Though Ginger is prepared to perform as Jasmine's rescuer, she is barely self-sufficient herself. Her divorce from Augie, in the wake of the investment fiasco, leaves her with one grocery bagger's income to live on and two young sons to provide for. She has collected Chili as a prospective partner for remarriage, in spite of his crude manners and a propensity for violence. She sees him more as a breadwinner and male presence in the home than as her ideal romantic partner. Jasmine is mentally unhinged (as evidenced by her obsessive drinking and pill popping) but well dressed and with sophisticated social skills. Well aware of Jasmine's fragility, Ginger still sees her sister as someone from whom she might learn and reacts positively to the advice that she stop dating "losers." The search for new beginnings carries both women to a party where each finds a man who seems a potential rescuer (Allen 2013, 53:40/58:30). But as Newman would have predicted in *Falling from Grace*, Jasmine invests more in the "white knight" scenario than her streetwise sister, a trust that ultimately delivers a fatal blow to Jasmine's dream of recovery. Though Ginger is awkward and inept, she has hard-core survival skills that elude Jasmine, in spite of the New Yorker's elegant talk and superior taste.

Allen nimbly counterpoints the romantic strategies of the two women. Ginger is precipitous in attaching herself to Al (Louis C. K.), whom she knows only as "a fun-loving guy" who "brings music into people's lives." On the day of their meeting, she launches a love affair with him, conspicuously enough that word drifts back to Chili, putting their relationship in jeopardy. Jasmine is much more circumspect with Dwight, setting the stage for a long-term relationship. They meet in a room they have entirely to themselves, each having deliberately separated from the other guests, and Dwight frankly acknowledging, "I'd rather be somewhere else" (Allen 2013, 55:15/58:25). His tie and jacket set him apart from the rest of the crowd, and he immediately notices Jasmine's designer handbag and upscale wardrobe. It's a moment of instant rapport, though their ardor is disciplined, muted, and controlled by unfailing good manners. Against a backdrop that includes a memorable view of the bay and the Golden Gate Bridge, they offer each other brief accounts of their lives, which in Dwight's case includes his career in the diplomatic corps, his political aspirations, and the fact that he has just purchased a swank home in Marin County, one of the choicest locations in the Bay Area. This last detail invites Jasmine to announce that she's an interior decorator, looking to make a new start in San Francisco, after the untimely death of her husband, a respected surgeon. In her account of herself, Jasmine claims a station she only aspires to, conceals the existence of her son, and extracts her husband's reputation from the morass of criminality, prison, and suicide. In spite of its duplicity and deception, the narrative succeeds admirably and Jasmine finds herself invited to Dwight's new home, where her expert eye will be called upon to advise him with the furnishings.

The scene at Dwight's home is sharp in its delineation of Jasmine's self-deception. Spacious and full of light, it immediately puts us in mind of Jasmine's sumptuous quarters in New York, which so impressed Augie and Ginger when they visited. Its patio is particularly striking, sun-drenched and open, much like the one Hal had provided for his much-indulged wife. It's also the diametric opposite of Ginger's more downscale apartment, where the rooms are too small, the walls too thin, and the décor is gaudy and overstated, what Jasmine called "homey" in a strained effort to be polite. The fact that Dwight's house is almost empty spontaneously prompts Jasmine to imagine herself in charge of it, making decisions about color and décor. It's where she is convinced she belongs. The home visit is the start of a whirlwind courtship that includes strolls through antique shops, affectionate moments in the car, and Jasmine's naïve assurance to Dwight, "I think when something's right you know it immediately." But for the moment everything falls into place and their next date will be a trip to the jeweler to pick out Jasmine's engagement ring (Allen 2013, 01:05:00/01:07:10).

What quickly follows is the cruel unraveling of Jasmine's grandiose plans, a piece of bad luck that dissolves the gauzy fantasy in which she has wrapped herself. Allen's universe is one of chance and happenstance, where sheer accident counts for more than careful design. The off-screen narrator of *Match Point* remarks at the outset that people are afraid to face how great a part of life is dependent upon luck. Later that point is underscored in the action as Chris Wilton gets away with murder because a ring that he has attempted to throw into the Thames bounces back from the top of a retaining wall in circumstances that incriminate the wrong man and direct suspicion away from the real killer. In *Blue Jasmine*, the much more innocent heroine is made guilty by the random appearance of Augie, Ginger's ex-husband, who rounds a corner with lethal precision to confront Dwight and Jasmine in front of the jewelry store, where they've come to buy her engagement ring. Had he come to that corner ten seconds earlier or later, there would have been no discovery and a radically different outcome for Jasmine's life. Augie, we discover, is in on his way to Alaska to help lay an oil pipeline, but this brief moment before his leaving is sufficient for a parting shot at Jasmine, whom he still blames (with some cause) for wrecking his life. Though Dwight is not directly caught up in the conversation, he can't avoid hearing about Jasmine's son, her husband's suicide, and the shady business transactions that sent him to prison. In spite of Jasmine's gasping explanations and apologies, the white knight hurriedly drives away, leaving the damsel in distress alone at the curbside, thrashing about to pick up the assorted items that have fallen from her purse.

Remarkably, Ginger's fate is quite different, in spite of her equally imprudent behavior. She, too, is disappointed by her new lover, who turns out to be a married man, looking for recreational sex and not a new partnership. Daunted but not dismayed, she quickly reconciles with Chili, invites him into the house to replace Jasmine, and hints that wedding bells will soon be ringing. Her safety net is efficiently mended, while Jasmine's continues to fray. The difference is that the more proletarian sister is accustomed to living close to disaster and better prepared to recognize and deal with it when it arrives.

Summing up the issue of "downward mobility in the age of affluence," Newman concludes that the victims of this process "do, for the most part, grope their way to stability," though it is a "stability devoid of promise, short of comfort, and surrounded by the feeling that there is little in life that one can rely on" (1999, 238). This outcome describes the fate of Ginger, but Jasmine's future looks much darker. The last moment of her disintegration comes when she visits her son in Oakland, only to find that he has completely renounced her, blaming her for the family catastrophe more strenuously than he blames his father. This response is paradoxical, since his father was the criminal and Jasmine no worse than an enabler. But the judgment springs, it would seem, from the gender-inflected point that Jasmine's exposure of her husband's crimes has nothing to do with justice and everything to do with her status as the jilted geisha. What Daniel finds unforgivable in his mother's behavior is that she seeks to punish her husband's chronic infidelity and ultimate desertion, not his unlawful business practices. Though Jasmine deserves to be judged harshly, she herself is something of a victim, fatally compromised by male dominance.

Linking white privilege and male privilege, Peggy McIntosh (2003) describes social advantage as "an invisible weightless knapsack of special privileges, assurances, tools, maps, guides, codebooks, passports, visas, clothes, compass, emergency gear, and blank checks" (148). These, she says, are the unearned assets of whiteness, though particularly male whiteness, which takes for granted "the inevitability of present gender relations and distributions of power" (149). In practice this means that many women gain and hold power through powerful men, whom they serve as wives or professional subordinates. Turning to herself, McIntosh notes, "most people I meet will see my marital arrangements as an asset to my life or as a favorable comment on my likeability, my competence, or my mental health" (158). Jasmine is a woman who has reaped impressive rewards from her "marital arrangements." As we see Jasmine luxuriating in her queenly bubble bath while she receives the golden bracelet from her husband, we should remember that her husband also bought her the bathtub, the upscale appointments of the room, the home itself, and the prime real estate on which it sits. Although she seems incredibly well situated, her power is illusory, fictive, the product of an unwritten contract never to challenge the judgment of her husband. On the one occasion when she questions his business practices, Hal's response is a version of, "Don't worry your pretty little head." The contract also includes a blind eye toward Hal's copious infidelities. What changes is the threat of divorce and desertion. When Hal speaks of "making plans" with his latest mistress, Jasmine rebels and plays whistle-blower, seeming not to realize the consequences this holds for her and her son.

The tragedy of Jasmine is that she is actually a woman of considerable talent, as Blanchett conveys in performing the role. Ginger is correct in recognizing her sister's aptitude for interior design and imagining that under other circumstances she might have turned this gift into a profitable career. Her character is flawed by a propensity to conceal and contrive, which compromises her ability to keep the trust of colleagues, friends, and family. But Jasmine is also the victim of the alpha male, seduced by the aura of invincibility that is one of the conspicuous badges of white privilege. In expanding his culture critique beyond ethnicity into the realm of gender, Allen has found a new theme to explore—the waste of intelligence and creative energy that results from forced exile, whether one is pushed to the edge by gender, class, or ethnicity. This point is not lost on the writer/director as he returns to his contemplation of American Jewry in *Café Society*.

If *Blue Jasmine* is a story of lethal exile, a plunge into the abyss of isolation and madness, *Café Society* is a tale of an exile's return. Bobby Jacob Dorfmann deliberately expatriates himself from the spare Jewish enclave in New York where he grew up, in order to build a career amid the glitz of Hollywood's golden age. Disappointed in love as well as with the celluloid dream factory, he returns to New York in a chastened state of mind, but ready for a new beginning, which ultimately achieves the "difficult redemption" that Macready sees as the principal concern in Allen's exilic period (2013, 101). Like most of Allen's best films, *Café Society* is a drama of human relationships that in this case reworks his analysis of American Jewry in a broader historical frame and with peripheral vision wide enough to catch many interrelated themes. Among these is Dorfmann's ability to "stage" his Jewishness so as to make it acceptable to a culture that has begun to unlearn its residual anti-Semitism but still is in the thrall of many surprisingly retrograde tendencies. Revisiting the Jewish family and its mixed bag of offspring, Allen also operates with more detachment than in his deeply personal New York films of the seventies, eighties, and nineties, farming out the aspiring celebrity role to the talented young Jewish actor Jesse Eisenberg. *Café Society* celebrates Bobby Dorfmann's largely triumphal return to New York. In a certain sense, it also celebrates Allen's return from his own place of exile.

Café Society begins with a lower-middle-class Jewish family, comical in its intramural bickering, but united in its concerted effort to advance its members by any means necessary. Rose (Jeannie Berlin), the stereotypical Jewish mother, sends her prize son Bobby to Hollywood, hoping her brother Phil Stern (Steve Carell) will show him the way to the celebrity and success he himself has enjoyed. Here she must override the protests of her husband, who insists, correctly, Stern "is not a Jewish man." Indeed, Phil Stern has turned his back on everything that might even hint at his Jewish lineage. As Bobby enters upon his new life, brother Ben (Corey Stoll), the gangster sibling, gives him tips on how to be street-wise, along with pocket money and the phone numbers of contacts who can provide him with prostitutes, any time his young-manly urges get the upper hand. Sister Evelyn (Sari Lennick), the Jewish schoolmarm, writes him encouraging letters, striking a moral tone that would leave Ben politely amused. Bobby's discredited father, who must feel somewhat humiliated by his son's abandonment of both his Jewishness and the marginal family business, seems to accept the general disregard for his opinions, not challenging Rose's succinctly negative verdict, "You're stupid." Stern, the Hollywood power broker and the family's one success story (his name in German means "star"), is visibly put off by Rose's phone call and defensively asks, "How did you get my number?" But despite his annoyance at the cheekiness of his poor relations in the Bronx, "Uncle Phil" is soon on board with Rose's plan for Bobby's advancement, extending himself rather energetically to find work for young Dorfmann and introduce him to people who know how to open doors. In Bobby's difficult hour, the vaunted Jewish sense of community, deeply rooted in the extended family, plays a decisive role in pushing forward their favorite son.

The family's determination to secure for Bobby the affluence and status they might barely dream of coincides, ironically, with a moment in American cultural history when Jews were suffering mightily at the hands of the hegemonic class, which in the late 1930s was preaching a political gospel of Anglo-Nordic superiority. The prevailing ethno-racial bigotry was directed primarily toward Jews and Southern Europeans, taking the abstract form of a racialized anthropology but extending into the practical realm of immigration quotas and border control, efficient tools of intimidation and exclusion.

In *City of Dreams*, Tyler Anbinder devotes a full chapter to the restrictions imposed upon immigrants by the National Origins Act of 1924, which he considers "one of the most momentous laws enacted in all of American history" (2016, 468). Intended explicitly to deny citizenship to Italians, Sicilians, and Eastern European Jews, chiefly from Russia and Poland, the statute's quota system reduced immigration from the targeted nations to approximately one-tenth of what it had been before its enactment (469). Inspired by the eugenics movement and an upsurge of xenophobia in the aftermath of World War I, the Congress of this era yielded to the alarmist conclusions of public intellectuals like Madison Grant, who wrote furiously in *The Passing of the Great Race* (1921) against the threat to national identity posed by the "the hyphenated-aliens in our midst" (xxxii). Convinced of the "immutability of psychic predispositions and impulses," he raged against "the folly of the Melting Pot theory," insisting that any ethnic hybridizing outside of the Nordic lineage would result in the production of a "mongrel race" (xxvii). Closed borders were the nation's last line of defense, borders closed particularly against "Jews, whose dwarf stature, peculiar mentality, and ruthless concentration of self-interest are being engrafted upon the stock of the nation" (16). In his nightmare vision, true Americans were being "driven off the streets of

New York by swarms of Polish Jews" (91), threatening the nation in the same way that Syrian mongrels had brought down classical Rome and blacks had racially polluted the Confederate South. As Grant would have it, this drastic breach of racial hygiene was turning metropolitan America into "a kind of cloaca gentium, which will produce . . . ethnic horrors it will be beyond the powers of future anthropologists to unravel" (99).

Grant's anxiety so captured the public mood that his book went through four editions between 1916 and 1936. In the post-1924 editions, he even congratulated his Anglo-Nordic comrades for the racialized quotas they had imposed to restrict the immigration of Jews, Poles, and other undesirables. By this time widespread anti-Semitic feeling had led to similar quotas in law schools and medical schools as well as an all-embracing suspicion of Jewish influence upon public life. This last point touches Bobby Dorfmann and his Uncle Phil, cultural aliens who seek to make their mark on a world in which the Jew is suspect.

Steven Carr in *Hollywood and Anti-Semitism* (2001) pursues the various ways in which the new spirit of "scientific" racism reinforced centuries of Christian prejudice against the Jews as "Christ-killers" and deceitful moneylenders. Conveniently, these sentiments received further support from the broad circulation of *The Protocols of the Elders of Zion*, a notorious forgery that testified to the existence of an international Jewish conspiracy against Christian culture. Spurred by these pseudo facts, one short-lived institution of the 1930s called the Anti-Communist Federation of America published posters seeking "Christian Vigilantes," who would boycott the movies," because the industry was controlled by "international Jewry" and "young Gentile girls are raped by Jewish producers, directors, [and] casting directors, who go unpunished" (quoted in Carr 2001, 112).

Religious zealots of all sorts lent their individual voices to the same crusade, united in their fear that a Jewish-dominated entertainment industry might degrade the moral fiber of small-town America. Fr. Charles Caughlin, a Roman Catholic priest, preached a virulent anti-Semitic message via his CBS radio show, hammering home the theme of Jewish control of mass media. Evangelical Christians performed in kind, none more doggedly than two disgruntled Hollywood writers, William Pelley and Kenneth Alexander. Both complained that Jewish producers, obsessed with the bodies of gentile women, had altered their scripts in the direction of prurience and sexual innuendo. Generalizing their personal experience through references to the *Protocols*, they insisted that every scandal and breach of sexual etiquette was evidence of a systematic effort to undermine the foundations of Christian civilization. As Alexander concluded, "Jews have penetrated all fields of entertainment to the point of saturation, but in Hollywood their domination is the most complete of all" (quoted in Carr 2001, 123).

Carr's analysis of the pushback against Jewish "interests" in Hollywood is completely congruent with the argument Neil Gabler conducts in *An Empire of Their Own* (1988), a careful examination of "how the Jews invented Hollywood." In fact, his description of the industry's founders makes clear they were of exactly the same ethno-racial stock as the "undesirables" that Madison Grant and the architects of the National Origins Act had intended to keep out of the country. "The Hollywood Jews," says Gabler, "at least the first generation that built the industry and form the core of this book, were a remarkably homogeneous group with remarkably similar childhood experiences" (3). Most were Eastern European: Adolf Zukor, founder of Paramount, came from a small village in Hungary; William Fox, who stamped his name on another major studio, was also Hungarian; Louis Mayer, the loudest of the roaring lions at MGM, was another creature of East Europe, hailing from a small town in Russia whose name he could not or chose not to remember; the Warners' lineage was Polish, the ethnic group whose deleterious influence upon American culture most worried Grant and the eugenicists when they contemplated "the passing of the great race."

Using the ties of their extended families to bind their resources together, the Jewish moguls defeated the Edison Company in the battle over patents and went on to create a vertical monopoly of production, distribution, and exhibition. This nearly airtight structure allowed them to divide up, among about half a dozen major studios, a rapidly expanding and hugely profitable mass media market. As Gabler concludes: "What gave each studio its distinctive personality was an elaborate calculus of economic circumstance, the location of its theaters, tradition, geography, and a hundred other things, but most of all it was the product of the personality of the man or men who owned and ran it. The moguls made the studios in their images to actualize their own dreams" (1988, 189).

What is paradoxical here, as Gabler remarks, is that these media entrepreneurs advanced their interests in the face of powerful prejudices against Jews, a situation that required the erasure of all explicit references to Jewishness in the Hollywood product. This practice persisted into the generation after the founding, when Mayer, Zukor, and Fox began to cede power to the new generation of more fully assimilated Jewish producers, like Irving Thalberg and David Selznick. The Hollywood Dream Factory produced the "American Dream," not the Jewish American Dream. There are no Jews hanging out with Andy Hardy or joining Dorothy on the Yellow Brick Road. Gabler drives home this paradox by noting that none of the country clubs in metro Los Angeles accepted Jewish members: "not the Lakeside Country Club, which was adjacent to the Warner Brothers Studio in Burbank; not the Los Angeles Country Club, which was a stone's throw from Fox Studios; not even the Santa Monica Beach Club, which was just down the road from Jesse Lasky's and Louis Mayer's homes" (273). The price of Jewish success in the industry was a low profile and a carefully crafted "Americanist" identity.

The protagonists of *Café Society*, Bobby Dorfmann and Phil Stern, have learned these lessons well. Even before he has met his celebrity uncle, Bobby has had his own introduction to code switching, when he is visited by "Candy" (Anna Camp), the young prostitute he has summoned to his quarters, using one of the phone numbers provided by his brother Ben. Candy is actually Shirley Garfinkel, a girl from Brooklyn, who has cast off her Jewish surname and dyed her hair blond. Their encounter goes badly, in part because Bobby seems embarrassed by their ethnic affinity and also by the fact that she is clearly uncomfortable in her new role, taking it up only because "my acting career wasn't going very well." Their prospective intimacy never recovers from Bobby's startled question / observation, "You're a Jew?" Uncle Phil has similar problems with his ethnic roots, but generally covers them more gracefully. He lives in a white stucco, art-deco style home, redolent of affluence but not gaudy or pretentious. He is annoyed by Rose's impertinent phone call, which he receives when he's expecting to hear from Ginger Rogers. And it distresses him even more that his Jewish family is burdening him with Bobby: "What the hell is he coming out here for?" But after berating his sister for a phone call that's "costing you an arm and a leg," he honors family obligations by making Bobby into his personal assistant and soon introduces him to industry contacts that are on the Sterns guest lists, some of them professionally valuable (Allen 2016, 01:40/04:05). After he meets Bobby, the only point he insists on is, "Stop with the uncle stuff—we don't want to advertise the nepotism." It's obvious that Phil has worked diligently to craft a gentile identity, which connects him to the movie-making colony, not to down-at-the-heels Jews from the south Bronx. His social skills make him Bobby's role model for professional behavior, but Bobby preserves closer ties to his blood family than his better-situated uncle.

The most obvious thing about Phil Stern is his absolute alienation from his relatives in the Bronx. Whatever there is of a personal relationship between him and Bobby, it never includes a mention of Rose's family or any memories of childhood that might recall the sidewalks of New York. Instead, the high-powered Hollywood agent has invested all his energy in building a surrogate family out of the business associates who populate his private world. His social skills are displayed to advantage at the parties he and his wife Karen regularly host for their many "friends." Seemingly childless, though he once speaks of his children, and in a marriage that will soon collapse, Phil presides over these gatherings as if the guests were cousins or siblings, taking his cue from the behavior of Louis Mayer toward the stars at MGM. Home and office lose their meaning as separate spheres. At one of the get-togethers he boasts that he discovered Paul Muni and soon may be representing Ginger Rogers. At another he assures a guest that Joan Blondell and Greta Garbo are somewhere circulating about. He talks to Bobby about Joel McCrea as if he were a personal friend. In the most fully articulated scene at his home the festivities sprawl over several floors and spread across an enormous patio, which gives Bobby's mentor the chance to weave smoothly among numerous partygoers, mixing business with pleasure, and eliding the roles of benevolent guardian and polished master of ceremonies. It also gives Bobby a chance to watch his moves, later adapting them to his own needs when he takes over management of his older brother's nightclub. We also see Bobby cultivating a friendship with Rad (Parker Posey), a New Yorker like himself, who runs a modeling agency in Manhattan. No hint of Jewishness inserts itself into Phil's parties, except that the highly observant Bobby notes, "it's the first time in my life I've ever had champagne with bagels and lox." To which his new friend, Rad, sharing the joke replies, "That's Hollywood" (Allen 2016, 21:50/25:40).

It is the case, however, that Phil also has a secret life, apart from his role as master of the revels. He craves and courts the mysterious Vonnie (Kristen Stewart), his secretary, seemingly an innocent prairie flower from Nebraska, to whom he has assigned the task of orienting Bobby to Hollywood. Though she impresses Bobby as a breath of fresh air in a chokingly artificial environment, she has no qualms about involving herself with a married man or in lying to Bobby in order to conceal her lover's secret. What Phil hasn't counted on is that Bobby will fall in love with Vonnie, who responds to his romantic affection sufficiently to cause her second thoughts about her relationship to Bobby's uncle. She is the most puzzling character in the film and the focal point of Allen's attention to themes of loyalty, family, and belonging.

Vonnie instantly fascinates Bobby, as she proves herself the knowledgeable Hollywood insider, but somehow one who stands outside the show business mystique. When he asks her which house in Beverly Hills she would choose to live in, she surprises him by saying she prefers her present home by the beach, where she can easily overlook the ocean. The overblown mansions of the stars, she tells him, usually just signify overblown egos. When they go out to dinner, she picks a small Mexican eatery that serves good tacos, and when she offers to fix dinner herself, it's spaghetti and meatballs, not a fancy French soufflé. Vonnie exudes spontaneity and naturalness, though confesses she is "just the same as every other girl in this town, same ambitions." Briefly, a window of opportunity opens for Bobby as Phil tells Vonnie he can't leave his wife and that he is breaking off their relationship. This news projects Bobby into a whirlwind courtship that involves intimate moments on the beach, serial visits to famous picture palaces, and finally a proposal of marriage. Unfortunately, from Bobby's standpoint, Phil changes his mind about the divorce, contemptuously dismisses Bobby as a rival suitor ("Where the hell's he going?"), and claims Vonnie as his new bride, who suddenly becomes a very rich woman. The rupture of their romance sends Bobby back to New York to heal his wounds, rejoin his family, and rebuild his life.

To a certain degree, Bobby's return to New York occasions a recovery of his Jewishness, at least as it is mediated by his family and touches upon Jewish habits and the Jewish conscience. He comes during Passover and dines with his parents and siblings as they celebrate what Rose calls her "Seder." It is a completely secular event, with no prayers, no ceremonial garments or food, and no Elijah Cup at the open door to welcome the stranger. It's simply a family dinner. But it resembles a Seder, as the conversation turns upon ethical themes and interrogates behavior. The theme is Uncle Phil's desertion of his wife and children. Rose's husband, Marty (Ken Stott), who again charges that Phil is "not a Jewish man," is most aggressive in condemning his brother-in-law: "What kind of man throws out his wife of twenty-five years and runs off with his twenty-five-year old secretary?" He wants respect for "loyalty" and "character." Evelyn is of the same turn of mind, insisting, "a wife is not like a car, you don't just trade her in for the latest model." Evelyn's bookish husband, Leonard (Stephen Kunken), adds his abstract wisdom, muttering something about "the premise of common humanity." Ironically, whatever support the transgressive couple receives comes from Bobby, who comments that Vonnie is "very lovely" and the new love relationship might be "good for Phil." Though in this scene he plays devil's advocate, the conservative moral stance of the family ultimately has a bearing on his own behavior when Vonnie unexpectedly re-enters his life several years later (Allen 2016, 51:30/54:15).

Bobby's psychic recovery is bound up with his immense success in running his older brother's nightclub, which he renames and redecorates on the good advice he gets from Rad, his favorite friend from Hollywood. She also introduces him to Veronica Hayes (Blake Lively), another "Vonnie" who turns up in his life, as if a providential symbol of a second chance. By the time he meets Veronica, Les Tropiques is already famous as the "in" place for music and dining in Manhattan, and Bobby, plying the same self-promotional skills as his uncle Phil, is apparently the best known maître d' in the borough. It's interesting, though, that he chooses to include his Jewishness in the representation of himself, even applying it strategically as a means to project an aura of magic and mystery. Unlike Alvy Singer in *Annie Hall*, Bobby Dorfmann sees his Jewishness as an asset to his public persona more than a perpetual source of anxiety.

Undoubtedly, New York in the late 1930s was friendlier to Jews than Los Angeles, simply because of the demographics, but the generic taboos

were fully operative in both locales. When Bobby visits Rad and her husband at their suburban estate just outside New York City, she reminds
him that the golf course he has spoken of joining doesn't admit members
"who have been circumcised." The ethno-racial protocols of the time require formal acceptance of the restrictions, but the unspoken assumption
is that sophisticated people know the exclusions are slightly ridiculous.
This state of affairs is pertinent to Bobby's fast-paced courtship of Veronica, which is transacted largely in one very late evening (actually early
morning) at a black jazz club. The relevant conversation begins with Veronica confessing she is a liberal Democrat and hopes that doesn't disturb
her escort. Bobby responds that New York Jews, like himself, are predictably Democrats, which persuades Veronica to say, "that plays right into
my rebellious streak." She goes on to add, "I didn't see a Jew till I came
to New York, and in Oklahoma we weren't even allowed to mingle with
Jews. . . . You guys are money-lenders." Instead of taking offense, or trying to explain and rebut, Bobby jovially accepts the premise, remarking,
"Yes, we control everything, actually." But then notes that he has "no
horns." Undaunted, she continues to celebrate his fascinating otherness:
"I find Jews exotic, mysterious, and I wouldn't mind if you had horns."
She knows most of this is in jest, but seems more in earnest when she says,
"It's true what they say, you people really are pushy." Bobby clearly en-
joys the exchange and has the perfect comeback: "It's part of my charm"
(Allen 2016, 58:00/01:01:05).

Later, Veronica is assimilated into the Jewish family, albeit a completely
secular one. At the outset, it's not clear what she expects from her new
relationship, because she seems surprised that Bobby is interested in marrying her, even after she becomes pregnant with their first child. In fact,
she offers to terminate the pregnancy with a quick trip to Mexico, but is
dissuaded by Bobby who suggests that their destination really should be
Niagara Falls. A little less romantically, they settle for a wedding at City
Hall, but it's a major family event, particularly for Bobby's family, all of
whom attend and pose for the iconic group photo. Similarly, the birth
and homecoming of daughter Susan is a festive, ceremonial occasion, attended by Rose and Evelyn, who gather round the baby basket to rejoice
at the arrival of the young niece and grandchild. The contentious ethnicities blend, apparently with no friction.

Bobby is also bound to his family through Les Tropiques, which—like
his Jewish "exoticism"—garners word-of-mouth celebrity by seeming slightly illicit, probably because of its association with his gangster
brother, "Benny from the streets." The club also draws politicos, business
executives, gossipmongers, and tainted celebrities who come to dine and
dance with their trophy wives and bejeweled girlfriends. Bobby is expert
at managing this diverse clientele, soon displacing his brother as the real

proprietor of the club. This transfer of power becomes complete when Benny's criminality is exposed and he is charged with murder. Strangely, this too adds to the cachet of Bobby's nightspot and his own reputation as a *macher* in the social world. Meanwhile he serves the family dutifully, securing legal counsel for his threatened brother and later, after the conviction, trying to convince him he should be buried in a Jewish cemetery, instead of converting to Roman Catholicism. Ben's last days before his execution are a grotesque parody of second-rate 1930s gangster movies, but they show the Jewish family closing ranks around its imperiled son. This loyalty to familial commitments is at the core of Bobby's reluctant resistance to the overtures of Vonnie, when she unexpectedly reappears in the last twist of Allen's plot.

Spending a few weeks in New York en route to several European destinations, Phil and Vonnie pass an evening at Les Tropiques, perhaps because it's a famous destination or perhaps because Vonnie presses her husband for a chance to renew her friendship with Bobby. As they are reacquainted, some of the old fire flares up, though Bobby resents the extent to which his prairie flower has adopted the manner and patois of the Hollywood wife. Yet when she is apart from her husband, she reverts to her earlier identity and they again feel drawn to each other. This leads to one long evening together and a renewal of romantic affection that includes a special dinner and a lovingly protracted carriage ride through Central Park. Indeed, virtually everything except physical consummation. It's obvious that Bobby still prefers his former girlfriend to his present wife, now pregnant with their second child. Significantly, however, he won't let his passion compromise his husbandly behavior. When he returns home from his tryst with Vonnie, he presents his wife with a large bouquet of red roses, explaining only that he hasn't given her any presents recently. She asks if he has ever been unfaithful, and he asks why this question has come up. She claims she dreamed he "slept with [his] old girlfriend," to which he replies, "Dreams are dreams."

We know that this dream will linger forever in Bobby's imagination: Vonnie's face is momentarily superimposed upon Bobby's own, as they ring in the New Year on separate continents and in totally different life worlds. But Bobby's commitment to home and family, really his indestructible Jewish conscience, won't allow him to act on the feelings he continues to have for his lost love.

Café Society could serve as a capstone for Allen's reflections on Jewish culture in New York City as well as a fantasia upon motifs from his earlier New York films. Vonnie recalls Annie Hall as the tantalizing *shickse* who hovers unforgettably, just beyond reach; the festive New Year's Eve party, which suggests loss as well as promise, harks back to *Radio Days*, with its image of Joey's Aunt Bea sitting alone by the radio, wishing she had a permanent partner, so she could join the dancers and romancers at the King Cole Room; Allen's love letter to the city recovers the tone of *Manhattan* and leaves Bobby Dorfmann in the same frame of mind as Isaac Davis: "New York was his city and it always would be." But the action in *Café Society* is a little less flamboyant, the mood a little darker and more resigned. Musing on his contorted relationship with "Aunt Vonnie," Bobby remarks that "life is a comedy written by a sadistic comedy writer." His hyper-intellectual brother-in-law, Leonard, makes much the same point in more philosophical language: "Socrates said the unexamined life is not worth living. But the examined one is no bargain either." Bobby assimilates comfortably to his multi-ethnic world and enjoys the fruits of his entrepreneurial success. He also seems genuinely fond of Veronica and glad that his life includes marriage and family. But this doesn't ease his yearning for what might have been, if blind luck had smiled on him or there had been a more favorable conjunction of the stars.

Allen's stoicism is also reflected in his present view of Jewishness and the stress of living in a world that still sees Jews as the problematic "other." Asked about anti-Semitism in a recent interview with *The Guardian*, Allen said simply, "it's in the nature of people to have someone to scapegoat." He added that "Freud said there would always be anti-Semitism because people are a sorry lot. And they are a sorry lot" (Shoard 2016). That said, he doesn't see Jews as the unique victims of ethno-racial hostility, rather as fulfilling a broader paradigm in which difference and otherness inevitably provoke unease, suspicion, and sometimes explicit hostility. Were there no Jews, he observes, the dreaded other would be blacks, or Catholics, or whoever else might play the scapegoat role. Like their creator, Allen's protagonists are increasingly at peace with their Jewishness, as it slowly morphs into a trans-ethnic modernism: Alvy Singer is close to hysteria as he tries to cope with Annie's insensitive family and the wastes of rural Wisconsin; Bobby Dorfmann meets and masters both Nebraska and Oklahoma, untroubled that people from these far-flung places might put mayonnaise on corned beef sandwiches. He also handles California greatly better than Alvy, though he too leaves no doubt that he much prefers New York.

From his present vantage point, Allen would probably accept Zygmunt Bauman's conclusion that the current consensus in the United States is "allosemitic," meaning that the Greek prefix "allo," or "other," more accurately describes prevailing attitudes toward Jews than "anti," though the more neutral term still sets the Jews "apart as a people radically different from all the others, needing special concepts to describe and comprehend them and special treatment in all or most social intercourse" (1998, 143). Bauman sees this attitude as slightly disquieting, in spite of its seeming neutrality, because it casts the Jew as "someone that does not fit the structure of the orderly world, does not fall easily into any of the established categories, emits therefore contradictory signals as to the proper conduct—and in the result blurs the borderlines that ought to be kept watertight" (144). In most of his social behavior, Bobby is trying to neutralize such feelings, as when he assures Veronica that he doesn't have horns and that perhaps she shouldn't treat him as an exotic. This issue is left open in the last scene of *Café Society* as Bobby is separated from the revelers at Les Tropiques by being lost in his private musings. But he has blended almost completely into the Anglo-Nordic world, at least in the advancement of his public professional career. And he has achieved this place for himself, without disowning his Jewish family of origin with whom he continues in contact.

Characterizing Hollywood's "image of the Jew" at the moment of Allen's emergence as a major American film director, Lester Friedman credited him with "a sense of the absurd and a knowledge of contemporary philosophical thought" (1982, 274) that allowed him to create more realistic and more complex portraits of the Jew than had previously appeared on American screens. Four decades later, we can now see that, in addition to fashioning these vivid individual personae, Allen has also charted the trajectory of Jewish culture through the twentieth century, recording its hesitant but relentless integration into mainstream American society.

THREE

Spike Lee

When Spike Lee began to produce films in New York in the mid-1980s, critics and scholars saluted him as part of a new wave of African American talent that was reviving independent black filmmaking after the blaxploitation films of the 1970s had run their course and a new generation, a film school generation, actually, was ready to make its mark. Arriving at this moment, Lee gained support and professional traction from the valuable precedents in independent production set by directors like Scorsese and Allen, as well as new initiatives from the black community represented by filmmakers such as Charles Burnet, Julie Dash, and Robert Townsend. The NYU Tisch School of the Arts provided an even more decisive assist to Lee's career by promoting work he produced en route to his degree, notably *Joey's Bed-Stuy Barbershop: We Cut Heads* (1983). This sixty-minute slice of black urban life won a prize for student filmmaking and premiered at Lincoln Center, showcased as representing the accomplishments of "New Directors." The film program at NYU also introduced Lee to Ernest Dickerson, a black classmate, who immediately distinguished himself as a cameraman and performed as director of photography for all of Lee's early features, before moving on to his own career as a director. Soon Lee would found his own production company, Forty Acres and a Mule Filmworks, Inc., which now does business from a choice location in the increasingly gentrified Green Park neighborhood of Brooklyn.

Lee's self-assigned role as a politically engaged black filmmaker quickly drew critical attention. In *Framing Blackness* (1993) Ed Guerrero named him as a promising black director whom he hoped would "frankly explore the great unspeakable repressed topic of American cultural life: race and racism" (146). Manthia Diawara in *Black American Cinema* (1993) placed Lee among a small cadre of independent black filmmakers who were providing "alternative ways of knowing Black people that differ from the fixed stereotypes of Blacks in Hollywood" (7). Diawara was also impressed by his shooting and editing style, borrowed in part from Scorsese and new wave French directors like Jean-Luc Godard.

197

Certainly Lee has set ambitious tasks for himself over the past three decades, though not always to the complete satisfaction of himself or his critics. Guerrero complains that Lee has been too eager to learn "the conventions and clichés of market cinema language" (1993, 148) and Amiri Baraka indicts him for responding to "the vibes of NY pop art, NYU film school chic" (Diawara 1993, 148). More sympathetically, Paula Massood in *Black City Cinema* (2003) credits Lee with a "rearticulation of the Black Urbanscape," which includes location shooting as well as "references to the fashions, urban patois, and politics (such as black nationalism) contemporaneous with African American urban experience" (117). Of particular importance to Massood has been Lee's "shifting of East Coast city films from Harlem, the black cultural mecca of the past, to the borough of Brooklyn, a move that acknowledges larger African American demographic shifts that took place during and after World War II and that underscores Brooklyn's geographic significance for present-day African American cultural life" (121). This quest for authenticity is perfectly consistent with the compromises Lee has made with backers and studio executives to secure fiscal support and distribution arrangements for films that might seem to challenge prevailing racial codes. From this standpoint, Lee's work is an ongoing negotiation of the changing relationship not only between African American culture and the corporate class, but also between black culture and various "off-white" subcultures, particularly Jewish and Italian.

While Lee has gained much from the greater openness to independent filmmaking that has characterized American cinema since the 1970s, he has also been constrained by the conservative drift of American politics during the 1980s and beyond. Film historians have often remarked the turn toward masculinity, patriarchy, and militarism during this period (*Top Gun* and the Rambo vehicles come quickly to mind) as well as the implicit racism of the Rocky Balboa cycle, a sure fire moneymaker from the mid-1970s through the 1990s. This rightward inflection of commercial taste that marked the Reagan era marginalized all minority cultures, as did the recuperation of power by the studios, now restructured as finance managers and distributors, with censorial power over filmmakers they support. Hence Lee's problems with the financing of his first commercial release, the low-budget story of a young black woman with artistic ambition and an expansive sexual appetite. *She's Gotta Have It* (1986) seemed seriously at odds with mainstream sensibilities of the period, radical enough that the New York State Council on the Arts withdrew an $18,000 grant they had awarded Lee, when he replaced the first script he had proposed with this more daring exploration of female agency (see Aftab and Lee 2006, 35–64). Speaking of his financing, Lee says, "We had to put the money together nickel by nickel, it was one of the hardest things I ever had to do" (41). Staying one step ahead of his creditors and poaching the skills of his talented family (Bill Lee, his father, composed the music and played a minor role, as did his sister Joie), Lee created a rough cut credible enough to attract a few private investors. With this combination of private backers and another $10,000 from the Jerome Foundation, totaling approximately $175,000, Lee finished the film in time to get it placed in the Cannes Festival, after which time he contracted for distribution through Island Pictures. Despite the vestigial stigma of race and the adverse political climate, Spike Lee was launched into filmmaking.

SEGMENT 1: CONTESTED TERRAIN: *DO THE RIGHT THING* (1989) AND *JUNGLE FEVER* (1991)

While Scorsese and Allen have constructed ethnicity largely as a relatively smooth assimilative process, concentrating on what implications it holds for Italians and Jews in a multicultural society, the persistent racial taboos in contemporary America have almost inevitably dictated that Lee would construe ethnicity in adversarial terms, always imagining black culture competing against rival ethno-racial minorities as well as against the hegemonic class, which still manipulates most of the levers of power. Aptly, Catherine Pouzoulet (1997) speaks of the "territorial inscription" (33) of Lee's films, which implies his determination both to situate his production company in the borough where he lives and to use neighborhoods familiar to him as sites for staging the urban African American experience. As William Grant reports, respecting the financing and production of *Do the Right Thing*, Lee was determined to write into his contract with Universal the provision that the film be shot on location, in the near neighborhood of Forty Acres and a Mule Filmworks, so that he and his associates could build the film sets into the living world of Bedford-Stuyvesant. He also bargained sharply to retain control of the final cut and to secure a budget (ultimately about $6.5 million) sufficient to give the film a fully professional look (see Grant 1997, 16–30). As a mark of his independence, he seeks a property right to the "Spike Lee Joints" he is bent on creating.

Do the Right Thing is topical in the sense that it reflects a particularly tensive moment of race relations in New York City, during the last year of Mayor Ed Koch's twelve-year term. Though Koch had figured importantly in the city's broad economic and cultural recovery of the 1980s, the mayor's popularity declined during his fourth term, particularly among black voters. He had opposed Jesse Jackson when the African American evangelist sought the presidency in 1988, and in the local politics of the late 1980s Koch turned decisively toward a law and order agenda. Rightly or wrongly, Lee held him responsible for abuses of police behavior that led, in one case, to the death of Michael Stewart, a black prisoner in police custody who, according to some accounts, died as the result of a police chokehold. He is one of three victims of racial violence to whom the film is dedicated. Another, Eleanor Bumpers, also died at the hands of the New York police, as they undertook to evict her from an apartment on which she refused to pay rent. The third, Michael Griffith, was the victim of Italian American vigilantes who chased him with a ball bat from a local pizzeria, into fast traffic, where he was struck and killed by a car. All three of these incidents are noted obliquely in Lee's film, with references to eviction, ethnic aggression, and police violence. "There's a complete loss of faith in the judicial system," he told Cynthia Fuchs, shortly after finishing the film, "and when you're frustrated and there's no other outlet, it'll make you want to hurl a garbage can through a window" (2002, 17–18).

The man who eventually hurls the garbage can is Mookie (Spike Lee), a largely unreflective young African American who makes deliveries for Sal's Famous Pizzeria, an Italian proprietorship in a nearly all-black Brooklyn neighborhood. "Mookie," says Lee, "is an irresponsible young black youth. He can't see beyond the next day" (Fuchs 2002, 17). He has a Latina girlfriend, Tina (Rosie Perez), by whom he has fathered a son. Tina still lives with her mother, complaining of Mookie's inattention to parenting and of his inadequate support. Mookie speaks mostly of his need "to get paid." On the more positive side, Mookie is open, friendly, and on good terms with the neighborhood, promoting Sal's interests by informally negotiating race relations on behalf of his employer. Significantly, we usually see him wearing a #42 baseball jersey, the number Jackie Robinson wore as the Brooklyn Dodgers' infielder who integrated major league baseball in the spring of 1947. In _Do the Right Thing_, Mookie is the character who crosses the color line to "integrate" Sal's pizzeria. Without seeking this role, Mookie becomes the focal point of a dialogue between the Italian and African American communities, having to do with autonomy, agency, and the right of self-defense. This is the dialogue that breaks down as the action takes increasingly darker turns.

On one level, _Do the Right Thing_ is a kind of turf war, the struggle between a black neighborhood and an independent Italian proprietor who makes no place for the claims of the community toward defining neighborhood institutions. The film represents a contentious dialogue about personal and public space. The site of conflict is Sal's (Danny Aiello) Famous Pizzeria, whose self-consciously Italianate identity has become a sore point for black activists of the neighborhood. The specific bone of contention is Sal's "wall of fame," a picture gallery of Italian celebrities that ranges from Frank Sinatra to Joe DiMaggio, but conspicuously omits any portraiture of African American athletes or musical celebrities. As

J. T. Mitchell observes, "Sal's wall stands on the threshold between the aesthetic and the rhetorical, functioning simultaneously as both ornament and as propaganda, both a private collection and a public statement" (1997, 110). From different points of the racial compass, forces gather throughout the film to protest against Sal's segregated gallery, an encounter that ends in tragedy.

Though *Do the Right Thing* is intensely realistic in its vivid portrait of a neighborhood, Lee also uses various expressionistic devices to relate local tensions in Bed-Stuy to a much more abstract formulation of racial conflict in the nation as a whole. One of the most effective of these is provided by in the opening scene, which accompanies the credits, much like the musical sequence from *Cavaleria Rusticana* that opens Scorsese's *Raging Bull*. Lee's forceful prologue features Rosie Perez, entirely detached from the role she plays in the film, performing a violent street dance to the rhythm and lyrics of Public Enemy's "Fight the Power."

The Perez dance is provocatively physical, aggressive, almost threatening, full of grimaces and bodily distortions. The controlling metaphor is a boxing match, the dancer's arms making thrusts toward the camera that simulate a boxer's jabs. She is first shown wearing a red dress, but this costume morphs into the garb of a female boxer. Her bright red boxing gloves fit perfectly with lyrics from the musical tract, where lead vocalist Chuck D. demands that we "fight the powers that be." Lee's use of musical cuts from the controversial hip-hop group Public Enemy is of a piece with his interest in the black power movement, which would culminate three years later in his biopic of Malcolm X. Here the boxing motif evokes Muhammad Ali, the black heavyweight champion who forfeited his title when he converted to Islam and refused to be drafted for the Vietnam War. Mike Tyson, the boxer who figures later in the urban graffiti of the film, is another icon of black masculinity. The décor of the scene is starkly anti-realistic, drenched in red so as to render nightmarish what might otherwise be non-threatening images of stately homes and ornate staircases. Much of the backdrop is more sinister— closed doors, shade-covered windows, a confusing riddle of shapes, legible only as blood red architectural fragments separated by black shadows. Throughout Perez's four-minute performance, the rapper insists that someone's "gotta give us what we want, gotta give us what we need." Though the lyrics indict "white power," we are left—somewhat ominously—without guidance as to how this might apply to everyday commerce with our neighbors (Lee 1998, 00:30/04:20).

Lee assimilates the persona of Public Enemy into his own editorial voice. Like the hip-hop artists who are singing, he would lead the African American community to a new level of insight. Chuck D's angry lyrics provide the soundtrack of Rosie Perez' dance: "I'm black and I'm proud," says the rapper, as he insists on "our freedom of speech." This persuades him to disown the icons of white pop culture, which glorifies figures like John Wayne and Elvis Presley. Presumably, it is time for black culture to build its own iconography: "What we need is awareness," Chuck D. continues, "to make everybody see." Surfeited by images of white affluence and arrogance, he is angry that "most of my heroes don't appear on no stamp." Neither do they appear on the wall of Sal's pizzeria, which is why a matter of such little importance becomes a duel to the death in *Do the Right Thing*. Lee shows great skill in dramatizing how racialized mindsets corrupt interpersonal relations, leading to suspicion, exaggeration, and violence.

Do the Right Thing is structured around the conflict between a tightly knit ethnic enclave and intrusions from nearby neighborhoods as well as larger units of civic power, chiefly the police. The neighborhood is represented by storefronts, pedestrian traffic, and continuous personal encounters; the larger world is shown as motorized—private cars but also official vehicles, like police cruisers, personnel vans, and fire trucks. Bed-Stuy is an overwhelmingly black neighborhood, though with a small Latino contingent, at least one Caribbean islander, and one very conspicuous white yuppie, who personifies the spirit of gentrification that may be coming. The street is the common property of the neighbors, with businesses and tenements that open onto Bedford-Stuyvesant Avenue, often by way of a stoop or staircase that facilitates the gathering of small groups of residents. Because of the weekend, most people are home and because of the brutal heat, they are likely to be outdoors. We meet most of them through Mookie, who moves casually about the neighborhood while making his deliveries. Though the neighborhood is not free of bickering, people seem generally on good terms, going about their particular business. The collective voice of the neighborhood is supplied by Señor Love Daddy (Samuel Jackson), a jovial disc jockey representing Station FM 108, who chats about neighborhood concerns and plays "the platters that matter" for listeners who call in their requests.

Lee evokes the neighborhood memorably in one scene where a slightly delinquent teen turns on a fire hydrant, allowing cool water to stream profusely into the street, much to the delight of all the young people and most of the adults. This is a juvenile prank, but also a political act that attests to neighborhood solidarity. At this stage of the film we have looked in on several stifling interiors, where Mookie, Da Mayor (Ossie Davis), and others swelter in buildings that lack ventilation or air conditioning. Headlines scream from the local dailies: "*QUE CALOR!*" The only refuge seems a cold shower. Now Bed-Stuy finds a collective solution: the improvised public swimming pool. Suddenly people are rushing in and out of the cascading water, racing back to grab hesitant comrades and pull them

Spike Lee, *Do the Right Thing*. The black community of Bed-Stuy gathers the neighborhood into the cooling hydrant water that relaxes them on a hot summer day.

Source: This frame-capture is the work of James F. Scott, with technical support from the Instructional Media Center, Saint Louis University.

into the communal cool-out. Love Daddy can't forsake his responsibilities at FM 108, but he joins the water games in spirit by dancing gleefully in front of the plate glass windows of his storefront. A few characters engage the festivities with less enthusiasm: Smiley (Roger Guenveue Smith), the speech-impaired young man who is trying to sell pictures of Malcolm X and Martin Luther King, seems oblivious to the celebration around him; another discordant spirit, Radio Raheem (Bill Nunn), cannot be distracted from his ghetto blaster, which obsessively plays Public Enemy's "Fight the Power." The two youths who control the flow of the water respect this detachment and do nothing to splash either Smiley or Radio Raheem (Lee 1998, 26:30/30:10).

This is the film's most dramatic moment of solidarity, when the neighborhood asserts its agency and collectively solves a common problem. But in its last turn the action sounds a dissonant chord. In the midst of the water party, a self-important Italian approaches the fire hydrant site in a "classic car," which—by his reckoning at least—is far finer than anything that anyone in the Bed-Stuy neighborhood could afford. Having boasted lengthily of its value and threatened anyone who might compromise its elegance, he undertakes to drive through the intersection, after securing the unreliable promise that his priceless convertible will be safe. But it isn't! The masters of the revels take special delight in drenching the vehicle and its owner as completely as possible in a matter of a few seconds. The driver emerges cursing and screaming, much to the delight of the unsympathetic crowd. We see there is solidarity in the neighborhood but no inclination toward interethnic cooperation. The Italianate dandy is regarded as a trespasser and turned into an object of ridicule.

What happens next is equally instructive. A police cruiser arrives with sirens blaring, its crew concerned only with turning off the hydrant water. This comes with a scolding and with the cynical non-advice, "if you want to swim go to Coney Island." The sweltering multitudes are robbed of the relief they contrived for themselves and warned that if these transgressions are repeated punishments will be meted out. The hapless motorist receives no sympathy either, though the police conduct a perfunctory investigation. Basically, the mood is one of unrelieved cynicism: this is a neighborhood that has been written out of civil discourse. The police respond to emergencies, since that is demanded of them, but in no sense do they think of themselves as part of the community. After issuing their threats and performing their minimal intervention, they are back in their squad cars driving quickly away.

The police will return twice to this neighborhood before the cataclysmic finale. Their first visit is one of surveillance: the slow motion footage of their close scrutiny of people on the street indicates the spirit of suspicion that inspires their watchful glance. The second visit takes them out of their cruiser and into Sal's place, but only to chide him about how much longer he intends to do business in a questionable neighborhood.

Though Mookie's Bed-Stuy neighborhood looks safe and self-sufficient (Lee has been accused of deliberately erasing references to drugs and homelessness), what it clearly lacks is black-owned businesses and property owners. Mother Sister (Ruby Dee) apparently owns the apartment building from which she keeps watch over the street, but ownership is exceptional and commercial capital is largely imported from the outside. Sal's pizzeria is the most obvious case in point, though he has done business in the neighborhood for a quarter-century and prides himself on having fed a generation of young blacks and Latinos, whom he treats respectfully but keeps at arm's length. He and his two sons come into the neighborhood by automobile from Bensonhurst, a nearby Italian enclave, and make a point of removing the lock and chain that ensures the security of their property. They also busy themselves with cleaning up the sidewalk in front of the store, a task finally assigned to Da Mayor, a neighborhood alcoholic, after both of Sal's sons disown the work as too menial for them. Sal strives to be welcoming to his patrons, though he is dismissive of suggestions that there should be "some black brothers" on his wall of fame. Sal stands in contrast to Kim (Ginny Yang) and his wife, a family of Koreans who run a green grocery and flower shop directly across the street from the pizzeria. They are the objects of slurs from the "corner men," three problematic characters, one conspicuously from the islands, who hang out under a large umbrella and make incidental comments on their neighbors' business. These choral figures marvel at the ease with which the Koreans raise money to buy a business and profit handsomely from the sales they make to a reasonably large black clientele. They resent the foreigners and are eager for the day when black entrepreneurs will occupy these storefronts. A little ironically, they don't find fault with Sal.

Though the Koreans have issues with the language and are slow to master the protocols of the black community (Kim is bewildered by Da Mayor's resentment of "lite beer"), they are flexible and adaptable in ways that Sal is not. They seem to instinctively understand that their patrons should play a role in how the proprietorship conducts business. In an amusing encounter with Radio Raheem, probably the angriest black man on the block, Kim enters into a duel of American obscenities, losing as would seem inevitable, but earning Raheem's respect, even drawing from him one of the few smiles that come to his face. In the film's violent finale, Kim saves his store from the rioters, by claiming to be "black," an identity which is not quite accepted, but comes close enough to fulfilling the American racial code to earn an amnesty from the unruly crowd. In a show of solidarity with that crowd, Kim also pounds his fist on the police squad car that has come to quell the disturbance. Sal, on the other hand, is quick tempered, refusing to serve Radio Raheem until he turns down his boom box and rudely pulling the cheese dispenser from the hands of Buggin' Out (Giancarlo Esposito) when he tries to add extra cheese to his slice of pizza. These are trivial things but they add to the weight that ultimately becomes a tragic burden.

The film progresses as a dialogue between the storefront and the street, with Sal striving to be cordial to his customers of long standing but harboring racial attitudes that flash dangerous warning signs. He keeps a baseball bat (shades of Michael Griffith) behind the counter and has it in his hand early in the film, when Buggin' Out first complains about the absence of a black presence on the wall. Sal's double-sidedness reveals itself in his attitude toward Mookie, whom he sometimes describes as a "son" but treats as a servant. His racial ambivalence is reflected in his two sons, Pino (John Turturro) and Vito (Richard Edson), the first a fierce racist, the other more open and accommodating, friendly to Mookie, and inclined to keep company with him. Pino, on the other hand, always berates Mookie, attaching to him all the black stereotypes of laziness and unreliability. In one memorable scene, Sal asks his older son why there is "so much hate" in him and is told he "detests [the neighborhood] like a sickness." Their conversation unfolds in a continuous wide shot, where Sal and Pino sit down together in front of a large plate glass window, which offers a full view of the street. It's a liminal space that blurs the division between indoors and the outside, rendering untenable Pino's *apartheid* attitudes toward race mixing, but also problematizing Sal's hope for an easygoing business arrangement between the pizzeria and its black clientele (Lee 1998, 57:45/01:02:05).

Obviously, Sal is proud of his pizzeria and sees it as a family business he would like to pass along to his sons. But Pino is contemptuous of the thought: "I'm sick of niggers. It's like I come to work, it's *Planet of the Apes*. . . . My friends, they laugh at me. They laugh right in my face." He wonders why they couldn't sell the pizzeria and "open up a new one in our own neighborhood." Sal's rejoinder is that Bensonhurst is already saturated with pizza parlors and that the Bed-Stuy address gives them a market niche they would not otherwise have. Sal also admits he is too old to venture into another kind of business endeavor: "I've been here twenty-five years. Where am I going?" Besides, says Sal, "I never had no trouble with these people. . . . I mean, for Christ's sake, Pino, they grew up on my food. On my food! And I'm very proud of that."

While father and son converse at cross-purposes, the life of the street imposes itself upon them in ways that neither could have predicted. Just as Sal announces, "what I'm trying to say, son, is that Sal's Famous Pizzeria is here to stay," their conversation is interrupted by the sudden appearance of Smiley, the stuttering idiot-savant who spends his days trying to sell photos of the famous handshake between Malcolm X and Martin Luther King. Smiley is harmless, but disruptive, immediately calling into play the conflicted attitudes of the proprietorship, as Sal and Pino respond to his presence. For Pino, Smiley's intrusion is positive proof that Bedford-Stuyvesant Avenue is planet of the apes, an alien universe where Sal and his family will never feel safe or comfortable. Taking up the challenge, the elder son rushes outside to drive Smiley away from the window and threaten him with violence if he returns. For Sal, however, the encounter cues another desperate effort to affiliate with the neighborhood, to keep an uneasy peace, even if it amounts to little more than making small pay-offs to people he distrusts, but is determined to get along with. Ultimately, Sal is outside his shop, making a futile public relations gesture, while his son is inside the pizzeria, full of rage at his father's stance of appeasement. This ambiguous stage picture, the image of a house divided against itself, bodes ill for the fate of Sal's Famous Pizzeria.

Though this scene seems to make Pino the racist and his father the racial conciliator, Lee in his personal commentary is quick to point out that Pino's racism is likely to have been created within the family. Later, when Sal screams his racial obscenities at Radio Raheem, Lee notes that "it didn't come out of thin air. It was there. It just had to be provoked" (Fuchs 2002, 19).

The violent finale of *Do the Right Thing* results from another incursion from the streets, as much a surprise as the unexpected appearance of Smiley. Throughout the day, we have watched Buggin' Out make what seems a failing effort to organize a boycott of Sal's place, in response to his refusal to add black celebrities to the wall of fame. Da Mayor scoffs at the initiative as "black foolishness," and the corner men are equally dismissive, advising that perhaps Buggin' Out, who sports a strange-looking hairdo, should "boycott the barber who cut your hair." The most telling critique comes from Jade, Mookie's sister, who is one of the most levelheaded characters in the film. She says that it would make sense to undertake something "more positive," if the neighborhood is truly in need of a consciousness-raising project. By and large, Bedford-Stuyvesant Avenue has no quarrel with Sal and sees no reason to boycott the pizzeria. In spite of the lack of support, however, Buggin' Out resolves to confront

Spike Lee, *Do the Right Thing*. In the climactic scene at Sal's pizzeria, the severe angularity of the framing portends the tragic outcome of events. The composition also isolates the intruders.

Source: This frame-capture is the work of James F. Scott, with technical support from the Instructional Media Center, Saint Louis University.

Sal and gathers momentum from Smiley and Radio Raheem, two characters whom Sal has explicitly offended. The trio of malcontents arrives after the official closing hour, but manages to get in because the door was accidentally left unlocked. Their problematic intrusion is signaled in Lee's composition: the disruptive latecomers are framed in series of canted angles, which make the whole set look tilted and off balance, a place where finding one's footing might be chancy. Thereafter, events spiral out of control, as good intentions give way to deep-seated hostilities founded upon attitudes of "us and them."

The *leitmotif* of the confrontation scene (Lee 1998, 01:29:30/01:33:00) comes from the blaring lyrics of "Fight the Power," as Radio Raheem with his massive boom box again brings Public Enemy to the center of the stage. Predictably, Sal responds to this affront to his proprietary rights by seizing his baseball bat and demolishing the radio. In turn, Raheem assaults Sal, dragging him over the counter and eventually out into the street. By this time a massive fight is in progress, which becomes a matter for the police as it spreads across the threshold and into public space.

At this point mass mayhem might still have been averted, but after the police intervention, diplomatic solutions have no chance. It's not clear that the police intend to kill Raheem, but he is deliberately brutalized, because he fulfills the favorite racial stereotype of white middle-class culture, the muscular, violent black male. Caught in a lethal chokehold, he dies as one of the arresting officers lifts him off his feet and holds him in that position, in spite of some effort from a fellow officer to restrain his partner. Furthermore, the police detail makes no effort to quiet the crowd. Instead, they flee the scene immediately, bearing Raheem's body, presumably more worried about their own safety than about the chaotic scene they are leaving behind. In spite of Da Mayor's effort to disperse the crowd, the torching of Sal's place of business seems the predestined outcome. That Mookie initiates these reprisals against Sal is the most ambiguous act of the film and ties closely to Lee's feelings about racial confrontation. In light of the film's title, it's inevitable that we would ask, is Mookie correctly responding to the command, "Do the right thing?" For Lee, the question is part of the larger issue of neighborhood self-defense.

In *Place Matters* (2014), Peter Dreier, John Mollenkopf, and Todd Swanstrom speak at length of a "metropolitics" that disadvantages communities of color, while unfailingly describing these policies as racially neutral (see particularly, 103–35). These authors speak of a pattern repeatedly displayed in American cities, whereby federal and local initiatives have favored "investment in suburbs and disinvestment in central cities" (104). In practical terms, these initiatives have "encouraged competition and political fragmentation within metropolitan areas, primarily by allowing local autonomy over taxation, land use, housing and education, but also by failing to provide incentives for regional governance or cooperation" (104). New York's Mayor Koch was caught up in these controversies throughout the 1980s, to some extent supporting a progressive agenda. But in his final term (1986–1989) he "refocus[ed] his electoral coalition on white voters, particularly the reform-oriented middle-class professionals in Manhattan and adjacent parts of Brooklyn and the more blue-collar, white ethnic neighborhoods of the outer boroughs" (Dreier, Mollenkopf, and Swanstrom 2014, 226). Lee turned furiously against Koch at this time, charging him with explicit race baiting: "Anytime you hear Mayor Koch talk about 'savages' and 'animals,' you know he is talking about young black males" (Fuchs 2002, 20). Ultimately, as Lee sees it, the mayor's suspicion of ghettos and "bad neighborhoods" and his decisive tilt toward law and order is what legitimates the vigilante tactics of the NYPD practice in the climactic scene of *Do the Right Thing*.

This is the context into which we must fit the on-screen quotations of Martin Luther King and Malcolm X at the film's conclusion. King's insistence that violence is self-defeating needs to be measured against Brother Malcolm's rejoinder that he would not characterize self-defense as "violence," but simply as "intelligence." Expanding upon these citations in his *Film Comment* interview with Marlene Glicksman, Lee comes to the defense of Bed-Stuy, *vis-à-vis* the intrusion of the police: "It would be a fallacy to say that lower income people always live in burned out buildings. These are hard-working people and they take pride in their stuff just like everybody else. So there's no need for the set to look like Charlotte Street in the South Bronx" (Fuchs 2002, 21). Lee regards the violence that erupts after the death of Raheem at the hands of the police as something more like self-defense. He is aware, of course, that Sal is not the primary culprit in this situation and that the crowd's response damages the neighborhood more than it hurts the police or Mayor Koch:

> That always happens. . . . Any time there's a riot . . . they always make sure they confine that riot to the ghetto. And so the buildings they burn down will never be built back. When there were riots in New York City, they were never on Fifth Avenue. There's never been looting in Lord & Taylor's or Saks. It was on 125th St. So in a way we do lose out. But people don't feel they lose out, because they feel lost already. (Fuchs 2002, 21)

As Lee understands it, the rage is justified, though its efficacy might remain a matter of debate.

One further point should be made in considering this deeply ambiguous scene. When Mookie throws the trash can through Sal's plate glass window, he shouts the word "hate." We should remember that this word not only conveys personal anger but harks back to a conversation between Mookie and Radio Raheem, where Raheem, displaying his fist ornaments, sums up life as an ongoing battle between love and hate, words which are engraved in metal on his right and left hands. In the boxing match between these two forces that Raheem describes, hate strikes the first several blows, but then love recovers to win the fight. In other words, "hate" is only one pole in a dialectical pairing of hate and its opposite—love. With that relationship in mind, we can return to the scene after the riot, where the neighborhood begins to put itself back together. Señor Love Daddy dedicates a song to Radio Raheem ("We love you, brother") and Da Mayor makes peace with Mother Sister, allowing them to confront the tragedy of the neighborhood as a team, not as scratchy, carping antagonists. And whatever their shortcomings, they are the godparents of Bedford-Stuyvesant Avenue, urging its residents to "do the right thing." The Kim family, though they make no final appearance, seem to have won recognition as "belonging" to the neighborhood in a new way, having joined their neighbors in opposing the police. Even the tensive exchange between Mookie and Sal goes better than anyone would have imagined, with Sal giving Mookie his wages and Mookie assuring his former employer that with his insurance money he will be able to rebuild his store. There's nothing here to suggest that love has won the day, but the morning sunshine augurs for a future that is open to possibility.

Having explored with painful authenticity the conflict over the claims of property in a racially conflicted neighborhood, Lee moved on two years later to the more delicate subject of interracial sexuality in *Jungle Fever*. Though generally a little less deeply imagined than *Do the Right Thing*, the latter film is memorable for its audacity in venturing into the intimate space of a cross-racial love affair between a black professional and his subaltern Italian secretary. The films share in common the sense of personal feelings being overwhelmed by the burden of racialized habits surviving from the remote past.

The core theme of *Jungle Fever* is oddly anticipated in *Do the Right Thing* in a puzzling scene that constitutes a loose end in Lee's earlier narrative. For no apparent reason, Mookie's sister, Jade (Joie Lee), turns up at Sal's pizzeria and is greeted with effusive friendliness. Sal, who tends not to mix casually with his patrons, insists on making her a special slice and then joins her at the table as she eats. He also remarks on how much he has missed her recently and wonders why he has seen so little of her. Though she is in no sense flirty or emotionally engaged with Sal, Mookie flies into a rage and virtually drags her out of the store. Outside, he further scolds her, clearly suspecting that Sal seeks to recruit her as a romantic partner. The scene is further complicated by the graffito on the wall behind Mookie and Jade, which says, "Twana told the truth." The reference is to Twana Brawley, a black woman of the time who falsely claimed that she had been raped by a white street gang. What the action seems to imply is that interracial sexual taboos loom so large all engagements between African Americans and whites are corrupt and deceitful, almost foreordained to end in catastrophe. This is the burden that Angela Tucci (Annabelle Sciorra) and Flipper Purify (Wesley Snipes) carry into their short-lived romance. Sounding this note in his personal commentary, Lee says that his lovers wreck the chances of a positive outcome "because they are not drawn to each other by love but by sexual myths" (Fuchs 2002, 28).

Lee deserves praise for his ambitious effort to dramatize this powerful theme. But the film is compromised by the writer/director's insistence on fastening it to an altogether different narrative about the crack epidemic that bedeviled New York at the outset of the 1990s. Strangely, Lee felt the drug issue was paramount: "I just wanted to use the interracial thing as a hook. For me, the heart of the piece is the devastation of crack on families" (Aftab and Lee 2006, 168). Few would doubt that the crack plague is a worthy topic for cinematic exploration, or that Samuel Jackson, as Gator, gives a superb performance as Flipper's crack-addicted older brother, the straying son who is ultimately shot to death by his own father. But this wildly melodramatic subplot is completely tangential and almost impossible to integrate into the interracial drama, which cries out for nuance and more detailed exposition. After the fact, Lee himself seems to realized that he missed the opportunity to advance a much more meaningful subplot, built around Paulie Carbone (John Turturro) and his hesitant effort to launch an interracial relationship with his black friend and candy store customer, Orin Goode (Tyra Ferrell). Almost as an afterthought, Lee recalls that "there's another interracial couple in the film . . . I think they have a chance of having a better relationship because they have a real foundation of friendship, whereas Flipper and Angie's was based on myth" (Fuchs 2002, 29). Unfortunately for *Jungle Fever*, this valuable insight remains largely an abstraction, deprived of the conscientious dramatic development that might have made it seem more real.

In spite of its hurried exposition, *Jungle Fever* is a compelling film. Flipper is a memorable example of an upwardly mobile black architect, who feels entitled to claim a white woman as a sexual trophy, working into his behavior a subtle counterthrust against his self-important white employers, who refuse to regard him as an equal. Angie in her own fashion is equally memorable as the undereducated, but highly ambitious secretary, who finds in her lover a level of concern and sensitivity she has not found in her father or her brothers, all of whom treat her like a household servant. But Lee's talent also shows itself in the vivid collective portraits of their respective peer groups, the cadre of black women who gather around Drew, after she throws her unfaithful husband out of their home, and the gaggle of young Italian males, who hang out at Paulie's candy store to complain about the newly elected black mayor of New York City and what they take to be the encroachments of the black community upon the white privileges they cherish.

Writing of "inter-ethnic and interracial romantic relationships," Amadu Kaba makes use of "status caste exchange theory" to analyze the broad social dynamics of interracial unions, whereby "highly educated blacks would trade their educational status to reap the benefits associated with the racial status of a potential white spouse" (2011, 123). This is a reformulation of Karen Brodkin's argument in *How the Jews Became White Folks* that cultural capital is employed to overcome ethno-racial taint. From the opposite perspective, partners representing the majoritarian culture consent to relationships with "devalued ethnics" only when it is clear that these prospective partners have shown willingness to "acculturate to the norms and values of the host society" (123). Though neither Flipper nor Angie perfectly answers to this template, both are urged by these forces as well as by the special factors of temperament and circumstance that work upon them.

Flipper is the upwardly mobile black professional of the post–civil rights era, relieved of the legal oppression of segregated America but still the subtle victim of social prejudice, never acknowledged, yet everywhere in force. A point is made about his specialness, as we see a copy of the *New York Times* thrown up to his door and no other. That point is reinforced sometime later, when Orin, another black professional, remarks to Paulie that his news and candy store should stock "at least the Sunday edition" of the city's iconic newspaper. Though the *Times* is surely not a "white" newspaper, it speaks for the professional elite of New York City in a way that *Emerge* or *The Amsterdam News* could in no way match. Flipper is also in flight from his blood family, estranged from his father, a rigid Evangelical clergyman, and even more completely from Gator, the older brother who has turned to drugs and disgraced his kin. Flipper also works for a white architectural firm, whose executive partners respect his design skills but are suspicious of his racial attitudes, imagining (quite foolishly) that he's a secretive black activist, perhaps betraying them in underhanded fashion. They bristle when he asks them to hire a black secretary as his assistant and make a decisive point of refusing to do so. These factors alone do not foredoom Flipper's romantic liaison with Angie, but they marginalize him sufficiently to put his marriage at risk.

For her part, Angie encourages the relationship because her family situation is more desperate than Flipper's. At home, she not only supports her father, who is presumably retired, but also is made to feel responsible for her two brothers, neither of whom gives evidence of being gainfully employed. Though she works in Harlem and must commute from Brooklyn, she is expected to keep house and prepare meals for all the males of the family who constantly make demands upon her. She is in a romantic relationship with Paulie, but neither partner seems inclined to carry it forward with energy. At first glance, Angie's attraction to Flipper is a little difficult to account for, since it is burdened with serious risks to her personal safety. Apparently, Lee and his female lead, Annabella Sciorra, disagreed about interpreting the role. The director thought of her as motivated by erotic fantasy, what Celia Daileader calls "Othellophilia," which attaches magical powers to black male sexuality (2005, 1–13). Sciorra, on the other hand, thought of her character's motivation as more complex. "I was under the impression," Sciorra says, "that she was falling in love with the man. He was different from what she was used to. She had these brothers who were kind of bullies and racists, and so was her dad, and she was the girl who came home from work and cleaned and cooked for the family. I think that in Flipper she saw something that she hadn't come close to before. He was educated and opening up another world for her" (quoted in Aftab and Lee 2006, 162). These comments don't exclude sexual curiosity, but add density to our understanding of her behavior. In the end, she seems the more seriously damaged of the two parties.

Whatever propels the couple into their relationship, however, Lee gives most of his attention to the responses of their respective peer groups, which are uniformly negative. Lee also makes clear that these choral figures represent the deeply engrained racial prejudices of Harlem and Bensonhurst, respectively. In the expressionistic montage of maps and road signs with which the film opens, Bensonhurst posts signage that forbids entry to African Americans, while Harlem represents itself as "a guinea free zone." Bensonhurst was also the site of the murder of Yusuf Hawkins, the black teen to whom the film is dedicated. He was killed by white vigilantes when he accidentally crossed an invisible border separating "white territory" from "black."

Fully in keeping with the spirit of the rival clans, the individual voices give their particular inflection to the ubiquitous sentiment. Cyrus (Spike Lee), Flipper's friend and confidante, describes the romantic liaison as a "nuclear holocaust." He immediately tells his wife, who in turn informs Flipper's wife. Gator greets the news derisively, mocking his younger brother for choosing a white girlfriend who has neither wealth nor social status. Flipper's attempt to introduce Angie to his parents is an unmitigated disaster. Angie's personal circle is equally hostile. Her girlfriends are bewildered and scoffing, her family angry and violent. Her father beats her mercilessly, before he and her brothers drive her out of the family home. Even in public space, the mixed race couple is scorned, conspicuously in a Harlem restaurant where they have difficulty placing their order. Lee's depiction of their abuse at the hands of friends and family bears out the research of social scientists, like William Graziano and his colleagues concerning "Peer Influence and Attraction to Interracial Relationships" (Graziano, Lehmiller, and VanderDrift 2014). They conclude not only that "peer disapproval" usually predicts the failure of interracial relationships but also that "broader social pressures against interracial dating" (127) materially affect the way the couples themselves regard each other.

Though some critics remain persuaded that Lee believes in a biologically pure black essence," Lee's own words call this assumption into question:

> One thing a lot of people are not picking up on is that the film is not just about interracial marriages and relationships. It's about identity. There are people in the film who are products of mixed marriages. My character's wife in the film has a black father and a white mother. The same is true of Flipper's wife. The people in the film are constantly talking about their identity, where they belong. They make a distinction between mulattoes, quadroons, and octoroons. (Fuchs 2002, 28)

It's no doubt ironic that language surviving from the slavery era is still being used to describe the radically new culture of ethno-racial hybridity. But there's no evidence that Lee himself worries over drops of "black blood." In fact, the vocabulary of the plantation culture is introduced to the film by Flipper's hypercritical father, as he explains to Flipper and Angie why mixed race relationships are a moral abomination. The Baptist minister's narrow code is surely not the moral norm of the film.

Nor are there grounds for thinking Lee necessarily disapproves of interracial relationships, though he deeply resented his father's marriage to a white woman shortly after the death of his mother. He also has reservations about the romantic involvement of Angie and Flipper, but he is prepared to make an important distinction: "They didn't really love each other. I think if they had, love would have enabled them to withstand the onslaught of abuse they were getting from their family and friends and the two neighborhoods they live in—Harlem and Bensonhurst. In the end, Angie comes to love Flipper, but he still loves his wife" (Fuchs 2002, 29). Ultimately, Lee is far more concerned with the onslaught of abuse heaped upon the transgressive lovers by their peers than he is with the issue of miscegenation.

One of the best scenes in the film is the one where Drew's friends gather to support her after she has banished Flipper from their home, spectacularly pitching his belongings out of a third-story window in front of a jeering crowd. The women collectively extend their support to Drew, but their remarks carry us on wild tangents, having as much to do with their personal insecurities as with devotion to their friend. To his credit, Lee made no effort to script this scene but left his female actors free to play broadly on the question of black female romantic relationships. "It was completely improvisational," he says. "We did between twenty and twenty-five takes. I find the more you talk the more honest you get" (Fuchs 2002, 29).

What we take away from the scene is that "black" women are in no way a monolithic group, but are highly self-conscious of a color code that is layered from lighter to darker, almost always with a preference for the lighter hues. We also understand that the social landscape is changing and cannot be deciphered without considering race in conjunction with class, education, and acculturation. The girl talk is oriented toward finding romantic partnerships but carries implications beyond personal expectations. Drew admits that her lighter skin tone once gave her romantic advantage, but now fears she has lost her man to a "white trash" woman who "probably didn't finish high school." Which seems a way of saying, she once trusted her ability to attract black men who were drawn to fair-complexioned women, but doubts that this assumption remains reliable. Linda confesses that she always felt slighted because of her darker skin; she also complains of men that "can't deal with a black woman who has more education and makes more money." Inez wants black women to broaden their search for romantic partners to Chinese, Jews, Latinos, or anyone, who might "be nice to me, sweet to me." Another voice speaks of the "self-hate" going on among black men who can't deal with their black sisters, because they are embarrassed by their own failings. All worry that crime and addiction have taken a monstrous toll on black manhood in the late twentieth century (Lee 1996c, 58:30/01:03:30). Though Angie and Flipper think of themselves as outcasts, we are urged to see them as one aspect of a much larger cultural shift that is convulsing urban America.

The counterpoint to the doomed relationship between Angie and Flipper is the tentative but credible romance between Paulie and Orin, which Lee fails to fully articulate. This pairs the well-dressed, well-spoken upwardly mobile black woman with the limited but open-minded Italianate child of Bensonhurst. Their romance is a mirror image of Angie's relationship to Flipper. Lee seems to have become aware, after the fact, that this subplot is a missed opportunity: "We're not trying to condemn interracial relationships. . . . I think if two people love each other that's great. There's another interracial couple in the film. The John Turturro character named Paulie and the character Orin. I think they have a chance of having a better relationship because they have a real foundation of friendship" (Fuchs 2002, 29).

Apparently Turturro thought that Lee was planning to make the Paulie/Orin romance the centerpiece of the film and notes that "to this day I still think that this would have made a better movie" (quoted in Aftab and Lee 2006, 157). This is less obvious than the fact that the drug plot, featuring Gator, seriously impairs Lee's ability to give his subplot the expansiveness it deserves.

Be that as it may, the presence of Orin and Paulie helps balance Lee's portrait of two communities in transition. Bensonhurst is as troubled about skin tones as Harlem, as is clear from the chaotic shouting about the topic in Paulie's candy store. "I'm not black," says Frankie, one strident voice among the clique of young men who hang out there. "My mother's a dark Italian. I'm as white as anyone here." They heckle Paulie about his friendliness to Orin, insisting that a black woman is a legitimate sex object, but under no circumstances can be acknowledged as a friend. When they realize that Angie has deserted him for Flipper, they unanimously recommend he should beat her, so she might serve as an example to other straying girlfriends. These racial encroachments are imagined in terms of property, much like the wall of fame in *Do the Right Thing*. One of the most frustrated of the candy store chorus complains that blacks have already taken over sports and, more recently, the mayor's office and police department. "Protecting" their womenfolk, even if it means assaulting them violently, is their last line of defense against the multi-faceted border crossings that have now found their way even to enclaves like Bensonhurst (Lee 1996c, 01:16:10/01:20:45).

But Paulie stands his ground. He refuses to denigrate Orin, even when he is alone with his friends and resists his father's rage, when the parent demands that he stop keeping company with a black woman. In one of the last scenes, he is physically assaulted by the candy store vigilantes, but survives with a few bruises and carries on to find refuge with Orin. She too is aware she is code breaking and is hesitant about launching a cross-racial relationship. But when Paulie turns up at her door, looking a little scarred and battered, she cordially welcomes him in, leaving their future open to further negotiation.

Do the Right Thing and *Jungle Fever* effectively propel Lee into the ethno-racial cauldron of contemporary urban culture. However different they may be, both films share a sense of a changing of the guard. Older adults, like Sal, the elder Carbone, and Flipper's father, are steeped in habits they can never break, but their sons and daughters are ready to venture upon *terra incognita*. The trouble is that neither culture has developed a language of mediation. As Erica Childs gleans from her research in *Navigating Interracial Borders* (2005), many communities render interracial relationships as "outside the realm of what is speakable; in other words, interracial relationships were not part of the available discourse or script that they as a group drew upon" (50). The unresolved conflicts we are left with at the end of *Do the Right Thing* and *Jungle Fever* impel Lee to probe more deeply into the conflicted identities of the black world, which are at the center of *Malcolm X* and *Get on the Bus*.

SEGMENT 2: EXPLORING BLACKNESS:
MALCOLM X (1992) AND *GET ON THE BUS* (1996)

Having established himself as a director who challenged the racial com-
placencies of the Reagan era, Lee then embarked upon the most ambitious project of his career, a lavishly produced, three-hour biopic of the
controversial African American Black Nationalist Malcolm X, a powerful
leader slain in the prime of his career. Not only was this undertaking
an important filmic event, it was also a political and public relations
phenomenon of the first order, involving custodianship of the image of
Malcolm as well as a tense battle between Lee and Warner Brothers over
funding and marketing. Determined to have a budget that allowed for
an expansive high-gloss portrait of this charismatic but deeply divisive
figure, Lee alienated many notables in the black community, even while
he actively solicited and received support from black celebrities, like Michael Jordan, Magic Johnson, and Oprah Winfrey. Though black activist
Amiri Baraka, among others, denounced him for betraying the leader he
purported to commemorate, Lee's slightly cosmeticized treatment of his
subject allowed him to present the Nation of Islam radical to middle-
class audiences worldwide as the "black shining prince" of Ossie Davis'
funeral elegy. David Sterritt catches the basic paradox of the film when
he describes how, in the first few minutes of screen time, the brutal images of the Rodney King police beating give way to "a biopic in the old
Hollywood tradition, telling the story of a hero's life in straightforward,
conventional terms" (102).

Lee approached this project fully aware of the difficult environment
into which he had inserted himself. Essentially, his task was similar to the
challenge Buggin' Out forces upon Sal in *Do the Right Thing*: Lee wanted
to attach the image of Malcolm X to the screen of Warner Brothers' "wall
of fame." This is the substance of his insistence that the studio fund an
"epic" production of Malcolm, meaning, in practice, that Warner Brothers
should support Lee's film at the same level they had supported Oliver
Stone's *JFK*, a $30 million dollar blockbuster about the assassination of
President Kennedy, released in 1991. Such support would guarantee three
hours of screen time, location photography, and a spare-no-expenses look
that would qualify the picture for mainstream suburban distribution and
access to the international market. More importantly, from Lee's vantage
point, it would elevate Minister Malcolm, the Muslim activist, to the
status of a media icon, roughly on the same cinematic plane as *JFK*, or
earlier big budget biopics like *Lawrence of Arabia* (1962) and *Patton* (1970).
But the studio was unwilling to authorize more than $20 million for the

production, $10 million less than Lee felt was essential. Warner Brothers also sought to soften the portrait of Malcolm X, bending him toward the more moderate political figure who, they assumed, would be more palatable to mainstream film patrons. This led to Lee's angry charge that Warner Brothers was an updated version of "the plantation," dramatizing a quarrel with the studio that he expanded to book length in *By Any Means Necessary: The Trials and Tribulations of the Making of Malcolm X* (1992).

Further complications came from the engagement of the black community in the intramural controversy between the studio and the ambitious Spike Lee. As Graeme Abernethy argues convincingly in *The Iconography of Malcolm X* (2013), Malcolm's image, and the cultural freight that it bore, became in the years immediately following his assassination "a near-divinity to be propitiated by the embrace of a revolutionism conceived at least partly in his honor" (125). Ironically, however, this overweening reverence for the martyred leader led in the next decade to "Malcolm's ubiquitous commodification as a Black Power icon" (125), whose image—in photography, journalism, theater, and pop art—almost overshadowed his political legacy (see particularly Abernethy 2013, 125–67). After two decades of hesitancy, and the preparation of several scripts, including two fashioned by prominent black writers James Baldwin and Charles Fuller, Warner Brothers opted to press forward with a film production that would capitalize on Malcolm's increasing fame. Not eager to court controversy, the studio tentatively chose Norman Jewison, a white, mainstream director, to helm their highly publicized project. At this time Lee confronted Warner Brothers, protesting loudly that the project demanded a black film director, who presumably would have superior insights into African American culture and who was prepared to acknowledge the radical, anti-establishment stance of the Muslim activist. Following a brief back-and-forth between Lee and Jewison, the latter bowed out gracefully, conceding that Lee perhaps had the better credentials. But in his campaign to oust Jewison from the director's chair, Lee encouraged the expectation in certain quarters of the black community that his portrait of Malcolm X would be much more angry, much more given over to "black power" than it turned out to be. Of Lee's critics, none was more strident than Amiri Baraka. He derided Lee as a self-serving "quintessential buppy, almost the spirit of the young upwardly mobile, Black petit bourgeois professional," who looked after his own personal advancement at the expense of what Baraka hoped for in the Black Arts movement (Baraka 1993, 146).

For Baraka, and a sizeable cadre of writers and artists who had been active since the late 1960s, Lee defaulted on his obligation to assert full-fledged racial autonomy, what Baraka called "the fundamental requirement for a Black democracy." This requirement, according to Baraka, was "to have a broad and effective communication front: art, culture, media, film, and so on, expressing with maximum force and skill the beautiful (albeit tragic) and politically revolutionary (albeit drenched in backwardness) lives, history, and culture of the African American people" (Baraka 1993, 145–46). Lee could not fulfill this agenda while under contract to Warner Brothers, since Baraka had in effect insisted that Lee stage a *coup d'état*, turning the assets of the studio toward the founding of an independent African American film industry. Ultimately, Lee settled for something much less radical, but in its own way transformative.

In retrospect, the conversation that ensued in the *New York Times* between Lee and the Black Studies scholar Louis Gates shortly after the release of *Malcolm X* is instructive for the light it sheds on Lee's angle of entry into the national debate on autonomy and self-determination in the black community. Questioned by Gates about Warner Brothers' control of the film, Lee fiercely defends his independence: "They just make suggestions. I have the final cut." What gave Lee considerable leverage is the fact of his personal fundraising, first in the sale of related merchandise (caps, T-shirts, key-chains, etc.), later in the negotiation of international rights, and finally in direct solicitations from celebrity donors. Altogether, he may have garnered as much as $8 to $10 million (see Aftab and Lee 2006, 179–214).

But the reality is, Lee wasn't as seriously at odds with Warner Brothers as first might seem. "I know for sure Warner Brothers is trying to stress the Malcolm after Mecca," Lee says, as if this were a major source of friction. But as Gates probes ever so slightly, Lee admits that "they have a point. Because Malcolm post-Mecca is the Malcolm who evolved the most. I think Malcolm came to the point where he thought we were all brothers." Though he refuses to negate "what Malcolm did when he was in the Nation" and cites his "speaking important truths about oppression and resistance," like Warner Brothers, Lee is more comfortable with his protagonist after "he stopped calling white folk blue-eyed mutant devils." In response to Gates' further queries, Lee lays emphasis upon Malcolm's role as educator: "One of the things that Malcolm stressed was education. . . . We're just not doing it. It's such a sad situation now, where male black kids will fail so they can be 'down' with everyone else, and if you get A's and speak correct English, you're regarded as being 'white.' Peer pressure has turned around our whole value system" (Gates and Lee 1992).

The Malcolm who is a role model for self-help and adult education and directs us to the niceties of English grammar is worlds removed from the threatening black revolutionary who lives in the lyrics of Public Enemy and in the political imaginary of the white suburban middle class. In the face of Gates' skepticism, Lee insists he can present Malcolm authentically to both black and white audiences: "I've always found it interesting to view my films as having two different audiences, one black and one white. . . . This film's about America, and all Americans can learn from it. Like Malcolm, we're taking a global view of this film: it's not just about the United States; we're thinking about the world" (Gates and Lee 1992).

Though Lee won control of the project by emphasizing its transgressive theme, he ultimately rendered Malcolm as a figure not much more radical than Bayard Rustin, James Farmer, or even Martin Luther King Jr.

The framework of Lee's film derives from Alex Haley's *Autobiography of Malcolm X*, which itself strives to turn Malcolm into a mainstream cultural presence. "The image of Malcolm established by the *Autobiography*," says Abernethy, "can be identified, above all, with the myth of transformation" (2013, 75). The conventions of the conversion narrative distanced Haley's protagonist from his crime-ridden, drug dealing past, allowing a more principled and politically responsible figure to emerge. Haley's privileged relationship to his subject also allowed him to claim he had written Malcolm's official narrative, especially since it was published after the assassination, granting Haley the right of last review. But, according to Abernethy, "Malcolm was coming to regard African American identity and struggle more clearly in the context of global politics—a shift revealed more explicitly in Malcolm's late speeches than by the *Autobiography*" (85). This open-endedness in the closing chapters of the *Autobiography* allowed Lee to claim he was adhering to Haley's "authorized version" of the black culture icon, while taking advantage of the relative malleability of the narrative to significantly expand and update the summation Haley had made in the middle 1960s.

Much like the *Autobiography*, Lee divides Malcolm's life into the binaries of fall and redemption, closely adhering to the tropes of his "Detroit Red" period, but taking more liberties with Haley as he recounts Malcolm's conversion to Islam and the conflicted spiritual pilgrimage that followed. What he admired in Baldwin's script, he tells us in his well-known interview with *Cineaste* (1993), was the way "he really captured Harlem and that whole period" (Fuchs 2002, 66). In the process of dramatizing this journey, Lee luxuriates in Malcolm the zoot-suiter, vividly records his prison experience, renders his discipleship to Elijah Muhammed in slightly ironic terms, and ventures ambitiously into the uncharted waters of the assassination and its aftermath. He softens Malcolm's anti-Semitism, excuses his misogyny and homophobia, but otherwise renders an honest portrait of an extraordinarily complex man. Jason Vest catches most of this complexity when he calls the film "revolutionary and traditional, progressive and regressive, libertatory and restrictive" (2014, 61).

Though Lee has never been friendly to Black Nationalism, throughout his career he has shown profound interest in recognizably black cultural forms—jazz, rap, blues, hip-hop, black athleticism, and celebrity, together with the emerging canon of black cinema and drama. As Michael Dyson explains in *Making Malcolm* (1995), these institutions figure importantly in "the myth and meaning of Malcolm X." Describing "masculinity and the ghetto in black film," Dyson maintains that "the themes they treat, the styles they adopt, the moods they evoke" are almost unintelligible without recognition of "Malcolm's impact on a generation that has driven and seized on his heroic return." Black ghetto films of the late 1980s, which comprise the immediate backdrop for Lee's *Malcolm*, brood solemnly upon the tension between emasculation and virility, poverty and fast money, braggadocio and vulnerability personified in Malcolm X. In Dyson's summation, "Malcolm is black manhood squared, the unadulterated truth of white racism ever on his tongue, the unity of black people ever on his agenda, the pain of black ghetto dwellers ever on his mind" (Dyson 1995, 107–27). Malcolm the street-wise Harlemite, Malcolm the conked, self-fashioned Detroit Red, Malcolm the sexual gigolo to Sophia, Malcolm the crafty subaltern of West Indian Archie: these are the personae Lee developed from the black ghetto film and remade into the reprobate spirit of Malcolm before his conversion to Islam. Though perhaps a little too long, this opening movement of Lee's film provides him with the tropes that display his "blackness" as well as hint at the transgressive politics of black pop culture.

One of the most memorable passages of Haley's *Autobiography* gives us Malcolm's first view of Harlem:

> Up and down along and between Lennox and Seventh and Eighth avenues, Harlem was like some Technicolor bazaar. Hundreds of Negro soldiers and sailors, gawking and young like me, passed by. . . . Every man without a woman on his arm was being "worked" by the prostitutes. "Baby, wanna have some fun?" The pimps would sidle up close, stage-whispering. "All kinds of women, Jack, want a white woman?" And the hustlers were merchandising: "Hundred dollar ring, man, diamond; ninety dollar watch, too— look at 'em. Take 'em both for twenty-five." . . . In another two years, I could have given all of them lessons. But that night I was mesmerized. This world was where I belonged. (Haley 1993, 84)

The seductive spectacle of a noir city sets the stage for Malcolm's first iteration of himself as "one of the most depraved parasitical hustlers among New York's eight million people" (Haley 1993, 84).

In keeping with the conventions of the black ghetto film, particularly the tropes of Mario van Peebles' *New Jack City* (1991), Malcolm (Denzel Washington), who now calls himself "Red," is defined by violence, greed, and sexual conquest, specifically the conquest of white women. It's his spontaneous fury that first draws him into the orbit of West Indian Archie (Delroy Lindo), a major player in the Harlem rackets. The occasion

Spike Lee, *Malcolm X*. The consolidated black power of Harlem is the launch point of Malcolm's crusade for black autonomy. Racial pride in Joe Louis also foreshadows a more muscular assertion of black identity.

Source: This frame-capture is the work of James F. Scott, with technical support from the Instructional Media Center, Saint Lous University.

of their meeting is one of Malcolm's early visits to Small's Paradise (Lee 2000b, 29:50/35:00), at a time when he is regularly riding the train from Boston to New York as part of his railroad job. The décor of the scene is dominated by harsh red light, picked up in Red's flamboyant costume, an outlandish zoot suit with red and black stripes. The lighting is also low key, which produces a strobe effect, where the protagonist is lit almost to incandescence, then vanishes into deep darkness. What attracts Archie's notice is Malcolm's hair-trigger violence, evidenced in an argument with a customer at the bar, who mocks his wardrobe and insults his mother. Red seems to turn away from the fight, but only to grab a bottle from the counter and flatten his antagonist with a fierce blow to the head. Archie is sufficiently impressed by this response to buy Malcolm a drink and invite him to their table. Because Malcolm introduces himself as a West Indian, there is also an ethnic bonding, reflected in Archie's quick friendliness and hearty laughter. Before they part company, Red has pledged to quit his train job, apprentice himself to Archie's gang, and take some lessons in tailoring from the older, more seasoned gangster, because as one of

Archie's henchmen says, "those threads are puttin' a hurt on my vision." The pact is sealed a short time later as Malcolm is re-costumed in a much more conservative style and receives a present of Archie's first gun, a small caliber weapon, easily concealed in the new wardrobe. We have just witnessed a laying on of hands.

In spite of the vibrant cordiality of the scene at Small's, and immediately thereafter, the relationship to Archie is inherently unstable, since Malcolm carries a massive burden of rage, borne from the near past as well as from his more distant childhood. On the train trip that carries him to Small's, Malcolm has had an altercation with both his supervisor and one of the passengers. While in transit, the blacks who are servicing the train are berated for being noisy, as they listen to a fight broadcast of Joe Louis successfully defending his heavyweight crown. Of the small klatch of black porters, only Malcolm makes an ironic comment to his supervisor, prompting all the other blacks to censure him strongly, imagining that he might compromise their ability to get along with "good white folks." Moments later, Malcolm is consumed by quiet rage as he must smile foolishly while he hawks ham sandwiches up and down the aisles. He imagines himself mashing a creamy dessert into the face of a prospective customer, but in reality suppresses his anger, gliding by rote into a conventional Uncle Tom routine. The championship fight, of course, is also a symbol of black resistance, a point underscored when Red gets off the train in Harlem, mingling with a crowd that is ecstatic over the boxing exploits of Joe Louis.

Lee also skillfully introduces flashbacks into this sequence where Malcolm affiliates with Archie. The bar scene and its aftermath is broken up by references to Malcolm's childhood where the family is burned out of its home by Klansmen and his father is murdered by being thrown, semi-conscious, in front of an oncoming tram. The blow Malcolm delivers to the cocky bar patron who insults his mother is also payback to the insurance company who refused his mother's claim to her husband's life insurance and the social welfare agency that broke up the family by assigning the children to foster care. As Lee manages these details of the biography, we see that Malcolm's violence is a form of political resistance, albeit resistance too chaotic and unfocused to be anything other than meaningless hooliganism.

The sexual adventure with Sophia (Kate Vernon) is similarly tarnished by ulterior motives. Neither partner cares for the other in the slightest. Their intimate moments are mutually exploitative, in spite of sentimental pop lyrics crooning glibly that "My prayer is to linger with you in a world far away . . . in a dream that's divine" (Lee 2000b, 16:25/17:00). Sophia delights in vanquishing her black rival, Laura (Theresa Randle), glad for the advantages white privilege confers in the realm of Eros. But she seems not the least to mind that Malcolm arbitrarily demeans her. Their relationship is the diametric opposite of the bond between Pauli Carbone and his black girlfriend in *Jungle Fever*, where it is clear that each of them genuinely likes the other. Tellingly, Malcolm uses Sophia as a trophy to parade in front of Archie, a ploy that helps undermine the initial comradeship between the two men. She is also the enabler of his increasingly out-of-control drug habit and seems to collude with him to cheat Archie out of some of their earnings in the numbers racket. This leads to a breach with Archie and an attempt on Malcolm's life. When he and Shorty (Spike Lee) return to Boston, resolving to loot the city, Sophia is again a disruptive force: Malcolm humiliates Rudy (Roger Smith) in order to impress his white girlfriend with his devil-may-care courage, the act that impels Rudy to betray them to the police.

Up to this point in the film Lee has drawn heavily from the tropes of blaxploitation and film noir, filling the screen with macho posturing, sleazy sexuality, and explosive action. But with the protagonist's arrest and imprisonment, *Malcolm X* becomes a conversion narrative, fixated upon the birth of a "new man." The cocksure defiance that served him well as a small-time gangster now earns him only beatings and long stays in solitary confinement. The colorful world of Harlem fades into the gray tones of his prison cell and the utter blackness into which he is cast during his time of isolation. Steel bars and confined spaces dominate the décor, as Malcolm struggles with both his confinement and his unsatisfied craving for drugs. His rescuer is Baines (Albert Hall), a composite and largely fictional character, who eases Malcolm's withdrawal symptoms, counsels him against self-hatred, and introduces him to the thinking of the Honorable Elijah Muhammad (Al Freeman Jr.). Baines is the film's pivotal character, saving Malcolm from his self-destructive tendencies, but later betraying him as he strays from the teachings of Elijah. Under Baines' tutelage, Malcolm defeats his drug habit, adopts a pork-free diet, and begins to resist the Christian message of the prison chaplain. The capstone of this sequence is a mystical visitation from Elijah Muhammad: suddenly the bars of Malcolm's cell melt away as the Messenger of Allah, enveloped in golden light, calls the convert to his new mission in the world.

Malcolm's mission is the subject of what Lee calls "Act 3" of the film, the deeply ambiguous behavior of the convert after he has heard the call of Allah. Here Lee moves well beyond the orbit of Haley's narrative and also beyond the James Baldwin/Arnold Perl script from the 1970s, the closest text he had to the screenplay he himself was now preparing. Lee says in *By Any Means Necessary* that "the last act was weak because of the uncertainty of how to portray Elijah Mohammad in the context of the film" (Lee with Wiley 1992, 27). But Lee found as he addressed this question that he was thrust into controversy with the Nation of Islam and its new leader (as of 1985), Minister Louis Farrakhan. Farrakhan was hostile to Malcolm X and dismissive of the charges of sexual impropriety he had leveled at Elijah Muhammad. While the film was in production, Lee acknowledges that "I flew to Chicago to discuss the film with Farrakhan. . . . He didn't want us to trash the image of the Honorable Elijah Muhammad. He let me know he would be very upset if we did" (Fuchs 2002, 84). In light of Farrakhan's concerns, what view should Lee take of the sexual scandals surrounding Elijah? How should he interpret Malcolm's Mecca experience? How should he handle the assassination itself?

Lee understood that the passing of a quarter century brought with it the opportunity to see Malcolm X from a perspective unavailable to either Haley or Baldwin. But Farrakhan's determination to protect the image of Elijah from criticism at the hands of Malcolm, or now Malcolm's "biographer," Spike Lee, undoubtedly complicated the director's creative task.

In *By Any Means Necessary*, Lee gives a more detailed account of his "audience" with Farrakhan and their effort to find common ground in interpreting the behavior of the fallen black leader, especially during the period after his African journey and his pilgrimage to Mecca. But what Lee discovered was Farrakhan's complete intransigence. While conceding that Lee's film had "the potential of becoming one of the most powerful movies ever done by a Black person," showing "the ability of our people to make the transition from ignorance to knowledge, aimlessness to purpose," Farrakhan also worried that "the consequences of the mishandling of this film could be very, very grave for all concerned" (Lee with Wiley 1992, 50). Which meant, in effect, that Farrakhan would accept no criticism of Elijah's behavior toward Malcolm and contend instead that Malcolm's break with the Messenger of Allah was precipitous and wrongheaded. Dismissing Elijah's sexual delinquencies with his young secretaries as irrelevant, in fact, the scriptural prerogative of a patriarch and prophet, Farrakhan also rejected Malcolm's "Mecca experience" of human brotherhood and his confession that it had been wrong to demonize the white race. Instead, Farrakhan accused Lee of approaching Elijah "from the mind of a Christian who is not familiar with Islam nor with the lives of many religious prophets," many of whom had "a number of wives" (52). Lacking the requisite Islamic perspective, Lee would not be "interested in digging deeply enough to give this thing the balance that it should be given" (54). For this reason Farrakhan feared Lee's film might have "a terribly divisive effect" (56) upon black solidarity, unraveling much of the careful work the Nation had done over the previous three decades.

Farrakhan's unsympathetic view of Malcolm is incorporated into the film through the character of Baines, first established as Malcolm's savior during their time together in prison, but later alienated from his close

friend when Malcolm rises spectacularly in the ranks of Elijah Muhammad's chosen ones. It is Baines who suggests to Elijah that Malcolm is
promoting himself at the Nation's expense and Baines who arouses Betty's (Angela Bassett) suspicion that he is the chief voice of sinister rumors
about Malcolm's loyalty. When Malcolm speaks publicly in the name of
the Honorable Elijah Muhammad, Baines conspicuously withholds his
applause. As Malcolm and Baines finally confront each other, the scene is
drastically underlit, with both characters moving about in deep shadow
(Lee 2000b, 02:20:50/02:23:05). During their meeting, Baines makes no
explicit threat, but warns Malcolm to "be careful." As the crisis plays out,
with Malcolm's home devastated by a fire bomb, Baines smugly dismisses
the assault on his family as a "publicity stunt," engineered by Malcolm
himself to cast blame upon the Nation of Islam. Lee is not neutral on this
point, however, openly avowing that the "Nation of Islam was behind the
assassination" (Fuchs 2002, 85).

Despite his personal feelings, Lee was circumspect enough to avoid
explicitly indicting Farrakhan in his narrative. Threatened by the official
voice of the Nation of Islam, he made a diligent effort to avoid a caricature
of Elijah Muhammad and largely represents Malcolm as his loyal disciple.
Still, irony inflects both the editing and the composition of the film segment dealing with Malcolm's absolute discipleship to Elijah. When he
is instructing his future wife Betty about the proper age and stature of
a woman seeking a marriage partner, Malcolm's remarks—spoken as if
they were his own—are juxtaposed to exactly the same pronouncements
Elijah has made to Malcolm, as he teaches gender orthodoxy to his favorite
disciple. After reciting a grocery list of other platitudes, Malcolm warns
Betty that Samson was destroyed by a woman who claimed to love him,
using a favorite parable from the Messenger of Allah to remind his wife of
her duty to be subsurviant. Later, when Betty admonishes Malcolm to be
more wary of false friends, he silences her by again citing Elijah's precept
about man's supreme authority over his spouse. Similarly, when Malcolm
is on the podium addressing an assembly of partisans who represent Nation of Islam, we see him framed by the slogans and iconography of the
movement, as if his individual feelings had no substance apart from the
ideology that was threaded through all that he thought and said. In one
memorable image that is held and repeated (02:09:15/02:09:35), Malcolm
is framed against a massive poster of Elijah, so that he stands between
the eyes of his mentor, as if eternally under the scrutiny of the Nation
of Islam's peerless leader. These ironic touches underscore the extent to
which Malcolm at this time is Elijah's creature, a servant whose absolute
loyalty permits him no analytical distance from the spiritual master he
has allowed to form his mind.

For Lee, Malcolm's true conversion was what he experienced in Egypt and at Mecca. That's why he resisted so strenuously Warner's cost-cutting suggestion that he might stage the Middle East in Arizona or—even more laughably—in New Jersey. Complaining vehemently, Lee held the high ground when demanding, "How can you have 160 minutes of Malcolm saying white people are blue-eyed devils and then not go spend the time or money to shoot the pivotal moments to turn around on that line of thinking, which occurred in Africa and Saudi Arabia" (Lee with Wiley, 102). After these intramural battles were fought and won, Lee set out to render Malcolm's Holy Land pilgrimage as the most decisive event of his life. Not only does he acquire a new understanding of Islam, he also asserts a new selfhood, a sense of identity that he has not felt since he ceased to prowl the back streets of Harlem as the sinister "Detroit Red."

Malcolm's journey is double-sided, reflecting his dawning awareness of a political mission that is separable from his religious quest. This division is marked by his two distinct destinations, Cairo and Mecca. Edward Curtis, writing of *Islam in Black America* (2002), reminds us that at this moment in its history, Egypt under the leadership of Abdel Nasser had taken a notably secular turn, suppressing (and eventually executing) radical clerics like Sayid Qutp, who would posthumously reemerge in the 1990s as an inspiration for jihadist Islam. According to Curtis, the students of Islam who instructed Malcolm in the Sunni faith, chiefly Abd Azzam and Youssef Shawarbi, convinced Malcolm that if he "were a true Muslim, then he could not mix his Islam with his pan-Africanism" (104). These divergent paths are embedded in the shooting strategy of the two scenes. Cairo is energetic, colorful, slightly chaotic, not altogether different from the Harlem of Malcolm's days as a hustler (Lee 2000b, 02:40:00/02:43:00); Mecca, by contrast, is controlled, ceremonial, and respectful of transcendent forces (02:43:00/02:46:00). In Cairo, Malcolm is an outgoing tourist, trying to make friends, pricing fruit at the public market, giggling when a new acquaintance thinks he has come to see dancing girls, finally improvising a trip to visit the pyramids. At Mecca, he dons the white costume of a pilgrim, spends virtually all his time in places of ritual, and cleanses himself at a fountain dedicated to that purpose. Here, as he writes home to Betty, he "stood before the Creator of all and felt like a true human being." These two faces of selfhood are congruent, however, because in his new formulation of an agenda, Islam must mend the moral character of the African American before it will be possible to proceed with the enactment of broader political goals. Malcolm returns from his international journey with a newfound openness and cooperative spirit, though this positive transformation makes him all the more vulnerable to the angry spirit of Nation of Islam.

Spike Lee, *Malcolm X*. The pilgrimage to Mecca is the culmination of Malcolm's quest to know the spiritual essence of Islam.

Source: This frame-capture is the work of James F. Scott, with technical support from the Instructional Media Center, Saint Louis University.

Lee also treads carefully in assigning blame for Malcolm's assassination, in spite of his personal convictions. Malcolm himself accuses the Nation in an excited comment to reporters after his home is firebombed, but he later second-guesses himself, wondering if other actors (the FBI or the CIA?) might share the blame. What the imagery does show is that Malcolm was certainly under surveillance, as we first observe in the pilgrimage sequence where he is stalked by a man with a film camera. It's also evident that his phone is being tapped and recordings made of conversations with his wife and their supporters. Lee does not interpret this data, leaving as an open question whether federal authorities were perhaps complicit in the assassination by taking no steps to prevent it. But the scene in the Audubon Ballroom is one of sheer chaos with multiple shooters coming forward out of the audience, giving no clue as to their affiliation or their motive for murdering the speaker at the podium.

Lee is more interested in the aftermath of these events, not with reference to the Nation of Islam but in the broader working out of the American civil rights movement and the dismantling of European colonialism in Africa, particularly in the struggle against apartheid in South Africa. Lee sought to include Nelson Mandela in his epic of black liberation and engineered an on-screen role for the South African patriot, who in 1991 had just been released after nearly thirty years in prison. He would not step forward as South Africa's first black president until 1994, but he was already involved in negotiations to dismantle the apartheid regime. We see him gathered with a small detachment of school children, whom he quietly lectures on respect for the human person. Lee sees the martyred Malik El Shabazz as an American Nelson Mandela, and the American civil rights movement as analogous to the anti-apartheid struggle that freed Mandela from prison and would soon promote him to the highest office in the land. The last scenes of *Malcolm X* are organized around Ossie Davis' eloquent funeral oration, which is cut together with images of Martin Luther King Jr., Bobby Seale, and the black athletes who protested at the 1968 Olympics. Together they are gathered under Davis' rubric of "our black manhood, our living black manhood." Davis' words are also intended as a rationale for reconciliation: "However we might have differed with him, or with each other about his value as a man, let his going from us serve only to bring us together now" (Lee 2000b, 03:07:45/03:11:05).

Appropriately, *Malcolm X* ends in Harlem, the *locus classicus* of the Minister's life and work. True to the theme of education, we are remembering Malcolm X in a public school classroom where a black schoolmarm is advising her young charges to imagine themselves as extensions of Malcolm X. Then each rises energetically to proclaim directly into the camera, "I am Malcolm X." While there is no literal possibility that any of these children could grow up to be clones of Malcolm, there is great likelihood that each child might build into his or her own life some sense of what Malcolm exemplified—courage, honesty, resilience, and determined political engagement. How might these virtues express themselves across the boundaries of culture, ethnicity, and gender over the next half-century? Wisely, Lee declines to offer anything resembling an answer. But the images of assertion, and even defiance, culminating in a final archival image of Malcolm himself, avow that the black liberation movement will go forward, "by any means necessary."

Lee returned to the issue of black identity and racial progress in *Get on the Bus* (1996), a much less spectacular and decisively low-budget film marketed by Columbia pictures. Lee was proud to announce in the credits that the film was paid for by donations from African American benefactors, notably Danny Glover, Wesley Snipes, and Lee himself. Carried out on a budget of less than $3 million (as opposed to the $30+ million lavished upon *Malcolm X*), it could hardly compete against the pyramids, Mecca, and the sands of Arabia in making a visual impression. But, like *Malcolm*, *Get on the Bus* is a journey of discovery, a "pilgrimage" with religious overtones, which follows a diverse assortment of young black men, as they make their way to Washington, DC, answering Louis

Farrakhan's call for a "Million Man March" on Washington to dramatize the unfulfilled expectations of the civil rights movement. The film
affords Lee the opportunity to again explore (and critique) Farrakhan's
leadership of the resurgent Nation of Islam and at the same time to present his own outsider's perspective upon losses and gains in the black
community in the generation after charismatic leaders like Malcolm and
King have left the stage.

Get on the Bus was kind of an improvisation in the sense that this production interrupted the making of another film Lee was already at work
on, *Girl 6*, which he would return to and also complete in 1996. The film
responded specifically to Farrakhan's summons, not in the manner of an
endorsement so much as skeptical commentary, though a commentary
that respected Farrakhan's power to mobilize public opinion and raise issues that were not being reflected in the national discourse. For better or
worse, Farrakhan beamed his remarks exclusively toward black males and
preached a salvation anchored in the core principles of Elijah Muhammad,
which were inherently sexist and anti-Semitic. As Farrakhan would have
it, "we wanted to call out men to Washington to make a statement that we
were ready to accept the responsibility of being the heads of our households, the providers, the maintainers and the protectors of our women
and children" (quoted in Aftab and Lee 2006, 272). Though Lee remained
angry at Farrakhan for his subversion of Malcolm's political mission and
was at odds with the obsessively familial focus of the Nation of Islam, he
felt, like many others in the black community, that Farrakhan had touched
a powerful chord in encouraging greater concentration upon black self-
fashioning and in resisting the "benign neglect" of African American
concerns in the national discourse. The busload of cross-country travelers
who board the Spotted Owl charter in Los Angeles all have mixed feelings
about Farrakhan and limited awareness of his preachments. But most embark with a sense of search and the hope of transformation.

As in other Spike Lee "joints," perhaps most memorably in *Do the Right
Thing*, Lee uses the sequence of preliminary credits to introduce crucial
motifs of the film. In the case of *Get on the Bus*, the theme is captivity, visualized as shackles that curtail the mobility of the black body—a metal
clamp for the neck, chains that cling to the torso, further metallic restraints
on the ankles. Included among these historically framed and sepia-toned
allusions to the slave trade and American slave culture, there are several
images of modern handcuffs, reflecting the contemporary oppression
of mass racialized incarceration, a phenomenon that was beginning to
declare itself in the mid-1990s and would grow to epidemic proportions
in the years to follow. Mixed with the detailed imagery of bondage are
various tight shots of African American eyes staring at unseen objects,
while the vocal musical score advises whoever is listening to "look at

yourself in the mirror (and) see if you like what you see" (Lee 1996a, 00:30/03:00). This montage speaks eloquently of the need for introspection and self-critical analysis. Perhaps it also implies a need for concerted action, epitomized in the huge march on Washington that is planned. But as the credits give way to the narrative that follows, the first images of the marchers undercut our expectations of solidarity, when we see a son handcuffed to his father, while the father leads his reluctant offspring toward a bus the boy is conspicuously unwilling to board (03:00/05:05). The driver immediately notices the unlikely pair and wonders aloud which "plantation" they've escaped from. The explanation that Junior (De'Aundre Bonds) is a prisoner in the temporary custody of his parent is legally clear, but in no sense morally satisfactory. It seems that the black underclass has simply exchanged one form of bondage for another, now even consciously oppressing itself.

Another discordant note in the first scene strikes at the conception of the march itself, a summoning of male power to the neglect, really the deliberate exclusion, of a female presence. This assertion of male privilege is in keeping with the fundamental tenets of the Nation of Islam and Farrakhan's own preachments, which enjoin African American men to "protect" their women but not to grant them public or professional agency. This stricture immediately sets at cross-purposes the two characters we next meet, as the camera pans from Evan and Junior to Gary (Roger Smith) and his girlfriend Shelley (Kristin Wilson), who is delivering him to the Million Man March. Shelley is a well-dressed, well-spoken, and professional-looking woman who strenuously resents the fact that women have been denied the chance to offer their perspective upon the needs of the black community in the 1990s. "This whole thing is sexist and exclusionary," she charges, arguing that any large-scale transformation of black men will require the active engagement of black women. She also wonders if Gary, a decidedly fair-skinned African American, would be comfortable with a march to which only "dark-skinned brothers" had been invited. As she reluctantly releases Gary to his all-male cohorts, she insists that "we're not finished talking about this" (Lee 1996a, 04:00/04:55). Nor is Lee. The issue is raised again in a scene at a rest stop in Little Rock, Arkansas, and once more in the closing minutes of the film, when the bus is diverted from its assigned destination to deal with a medical emergency on board. This plotting allows Lee to omit coverage of Farrakhan's keynote speech and acknowledge instead one of the few female speakers sharing the podium with the radical minister, the black poet Maya Angelou. This last turn underscores Lee's determination to endorse the march but not the minister who has called the crowd together.

Lee's overriding purpose in *Get on the Bus* is to reveal the diversity of the black community, foregrounding not only its richness and density, but also its cross-purposes and internal contradictions. In her discussion of "Realism, Representation, and Essentialism" in Spike Lee's "discourse," Wahneema Lubiano worries that this director, particularly in his portrait of Malcolm X, accidentally formulated a "symbol of blackness" who inadvertently came to represent the race, with the result that "we've backed ourselves into a religion of 'essential blackness' and away from a historical analysis or exploration of its complexities, its constructedness," adding that "iconography and fetishization is no substitute for history and critical thinking" (2008, 48). The detailed roll call of characters in *Get on the Bus*, together with the specialized and impromptu agendas they attempt to carry forward, is Lee's rebuke to the search for a universal black "essence."

The film is a picaresque adventure with narrative centers that change moment by moment and also yield to external events of the journey as these alter and complicate the storytelling priorities. Among the various themes Lee singles out for attention, we are asked to take note of ethno-racial fractures, of spiritual commitments, of class and caste divisions, of law and law enforcement, of parental and spousal relationships, of homosexuality and homophobia, even the rights and responsibilities of black media, but above all, of prospects for a future relieved of at least some of the burdens of the past. Inevitably, talk sometimes overwhelms action, though Lee is reasonably successful at inventing stage business and creating musical bridges appropriate to maintain a brisk pace.

The last major figure to take the stage in the opening scene is the Rev. Jeremiah Washington (Ossie Davis), whose seniority accords him a leadership role, though his fragile health and generational distance from the other marchers make him a slightly more problematic figure. We first see him cutting a medical band from his arm as he shambles down a short flight of stairs to catch a cab for the march. Joining the brothers, he claims to have "never felt better in my life," but is described by one of his bus mates as "an old man stuck in the sixties." His clenched fist is rather limp as he shouts for "black power," though most of the travelers honor his greeting by returning the call. There's also a hint of anachronism in his offer to say a prayer, but no one explicitly objects and all bow their heads reverently. His invocation makes the predictable references to Moses parting the Red Sea and King going up to the mountain, but he also remembers "Malcolm when he went to Mecca" and soon is in a serious conversation with Jamal (Gabriel Cassius), a devoutly orthodox Muslim, who was a gang member before he converted to Islam. While improvising his prayer, Jeremiah is momentarily interrupted by Flip (Andre Braughter), a self-important young actor, who boards the bus late. Unfazed, the preacher completes his call for God's blessing (Lee 1996a, 05:05/10:00).

This opening vignette underscores the mood of transition and the search for new leadership that characterizes the journey and the film. Lee is careful not to endorse one faction over another but to amplify a rich mix of contending voices, none of which constitutes a fixed and final dogma, such as preached by Farrakhan and the Nation of Islam.

Several story lines energize incidental moments in the action. Other strands of the narrative are through-lines that create the longer arcs of the film. Early on, we discover that one of the "pilgrims" is Xavier (Hill Harper), a filmmaker in the making from UCLA who is shooting and editing the trek to DC as his thesis project. His assignment invites him to intrude upon the privacy of others, linking one marginalized life world to another. Xavier and his probing camera get a hearty share of screen time, and he becomes one of the principal voices of the march. Commenting on his feverish action, one of the marchers endorses his work, as an antidote to media stereotypes, which reduce black culture to crime, gangs, and general disorder. From time to time, Lee cuts from the color stock that carries the official story line to the gray-scale images shot with Xavier's handheld camera, suggesting the young man's status as a subnarrator, who partners with Lee to chronicle events of the six-day trek. The other story that commands attention is the evolving relationship between Junior and his Dad, conspicuously bound together by handcuffs. Though they do not relish each other's company, they gradually grow more sympathetic to one another, so that by the end of the film, the son is free of his shackles and something like a family relationship seems possible. Gary may be the most conflicted character traveling to DC. Beyond his frictional relationship to a girlfriend who has disowned Farrakhan's project, Gary is a biracial child, with a black father who was a police officer murdered by a black gang member. He identifies with his father, both in calling himself "black" and choosing his father's career in police work for his own.

No sooner is the bus on the road than arguments and signs of fissure begin to reveal themselves. One contentious topic is black homosexuality, which is introduced into the narrative by two lovers who are publicly dissolving their partnership. Though Kyle (Isaiah Washington) pleads with his partner to "keep your voice down," it proves impossible to hold a private conversation. Issues of masculinity quickly come into play, because—according to his accuser—Kyle refuses "to let your macho ass out of the closet." Fleeing the argument, Kyle takes a new seat, but the greater separation simply makes the dispute more public. Soon the recalcitrant Junior is cursing his father for taking him on the "Million Man March with a bunch of homos" and Flip, the priggish actor, complains loudly of "faggots on the bus." Xavier, the filmmaker, intervenes on the side of the gay couple, asking, "Don't gays have a role in the black community?"

After insults fly in several directions, Jeremiah notes that, though the Bible condemns homosexual behavior, he's not sure how he would handle a son with homosexual tendencies. Or how he himself would behave if he had been "born that way." One of the lovers will later have to prove his manhood by besting Flip in hand-to-hand combat, but the issue of homosexual behavior is left unresolved. Like most of the issues the film addresses, Lee intends to bring the topic to the table, not push for premature consensus (Lee 1996a, 16:30/18:40).

In keeping with the conventions of picaresque narrative, Lee depends considerably upon adventitious events to propel his loose and baggy story line. Relatively early on, the driver, in a distracted moment, lets the bus run off the road. This collects the group into the common task of pushing the vehicle out of the ditch. After some huffing and puffing, they succeed, but only to find that the axle is broken and that they can't go further without a new vehicle and a new driver. So the Million Man March begins with an acknowledgment of dependency, in effect, stranded and in need of roadside assistance. The charter service responds to their needs, but replaces the disabled bus with one piloted by a Jewish driver who is completely unsympathetic to Minister Farrakhan and resentful that he has been called upon to perform this emergency rescue. Nor does this substitution work out smoothly. Richard (Richard Belzer) promises to take the wheel simply as a professional responsibility, but finally can't morally accept the task at hand. After wrestling with the problem for several hours, he tells George (Charles Dutton), the organizer and spokesperson of the march, "You wouldn't expect a black man to transport Klansmen to a Ku Klux Klan rally." Reluctantly, George concedes his point and agrees to complete the drive himself (Lee 1996a, 53:35/55:50). In this sequence, autonomy triumphs, but not before the narrative takes several ironic turns.

The trek is also burdened with a particularly obnoxious passenger, whom they pick up in Memphis, after he announces his eagerness to join the march. Though George is reluctant to let him sign on, Jeremiah and Xavier intercede on his behalf and Wendell (Wendell Pierce), a rich, cigar-smoking car salesman, becomes one of the pilgrims.

This character is presumably introduced for comic potential, but he is a woefully crude caricature of black conservatism. Very much a free market capitalist, he scorns affirmative action, mocks Jackson's Rainbow Coalition, and speaks derisively of black colleges he is proud not to have attended. More a cartoon character than a full-bodied person, Wendell's chief contribution to the rhetoric of race discourse is that he elicits from George a defense of Farrakhan for his service, however ambiguous, to the cause of black advancement. In his eight minutes on screen (Lee 1996a, 01:01:50/01:09:50), Wendell alienates almost every other rider, charging that the march itself is a scam and dismissing racism as "a figment of the black man's imagination." Kyle briefly defends his critique of black dependency but soon realizes that they are not really cultural allies. No one contests his admiration of Colin Powell but all are offended by his obsessive use of the N-word. When Xavier asks why he's attending the march, he admits it is simply an opportunity to broaden his business network. Convinced that African American males can't resist sexy-looking cars, he apparently sees the great gathering in DC as the sales opportunity of a lifetime. Weary of his insults and the fog of his cigar smoke, the travelers forcibly eject him from the bus. In spite of its contribution to the film's multisided conversation, the scene falls rather flat and seems out of keeping with the general tone of the film.

The last intrusion comes as the travelers reach Knoxville and are visited by Tennessee state troopers conducting a drug patrol. Their stop and search of the bus is completely arbitrary, since we see no other traffic pulled over and there is no evidence of an infraction on the part of the driver. It seems a clear case of suspecting all large congregations of black men. As the troopers board the bus, Gary displays his badge and shield, introducing himself as a member of the Los Angeles police department. But his credentials count for nothing, as he is reminded that Tennessee is not Los Angeles. George has fervently insisted that the marchers carry no illegal substances to DC and fortunately his advice has been heeded. The troopers bring dogs on board and are disrespectful at every turn, rummaging through everyone's belongings and urging the marchers to confess and reveal their stashes before the dogs sniff out their crime. When the drug search turns up nothing incriminating, they depart on a cordial note, remarking that if the marchers ever need "law enforcement assistance," Tennessee's finest will be there to protect them. All faces freeze in close-ups lit by an eerie blue light until it is clear that the troopers actually have departed. At that point the bus pulls back onto the interstate for the final leg of the journey (Lee 1996a, 01:23:30/01:26:25).

Meanwhile, the long hours of cross-country travel provide occasions for the deepening of interpersonal relationships and the advancement of thematic concerns. The visual production values are negligible, but the bus provides a minimalist stage for several consequential conversations. Little clusters of men gather, talk passionately for a moment or two, then disperse, as another exchange begins elsewhere. Flip speaks of being beaten fiercely with a belt reserved for no other purpose, and Jamal confesses that as a member of the Crips he had carried out several gangland-style executions.

Of these impromptu discussions, the tense dialogue between father and son, still manacled to each other, is one of the most revealing. After Evan offers to take over the driving (he claims to have been a professional truck driver), George points out that this will be possible only if he releases

Junior from handcuffs. When he shows reluctance, George pleads that "you can't ride into DC with that boy in shackles." He's also persuaded that "you've got yourself a good boy" who deserves a second chance. Unfortunately, when Evan does give his son his freedom, the boy runs away at the first opportunity, forcing his father to chase him down. But the episode has a better outcome than we might have expected, as their private moment together leads to the most meaningful conversation they've had. Evan confesses his failure as a father, acknowledging that he "was not man enough to take on the responsibilities" of parenting. In turn, Junior admits his own fear, and remarks how his urge to flee mimics the behavior of his father. The scene ends in an affectionate embrace, but in spite of this newfound rapport, Junior goes back into handcuffs, which he is still wearing when they step off the bus in DC (Lee 1996a, 01:35:20/01:38:30).

The other long arc of the plot that Lee fashions is the evolving relationship between Jeremiah, the faltering prophet, and Xavier, the energetic young filmmaker who seems destined to replace him in the leadership role. They grow significantly closer when Xavier interviews him on camera and incorporates his backstory into the history of the march (Lee 1996a, 01:27:40/01:31:25). We find that his persona as elder statesman of the black power movement is largely a fiction, that in reality he missed King's March on Washington in 1963 because he was settling into a well-paying job and wished not to offend his white bosses. He says he also made a point of distancing himself from Malcolm X and the political activism of that decade, again in fear of reprisals. He now feels discarded from the corporate culture he served faithfully and seeks a "second chance," in the same way that Evan seeks a second chance to be a father. His eleventh-hour determination to affiliate with a movement he had been too timid to embrace leads effectively to the film's climax, where the travelers reach DC and we mingle with a truly massive crowd, feeling the force of its energy. In this scene, Xavier is busy with his camera, leaning out the window and clamoring to the roof of the bus (Lee 1996a, 01:40:00/01:42:00). Tragically, when he tries to rouse Jeremiah to share this lyrical moment, he finds him in a state of cardiac arrest, barely clinging to life. Jeremiah dies in the emergency room, having lived just long enough to link his name to the march and inspire a small cadre of like-minded spirits to carry on in his name.

The effort to save Jeremiah carries the action in a new direction, allowing Lee to deftly avoid Farrakhan's rally, reducing it to a few incidental images seen on television in the hospital waiting room. Farrakhan is nowhere to be found, replaced chiefly by Maya Angelou, who represents the female voice that several critics of the march had wished for. Lee's maneuver around the rally lets him concentrate, in the closing scenes of the film, not on the official agenda of Farrakhan, but on more personal agendas, typified by Evan, Xavier, and George.

Though he is no longer among the marchers, Jeremiah speaks the last words of the film. Having missed the rally, the bus mates gather at the Lincoln Memorial for their private meditation before beginning the journey home. George awards to Xavier the tribal drum that Jeremiah much prized, assuming that he is the man best qualified to speak for the rising generation. He also exhorts the group to be a force for good in their communities, resisting "crime, drugs, guns, gangs, and children killing children." Lastly, he reads the prayer that Jeremiah had intended to offer at the conclusion of the march. As he does the reading, his voice gives way to that of Jeremiah himself, while Xavier begins to tap out a musical message on the tribal drum. The prayer speaks of "the scent of water" that will coax the dead stump into new sprouts of life that emerge from its roots. The last lingering image is a slow tilt down from the face of Lincoln to the space immediately in front of the monument. That space frames a single object—the shackle that once tethered Evan's son (Lee 1996a, 01:54:00/01:56:45).

SEGMENT 3: REPRESENTING BLACKNESS:
GIRL 6 (1996) AND *BAMBOOZLED* (2000)

Himself a maker of images, Lee from the outset of his career has been sensitive to the role of representation in defining the black community. That's why he pushed back so insistently when he felt that Warner Brothers was bent on taking from him the opportunity to portray the black world's most charismatic culture hero of the late twentieth century, Malcolm X. Lee's antipathy to blaxploitation films of the 1970s springs from the same set of assumptions. But his interest in the image extends beyond product to process: How do African Americans fare when, like Xavier in *Get on the Bus*, they attempt to make themselves architects of their own images by launching careers in film, media, and other forms of public art? These themes find expression in two films at the turn of the century, *Girl 6* and *Bamboozled*. As Jamie Barlowe argues in "'You Must Never Be a Misrepresented People'" (2003), Lee feels that, "although African Americans have earned positions as actors, directors, writers, and even producers, in the film and television industries, the 'gate keepers,' the real power behind the camera, are all white" (4).

Recent scholarship has been highly attentive to the role of stage and theater in the formulation of ethno-racial identity. In *Staging Blackness* (2006), Karen Sotiropoulos reaches back to "black performers in turn of

the century America," particularly black musicians, to find early examples
of "a commitment to using 'real Negro melodies' for racial advancement"
(83). But the difficulty, she observes, is that black artists of this period,
with Will Marion Cook and others as cases in point, found that as they
struggled to present an authentic "Negro song" they were competing
against radically different representations of black culture that were the
work of white artists and majority institutions. In Moody's case, the musical material he sought to market as "real Negro melodies" were sold as
"coon songs," advertised as something indistinguishable from the crud-
est minstrel caricatures of black life and entertainment (see Sotiropoulos
2006, 81–122). As Cook and others came to understand, the framing devices that staged the art and the marketing vehicles that delivered the art
to the public were ultimately more important than the art itself. Nearly
a century later, Lee encounters a similar artistic environment and makes
it the subject of two of his most ambitious films, *Girl 6* and *Bamboozled*.
The first records the defeat of a would-be black actress, undone by the
casting process and a pair of exploitative producer/directors. The second
recounts the ruin of a black television writer, who suffers at the hands of
the network manager and from his own self-inflicted wounds.

According to critical consensus, *Girl 6* is not one of Lee's better films.
David Sterritt berates it as "neither a popular movie nor an artistically
successful one," remarking that the faults of the film "are attributable to
the script as well as to Lee's handling of it" (2013, 135). For the first time
in his career, Lee had given over his role as writer to Suzan-Lori Parks,
a young black playwright who was earning critical acclaim for her bold
theatrical experiments and her articulation of racial and feminist themes.
Though the partnership seemed promising (and Lee surely needed help
in the delineation of his female characters), writer and director failed to
enter into a completely satisfactory relationship, with the result that the
whole is somehow less than the sum of its parts. Parks says little about
her collaboration with Lee, except that "Spike added stuff" to the script
of *Girl 6*. We gather this is "stuff" she herself would have never included,
but "it was his baby and you just had to let it go and not worry about it"
(Kolin and Young 2014, 90). Among other things, she didn't want her protagonist, the Theresa Wrangle figure, to bare her breasts to the male gaze
in an early interview scene. Actually, I think Lee's decision in this case is
defensible (see below), but his quarrel with Parks over details of this sort
advertises their inability to achieve a harmonious partnership, in spite of
broad agreement about racial stereotypes in the media. Lee himself defends his film, but a bit left-handedly. "I think it is very experimental and,
unfairly, the most underrated of all my films" (Aftab and Lee 2006, 267).
The first clause is directly on target, the second perhaps more like wish-
ful thinking. The film's significance to the Lee canon, however, is that in

many ways it foreshadows the much more substantial *Bamboozled*, which Lee created four years later.

Girl 6 is a study in role-playing and a critique of ethno-racial assignment. The protagonist, Judy, aka Lovely Brown (Theresa Wrangle), is a black actress trying to launch a career in New York and dogged by stereotypical expectations that follow her as she seeks opportunities for herself via stage or screen. In keeping with this theme, the film features wigs, hairstyles, costumes, make-up, and other cosmetic paraphernalia that underscore the plasticity of the human person, particularly the racialized female. Shots of mirror reflections also abound, drawing attention to how people compose an identity from moment to moment, while studying their own reflections. The opening montage presents the heroine as a collection of body parts—lips, mouth, teeth, eyes—images cut together with items from the "personals" section of a newspaper, which lay out the psychosexual agendas of lonely New Yorkers. Judy is a human Lego set, ready for assembly or disassembly. In the first scene, we watch her audition for a white director who promises he is producing "the greatest African American film ever made," one that will be told "from the point of view of an African American woman" (Lee 1996b, 02:50/07:00). Though seeking a black actress, the director (Quentin Tarantino) seems at best marginally interested in the dramatic script she performs. Judy herself has no inkling of what role she will play, but she is told simply that baring her breasts is the one non-negotiable demand that she must meet. Thus commanded, she complies under protest, while the camera stares voyeuristically at her ample breasts. So much for the point of view of the African American woman! This insistence on her nudity disturbs Judy so seriously that she leaves the interview in tears, only to be further humiliated by her acting coach and her professional agent. Both scold her intemperately for refusing to recognize the rules of the road, which recognize relevance in black bodies only when they are largely unclothed. Significantly, the figure least sympathetic to Judy's feelings is herself a black woman, completely compliant with the system and angry that anyone would have the temerity to resist. From the outset, Lee and Parks are bent on showing that the problem of casting black characters or generating black scripts is structural, not personal. The issue will not be settled simply by having a fuller black presence either in front of or behind the camera.

In some ways Parks was the ideal scenarist to create this script, since her work in theater entails masks, impersonations, reenactments, and various other devices of costume and performance that relativize identity, particularly racial identity. She is also an ardent feminist. These signatures are evident in the two plays she wrote for the stage immediately before creating the script for *Girl 6*. *The America Play* (1994) features a black gravedigger who bears a striking resemblance to President Lincoln, exhibiting the same gaunt and gangling physical frame, though clearly the wrong skin tones. Representing himself both as "The Founding Father" and "The Lesser Known," he is a living oxymoron that reflects the cognitive dissonance of American political life. On the one hand, African American culture reaches back to the founding moments of the nation; on the other, it is nowhere advertised as a fundamental element of the national culture. The role of gravedigger associates him with burials, hence with repression, submergence, and the realm of subterranean forces. In fact he tends the "Great Hole of History," which alludes to all the unacknowledged black history that is interred under official versions of the historical record. While working on the script of *Girl 6*, Parks was also writing *Venus* (1996), a radical feminist play that is also intensely anti-colonial. The protagonist, also a victim of sexual exploitation, is the so-called "Hottentot Venus," part of a nineteenth-century sideshow that renders her as a spectacular sexual object. A central figure in "Mother Showman's" traveling carnival, the hapless black woman is endlessly on display for the exaggerated development of her buttocks and genitals. Though she escapes into the company of "the Baron," who is also a man of science, she quickly contracts gonorrhea from her new master and eventually dies in prison. In a metaphoric sense, she has never been anything other than a prisoner, a captive of the racialized colonial culture that holds her enthralled.

Rightly, Parks saw the concerns of *Girl 6* as a variation upon themes that fully engaged her, particularly the question of identity. In the interview quoted above, she details her perception of Judy's situation: "She's everybody: 'Who am I? Who do you want me to be? You want me to be blond? I'm blond. I'm brunette. I'm Asian too.' So that's really how it lines up with the rest of my work, how the self is malleable" (Kolin and Young 2014, 90).

What went wrong? While there is no definitive answer, it would seem that Parks was unable to write within the conventions of realism, with the result that the real and the surreal sometimes compete with each other, even disturb and displace each other. The first hour of the film represents one wing of the New York sex workers' industry with striking fidelity, sometimes almost documentary in tone. But as Judy is drawn more and more deeply into a world of psychic derangement, the landscape becomes nightmarish, hopelessly distorted by illegible shapes, gathering shadows, and garish blobs of color that have no reference points in the daylight world. Significantly, when Judy meets Lil, her first sex trade mentor, she impresses her soon-to-be employer by solving a crossword puzzle that asks for a seven-letter word that might describe "a body falling." The answer is "vertigo," which also alludes to a Hitchcock film about the loss of psychic balance and the threat of a descent into madness. The allusion seems intended to bring the real and surreal together, much as Hitchcock wove them together in his classic thriller of 1958. But *Girl 6* suffers from comparison to *Vertigo*, though both have sexual exploitation at their core. Whether the blame for the flaws of the film falls principally upon Lee or Parks is an open question. Whatever its faults, however, *Girl 6* is remarkably sensitive to the ways that race and racial perception deform the aspirations of a talented black woman.

The narrative thrust of *Girl 6* carries the action in two directions: Judy's struggle to persuade herself that her performance as a phone sex "friend" is the equivalent of an acting career and the impact that this job has upon her personal relationships. Seeking love, or at least a sense of belonging, she is convinced that she can't get it in real life and is ready to look for it on the job. That proves dangerous.

One of the more memorable achievements of *Girl 6* is its credible treatment of the underclass of sex workers who comprise part of the new service economy of New York City. Presumably these character sketches owe more to Parks than to Lee, but the director contextualizes them in a convincing way. In *Understanding Suzan-Lori Parks* (2012), Jennifer Larson remarks with reference to *Girl 6* how well the playwright and screenwriter "depathologizes abnormal sexuality and sexual fantasy, especially for women, while simultaneously questioning Hollywood's sexualization of black women" (103). This point applies not only to the clients who seek eccentric sexual fulfillment but also to the women who struggle to maintain their own "normalcy," while they construct roles that implicate them in their clients' off-center demands. Judy, of course, is the primary case in point.

After her humiliation at the interview and the meltdown with her agent and acting coach that follows, Judy resolves to explore the sex trade as a venue for her talents, hoping that she can avoid compromising herself by building a firewall of professional distance between what she pretends to do and what she actually does. First she visits a strip club that apparently also functions as a phone sex hub, even though they want the women they employ to work out of their own homes. Judy is troubled by the lack of privacy this arrangement implies, though she is assured every effort is made to protect the sex workers' personal safety. But the atmosphere also looks terribly unwholesome (Lee 1996b, 19:10/21:00). Throughout the interview, while Judy is being assured of the respectability of the job, the background is full of semi-nude women twisting themselves provocatively around dancing poles. At regular intervals, great jets of steam erupt to drench the stage with surrogate bodily fluids. Fortunately, the fact that Judy lacks a private phone line allows her to move beyond this environment leaving no hard feelings behind.

The protagonist settles upon what looks like a more professional operation when she finds a venue that offers a workplace apart from her residence and a cadre of co-workers who support each other and exchange information about their job experiences. At the orientation session, we also learn that the agency provides a set of scripts that compel each girl to adopt several prospective identities to fit the preferences and fetishes of the callers who seek their services. Judy positions herself to play either the Dominatrix or the Girl Next Door, but finds that she settles most comfortably into the latter role, designating herself "Lovely Brown," a name which plays upon both her race and her personal disposition. Ironically, all the women Lil has recruited are asked to be "white," an odd stipulation considering that they will be performing their "whiteness" over the telephone. What does it mean to sound white?

Faedra Carpenter has met this question head-on in *Coloring Whiteness* (2014). Concerned with the personae that voice-over artists project for radio (and television featuring an off-screen narrator), Carpenter is struck by how few performers have succeeded in their "racial ventriloquism," wondering at length about "aural whiteness, linguistic whiteface, and the economics of opportunity" (2014, 194; see also 194–224). What Carpenter's research established was that generic voices were assumed to be "white voices" unless there was a disconfirming image attached to a voice advertising a "white" product. She cites the case of Nancy Giles, an African American actress who did off-camera voice-overs for clients such as Folgers coffee, Office Depot, and the *New York Times*. Giles remarks her success in these crossover roles until prospective sponsors realized that she was Private Frankie Bunsen, a black female character from the television drama *China Beach* (1988–1991), which reprised the Vietnam War. Thereafter she experienced at least temporary difficulties in securing further contracts to voice so-called "white" parts. From these and other instances of similar responses, Carpenter describes a "racial synesthesia," which causes an image to be automatically associated with a voice when the vocal cues are inconclusive. This persuades her to distinguish between "linguistic whiteface" (which conspicuously exaggerates the qualities of the white voice) and "presumed aural whiteness" that achieves a true "racial ventriloquism" (210–15). Exactly this distinction is enacted in Lee's film, as Judy's performance of whiteness is contrasted with that of her one black female colleague.

Judy's co-worker is also successful in her racial impersonation, though she enacts it in a much more self-conscious way, playing the Dominatrix by simulating a West Indian accent conspicuous for its British imperial inflections. Using what seem to be native Caribbean voice rhythms, she flavors her speech with discernibly British vowels that suggest a private girl's school education in Jamaica or elsewhere in the English-speaking islands. It proves to be a fully convincing performance, adding the authority of Empire to the sexualized demands she makes upon her hapless client, who is completely drawn into the "naughty child" role in which she casts him. Hers is a perfect articulation of linguistic whiteface. But Judy (as Lovely) outperforms her co-worker, as she glides fluently into her first iteration of the Girl Next Door, showing little sense of self-consciousness as she accommodates her New York City accent to the norm of "presumed oral whiteness." With her first client, Judy scores a success that sets the bar for her much-impressed colleagues. While other sex workers step out of their own booths to listen in on Judy's performance, she masterfully coaxes "Steve" into sexual enthrallment. Perfectly intuiting the voice of his girl-next-door seductress, Judy guides Steve step by step from getting acquainted, through erotic arousal, to orgasmic climax. Lil, the Madame, is so pleased by Judy's launch that she pins a corsage on her prize recruit, while all stand about applauding. The downside of this impressive beginning, unfortunately, is that it causes her to become more caught up in the role than she should have been. Eventually, it even leads to profound humiliation as she imagines she falls short of proving herself "white."

Success in Judy's phone sex career is measured in terms of callbacks, particularly from clients who request sought-after conversation partners by their number. On the evening of which she is most proud, Judy's "Girl 6" receives seventeen of the thirty-eight calls that come in. Her landlord Jimmy (Spike Lee) doesn't approve of her occupation (which he derisively refers to as "phone bone"), but even he is impressed by the ease with which she outdistances her colleagues.

Judy gains substantially as a phone sex operator because of the seriousness with which she approaches her job. Unlike the other women in her unit, she carefully attends to her roles, refining and polishing them while her colleagues eat cookies, do charcoal sketches, or read romance novels. She is proud of her routines and on one occasion shows them off to a male acquaintance, who is angered by the seeming authenticity of her performance. In this sequence, Judy visually morphs into the characters she pretends to be, suggesting the ease with which she can bring her fantasies to life. One of her teammates warns her not to "get hooked," but Judy feels it would demean her theatrical training, if she refused to take her various identities seriously (Lee 1996b, 01:13:30 / 01:15:30).

The other dimension of Judy's spectacular success is the active fantasy life she lives apart from her professional performances. Her personal idol is Dorothy Dandridge, a rare black starlet of the 1950s (heir to the kingdom of Lena Horne), but a woman whom the Hollywood establishment soon discarded, after the exoticism of her tabooed beauty lost its immediate shimmer. Dandridge leaped to early fame on the strength of her starring role in *Carmen Jones* (1954), a black musical adapting and repurposing the music from George Bizet's 1875 opera, *Carmen*, itself a tale of seduction and intrigue, invoking ethnic exoticism. Ominously, Dandridge's role was drenched in vagrant sexuality, trafficking in long-standing black stereotypes of women without boundaries or emotional controls. After her stunning triumph in the middle 1950s, Dandridge's star quickly plummeted, leaving her dead of a probable drug overdose in 1965, while barely past forty. Judy's apartment displays a life-sized poster of Dandridge, and—early on in the film—she fantasizes herself into a performance of one of Carmen's most sultry dances, a prelude to the seduction of one of her lovers. She also receives as a gift the famous cover of *Life* magazine, which pays homage to an African American actress for the first time. Judy's urge to identify with this doomed celebrity reveals the weakness that undermines her seeming strength.

Her more aggressive persona is that of Foxy Brown, modeled upon a young Pam Grier, the heroine of a 1974 blaxploitation film of that name. Grier is the violent, vengeful star of several films from the early 1970s, including *The Big Bird Cage* (1971), her iconic debut as the inmate of a women's prison, the tough-girl role, quickly reprised in *Coffy* (1972), and *Sheba Baby* (1975). In each case she's an action figure come to life in the defense of what she thinks is justice, but it's a justice with no place for due process or the patient prosecution of criminal charges. Grier's publicity pictures of that period typically show her with a massive Afro hairdo reminiscent of the styles worn at the time by political activists like Kathleen Cleaver and Angela Davis. The persona invades Judy's life world as her early success fades and she becomes more discomfited by crank callers who abuse her. In this iteration of herself, she is seen fighting off four or five tough-looking black males with martial arts moves that would do credit to a karate black belt (Lee 1996b, 01:02:00/01:04:30). But this identity too is problematic, since it provides no conduit to channel rage into a truly transformative force. It's the equivalent of screaming into the telephone at a caller who insults her.

Judy's construction of her work leads over time to increasingly greater enmeshment in the lives of her clients and less contact with her friends and co-workers. Some of the women clearly have private lives, as we learn from one of the "girls" who turns up at the job site sporting an engagement ring and welcoming the well wishes of her colleagues. Judy misses this festive occasion because she is servicing a client in her own phone booth. Jimmy complains that he rarely sees her, though he phones her and tries to insert himself into her life. Meanwhile her relationship to her clients deepens, particularly her ties with "regular Bob" (Peter Berg), one of her most frequent callers. He is a pivotal figure, one of several successful businessmen with whom she converses more than occasionally. Though most of her clients are interested only in sexual stimulation, Bob is a more complex figure, looking for permission to talk about his mother, who is a terminal cancer patient. He differs from the rest of her clients, because he is emotionally numb, more than sexually unable to perform within conjugal channels. Through Judy's/Lovely's intervention, Western "manliness" is coaxed into softness, and each seems comfortable with the other. Wading deeper into murky waters, Lovely gives Bob her personal phone number.

The relationship with Bob culminates in a failed encounter at Coney Island, which is proposed when Bob announces he will briefly be in New York on professional business (Lee 1996b, 01:02:00/01:04:30). Judy agrees to the meeting (after consulting with no one), presumably because Bob has shown no particular interest in sex, "pathological" or otherwise. His phone sex friend has done the work of a therapist by being a sensitive listener who has helped him with the grieving process as he confronts the loss of his mother. When they attempt to meet in person, we find Lovely sitting absolutely alone on the boardwalk, discovered by the camera after a long tracking shot, which in a kind of intensified realism is inexplicably repeated twice. The emptiness of the scene, underscored by a long succession of vacant rectangles where the camera simply stares out to sea, marks her as isolated and vulnerable. She waits for an extended moment for Bob to appear, adjusting her nametag to make it easier for someone to read it from afar. But no one is visible in either direction. Finally a man whom she assumes is Bob appears at the far end of the boardwalk and moves slowly toward her. He glances in her direction with a warm smile, but then turns away and walks on. She calls his name softly, then more loudly, finally as a shout to summon him to her side. But he never turns back to her. Having been given an image of Bob on the phone, we realize this particular stroller is not Bob, but a different man, who realizes they are not acquainted. Lovely, however, feels she has been examined and found lacking, perhaps because, exposed in reliable daylight, she can't possibly masquerade as "white." The last shots of the sequence frame her with the carousel in the background and its movement nicely conveys the unsettlement Judy feels as she recognizes her simulated identity has failed her, exploding the illusion that she might somehow live in her role (01:03:40/01:08:10).

At this point, Judy's more or less stable universe begins to go seriously out of control. The last phase of her phone sex career is nightmarish and phantasmagoric, metaphorically deforming the well-worn pathways of her life into the fateful elevator shaft down which a young child has fallen and now hovers between life and death. This image of the life-threatening elevator shaft is repeated several times in the ensuing sequence, always associating Judy with the imperiled child. In a long, surreal fantasy, *Girl 6* is lost in a garishly lit tunnel, presumably a subway, but grotesquely transmogrified by distortions of perspective and unnatural bursts of red and blue light. During this period, Judy has made herself more vulnerable by giving up the protective distance of her business address and working as a "homegirl," dangerously close to her clients. Soon she has fallen prey to a stalker (Michael Imperioli) who has her address and threatens to strangle her to death. In terror she flees to Jimmy's apartment, reconnecting to the world of sanity and finally persuaded that she must abandon her phone sex career. In one of the film's few comic moments, a deluge of telephones (pink, blue, lime green—most of the color spectrum) now fall in slow motion from the sky, breaking to pieces as they crash against the hard reality of the New York streets (Lee 1996b, 01:28:40/01:34:20).

This is a moment of awakening, in which Judy resolves to leave New York for Los Angeles, hoping for a new beginning at the other side of the continent. In keeping with the spirit of healing, she visits little Angela King (Jacqueline McAllister), the child-victim of the elevator accident who is now recovering from her near fatal fall.

Though the film seems to turn toward a positive outcome, the ending is puzzling and denies us clear resolution. Resuming her acting career in Los Angeles, Judy is blocked by the same prejudices that defeated her in New York. The patois of the sunbelt city is different, but the demands are the same—objectification of the black body and the lack of serious interest in Judy's theatrical ability. Once again she will be on display, a prisoner of the male gaze. Again she walks away from the casting interview, more poised than when she confronted the white male hegemony of Manhattan, but no better positioned to resist or reorient herself more effectively in her matchup against white power. Soon she is out on the street, threading her way through a crowd of Los Angelenos, without apparent purpose. We do notice, however, that she has found her way to the iconic sidewalk that honors the celebrities of yesteryear with stars commemorating their achievements in film. For a moment she stands with one heel planted firmly upon the star that remembers Dorothy Dandridge, the tragic "lovely brown" queen of the 1950s, whose image had graced Judy's New York apartment, as her role model and template of theatrical achievement. She then springs forward toward a new destination, which might be interpreted either as walking in the footsteps of Ms. Dandridge or as striking out on a new path. The same ambiguity is built into the last image of the film, which incongruously shows us the marquis of a cinema house that is playing a film called "Girl 6." Does this mean that Judy is destined to see her name in lights as a black celebrity of the near future? (In one sense that's precisely what Lee has done for actress Theresa Wrangle.) Or does it mean that Lee's protagonist is caught in a time loop, a "lovely brown" Flying Dutchman who will live out her life endlessly repeating the cycle of entrapment we have just watched her get caught in? Lee closes the film without closure, leaving Judy's prospects and direction very much in doubt.

Although *Girl 6* enjoyed neither critical nor box office success, it led naturally, if not inevitably, to the production of *Bamboozled*, a far more substantial project that indicts the once venerable tradition of black minstrelsy. As the earlier film recounted the commodification of a female black performer, *Bamboozled* explores the mental colonization of a black male television writer, the would-be black voice of a conspicuously white network that exploits his talent in the name of the Continental Network System's political and commercial purposes. What enlarges the social and political implications of the latter film is Lee's imaginative use of the minstrel show metaphor to illustrate how American corporate media constrains and domesticates black artists by framing them through the homogenizing conventions of genre.

Despite differences of gender and class, Lovely Brown and Pierre Delacroix share the humiliation of African American artists that Ed Guerrero sees reflected "In the Mirror of Abjection" (2012). More expansive than the demeaning of a single individual, *Bamboozled*, says Guerrero, traffics in the "vexed issues and devalued images of African Americans," in the media, images and issues that may sometimes "arise as the creations of ambitious blacks themselves, squirming for a break," in an industry that limits the menu of available visual representations: "White Americans tend to work out the narratives and scenes of their lives through a general process of *affirmation*, whereas Black Americans struggle with the mysteries and tangles of their big screen issues and images through a general process of *negation*" (Guerrero 2012, 109–10). With his ridiculously affected accent and his pseudo-French identity, Pierre Delacroix might seem the classical race traitor, consumed in self-hatred. Yet Guerrero correctly recognizes Lee's film not as an indictment of isolated cases of self-delusion but as a broad critique of the American image industries: "Disastrously for all the out-groups concerned, the production and dissemination of the images, narratives, caricatures, and ideologies that have so much to do with mapping social destinies and negotiating political power have been kept beyond these out-groups' control, and mostly deployed against their self-interest" (112). Voicing largely the same sentiment, Lee says of *Bamboozled*, "I want people to think about the power of images, not just in terms of race, but how imagery is used and what sort of social impact it has—how it influences how we talk, how we think, how we view one another" (Fuchs 2002, 217).

Lee claims to have had this film in mind through most of his filmmaking career. One of his student projects at NYU was a film called "The Answer," which rebuked the stereotypes of black culture in D. W. Griffith's *Birth of a Nation* (1915), a film much admired for its formal brilliance, in spite of its crude caricatures and racist ideology. "Representation" is also the bone of contention in *Do the Right Thing*, where access to Sal's wall of fame tragically becomes a cause to die for. But the more immediate inspiration comes from two more recent films: Melvin van Peebles' *Classified X* (1998) and Lee's *The Original Kings of Comedy* (1999). Van Peebles' history of black images in the cinema scored a coup by making public a body of footage that showed how blackface and the conventions of minstrelsy had hybridized and taken root in classical Hollywood, thereby shaping the racial conventions of comedic cinema. Lee's own *Kings of Comedy* (2000) enjoyed box office success well beyond its sponsors' expectations, proving to Lee that the size of crossover audiences for authentically black films was much larger than the numbers the "gatekeepers" typically used to impose caps on the funds they were willing to put behind his productions.

Predictably, funding issues quickly surfaced as Lee sought production money for *Bamboozled*, a film already in the making when *Kings* was released. After shopping the work to several unresponsive backers, Lee finally secured modest support (about $10 million) from New Line Cinema, for which he was clearly grateful. "Thank God for New Line," he blurts out in a 2001 interview with *Cineaste*, "because no one else wanted to finance this film" (Fuchs 2002, 212). But this upbeat moment is coupled with considerable cynicism about how difficult it is "to operate within the system, . . . something I've been able to do, even though I am on the fringes of it" (211). New Line presumably represents "the fringes" of Hollywood production, because since its founding in the late 1960s the studio has never quite defined its brand. Its promotion of "fantasy" themes was broad enough to embrace *Lord of the Rings* (2001–2003) and the studio reaped good returns from *Teenage Mutant Ninja Turtles* (1990) in its several iterations. New Line also underwrote and distributed offbeat dramatic works like *Seven* (1995) and *Boogie Nights* (1997), but—according to Lee—they were flummoxed by *Bamboozled*. "They never knew exactly what they had," he reports, "I don't think they ever really understood the film or who the audience was. At the time they were going through a very serious financial situation, so there were a lot of restraints about how much money would be spent" (212). The upshot of the studio's extreme frugality was that Lee was obliged to work in digital video (DV), instead of the more fine-grained 35mm, or even 16 mm cine. Eventually he struck a compromise that allowed him to shoot the scenes of *The New Millennium Minstrel Show* in Super 16 cine. Here he achieved higher production values in those specific sequences, and it's not obvious that the DV footage damaged the finished product. But Lee also felt the studio "botched the release" (Fuchs 2002, 212) of the film, failing to insert it into the market with the most appropriate advertising. It would not be a mistake to surmise that Lee sees himself as standing in approximately the same relationship to the Hollywood establishment as Pierre Delacroix stands to Thomas Dunwitty's faltering Continental Network System (hereafter CNS) television network.

Bamboozled opens with the lyrics of Stevie Wonder's lament that from their first days as slaves in the New World, African Americans have been "a misrepresented people." While the song describes centuries of oppression "in the so-called Land of God," we meet Pierre Delacroix (Damon Wayans), the would-be custodian of contemporary blackness, who chafes at his inability to fashion and present on national television a positive image of African American society—striving, confident, upwardly mobile. The image that we see of him, with an aura of bright light enveloping his head, represents the writer as he sees himself, a black champion in the service of his people, determined to uplift the race. But soon the camera turns away from this honorific shot that looks up to an overhead skylight. We now see him in a more quotidian image environment and hear the voice of a frustrated and embattled man. According to his own testimony, he is "a creative person" responsible for "what you view on your idiot box," but aware that his audience has deserted him, "like rats fleeing a sinking ship." He intends to answer with satire, reminding us it's the genre through which "human vice or folly is ridiculed." How this counter-attack on the prevailing tone of CNS might develop is by no means clear. Nor is it in the least obvious where Delacroix stands in relationship to the hegemonic culture, since his overly articulate speech conforms perfectly to what Faedra Carpenter calls "linguistic white face." In this sense, he is already one of the minstrels that his New Millennium Minstrel Show will hold up to ridicule (Lee 2000a, 00:30/02:00).

Very quickly it becomes evident that Delacroix is not quite what he seems. Well-dressed and impeccably groomed (we watch him shower and shave), he strolls to his job site as a confident young black professional. On the street he pauses to patronize a pair of down-at-the-heels black entertainers who receive a generous tip for their tap dancing act, before they appeal to him as a well-connected brother who might find them a job. He dismisses them with a good-natured smile. But his pseudo-power immediately evaporates when he arrives at CNS to discover that an important meeting he was unaware of is already nearing conclusion. Arriving "32 minutes late," he is singled out by his supervisor, Thomas Dunwitty (Michael Rapaport), as an example of the slipshod behavior that has caused the network to lose market share in the never-ending struggle for good ratings. Adding insult to injury, Dunwitty addresses him as "Monsieur Delacroix," sneering at whatever dubious connection with French ancestry he might pretend to have. Helpless in the face of Dunwitty's mockery, he can only retaliate by

browbeating his black assistant, Sloan Hopkins (Jada Pinkett Smith), a
well-focused African American woman who has been as systematically
excluded from the CNS power elite as Delacroix himself. Typical token
figures, hired to meet race and gender quotas (so much the better when
one hire fits both categories!), Sloan and Delacroix are united in their
separation from everything consequential (Lee 2000a, 04:50/07:05).

Delacroix's humiliation continues in the scene that directly follows.
Dunwitty charges that his one black writer is too "white bread" to play
the role the station has cast him in. Dunwitty himself claims to be completely in tune with the black world, pointing to his own office, which
is full to overflowing with black cultural memorabilia, chiefly images
of famous black athletes but also art objects that seem of African origin.
In advancing his claim to honorary "blackness," Dunwitty also speaks
of his African American wife and two biracial children. He feels well
positioned to chastise his corporate subaltern for his "pretentious buppy
ways." For Dunwitty, the crowning proof of Delacroix's incompetence
to represent black culture is that he can't identify jersey number 24 as
the iconic number of the New York (later San Francisco) Giants super-
star center fielder, Willie Mays. After administering this extended scolding, Dunwitty challenges the "buppy in residence" to produce a truly
innovative black show that will move the needle positively for CNS.
Angry and a little desperate, Delacroix, largely against the better judgment of Sloan, conceives and pitches *The New Millennium Minstrel Show*,
which he trusts will purge once and for all the demeaning stereotypes
of black popular culture (Lee 2000a, 7:00/10:40).

Lee's indictment of American media (music, television, cinema) is
fiercely expressed in the conception, construction, and presentation of
this electronically repurposed "coon show." Though Delacroix intends
that the outrageous distortions of black minstrelsy will hopelessly compromise Dunwitty's network, the real outcome is the opposite of his
expectations. Subtle interventions from Dunwitty (and a cadre of executives whom we never meet) excise or suppress the satiric thrusts of
the program, leaving us, without the benefit of irony, on an antebellum
plantation (rendered as a painted backdrop) inhabited by the "Alabama
Porch Monkeys" and two master buffoons of minstrelsy, Mantan (Savion
Glover) and Sleep'n Eat (Tommy Davidson). As inevitably as Hula Hoops
or pet rocks, blackface becomes an overnight cultural craze.

Beretta Smith-Shomade frames the film within a dialectic of "Paradox
and Authenticity" (2008), noting that "the invocation of authenticity,
'keeping it real,' permeates almost every interaction, every scene in *Bamboozled*" (229). She traces these concerns back to a debate "in black popular
culture that has been raging in both consumer and scholarly communities
for the past three decades" (229). When he is asked to perform in black-

face, Mantan (the newly minted stage name of the fast-stepping street dancer Manray) reluctantly accepts this demeaning self-presentation "so long as the hoofin' is real." Delacroix in turn buys into the cult of authenticity by gifting to Mantan a pair of tap-dancing shoes that actually belonged to Bojangles Robinson, the celebrity black minstrel who danced on screen with Shirley Temple. Apparently if the shoes are authentic, so is the performance. Later, as the show comes under fire for its reliance on black stereotypes, the network fights back by pointing to the number of African Americans it employs on either side of the camera. For good measure, the Jewish media consultant Myrna Goldfarb (Dina Pearlman), whom Dunwitty calls in for image control, also recommends that CNS wrap its operation in kente cloth, a much-revered African textile, whose symbolism is associated with maturity, manhood, and African spirituality. If all else fails, she says, CNS can simply upset the chessboard by asking, "What is Black, anyway?" (01:11:00/01:14:15).

But how do context, genre, and product placement affect authenticity? Many of these issues had already been closely scrutinized in the culture wars of the 1990s. According to Smith-Shomade, Lee addresses

> the preponderance of African American representations (mostly sitcoms) that appeared initially on Fox [the Fox Network] and migrated to UPN [United Paramount Network], the WB [Warner Brothers] television network in the 1990s and BET [Black Entertainment Television] in the latter part of the decade. From advertisements to music videos, the humble, shuckin' and jivin' black is resurrected within these media offerings—ostensibly, but not exclusively—at the hands of whites, but for the pleasure of all. (2008, 230)

These would include programs like *In Living Color* (1990–1994), which originated at the Fox Network, emphatically right-wing in its politics, but enjoyed reruns on Black Entertainment Television, which served an entirely different racial demographic. The variety show made no explicit references to minstrelsy, but trafficked in racial caricatures that provoked widespread criticism. For three seasons the show featured Damon Wayans, whom Lee chose to play Delacroix, presumably because of his embroilment in controversies about creative control that were somewhat similar to those of Delacroix in *Bamboozled*. The vexed question to emerge both from Lee's film and the media culture to which it alludes is simply: Does the centrality of a black performer, or even a black writer, assure the production of an authentic "black" performance?

The issue of authenticity also comes up as Delacroix visits his father, June Bug, a black comic who has performed for several decades on "the chitlin circuit," a non-descript array of low-profile comedy clubs featuring more distinctly ethnic entertainment. In one sense June Bug is the personification of everything Delacroix seeks to be—except, of course,

a commercial success. He is a true grassroots comedian, powerfully satiric when he turns a sharp eye on all the "white people who want be
black." He muses out loud, to the delight of his small audience, how
desirable this fabricated blackness would be if the practice of lynching
were revived. While he performs smoothly in a black vernacular his son
could never match, June Bug confesses that he "can't do that Hollywood
stuff." When Delacroix asks where his father's life is going, June Bug assures his son of his personal self-sufficiency: he is secure with "a pretty
woman [and] a little money in my pocket." The trouble is that June Bug
is not as self-contained as he declares. Before the end of the evening he
has collapsed from heavy drinking and his son leaves in profound disil-
lusionment, pronouncing his father "a broken man." He's aware of his father's principled resistance to the media establishment, but cannot accept
"where it had gotten him." He returns to New York, ready to surrender
to Dunwitty (Lee 2000a, 00:57:10/01:03:30).

At its best, *Bamboozled* is a study in the way a creative artist loses control
of his (or her) program. In this instance, Delacroix is given the power both
to write the show and recruit its stars, but these seeming guarantors of
autonomy prove weak in the face of the network's right to revise, restruc-
ture, and, above all, reframe his material with an eye toward cultural orthodoxy. Dunwitty imagines himself more authentically black than Delacroix, and the sponsors who stand behind him expect to put money in the
bank, not expose racial stereotypes. After Delacroix successfully pitches
his "coon show," Dunwitty burdens his writer with a room full of white
flunkies, none of whom has the least understanding of his imaginative
universe. When Delacroix ignores Dunwitty's "team" and writes his own
script, his supervisor is immediately on hand with a rewrite specialist
who will "punch up" his material to give it more crowd appeal, no doubt
at the expense of any artistic substance it might once have had. To underscore how light is the footprint of satire upon the finished product, Lee
expands his attention to the advertising that shares the screen with Delacroix's minstrels. It's impossible not to notice that the sponsors see *The New
Millennium Minstrel Show* as an electronic storefront from which to sell
booze, sexual stimulants, and a prestigious line of ghetto gear, clothing
styles so "authentic" that they include bullet holes in the shirts and jack-
ets. In fact, the show's emcee, Honeycutt (Thomas Jefferson Byrd), who
would have to be a crucial figure in any satiric format, is co-opted by the
sponsors to help sell the industrial strength alcohol represented by "Da
Bomb." True to the most degraded conventions of minstrelsy, he breathes
fire after consuming his drink.

Whatever Delacroix's intentions, they are doomed from the start, as
his sidekick Sloan warns him on several occasions. His recruitment of
black talent is somewhat predatory, though he may see it as creating

job opportunities for the black underclass. Manray and Womack, now reborn as Mantan and Sleep'n Eat, are the first case in point. Manray is an exceptionally talented tap dancer performing for pennies on the street while Womack works the crowd, trying to hustle as much cash as possible out of the not-very-generous passers-by. How precariously they live is underscored in an early scene where their shabby tenement is raided by the police, who arrive in the early hours of the morning with helicopters, spotlights, and sirens. Presumably, this is part of the strategic harassment Mayor Rudy Giuliani pursued through the late 1990s to force the homeless to vacate neighborhoods that were ripe for gentrification. Next we see them as a dance and comedy team recruited by Sloan to star as the principals of the show Delacroix is pitching to Dunwitty. In a scene ominously similar to a slave auction, Mantan—re-costumed and deodorized—is ushered into Dunwitty's office and asked to show his skills for the benefit of his new master (Lee 2000a, 25:10/32:20). Mounting the stage, which is the elegant table in Dunwitty's office, he steps flawlessly into the role of "happy darkie," ready and eager to embrace the high cotton and ripe watermelon patches of Southern myth. Soon both Mantan and Sleep'n Eat will be burying their real-world faces under burnt cork and fire red lipstick, while explaining to an opening night audience why they have fled the century into which they were born, so as to recover their "roots" in the nostalgia-drenched landscape of the Confederacy: "I'm tired of the crack babies born out of wedlock," they tell us, immediately adding the inevitable cliché about "inflated welfare roles" (Lee 2000a, 50:50/55:45). What right-wing ideologue could have said it better?

This might be the proper place to remember that the "plantation" is Dunwitty's idea, the only modification he immediately forces upon Delacroix. The relocation from the hood to the rural world might not at first seem momentous, but an urban site would almost inevitably cast an ironic light upon the looming anachronisms of character and action we find on the set of the Old South. In *Darkest America* (2012), Jake Austen and Yuval Taylor wonder for several paragraphs why Delacroix doesn't make more effort to resist Dunwitty's strategic interventions, if his goal is "creating a show that will fail spectacularly" (288). These students of black minstrelsy note that Delacroix and Sloan work meticulously to find the very best talent to serve the perverse objectives of their showmanship. If a production disaster is the sought-after goal, why deny the stage to the barely coherent Mau Mau musical group represented by Sloan's brother Julius (Yaslin Bey)? Or how about the eccentric soloist who auditions on a didgeridoo? He could empty an auditorium in ten minutes. Unlike the "where-did-we-go-right?" masterminds of Mel Brooks' *Producers* (1967), Delacroix and Sloan seriously invest their taste and judgment in culling from the round-the-block line of underemployed black performers some few whose genuine talent shines through their blackface makeup and the shoddy scripts they are asked to perform.

Ironically, Sloan, Delacroix, and the anonymous casting director inadvertently do the bidding of Dunwitty and the network's executive elite. They assemble a remarkable collection of marginalized black artists who give *The New Millennium Minstrel Show* a professional tone the material really doesn't deserve. And though we have no data on the salary scales for this production, we can surmise that CNS brought it to the screen on a bargain-basement budget. Delacroix's plan to embarrass the network actually improves its ratings to a degree not even Dunwitty, in his most flamboyant boosterism, could have imagined. Delacroix's blind spots with respect to the show have to be sought, I think, in his private anxieties about his career. He despises Dunwitty and the network, but fears even more deeply that outside the system he may suffer the fate of his father, whom we last see sprawled in a drunken stupor on a dingy barroom floor.

By the time of the first pilot, Delacroix has already lost control of the production. In the last script conference before the program airs, Dunwitty and the rewrite man are pushing Delacroix away from his own project. Honeycutt survives as master of ceremonies, but there is no suggestion of satire in his lines. The versatile comic of the earlier interview has disappeared into the circus barker, whose role is to reconcile the live studio audience to material they at first feel uncomfortable with. Along with flashing cues that ask repeatedly for "Applause," he gently guides his viewers though the introduction of the Porch Monkeys and the rest of the minstrel chorus. And as Manray would have it, "the hoofin' is real," so the scene culminates in a spirited dance that, in spite of the demeaning costumes and make-up, shows poise, energy, and professional skill. While this subtle manipulation of the audience is going forward (we watch them gradually come to terms with the minstrel conventions), Lee's editing intercuts shots of Manray and Womack "blacking up" for their opening night caper, very reluctant to apply burnt cork and red lipstick in front of a mirror that makes them recognize the damage they are doing to their own humanity (Lee 2000a, 48:30/55:45).

As the show progresses from its pilot form to its place as a new network series, Delacroix's signature experiences further erasure. Someone has added a new opening, which now has the dance team emerge from a monstrous black mouth, as if regurgitating Mantan and his partner from the deepest recesses of the grotesque minstrel tradition. Insult to injury is added in the musical track, which blares out the lyrics of "Dixie." Watching in horror to what has happened to the show she helped create, Sloan confesses to Manray and Womack that she has no idea where this latest version of the program originated. Ironically, however, Delacroix is quickly seduced by the show's success, even though it no longer resembles what he first described to Sloan. He bristles momentarily when Myrna Goldfarb joins Dunwitty to clarify for the only African Americans at the CNS studio what it means to be black. But Delacroix never seems to fully take hold of Goldfarb's most devastating point, namely that the show's best answer to its critics is Delacroix himself, "a non-threatening black man" who has legitimated the revival of black minstrelsy by writing within its conventions. Not long thereafter, he is defending the program on local talk radio, complaining of the "slave mentality" that allows black activists to excuse their own shortcomings by retreating into victimhood. And he obviously enjoys the newfound prestige and respect he receives from colleagues at the station who have previously ignored him. At this point Sloan favors him with a highly ambiguous gift—a piece of racial kitch called the "Jolly Nigger Piggy Bank," which she describes as his reward for creating a palpable hit. Its ample mouth, which resembles the proscenium arch that frames the set, serves to swallow gold and silver coin, the welcome treasure earned by *The New Millennium Minstrel Show*. The icon is a symbol of Delacroix's self-serving success, but it also foreshadows the madness and tragedy that will soon overwhelm his life.

Tavia Nyong'o calls Delacroix "the film's internal scapegoat, one upon whom we can credibly lay blame" (2008, 223). No doubt Delacroix is blameworthy, but his lust for success is by no means the only moral failure of Lee's narrative. In fact, the house of cards collapses largely because of the impulse toward self-aggrandizement that grips all the major characters in varying degrees. Mantan is proud of the chic apartment his blackface earnings have won him and disowns Womack as an inferior freeloader who now holds back his career. The décor of his new home is a hymn to his own ego, full of the racial kitsch he himself personifies. When Womack voices his skepticism about the "coon show" that has won them national fame, Mantan interprets this behavior as envy of his own superior talent. He also turns on Sloan, who has made every effort to befriend him, dismissing her as the sleazy professional woman who sleeps her way to the top. Dunwitty proves himself absolutely unscrupulous, when he responds to Mantan's belated refusal to put on his black-face makeup by forcibly seizing him during his on-stage performance and having him expelled from the premises. This leaves him at the mercy of the mentally unmoored Mau Mau group, who kidnap and execute Mantan. Even Sloan, in some ways the conscience of the film, is not quite impervious to the success cult that controls the action. "I am on the rise, and you are embarrassing," she tell her ne'er-do-well brother, as she banishes him from her apartment (Lee 2000a, 21:50/25:00). Lee's point is not scapegoating, but exploring how African American culture cooperates in its own misrepresentation.

The bloodbath that concludes *Bamboozled* doesn't suggest much of a pathway to the future. When Delacroix bleeds out amid the debris field of black collectables strewn about him, we are left with a profusion of cartoons and caricatures spilling relentlessly onto a television screen that automatically displays them. Delacroix's killer is Sloan, his partner and close associate, who of course has effectively killed herself with her rash deed of futile retaliation. Together, they were the new generation of black artists who hoped to repair the damage to the African American image in the most vibrant of the public arts. Now the reformers are dead, while the stereotypes remain full of perverse vitality.

In summing up the film, Nyong'o perceptively observes that Lee pays homage to "the immense skill trapped within minstrelized iconography" but never loses sight of the "double injustice done to audience and *performer* by the demeaning legacies of slavery and racism" (2008, 221, my italics). She is also aware of "the film's very pointed warning against black-on-black violence" (222). But we might get to a still deeper level of critique by combining these two insights: Lee seems to acknowledge the complete breakdown of cooperative impulses within the African American creative community. Malcolm X, Martin Luther King Jr., and certainly Huey Newton, another of Lee's personal heroes, had all preached racial solidarity and struggled manfully to shape the institutions that would make this sense of communal purpose a meaningful political force. Amiri Baraka upheld a similar ideal as the capstone of the Black Arts Movement. *Bamboozled*, on the other hand, grudgingly recognizes that individual striving, particularly when driven by wealth and celebrity, takes priority over shared heritage and collective goals. Stevie Wonder's compelling lyrics continue to warn his African American comrades not to be a "misrepresented people." But the protagonists of both *Girl 6* and *Bamboozled* prove unable or unwilling to resist the tide of racial assignment.

SEGMENT 4: RACE IN WIDER PERSPECTIVE: *25TH HOUR* (2002) AND *BLACKKKLANSMAN* (2018)

In *Redefining Black Film* (1993), Mark Reid argues passionately on behalf of "black filmmakers who resist the calls of fame and increased production budgets" in the name of "black independent filmmaking . . . in which empowered images of black women and men dominate the screen" (125). This thinking in no way advocates a return to the contrived heroics found in blaxploitation films of the early 1970s, which typically were distributed by the major studios and made no pretense of developing a new film rhetoric or exploring complex ethno-racial themes. Instead, Reid applauds those few black filmmakers of the later 1970s and 1980s, who were trained in university film programs and received their funding through grants, private donations, and federal agencies, as well as bilateral agreements to market their films overseas. Thus financed, they briefly enjoyed a production environment that "empowers black artists to include the rigorous and inhuman conditions of black life" in their representations of metropolitan America (132). A dozen years later, however, in *Black Lenses, Black Voices* (2005), Reid confesses that "black independent filmmakers are relegated to film festivals and college campuses" and that "the public has no knowledge of this black film culture, its alternative narrative style, and the sociopolitical world that many of its films explore" (116). Searching for cultural authenticity in films of what he calls the "post-Negritude era," Reid is reconciled to black-directed films that accept studio funding and in return produce narratives which "honor mainstream moral and aesthetic norms" (29). His scholarly analysis of production conditions has led him to the same conclusion that Spike Lee arrived at earlier through filmic practice—the grudging acknowledgment of the need to work within the media establishment, in Lee's case both within the Hollywood filmmaking tradition and more recently, through an increasing affiliation with the powerful entertainment companies, Home Box Office (HBO) and Netflix.

Although Lee remains attracted to narratives that feature black celebrities—James Brown, Huey Newton, and Michael Jackson are among his subjects in the new millennium—he is also mindful of the need to seek out an audience appreciably larger than his loyal base in the black community. This impulse has drawn him toward the genre film, like the highly successful *Inside Man* (2005), a "heist film," or the "war film," such as *Miracle at Santa Anna* (2008), which details the experience of black GIs in Italy during World War II. In either case the formula involves inserting black characters into recognizable roles (the stress-ridden detective, the courageous conscript), where their racial identity is not the film's primary concern. The more substantial re-centering of Lee's creative project entails focusing less on the flash points of racial conflict, as in *Do the Right Thing* or *Bamboozled*, and more with ways in which the web of racialized relationships plays out in the intercultural geography of contemporary America. Lee's new thematic landscape embraces both the multiculturalist New York City during the months immediately following the seismic shock of 9/11 in *25th Hour* as well as the much less familiar American West that he attempts to depict in the startling new departure of *BlacKkKlansman*. The first of these films evidences a new attention to racial hybridity and the pressure of racial anxieties in metro New York; the second takes the racial temperature of the more ruralized community of Colorado Springs, revealing a deep well of social and political extremism often overlooked in cultural portraits of the American West. Both films furnish further examples of Lee's gradual shift toward collaborative scriptwriting, in which he builds upon the scaffolding of narratives already published under other authorial signatures.

In *25th Hour* Lee worked in tandem with David Benioff, the Jewish author of the novel on which the film is based. What began as a tribute to emergency first responders, originally titled "Fireman Down," turned into one of the earliest attempts to assess the wounding of New York City by the events of 9/11. The notoriety of the event and the contractual commitments from established stars, principally Edward Norton and Philip Seymour Hoffman, guaranteed a comfortable, though not lavish budget (approximately $5 million), which allowed Miramax, by that time a Disney affiliate, to turn a decent profit. Lee used the text to dramatize a moment outside of time (a magical extension of the twenty-four-hour day) when ordinary New Yorkers, stunned by the attack on the Twin Towers, would be forced to take stock of each other, to see themselves not only as victims of inexplicable violence but as morally compromised agents who might somehow be implicated in the tragedy that had devastated their city. The film *25th Hour* scrupulously avoids all references to the public theatricals of Mayor Giuliani and official homage to the city's resilience. Instead, Lee evokes the private world of a convicted small-time drug dealer, Monty Brogan (Edward Norton), together with the friends and family who lend him support on the last day before he is sent to prison. Supporting the root metaphor of the film, Monty too is outside of time, in a "step-back" category, which allows him a small reprieve before he must deliver himself to the state prison. The metropolitan menagerie of Monty's family and friendship circle embraces chiefly the New York Irish, represented by his father (Brian Cox) and his friend, Frank Slaughtery (Barry Pepper), but also glances at a guilt-ridden Jew, Jake Elinsky (Philip Seymour Hoffman), and a gregarious, upwardly mobile Latina, Naturelle Riviera (Rosario Dawson), Monty's lover. Monty's "business" associates also include a sampling of the Eastern European Mafia, who are among the most recent arrivals to contest for power and privilege in the American melting pot.

Beyond this ample cast of characters, however, *25th Hour* represents the collective persona of a city in crisis. Describing his angle of entry, Lee says, "It was simple: we felt that in shooting a film like this in New York City, so close to what happened on 9/11, in being responsible filmmakers we had to reflect that in the film" (Aftab and Lee 2006, 355). This reflection, before all else, is powerfully visual, its imagery supported by Terence Blanchard's highly expressive musical score. "Spike told me," recalls Blanchard, "he wanted post-September 11 New York to be another character in the film, so my whole intention was to not let you forget that" (Aftab and Lee 2006, 358).

The credits sequence runs more than three minutes (Lee 2003, 04:15/07:45) and opens with images of the New York skyline shot from steeply canted angles, which cause fifty-story skyscrapers to lean at structurally impossible angles, suggesting a city radically off balance. While a sound score of pipes and strings achieves a plaintive, elegiac mood, Lee introduces a montage of light beams composed from shots of the memorial beacons that were turned on to mark the site of the fatal assault. As the music builds to its final crescendo, now augmented by choral elements, we experience more conventional wide-angle shots of Manhattan, which include the Statue of Liberty, Brooklyn Bridge, and the Empire State building, always with the memorial beacons fully visible. It's impossible to escape the point that the small personal story of Monty Brogan is part of a larger cultural narrative. The rupture of his life is an analogue of a similar rupture of the city, which won't be resolved even by Monty's acceptance of his seven-year incarceration.

The portents of this early scene are picked up about forty minutes later as we look directly into the crater where the Twin Towers once stood. Now we are in the company of Monty's two best friends, and former school mates, Jake and Frank, who have gathered at Frank's apartment, a south Manhattan high-rise that overlooks the ruined landscape where the towers once stood. Their conversation is largely about Monty, but the background is the debris field beneath Frank's window. The composition and choreography of the scene are elegant. Both men stand by the window but Frank turns his back on the crater. Defiantly, he announces that, even if "bin Laden could drop another one right next door, I ain't movin'." But this is the shallow bravado of a man who routinely deceives himself and uses his facile cynicism to conceal a deep insecurity. In the same breath he remarks that Monty is lost, without hope of survival and perhaps not worthy to survive. On the other hand, Jake is shaken by the sight of the wounded city. Yet he never turns his back on it, just as he never ceases to believe that Monty will persevere in the face of his incarceration. Significantly, as Jake steps closer to the window, his reflected image is superimposed on the ruined landscape, as if he were falling into the abyss that had already consumed so many. Caught up in Monty's personal tragedy, he becomes a tragic figure himself. Finally, the site of the crater takes on a life of its own. As the two friends move away from the window, the camera ignores them and dollies forward, then tilts down and zooms in. For roughly twenty seconds we watch the construction crews below, flying their tiny American banner but performing tasks that could as easily be associated with burial as resurrection. Once again Blanchard's theme music intervenes powerfully, while the anxiety-ridden friends are at a loss for words. Monty is in jeopardy, though he was once a young man of great promise. Monty's father is shattered, feeling not just disappointed but implicated in his son's fall. Jake too may be lost in guilt and grief, and Naturelle is losing her partner. The scar upon the city is a symbol of ruptured personal lives (Lee 2003, 44:30/50:30).

The focal point of the film is Monty's criminal behavior in the black market drug economy that has supplied him with a generous income since he left high school. In the conversation with Jake, Frank—himself a high-rolling, edge-of-the-envelope stock broker—remarks that Monty has made himself rich by addicting his fellow townsmen, which spurs Frank to a rare moment of moral indignation: "I love Monty, but he's getting what he deserves." This may be, but the film deftly points out that black market capitalism is alive and well in New York City, an integral part of the service economy Mayor Koch labored through the 1980s to create.

The drug dealers of *25th Hour* are Russian or Ukrainian. By now they have largely displaced the Sicilian Mafia of an earlier generation, though they share with their Mediterranean forebears a sense of ethnic solidarity coupled with the capacity to insert themselves into various legitimate business endeavors. In fact, they exemplify what recent scholarship on immigration describes as "negative assimilation," the phenomenon of the newcomer who affiliates with the criminal class, rather than with the right-living, hard-working immigrant who is the poster child of assimilationist theory. What results from this distortion, according to Cara Bowman, Nazli Kibria, and Megan O'Leary in *Race and Immigration*, is a "dysfunctional pattern of integration into disadvantaged urban minority cultures that are marked by an adversarial outlook of rejection and rebellion against mainstream norms and values" (2014, 120). In a worst-case scenario, the outcome is a perverse form of social integration in which the new, relatively unwelcome immigrants "melt" into a criminal underclass given to theft, drug dealing, extortion, and gang warfare. In *25th Hour*, the sorriest specimen of this culture is Kostya (Tony Siragusa), a dull-witted thug who is Monty's drug dealing partner. But behind him stands "Uncle Nikolai" (Levan Uchaneishvili), the gangster czar, whose fashionable nightclub in a gentrified Manhattan neighborhood lends a patina of millennial cool to his otherwise criminal enterprise.

The look and tone of Nikolai's nightspot, where Monty spends most of his last night of freedom, is emblematic of the extremes and incongruities that characterize contemporary New York. Its strategically dissonant music jars the ear, but calls writhing masses of youthful bodies to its spacious dance floor, including the unsettled and alienated Naturelle. Its bright lights and beautiful women prompt Frank to display his most aggressive macho persona, while he drenches himself in alcohol and scurries about from one flirtatious destination to another. It also offers private nooks where anxiety-ridden Jake can plant a kiss on the lips of his underage and oversexed student, Mary D'Annunzio (Anna Paquin) (Lee 2003,

01:10:00/01:43:15). Most importantly, it's the command and control center from which Nikolai ruthlessly wields his power. And because it's the focal point of Nikolai's criminal enterprise, it's inevitably the site where Monty must free himself from the tentacles of the mob.

Nikolai's syndicate clutches at Monty from two directions. The drug czar has recruited him to be the face of white middle-class respectability in the prep school world where the upwardly mobile Irishman was once a basketball star. Now that he is losing Monty to state prison, and in return for vague promises of support, Nikolai seeks to colonize his father's bar, a neighborhood gathering place, which has become a shrine to the first responders who lost their lives on 9/11. The display of images and artifacts at Brody's tavern is at once a memorial to the downtown fire fighters and to the ethnic Irish who disproportionately filled the ranks of the south city firehouses. As Nikolai perceives, the new, more working-class location would create an ideal further place of business from which the gang boss could reach another stratum of his potential Manhattan market. In one of his most courageous moral gestures, Monty successfully resists this sinister plan and saves his father from exploitation at the hands of the cartel. Lee's handling of the imagery contrasting the club and Brogan's bar accentuates the recovery of the relationship between father and son. Nikolai's nightclub is supremely a theater of moral compromise. Brody's bar, on the other hand, with its 9/11 iconography, is a center of honesty and rectitude. Significantly, Monty in this setting achieves his most straightforward moment of truth. Standing in front of a mirror in the men's restroom, he indicts himself for his irresponsible behavior and his impulse to blame marginalized ethnic minorities for problems springing from his own moral lapses: "Montgomery Brogan, you had it all and you threw it away." His father's domain and his father's presence are the keys to his eventual right-mindedness (Lee 2003, 35:00/43:30).

The other issue negotiated with Nikolai in their confrontation at the club (Lee 2003, 01:36:45/01:43:15) is the suspicion that Monty has skimmed profits from the cartel's revenue and perhaps given information on Nikolai to the police. The real culprit is Kostya, Monty's supposed friend, who has accused Monty to divert attention from himself. Monty's courage in facing down at gunpoint the accusations of Nikolai earn the crime boss' respect and the opportunity to resign from the cartel without penalty. But the exchange with Nikolai evokes the racialized character of personal relationships projected into the film by the presence of Naturelle (Rosario Dawson), a Puerto Rican woman who in the film identifies as white, though the role is played by an actress of Afro-Cuban lineage.

According to Mary Beltran, one of the editors of and contributors to *Mixed Race Hollywood* (2008), Dawson/Naturelle is one of several cinematic Latinas, who have risen to star status by specializing in ethnically

ambiguous roles. After playing a recognizably "black" woman in Lee's
He Got Game (1998), Rosario returned to the director's production team
in *25th Hour* to articulate a "New York-centric" urban persona, "strongly
rooted in the city and its polyglot, distinctly 'ethnic' cultures" (Beltran
2008, 261). Disruptive at several levels, Naturelle is Lee's first portrait of
a figure representing racial hybridity, an instance of what Eileen O'Brien
(2008) calls "the racial middle." Remarking "interracial border crossing,"
in the Latino culture, O'Brien points out that "negative stigma is still attached in the dominant culture to those in the racial middle who appear
to be attempting to retain aspects of their 'brown' cultures instead of leaving it all behind and assimilating completely into American culture" (95).

This charge applies tellingly to Rosario's character, Naturelle, even
though Lee's heroine performs "naturally" as a white woman, never
speaking Spanish, never alluding to her Hispanic family, and partnered
to a white lover. We also see her almost exclusively in white company.
The one conversation she has about her ethnic identity is with Monty,
who comments (while they are bathing together) on the "I love Puerto
Rico" tattoo that ornaments one of her thighs. In a friendly tone, he admonishes her for fetishizing a "homeland" that she has known only as a
tourist and that seems to play no role in her diet, dress, cultural tastes, or
spiritual formation. Seemingly of no importance at this point, the question of Naturelle's ethnic identity plays out in painful detail as Monty and
his circle of close associates wonder who has betrayed him to the police.
Naturelle's loyalty is the most suspect, apparently for no reason except
her ethno-racial "otherness."

Though Monty never accuses Naturelle of betraying him, his coldness
toward her is apparent in the days after his arrest. She notices his distance but seems unable to account for it. Monty expresses his doubts to
his father when they meet for dinner at the bar: "Maybe they got to her,
you know. Do I really know her? I don't know." Remarkably, however,
his father gives Naturelle a solid vote of confidence: "The girl loves you,
Monty. I can't believe she would betray you" (Lee 2003, 42:30/42:50).
Once again, the accuracy of his father's perceptions marks him as the
moral compass of the film. The surprise comes from Frank, Monty's old-
est and most intimate friend, but not his most reliable. He is full of positive sentiment on Monty's behalf when they are together. But privately
he insists that after this last night together it's "bye-bye, Monty." He is
similarly disloyal to Naturelle. Though they are overtly cordial to each
other (the hugs and smiles look genuine), he is deeply suspicious of her,
ultimately on racial grounds. In the extended conversation they have at
the club, he accuses Naturelle of having lived off Monty and "watched
him ruin his life." More than that, he tells her, "You knew where he hid
the money, you knew where he hid the drugs." The first point might have

some grounding; the second is completely gratuitous. And so of course is the ultimate racial insult: "I told Monty when he first met you, you were nothing but a spic skank greaser" (01:31:30/01:35:35). Fashionably multicultural in his outward deportment, Frank hurries back to the realm of white privilege the moment he is placed under stress.

Race and ethnicity also figure importantly in the performance of law enforcement, as we see Naturelle's ethnicity caricatured from the opposite pole of the racial binary. Sensing that Nikolai might be sleuthing out his profit skimming, Kostya looks for ways to divert suspicion from himself, finding in Naturelle the perfect target on whom to plant incriminating evidence. While he hides the drugs in Monty's apartment, then tips off the police as to their whereabouts, he encourages Monty to believe it was Naturelle who betrayed her lover. To Kostya, the American nation is a largely a mystery, but he certainly knows the racial code. "Mexicans can't be trusted," he tells Monty, that's why he should be careful of Naturelle. It's of no use for Monty to point out that Naturelle is from the Caribbean, not Mexico. Like Frank, Kostya has already pigeonholed her as the "spic skank," an ideal scapegoat for the criminal behavior the Ukrainian himself is guilty of.

The further point is that the detective who makes the drug bust, an African American, seems inclined to accept this racialized narrative of events. He has drawn his conclusions with help from the same ethnic stereotypes that inspired Kostya. At the arrest site, Agent Flood (Isiah Whitlock Jr.) is determined to keep Naturelle under close surveillance, though Monty is the leaseholder of the premises where the drugs are stashed. In the interrogation session, the same detective gives Monty every opportunity to cast blame upon Naturelle, making sure Monty knows that she too is being interrogated, and given the opportunity to confirm the incrimination of Monty. To Flood, Naturelle is "the Spanish broad," who can't be trusted because of her a south-of-the-border lineage. The federal agent is particularly eager to tease Monty with the thought that Naturelle, in keeping with her self-serving ethnic predilections, has played her sugar daddy for a fool. As Monty receives an exceptionally harsh prison sentence for refusing to implicate his romantic partner, the sly Caribbean woman will stage a "big celebration," now that she has "a whole fancy apartment to herself. The girl saw a pot of honey and licked it clean." Completely in sync with Kostya's racialized construction of Naturelle, Flood's effort to turn Monty against his girlfriend again evokes the "spic skank" as the all-purpose bad-girl whose miscegenated genes have locked her into disloyalty and betrayal (Lee 2003, 50:50/55:50). Ironically, the lawmen and the lawless share the common practice of slandering ethnic undesirables.

Racialized stereotypes impact Lee's film in one further way. As Derik Smith makes clear in "True Terror" (2012), *25th Hour* is haunted by ghosts of the of the "angry black male," whose familiar stereotype lurks "in a sepulchral prison system that efficiently disappears black male bodies from civil society and social discourse, while intensifying the terror they produce in the national psyche" (1). Moving into the substance of his argument, Smith claims for the film "a simmering understated power that distinguishes it from [Lee's] more noted films from the 1980s and early 90s," arguing that "Lee constructs the trauma of 9/11 and the nightmare of race in America as correlative subtexts that erupt into the narrative only in brief, dense, evocative flashes" (2). The point might at first seem a little far-fetched but on deeper reflection, the analogy is strikingly apt. What overwhelms the political imaginary of Monty and his friends is the thought that he is imperiled by the masses of violent black inmates at the state prison in the same way that New Yorkers are threatened by more terror from the sky in the days and weeks following 9/11. Not only is the danger the more menacing because it is completely random, it also reverses the conventional power equations of contemporary international culture. As the perverse good fortune of the Arab terrorists allowed a third world assault upon the impregnable fortress America, so the black underclass will have its vengeance upon Monty Brogan, the privileged preppie who carelessly made himself vulnerable to forces that should never have had power over him.

The threat of sexual violence to Monty is directly articulated on three separate occasions and reinforced by several other incidental references. Uncle Nikolai urges Monty to be resolved against dangers to his person and points to the word "survive," which the gangster tattooed on his arm when he first went to prison at the age of fourteen. Frank mentions the threat of homosexual rape more specifically when he cautions Jake not to imagine that their friend will survive his seven-year incarceration. But the more unsettling allusion to the same threat comes during the interrogation scene, when Agent Flood and his two colleagues remind Monty of this possibility as they try to make him incriminate Naturelle, or perhaps even Nikolai. Monty's resistance to their tactic again testifies to his basic decency, though it is clear he does not take the threat lightly. As with the slurs about Naturelle's ethnicity, the most ominous point here is how efficiently the police power and the criminal lawlessness of the prison collude to brutalize young Brogan. Finally, Monty appeals to Frank to beat him up badly on the morning of his surrender to the criminal justice system in order to assure that he will not immediately be perceived as a sexually desirable commodity. Like Cervantes' deluded Don Quixote, who once imagines himself attacked by a windmill, Monty takes desperate measures to ward off threats that may be purely phantasmal.

With respect to the fear of black-on-white rape, we are left to decide for ourselves whether Monty is as much at risk as he imagines or whether he is more the victim of his own racial fantasies. Neither Naturelle nor his father thinks Monty is at risk, nor seems to suspect that the beating he claims resulted from a street mugging was actually inflicted by a friend at Monty's bidding. What Lee pushes much more insistently is the fundamental unfairness of the criminal justice system, which subjects a low-level, first-time offender to a draconian punishment largely because he refuses to turn on an innocent woman. During Monty's interrogation, the federal agents repeatedly allude to the prosecutorial discretion allowed in the formulation of charges. The leniency extended to "cooperative" defendants makes the recommendation of the investigating officers exceptionally consequential. Detectives Flood and Cunningham hold out to Monty the possibility of more favorable treatment if only he will name the promiscuous Latina as the primary criminal. The assumption clearly is that a "spic skank" would be easier to convict than an Irish preppie, adding the further likelihood that she might be more willing to implicate figures of higher standing in the drug cartel. In this circuitous way, Monty becomes the victim of the ethno-racial prejudices that are still alive and well in post-9/11 New York.

What is the likely outcome of Monty's tragic misadventure with the criminal justice system? Not hopeful, we surmise, but perhaps not utterly despairing. As the elder Brody is driving his son to the Otisville prison, we are offered an alternative script of Monty's future, which entails his escape to the west and to a new life in a small town at the other end of the continent. This classical reference to Turner's frontier myth is perhaps offered in good faith, but it's contra-factual and probably not viable, even if we think of it as an option to evoke after Monty has served his time. It might more likely represent a fantasy of Brody Sr., the life he would like to have given to his son, free from the taint of New York City and blessed with the family he might found in partnership with Naturelle. But a more realistic script—half-jokingly proposed by Frank when he stops talking about doomsday—would keep Monty in New York as the proprietor of an Irish pub. Since his father already owns one, this might be a workable option, in spite of Monty's cultural suspicion of green beer. In any event, that hopeful scenario is in keeping with the theme of resilience, which is the leitmotif of Lee's homage to New York City.

The film *25th Hour* respectfully treats one other character, yet to be mentioned. This is "Doyle," an injured, non-descript dog that Monty rescues in the first scene and never ceases to provide for. Like Monty, Doyle is a creature who seems worth saving and, like New York, he is invested with a spirit that proves hard to kill. Though he is never associated with the site of the Twin Towers, he has a relationship with virtually all the main characters, who generally can be measured by how well they get on with him. Most conspicuously, he is identified with Monty, who gets him medical attention and gentles him out of his feral state. Soon he is on a leash and behaving appropriately as Monty meets Jake and his students at the prep school where Jake teaches. He is with Monty when the former drug dealer refuses to supply a client from times past, decisively severing ties with "the life." Doyle is suspicious of Kostya, definitely an unsavory character, and doesn't take kindly to the detectives who, acting upon a tip from the Ukrainian, intrude upon Naturelle and Monty at their apartment. Later, Jake's would-be girlfriend, Mary, immediately bonds with Monty as "the man with the dog." Though Doyle must be left behind during the long scene at Nikolai's nightclub, he is not forgotten, as the first toast of the evening goes "To Doyle." Jake remarks, slightly tongue in cheek, that it's a shame Monty can't take Doyle to prison with him, both to assure his friend of company and to keep him safe. Significantly, it is Jake who assumes responsibility for the dog when he and Monty must part company. With Doyle at his side, Jake enjoys the only moment in the film when a fully adult woman takes notice of him. A female jogger who has just rushed by him on the footpath turns back to say, "Cool dog."

Doyle's name playfully inserts itself into Lee's portrait of the city. It emerges from the cultural confusion of Kostya, who describes the finding of the dog (a victim of brutalization and abandonment) as an instance of "Doyle's law." When Monty points out, "everything that can go wrong will go wrong" is properly referred to as "Murphy's law," Kostya dismisses the correction as one piece of Irish nonsense being much like another. Monty, however, takes the Ukrainian's malapropism as a sign that the dog should be called Doyle and that "Doyle's law," apparently, alters the overarching wisdom of Murphy in a slightly more positive direction. In the last analysis, what Doyle stands for is a work in progress, but it involves the capacity to prevail in the face of unfavorable odds. Whether Doyle's law will bring Monty safely home from Otisville is an open question, but Doyle's city will mourn the loss of the Twin Towers and then rise to meet whatever challenges the new millennium presents. For Lee, the events of 9/11 demand a reformulation of the racial dialogue but by no means force the question of ethno-racial conflict from the center of the American stage.

The road from *25th Hour* to *BlacKkKlansman* is quite circuitous, though the apparent tangents eventually converge into an intelligible pattern. Lee's determination to remain viable in the commercial market ordained that in the new millennium he would direct his work toward more mainstream production, in order to put Spike Lee's Joints on more secure financial footing. In practice, this meant partnering with other filmmaking companies, most of which, in terms of their ownership, directorship, and viewership, would be described as "white." This business model served to produce *Inside Man* (2006) in partnership with Imagine Entertainment (where Ron Howard of *Happy Days* has a stake), a collaborative endeavor that earned close to $90 million, about double its generous budget of $45 million. *Inside Man* remains Lee's highest grossing film. It features a black protagonist in circumstances that validate black agency, but otherwise is a formulaic Hollywood thriller.

Perhaps Lee's most creative breakthrough at this stage of his career was his venture into television and his highly fruitful collaboration with Home Box Office and later Netflix. The first of these partnerships invited him to develop his instinct for documentary, a genre in which he has acquitted himself with distinction. The partnership with HBO was key to the financing and marketing of what Delphine Letort calls *The Spike Lee Brand* (2015), a slightly hybridized form of documentary that exports into cinematic reportage elements of the fiction film. According to Letort, however, the corporate leverage of HBO did not turn Lee away from his determination "to challenge racial stereotypes and prejudices [while] retrieving historical episodes and African-American figures from collective oblivion" (2). This body of work includes a series of memorable documentary productions, beginning with *Four Little Girls* (1997) and continuing through *A Huey P. Newton Story* (2001), *Jim Brown: All American* (2002), and *When the Levees Broke* (2007), a "requiem" for the victims of Hurricane Katrina. The subject matter of these films—the civil rights movement, black celebrities, and the Bush administration's seeming indifference to the plight of brown-skinned peoples—had enough general audience or "crossover" appeal to match up well with the HBO demographic. And the network's "subscription model," which spreads costs over the whole spectrum of programming, orients the network more to the general satisfaction of its audience than to a search for individual "hits" (see Santo 2008, 19–45). Lee's sidebar success in television has sustained his career for two decades, giving him access to financial resources and audiences that might otherwise not be available. Hence his television career continues with his multi-chaptered video sequel to *She's Gotta Have It*, ten segments of which were released by Netflix in 2017. Lee is now preparing the second season of Nola Darling's latest adventures in love, life, and art.

It remains clear, however, that Lee prefers the big screen experience of the theater auditorium, where he has also enjoyed much success. And *BlacKkKlansman* has already proved itself one of these successes. Borrowing from the thriller, typified by *Inside Man,* and attaching its tropes of frenetic action to the quieter narration of Ron Stallworth's memoir, Lee renders his version of this unlikely, but largely truthful story as a surreal, serio-comic buddy movie with powerful political and ethnoracial overtones.

Lee's imagination, soaring well beyond the conventions of realism, expands the narrative of a black police officer who infiltrated the Colorado

Ku Klux Klan into a vast mosaic of American racial history that carries us from the Civil War to the chaos of Charlottesville in 2017, when the white supremacists of the so-called Unite the Right movement clashed brutally with a large cadre of counter-demonstrators representing Black Lives Matter. From opposite ends of the political spectrum, these groups contest the issue of Confederate monuments in the twenty-first century. In spite of its wild leaps across time and space, the film is coherently organized around the powerful images that give it continuity and focus.

In terms of its origins, Lee's *BlacKkKlansman* represents another fruitful partnership, this time with Jordan Peele's ambitious production company, Monkey's Paw, and, even more importantly, Focus Features, whose chairman, Peter Kujawski, exulted in Peele's naming of Lee to direct the film: "If there's a dream director, Spike's the guy" (Thompson 2018). Focus has a reputation for investing in controversial themes going back to the unexpected but spectacular success of *Brokeback Mountain* (2002). These partners not only supported Lee's project financially (his budget is estimated at $15 million) but also shared Lee's politically progressive agenda. The contract with Peele and Focus also brought with it the prospect of distribution through Universal, which guaranteed further resources for advertising and promotion. Peele, a black producer/director, had burst onto the scene a year earlier with his award-winning, politically engaged horror film *Get Out* (2017). He trusted Lee to develop the script he had purchased from David Rabinovitz and Charlie Wachtel. These writers took Ron Stallworth's memoir, which they felt "read kind of like a police report," and gave it "a more Hollywood style conflict" (Rabinowitz and Wachtel 2018). Thereafter, Lee added his own more wide-ranging historical narrative, turning Stallworth's local and short-lived effort to disrupt the plans of the Klan in Colorado Springs into a national crusade against political terrorism from the Reconstruction Era to the Trump presidency.

From Lee's personal standpoint, *BlacKkKlansman* represents an enlargement of the arena in which he considers ethno-racial conflict. We are no longer in New York, or Chicago, or even New Orleans. We have left the metropolitan world for the much smaller and more ruralized city of Colorado Springs (population 135,000 by the 1970 census, though now much larger). Colorado Springs is also "the West," a vast land mythologized by Frederick Jackson Turner as the primary site of democratic possibility, but more accurately characterized by Patricia Limerick as a "legacy of conquest." Remembering the region's record of violence, especially against the indigenous peoples, she warns us to walk "with some caution in these historic regions: land that appears solid may be honeycombed, and one would not like to plunge unexpectedly into the legacy of Western history" (Limerick 1987, 18). Founded as a mining town in the late 1850s and later famous as a haven for wealthy English tourists, Colorado Springs was not remarkably friendly toward brown-skinned peoples and had a population that had always lived close to firearms and explosives.

The west of *BlacKkKlansman* is not the casually sketched and sometimes sentimentalized west we find in Lee's earlier films, in *Clockers* (1995), for example, when Strike Dunham (Mekhi Phifer) boards a westbound train out of New York City, imagining he might find a new beginning in the rural world that begins to unfold. Lee conjures a more detailed vision of a utopic west toward the close of *25th Hour*, as Monty Brogan's father imagines visually that his son might avoid prison by escaping to the western frontier. Here he would form new friendships, enjoy the stress-free atmosphere of small town America, and soon found a mixed-race family, after he is joined by his Puerto Rican girlfriend. In the wish-fulfilling fantasy of the elder Brogan, the west is welcoming and open, a New Yorker's dream of spiritual health and practical opportunity.

But in *BlacKkKlansman* Lee calls upon Ron Stallworth to help him imagine the real west, which is formed more in the image of Limerick than Frederick Jackson Turner. As the camera climbs above the iconic red cliffs of southern Colorado to look down in a wide shot at Colorado Springs, we are thrust into a society where everyone (including the police force) is slightly xenophobic, where fear governs much of the decision making, and where a disturbingly large number of socially disadvantaged people are ready to settle their real or supposed grievances with race-based vigilante justice. Stallworth's memoir starkly inscribes several of the more problematic racial attitudes in Colorado Springs. In his job interview, Stallworth was told, without excuse or apology, that the police department is "lily white." Then he is warned: "You're going to be up against a lot to make yourself a success. These people don't deal with blacks unless they're arresting them." As the "Jackie Robinson" of the Colorado Springs Police Department, the new police cadet realizes that not much has changed since #42 first took the field for the Brooklyn Dodgers in April 1947 (Stallworth 2014, 8–9).

Given the way the west is often depicted in legend and lore, we might be surprised to learn that states like California and Colorado were hotbeds of Klan activity during its popular resurgence in the 1920s. In *The Invisible Empire in the West*, Shawn Lay assembles a broad array of scholars to explore how a terrorist society, once largely confined to the Confederate South, was reborn and re-baptized in the period after 1915, now putting down roots in what might seem improbable places, like Anaheim, Denver, El Paso, and Salt Lake City. In his contribution to this volume, Robert Goldberg explains how the primary cell of the Denver Klan reached out in the 1920s to tie into its propaganda network most of the principal Colorado cities at the base of the front range of the Rockies, including Greeley, Boulder, Pueblo, and Colorado Springs. Because of the Klan's

decentralized structure, it was comparatively easy for the western cells
to detach themselves from Confederate themes and set their own agendas. But the Colorado Klan echoed the national message: According to
Goldberg, it offered a program of "Americanism, militant Protestantism,
fraternity, order, religious intolerance, and racial purity," all stirred into
a spiritually intoxicating witches' brew (Lay 1992, 40). Under the "Americanist" rubric, they crusaded on behalf of the strict racial quotas written
into the new national immigration statute of 1924. Its tenets cohered
perfectly with the fierce anti-Semitism that expressed itself in Denver as
complaints about "Jew Town" and "Little Jerusalem," derisive terms for
the Orthodox *shtetl*. These same forces were at work in reprisals against
blacks in Denver who sought to buy homes in white neighborhoods or integrate restaurants and movie theaters. Early on, the Klan expanded rapidly and wielded serious power. Klansman Benjamin Stapleton became a
long-term mayor of Denver and by the mid-1940s the Denver municipal
airport bore his name. But, says Goldberg, the Klan in Colorado declined
abruptly after the heyday of its power: "Members withdrew their loyalty,
time, money, and votes, and the coalition crumbled. . . . Simultaneously,
hostile community perceptions militated against the effort to reverse the
spiral through recruitment of former or new members" (62). But like the
toxic rats of Camus' *Plague*, they returned to their sewers with the implicit
warning that they would return at some moment more favorable to their
dark purposes. That moment came with the civil rights movement of the
1960s and its contentious aftermath. This is where Stallworth's memoir
and Lee's film pick up the tangled threads.

At the simplest level, *BlacKkKlansman* is a "buddy film," a subgenre of
the action/thriller, which Lee both evokes and subverts. These films celebrate male bonding and invite their protagonists to display heroic masculinity in action: two stalwart males, confront (not always successfully)
whatever obstacles might threaten their common purpose. In its alienated, late-sixties costume, the genre produces *Easy Rider* and *Butch Cassidy*
(both 1969). Intellectualized and citified, the same inspiration morphs into
All the President's Men (1974), but its basic tropes remain available to other
variations. One further subcategory that evolves in the wake of the Civil
Rights movement is the cross-racial buddy film, which is tentatively in
place when Sidney Poitier and Rod Steiger grudgingly become law enforcement partners in *In the Heat of the Night* (1967). But the archetype of
the form remains the relationship between Mel Gibson and Danny Glover
in *Lethal Weapon* (1987). Here two Los Angeles police officers, one white,
the other black, are improbably partnered in an investigation that valo-
rizes both protagonists, individually and as a team. Finally putting their
dissonant personalities together, they settle personal business and bring
down a particularly vicious drug gang. Typically in the interracial config-

uration of this genre, says Philippa Gates in her contribution to *American Masculinities*, "the African American is the sidekick to the white hero." In most interracial films of the genre, she concludes, the black male "offers his skills and bravery for the preservation of mainstream (white) cultural values" (Gates 2003, 74). In *BlacKkKlansman*, these motifs are introduced, ironically twisted, and ultimately transformed.

The first major twist is in characterizing the buddies themselves. Stallworth (John David Washington) is much more than a "sidekick" to his partner Flip Zimmerman (Adam Driver). He designs the scheme to infiltrate the Klan and makes first contact with the local Klansmen, responding to a newspaper ad. His improvised tirade against blacks, Jews, Asians, and "anyone who doesn't have pure Aryan blood coursing through his veins" not only startles his police department colleagues into rapt attention but immediately persuades the Klan recruiter to invite him to meet other members of "the organization." But the invitation, of course, immediately calls up the most problematic feature of Stallworth's plan: he must find a white body to give flesh-and-blood identity to the black voice that has so impressed the Klansman. That body belongs to Flip Zimmerman, already a friendly colleague and sometimes partner to Stallworth, but now drawn into a much more intimate and reciprocally dependent relationship.

This brings up a further dimension of the buddy relationship. Inverting the conventional hierarchy of white over black, Stallworth becomes Zimmerman's mentor, both as a speech coach and body language choreographer, when it becomes clear that Zimmerman has no idea of how to talk like a white racist. In one of the film's most appealingly comic scenes, Stallworth schools Zimmerman in "redneck speak," a dialect Stallworth handles with high fluency. By the time their brief seminar is over, Zimmerman has mastered the colloquial speech of the Mountain West. And, courtesy of Stallworth, he also knows what radio talk radio he should tune in, which Christian rock is most spiritually satisfying, even what beer he prefers. Together, Stallworth and Zimmerman convince Chief Bridges that they can weave together body and voice into a single fictive identity, allowing Zimmerman to join the Klan, mingle with its members, and perhaps ferret out their plans (Lee 2018, 28:20/30:35).

Ironically, the issue of language comes up repeatedly in the film, often with good comic effect. Captain Bridges seems skeptical that the young black detective can successfully maintain his white racist persona, because his voice will inevitably sound "black." Like Lovely Brown from *Girl 6*, Stallworth can maintain his cross-racial ruse only if he can convincingly code-switch when he speaks. This turns out to be much less difficult than Bridges imagines, because, as Stallworth insists, he speaks both "English and Jive." In fact, Stallworth performs so well in "standard" English that, later in the film, Grand Wizard David Duke, chief officer of the Klan in Louisiana, congratulates him on the quality of his English, noting that proper pronunciation was what immediately proved the young recruit was of pure Aryan blood. Students of language will be amused to hear that language skills flow through the bloodstream.

To everyone's surprise, what poses problems is not Stallworth's speech, but Zimmerman's body. Zimmerman is a Jew. His ethnicity further complicates the buddy relationship, but also puts the "white man" in deadly peril. Jewish ethnicity is barely mentioned in Stallworth's memoir, but it looms large in Lee's reformulation of the narrative, allowing Lee to tease out more loopholes in the American racial code. Like Naturelle, the "spic skank" of *25th Hour*, Zimmerman is ethnically ambiguous, not black yet not quite white. To the Colorado Springs police department (and certainly to Zimmerman himself!) the young detective's genetic profile is a matter of absolutely no consequence. But to the Klan, trapped in the time warp of the late nineteenth century, the Jew is not really a white man. He is an "Oriental." Furthermore, he is a spiritual degenerate more threatening than the Negro, because his moral corruption, as is clear from any number of neo-Nazi pronouncements, works in concert with a perverse, but high-level intelligence and a particular aptitude for business and finance. More completely than either of them realizes, the buddies, Zimmerman and Stallworth, are, in the ethno-racial schematic of the Klan, the greatest imaginable threat to white supremacy—the diabolic partnership of Africa and Asia Minor. While Lee later uses Zimmerman's Jewishness as a trope to inquire into "white" values, ethnicity has the practical consequence of quickly putting him in more jeopardy than he expects.

The danger unfolds suddenly when Zimmerman is invited to the home of one of the more fanatical Klansmen, Felix (Jasper Paakkonen), ostensibly in order to get acquainted with the rest of the brotherhood, but really because Felix suspects (perhaps on the basis of his name) that the new recruit might be a Jew. The suspicion takes Zimmerman off guard because his parents were completely secular Jews and he has no grasp of Judaic rite or ritual. Also, he has been well coached by Stallworth. His preparation and experience notwithstanding, he is spirited away by Felix to a private room, where Felix demands that he take a lie detector test, then asks to see if he has been circumcised. The last test is several exponents beyond laughable because at midcentury American medical practice made circumcision common in most hospitals, Jew or Gentile. But what discourages laughter is that Felix makes this request while waving a loaded handgun in Zimmerman's face. At this point Stallworth, who has been listening in on this conversation via the wire Zimmerman is wearing, knows he must intervene. Racing from his vehicle to throw a rock through the kitchen window of Felix's home, he turns attention away from Zimmerman and draws all the vigilantes out into the street in futile pursuit of the vandal. The distraction even allows Zimmerman to take a gun from a fellow Klansman and fire shots at his partner's fleeing vehicle. Though Zimmerman is rescued and the undercover operation conserved, the mishap is not without consequences.

The foremost of these is that Zimmerman himself is shaken, bewildered by the violent response to his ethnicity and angry that he, not Stallworth, has become the target of the Klan's unhinged rage. Their first conversation after the incident puts them on opposite sides of the racial divide: "For you, it's a crusade," says Zimmerman, "for me it's just a job." Stallworth's retort is powerful: "Don't you think you've got skin in the game?" What keeps Zimmerman from understanding that the Jews, as recently as the death camps of World War II, have been victims of racism as brutal and all-encompassing as anything visited upon American blacks during the era of slavery, or in the first phase of political terrorism unleashed by the Klan in the 1870s? Ethnically but not culturally Jewish, Zimmerman has trouble identifying himself with those who died at Auschwitz and Dachau. Puzzled but not really won over, Zimmerman walks away from the conversation down a long dark corridor, not ready to fully confront the dilemma of unwitting racial assignment. But in spite of the friction between the partners, the undercover mission continues and Zimmerman gradually shows more sympathy for Stallworth's "crusade" (Lee 2018, 55:50/57:00).

While these several themes are put in play, Lee also develops another arc of the plot, which further subverts the conventions of the buddy film. Unlike almost any other specimen of the genre, *BlacKkKlansman* assigns significant agency to a woman, the politically engaged black activist, Patrice Dumas (Laura Harrier). A figure who does not exist in the memoir, she makes her way into Stallworth's life as a friend, a lover, and ultimately a powerful antagonist to Lee's police detective hero. Her presence and impact overthrow one of the most fundamental premises of the buddy film, namely, that women do not figure importantly in mediating issues of the male world. They are sexualized distractions, threatening both male camaraderie and the mission that has caused two powerful men to partner. Patrice is certainly disruptive and Stallworth is frequently scolded for his romantic interest in her. But she is crucial to the political conversation of the film, which debates the long-standing issue of whether racial justice is best advanced from within or from outside the "white" bureaucratic structure. Patrice speaks for William DuBois, Kwame Ture (aka, Stokely Carmichael, who has just addressed the black student alliance), and Pan-Africanism, while Stallworth implicitly makes the case for Jackie Robinson, Martin Luther King, and his own version of racial integration. Unsurprisingly, this issue is not conclusively settled: Patrice cannot be reconciled to Stallworth's status as a police detective (just another "pig" in the lexicon of the black power movement) and Stallworth remains unconvinced that in-your-face activism ensures a progressive political agenda. Like the debates in *Get on the Bus*, this one is meant to show that the black community was not, and is not, monolithic, and hence cannot be expected to speak with one voice. Nevertheless, it is Patrice who ultimately replaces Stallworth's male buddy, when she stands at his side and they magically advance into an ominous future that neither can understand or control.

These separate strands of the plot converge as the film moves toward climax. The black student alliance, which is Patrice's political base, seeks higher visibility in Colorado Springs for its relatively small constituency of black citizens, mostly college students. Having brought Kwame Ture to the city for a spirited rally on behalf of "black power," the alliance now strives to maintain its forward momentum by featuring another black leader, in this case an elderly veteran of the civil rights struggle, Jerome Turner (Harry Belafonte). The Klan, meanwhile, is planning a dramatic welcome for David Duke, who is traveling to Colorado Springs to celebrate a rebirth of the KKK in the west, a formal event built around the induction of the Klan's new recruits, including Zimmerman. What the Klansmen first imagine as a series of cross-burnings turns sinister with the theft of military explosives by two hyper-zealous members who work for NORAD (North American Aerospace Defense Command). Suddenly the revised scenario is a terrorist plot against the black civil rights veteran and the gathering of black students.

The climax marks the last project of the of the Stallworth/Zimmerman team. Their undertaking to thwart the plot follows a brief conversation in which Zimmerman acknowledges, with a note of profound sadness, that he can no longer avoid thinking about his Jewish ancestry. In spite of its dire implications for those who dream of a "post-racial" America, Zimmerman's realization that he can't escape his ethno-racial identity makes him more supportive of Stallworth. What's more, while they are foiling the attack on the black students, Zimmerman has the opportunity to save his partner, thus repaying a debt owed to Stallworth from the earlier heroic rescue.

This time the emergency requires Stallworth's rescue from the Colorado Springs police. In another theater of the absurd moment, the black detective physically tackles the would-be bomber, a white female, thus neutralizing the terrorist threat. But two overeager white lawmen in a police cruiser mistake the bomb-bearing woman for a sexual assault victim and begin to abuse Stallworth, whom they take to be a rapist. This time Zimmerman intervenes, flashing his police shield and explaining to the arresting officers that their prisoner is a law enforcement officer and the real criminal is the woman whom they mistook for a victim. Fortunately for everyone, in this instance Zimmerman successfully passes for white and his authority is sufficient to secure Stallworth's release and take the bomber into custody.

The Stallworth/Zimmerman relationship invites Lee's most searching examination of the complex relationship between American blacks and Jews. In partnering, the two undercover agents discern that in some sense they are political and spiritual comrades. Unlike the Jewish driver in *Get on the Bus*, who refuses to transport the black pilgrims to a rally organized by the anti-Semitic Louis Farrakhan, or Myrna Goldfarb of *Bamboozled*, who has been hired explicitly to prevent Delacroix from enjoying full control of his own television show, Zimmerman and Stallworth are not automatically cast into adversarial roles. The buddy film context of equal professional skills allows their shared ethno-racial history of suffering and victimization to gradually build a sense of mutual respect and common purpose. But the prospect of long-term interracial cooperation is left in doubt. Though they are often seen as cultural aliens, the Jews have fared better in the United States than African Americans. They have experienced discrimination more in psychosocial than in starkly physical terms—in other words, as quotas, exclusionist covenants, and personal insults more than as lynchings and bombings. In terms of social status, they often face off as superiors to subalterns: teacher/student, lender/borrower, prosecutor/defendant, employer/employee. Above all, the color code remains irresistible, as evidenced in the scene where Stallworth thwarts the terrorist. In spite of his sterling police work, the black officer remains the racial alien, whom the "lily white" Colorado Springs police immediately mistake for a criminal as he struggles to subdue the fair-skinned bomber. Zimmerman's heroic rescue of his comrade ironically underscores the gulf that still separates them. Guilt and innocence are reducible to skin tones, and Zimmerman is on the privileged side of the color line.

The last focal point of Lee's narrative is David Duke (Topher Grace), Grand Wizard of the Klan, and the figure who connects the events in Colorado Springs with national politics. A notorious neo-Nazi who later won public office in Louisiana, Duke sought to create a broad anti-progressive coalition built upon white privilege and fueled by grievances related to integration, affirmative action, and the liberal immigration policy of the Johnson administration. One scholar credits him with an "effort to modernize the Klan and broaden its appeal," evidenced by his willingness to induct women and teenagers into the previously all-male organization (Bridges 1994, 44). Another commentator sees him as exceptionally savvy in "making use of the structural characteristics of the news media, especially television, to get the most and best coverage he can" (Lay 1992, 137). As Lee presents him, Duke is deceptively affable, cordial on the telephone, and comfortable with like-minded people, as he mingles with his

Klan cohorts in Colorado Springs. There is even talk of linking the west to the South, in a hospitable exchange of visits and recipes.

More than all else, Duke wants to assure the membership of the intellectual cogency of Klan doctrine. His formal lecture is inspirational, but fiercely insistent upon white supremacy. Drawing upon the preachments of the discredited sociobiologist William Shockley, an engineer who developed a late-blooming interest in genetics, Duke assures the white citizens of America that they have every right to say they are superior, because it is a "scientific fact" that the Aryan nation is indeed the master race. The Klan intends nothing more (but nothing less!) than that these citizens take back what properly belongs to them. In so doing, they will be advancing the interests of Christian morality and Western European civilization. Duke's speech clarifies the overwhelming sense of entitlement that drives every impulse of Klan loyalists. In *BlacKkKlansman*, Lee offers a powerful counterpoint to this narrative by intercutting Duke's inspirational lecture on white supremacy with the horrific story of a lynching told to the black student alliance by Jerome Turner, an eyewitness to the murder of an innocent black man. But Lee's more comprehensive rebuke to Duke takes the form of a complicated framing device, which places the brief upsurge of the Colorado Klan in a continuum that reaches from the Civil War to the new millennium.

Lee's rendering of Ron Stallworth's memoir is competent and engaging, heightened by dramatic devices imported from the thriller. But what adds a remarkably new dimension of political relevance to the events in Colorado Springs is Lee's representation of Stallworth's personal experience as a small shard of the national narrative of race. The resurgent Klan is the fulcrum on which the historical action turns.

That action proposes and then critiques what we might call a Confederate reading of our national identity narrative. Appropriately, the first sequence is a scene from *Gone with the Wind* (1939), the aftermath of a battle which has cost the South dearly. While the musical track intones "Dixie," played not as a bright marching tune but as a dirge, the camera rises on a crane to show a seemingly endless expanse of wounded soldiers, their sheer numbers assuring that they cannot possibly receive proper attention or medical care. It's a scene of massive injury and humiliation, from which the South seems entitled to ask redress. And no redress comes before Appomattox, nor immediately thereafter.

These events set the stage for the Klan, whose founding and mission are celebrated in another motion picture sensation from two decades earlier, D.W. Griffith's *The Birth of a Nation* (1915). More insistently than Margaret Mitchell, whose exposition is not overtly political, though decisively racist, Griffith stresses the grave wrongs done to the South in the Reconstruction era and the need for patriotic vigilantes to organize and forcibly resist the black masses, who had been prematurely granted rights they were incapable of exercising responsibly. Astonishingly, this one-sided narrative threatened to become the national narrative when President Wilson, the child of a slave-owning Confederate family, endorsed Griffith's film as "history written with lightening." Griffith had already paid Wilson the favor of quoting him, in one of the film's inter-titles, a sympathetic comment the president had made on the Klan in his *A History of the American People*: "The white men were roused," Wilson says, "until at last there had sprung into existence a great Ku Klux Klan . . . to protect the Southern country" (see Rice 2016, 11–13). Apparently, in the thinking of both Griffith and Wilson, the impulse to "protect" the South took priority over the directives of the Fourteenth and Fifteenth Amendments. The last element of the Confederate "grievance" narrative is supplied by the overheated rhetoric of the fictive Kennebrew Beauregard (Alec Baldwin), whose rants against integrated public schools give the racist convictions of the Klan its contemporary format. Their mission is no longer merely to "protect" the South. The de-segregation decision, soon followed by busing and affirmative action, nationalized the issue of race and broadened the right-wing political coalition that opposed black rights.

As the prologue gives way to the events in Colorado Springs, Lee effectively shows how the spiritual children of Griffith and Margaret Mitchell have ingested the stereotypes of the popular media and used them to advantage in building their white power world. When the Colorado Klan socializes, they gather in bars where a neon replica of the Confederate battle flag is the primary icon, and they never tire of recalling black encroachments upon white privilege, including the greater visibility of African Americans in athletics and on television. They sit enthralled when *The Birth of a Nation* is screened at the induction ceremony, giggling at the dysfunctional black legislature and shouting their approval when Griffith's Klansmen summarily hang a supposed black criminal. On another occasion, Duke tells Stallworth about how much he revered Hattie McDaniel, the deeply conservative "Mammy" of *Gone with the Wind*, and Stallworth, in his white-racist persona, counters with a story about his childhood friendship with "Butter Biscuit," the stereotype of an infantilized, non-threatening black male. Again and again, they wonder: What has happened to the docile, compliant blacks who once served the master race so willingly? No surprise that the black student alliance, shouting for "black power," arouses such virulent rage.

After the bombing has been foiled and its perpetrators arrested, the police department of Colorado Springs shuts down its investigation abruptly, declaring victory over the Klan. But Lee adds an epilogue, which leaps forward to Charlottesville in 2017, to show that the Klan and its sympathizers are still alive and well. In a surrealistic transition,

Lee projects Patrice and Stallworth into the new millennium, where they bear witness in time present to the massive Unite the Right rally, staged to save the Confederate monuments in Charlottesville. At this point Lee grafts a kind of magical realism upon documentary footage that details the violent events of the white power rally.

The scene is launched by one of Lee's signature camera movements, one that places Patrice and Stallworth on the same dolly (or a trailer dolly moving with it) that produces the long tracking shot of an empty corridor. This composition violates the optical perspective of the shot, since we can see that the protagonists are being visually separated from their immediate physical environment, as if wrenched from their historical time and place. From this trans-temporal vantage point, they can presumably see how many battles over racial justice are yet to be fought.

In Charlottesville, the Klan has gathered in impressive numbers, looking far more robust than they did in Colorado Springs, as they burn their cross and luxuriate in their bigotry. We also see a large cadre of neo-Nazis, having no relationship to the Confederacy, but waving Swastika banners and shouting "Jews will not replace us." If proof were needed, their signage assures us that anti-Semitism is also alive and well. Even David Duke is on hand, still looking ruggedly handsome and promising his followers that the time has come to "take back our land." Lee's reconstruction of events also includes the assault on the counter-demonstrators, which claims the life of a supportive white woman who has come to Charlottesville in the name of cultural pluralism. With few hints of how these grave cultural divisions might be overcome, Lee breaks off his narrative on a deeply disruptive note.

That the film ends with rival constituencies violently contesting the status of public monuments is singularly appropriate to Lee's reading of the nation's ethno-racial conflict. In one of the best books on the Black Lives Matter movement, David McIvor represents the current upsurge of racial unrest as a "politics of mourning," in which angry factions, ethno-racially inflected, struggle furiously for the public space required to mourn their losses and display their grief. Hence the Charlottesville epilogue returns us to the first image on the screen—the massive number of wounded Confederate patriots laid out after a lost battle and the wounds to white pride that these broken bodies symbolize. The Confederate monuments, of course, are concrete artifacts that assuage grief and mourn the demise of the great slave empire the Confederacy aspired to build. But McIvor intervenes with the most immediate and crucial point: in the space of pluralistic civic discourse, sculptural or rhetorical, "which and whose losses will be commemorated or honored, . . . whose pain is publicly registered" (2016, 4–5). The white supremacists have come to Charlottesville to safeguard Jefferson Davis and Robert E. Lee, to save the heroic legacy of the south from "erasure or misrecognition" (McIvor 2016, 48). But they will inevitably clash with those who would build monuments to Martin Luther King, Kwami Ture, and the Black Panthers, lest their cultural impact be forgotten or distorted. In this concluding moment, Lee comes full circle in his analysis of contested terrain. As in *Do the Right Thing* from three decades earlier, *BlacKkKlansman* ends without resolving the question of who controls the space of representation. Sal, Smiley, and Buggin' Out are still at war.

Of the three filmmakers discussed in this monograph, Lee seems the most likely to prolong his career for at least another decade, and perhaps longer. Having just turned sixty, he is still in midlife and might yet turn unexpectedly in a new direction. But spectacularly new initiatives seem unlikely. In the new millennium, Lee has gradually morphed his persona as the angry young man into an establishment filmmaker with an insistent social justice agenda, strikingly displayed in *BlacKkKlansman*. This tendency toward mainstream thematic concerns is even more evident in his recent commitment to Netflix, which issued in a ten-episode sequel to his first great success as a writer-director, *She's Gotta Have It* (1986). The new version of this film updates its heroine Nola Darling (DeWanda Wise) for the twenty-first century, retaining her polyamorous sexual impulses, but giving more attention to her credentials as a feminist and her determination to establish herself in the New York art world. In this work, Lee also displays a more evolved interest in other issues, among them lesbianism, cosmetic surgery, biracial child rearing, and the problem of neighborhood gentrification. This revised agenda implicates him more in the mediation of urban issues than in the examination of more strictly racial concerns. It's not that the director has "sold out" to commercial sponsorship (though this is almost certain to be charged), but that the search for a broader audience dictates a reformulation of the racial dialogue. The rigid binaries of *Do the Right Thing* and *Malcolm X* are giving way to the conflicted conversation between the burbs and the hood that is becoming increasingly central to the future of our cities. The outreach toward the west in *BlacKkKlansman* also indicates that Lee no longer thinks of himself as exclusively a New York filmmaker and wants to investigate other theaters of ethno-racial dialogue. Inevitably, he continues to seek secure funding for his directorial efforts. That need not compromise his artistic integrity and might contribute positively to his further endeavors.

Epilogue

Twilight of the Tribes?

In *Beyond Blood Ties* (2009), Jason Hill argues on behalf of a "cosmopolitan perspective" which postulates that "one's identity is not determined solely nor primarily by any racial, national, or ethnic background" (47). In the place of allegiance to the family, the tribe, or the clan, as well as the symbolic artifacts that define them, Hill recommends a "larger universal identity grounded in reason, moral purpose, and above all, human dignity" (48). Drawing particularly upon the thinking of Julia Kristeva in *Strangers to Ourselves* (1991), he insists that we "accept the foreigner within us" and use this submerged self as an antidote to a seductive but dangerous "tribalism" (49). Hill is aware, however, that in promoting the abstract values of individualism, universalism, and generality, he risks alienating his disciples from "the central features that inform the thick identity of people's lives—their moral beliefs and religious convictions" (50). If it is dangerous to trust in "the salvific quality of ethnicity," attributing to lineage and ancestry magically "restorative and redemptive qualities" (147), it might be equally problematic to put too much faith in a transcendental order of rationality that could easily be mistaken for the organizational arrangements and power distribution of a particular culture at a particular moment. The hesitancy and reluctance with which filmmakers like Scorsese and Allen have severed their ethnic roots betokens not so much their susceptibility to tribalism as their skepticism in the face of a majoritarian culture that has in no sense transcended its own totems and taboos.

This point applies even more powerfully to Spike Lee as he plies his craft on the other side of America's racial divide. Intuitively, he has fully grasped the central concern that Houston Baker and K. Merinda Simmons bring forward in *The Trouble with Post-Blackness* (2015), a scholarly anthology published during the second term of the Obama presidency. Standing on "The Dubious Stage of Post-Blackness," Simmons plunges directly into the controversy over black identity by wondering how one can find neutral or "transcendental" ground in the discussion of race,

281

when the discourse emanates from a racially conflicted society that still takes whiteness as its norm. She sees whiteness not as a norm but as a contingency, "forged from consistently changing boundaries and made up of its own codes that people perform," without admitting that the codes themselves are not fixed or stable. Instead they are treated as "the knowable space of identity (rather than an act of identification like any other) that we need not question because of its clear cohesiveness" (9). Later in the volume, Erin Kaplan echoes Simmons' suspicions respecting the racially normative when she asks, "why everyone is debating post-blackness and not post-whiteness." Ideally, post-blackness would mean release from the legacy of America's slave empire. But Kaplan fears "there is no post-blackness as long as whites continue to create the terms of black existence" (2015, 191–92). So long as these circumstances persist, so long is it likely that Spike Lee will continue to complain of the media establishment even while he remains an integral part of it.

Engaged from the wrong angle, Jason Hill's cosmopolitanism might look suspiciously like neoliberalism in a more tasteful costume. It's also the case that not every tribal impulse evidences "psychopathology" or "ends up elevating difference into a cult" (2009, 150). Ethno-racial self-consciousness is sometimes perverse and brutal, but may also express itself as a mother's song recalled from childhood, the aroma arising from a holiday meal, or the grieving process associated with the untimely death of a sibling. These powerful, flesh-and-blood experiences are densely textured and emotionally resonant, particularly when they are set beside the maxims of a civics book or a discourse on due process. As Scorsese, Allen, and Lee gradually fade from the scene, they are likely to be replaced by a new generation of Latinos, Indians, Chinese, or Native Americans, of female as well as male gender, who will use the parochial norms of their ethnic cultures as valuable countervailing forces against the chilly abstractions of cosmopolitanism, which are subtly related to formula films emanating from both the old and the new Hollywood.

Recent scholarship has rightfully emphasized the capacity of the film industry to reassert its power in the face of independent production. In *The Studios After the Studios* (2015), J. D. Connor examines at length how the celluloid empires of the 1930s and 1940s, with Paramount as the prime example, regrouped and redefined their influence upon production through various branding mechanisms, most of them related to the catch phrase of "high concept" (see 69–124). While surrendering some ground to the vogue of "auteurship," which itself capitalized on Paramount's earlier reputation as a "directors' studio," the new media moguls concentrated on subsidizing films that would have a particular look, ideally reducible to a few vivid images—the pram, so prominent in the marketing of *Rosemary's Baby* (1968) or the gaping mouth of the great white shark in *Jaws* (1973). For Connor, this makes the revamped Hollywood studio "an intensified space of collective aesthetic endeavor, a work place where we might fashion not only art but also a society in microcosm" (321). But a "society in microcosm" does not speak with one voice. In acknowledging "the qualms of empire" and "conglomerate overstretch," Connor admits to chinks in the corporate armor. Ultimately, he recognizes individual centers of creative energy, "the people who shape these stories—the people above and below the line, writers and designers actors and directors" (322), all of whom bring their often conflicted intentions to a work of many hands.

This concession argues for the continued relevance of Mikhail Bakhtin to film discourse, especially discourse related to ethno-racial themes. In his groundbreaking work of the 1980s, Robert Stam discerned that the cinema is inherently polyphonic, because of the multiple crafts and disciplines (writing, acting, shooting, sound design, editing) that must be harmonized in the finished product. Noting the cinema's historic derivation from magic shows and arcade events, both intimately related to the travesties and "discrownings" of European and New World carnival, he also pointed up the continuing affection of the film medium for anarchistic action and chaotic behavior, such as we find in the Keystone Cops, the Marx brothers, and Monty Python's Flying Circus. What serves our argument best at this juncture is Stam's recognition that both the film medium and the film industry are sites of cultural tension, that "within a Bakhtinian approach, there is no unitary text, no unitary producer, and no unitary spectator; rather, there is a conflictual heteroglossia pervading producer, text, context, and reader/viewer. Each category is traversed by the centripetal and the centrifugal, the hegemonic and the oppositional" (1989, 221). Two decades later, Martin Flanagan in *Bakhtin and the Movies* (2009) picks up this thread as he contrasts "the centripetal unifying impulse that produces cultural norms" with "the centrifugal forces [that] attempt to scatter and counteract that uniformity for the benefit of a more heteroglossic culture" (160). In extended critiques of two independently produced films that resist the culturally normative, Flanagan shows how David Mamet's *House of Games* (1987) relativizes the conventions of film noir, while John Sayles' *Lone Star* (1996) dismantles the classical Western. In both cases, the polyphonic rhetoric of the film works against the ideological orthodoxy of the genre, in the first instance, acknowledging the voice of the *femme fatale* and in the other, challenging the moral authority of the straight-shooting sheriff (see Flanagan 2009, 110–27, 145–54). What marks the discourse of these films as polyphonic is its multiplicity of perspectives, its refusal to name any single viewpoint as decisive, thus creating a text that is "open, mysterious, and resistant to our understanding . . . in terms of gender and ethical models" (148).

Bakhtin's precepts provide a conspicuous niche for the ethnic film. All aesthetic discourse is "relational," maintains Stam, and must be seen "in relation to the deforming effects of power." Bakhtin's "sympathies are clearly with the nonofficial viewpoint, with the marginalized, the oppressed, the peripheralized." Ethnic cinema is well positioned to "deploy myriad cultural voices—that of the indigenous peoples (no matter how suppressed that voice may be), that of the African American (however distorted), that of the Jewish, Italian, Hispanic, and Asiatic communities, each of which condenses in turn, a multiplicity of social accents having to do with gender, class, and locale, all flowing into a broader, nonfinalized polyphony of cultures" (Stam 1989, 230–31). Stam finds this potential clearly articulated in Allen's *Zelig* (1982), replete with mockeries and travesties, from the spoof of the documentary genre itself, to the transmogrification of the ethnic body, to the ironic teasing of the heroic celebrity, who is inevitably at the center of the Hollywood biopic. The relative autonomy of the independent producer / director, supported by a sympathetic ethnic community as his core audience (in Allen's case, the Jewish community of metropolitan New York), is well situated to make such films "a matrix in which centripetal-dominant and centrifugal-oppositional forces do battle" (221). Flanagan adds the valuable point that new high-resolution digital formats, which encourage Blue-ray releases, together with the special features they often include, alter the film marketplace, so as to favor tailoring "the Director's cut" to an increasingly more self-selecting audience, frequently that of a specific subculture (2009, 155–60).

Two decades into the new millennium, none of the three directors we have examined is ready to concede that his career is coming to an end. In spite of the fact that he is the eldest of the group, Allen remains the most active, maintaining a work regimen that produces something close to one film per year. More significantly, he has recently tightened a relationship with the Amazon corporation, which links him to the most dynamic new force in the pantheon of American entrepreneurship. As if to vouch for his continuing relevance, Amazon used Allen's *Wonder Wheel* (2017) to showcase its new presence in the marketplace as an independent distributor. Scorsese also maintains an active production agenda, gradually shifting his focus away from Italianate themes but continuing to apply his anthropological interests to other subcultures, particularly the Irish. At the moment, he is planning and organizing a major production that, in the manner of *The Departed*, would resuscitate the Irish gangster of the recent past, this time in a biopic that remembers Frank Sheeran, a notorious Irish hit man of the 1960s and 70s, who claims to have murdered Jimmy Hoffa. Scorsese's most recent creative effort, *Silence* (2016), is a credible effort to reconstruct the mindset of sixteenth-century Japan, as the island empire turns decisively against the Portuguese Jesuits who came determined to Christianize its people. Standing apart from the assignment of praise or blame, the film effectively dramatizes a clash of cultures in which a well-meant Christian message is utterly lost in translation. Lee too remains active, recently completing the ambitious ten-part series for Netflix that revises and repurposes the *She's Gotta Have It* saga of Nola Darling, now fitted to the priorities of the new millennium.

While cultivating the new marketing opportunities presented by Netflix and HBO, Lee also perseveres in the favorite Indie strategy of advertising his wares through the interest generated by prestigious film festivals. His most recent release *BlacKkKlansman* garnered important positive publicity from having won the *Grand Prix* at Cannes, one of the most coveted of film awards. The film itself also represents a significant reassertion of Lee's filmmaking talent, again venturing into the troubled waters of ethno-racial conflict, but remembering that this conflict is multidimensional and not monolithic. Unlike Malcolm X, who shuns every thought of common cause with the broader culture, the protagonist of *BlacKkKlansman*, Ron Stallworth, is an African American police officer working on behalf of law enforcement in Colorado Springs. Furthermore, his daring plan to infiltrate the Ku Klux Klan requires that he recruit a white double, whom he finds in his Jewish fellow officer, Flip Zimmerman. This partnership is consequential, in symbolic as well as literal terms, even eliciting from Stallworth the acknowledgment, "With the right white man, you can do anything." In order to make himself acceptable to the Klan, Stallworth must insist that, though he hates blacks most fiercely, he also despises "Jews, Irish, Chinese, and Mexicans" with almost equal fury. Which implies, of course, that other, historically disadvantaged ethnics constitute a constituency of potential allies. What *BlacKkKlansman* argues eloquently is that black advancement requires coalition building and outreach to marginalized subcultures as well as some support from establishment institutions, even institutions as problematic as police departments.

Lee will no doubt continue to call out white America for its ongoing insensitivity to an underclass that is predominately black and brown. But at the same time he will work within corporate structures, joining basketball buddies like Samuel Jackson and Charles Barkley as they make promos for Visa's Capital One: "What's in your wallet?" He may also shift his production interests more heavily to television, a partnership fruitfully begun with HBO and now enlarged though his contract with Netflix. Though Lee is in no way beguiled by the delusion of a "post-racial" America, he will almost certainly situate race in its larger social context, which demands more attention to hybridity and intercultural exchange.

Given their body of work and their continuing commitment to it, the durability of these artists seems assured, together with the Indie film-making movement they have been part of for the past half-century. It also seems safe to assume that Scorsese, Allen, and Lee will continue to spur the nation's ethno-racial conversation, a topic sure to remain at the center of American cultural life for the foreseeable future. In addition to their exceptional work ethic, unflagging after half a century, they have also shown themselves highly resourceful in adapting to changing production conditions. Their example, encoded vividly into their best work, will inspire a new generation of independent ethnic filmmakers, who are more than eager to follow in their footsteps, though very likely in a different style of shoes.

Reference List

Abernethy, Graeme. 2013. *The Iconography of Malcolm X*. Lawrence: Kansas University Press.

Abrams, Roger. 1982. "The Language of Festivals." In *Celebration: Studies in Festivity and Ritual*, edited by Victor Turner, 161–77. Washington, DC: Smithsonian Press.

Aftab, Kaleem, and Spike Lee. 2006. *Spike Lee: That's My Story and I'm Sticking to It*. New York: W. W. Norton.

Alba, Richard, ed. 1988. *Ethnicity and Race in the USA: Toward the Twenty-First Century*. New York: Routledge.

———. 1990. *Ethnic Identity: The Transformation of White America*. New Haven: Yale University Press.

———. 2009. *Blurring the Color Line: The New Chance for a More Integrated America*. Cambridge, MA: Harvard University Press.

Alexander, Ella. 2013. "Cate Blanchett's Help for Woody Allen." *Vogue*. September 24, 2013. http://www.vogue.co.uk/article/cate-blanchett-blue-jasmine-interview-woody-allen-film.

Allen, Woody. 1966. *Getting Even*. New York: Random House.

———. 1972. *Without Feathers*. New York: Random House.

———. 1975. *Side Effects*. New York: Random House.

———, dir. 1977. *Annie Hall*. MGM DVD Video. United Artists Release.

———, dir. 1979. *Manhattan*. MGM DVD Video. United Artists Release.

———, dir. 1980. *Stardust Memories*. MGM DVD. United Artists Release.

———, dir. 1983. *Zelig*. MGM DVD. MGM Pictures.

———, dir. 1987. *Radio Days*. MGM DVD. Orion Pictures Release.

———, dir. 1989. *Crimes and Misdemeanors*. MGM DVD Video. Orion Pictures Release.

———, dir. 1998. *Deconstructing Harry*. DVD Video. Fine Line Features.

———, dir. 2013. *Blue Jasmine*. DVD Video. Sony Pictures Classics.

———, dir. 2016. *Café Society*. DVD Video. Amazon Studios.

Anbinder, Tyler. 2016. *City of Dreams: The 400-Year Epic History of Immigrant New York*. Boston: Houghton Mifflin Harcourt.

Ashcroft, Bill. 2009. *Caliban's Voice: The Transformation of English in Post-Colonial Literatures*. New York: Routledge.

Austen, Jake, and Yuval Taylor. 2012. *Darkest America: Black Minstrelsy from Slavery to Hip Hop*. New York: W. W. Norton.

Baader, Benjamin Maria, Sharon Gillerman, and Paul Lerner, eds. 2012. *Jewish Masculinities: Germans, Jews, Gender, and History*. Bloomington: Indiana University Press.

Babb, Valerie. 1998. *Whiteness Visible: The Meaning of Whiteness in American Literature and Culture*. New York: New York University Press.

Bailey, Peter. 2001. *The Reluctant Art of Woody Allen*. Lexington: Kentucky University Press.

———, and Sam Girgus, eds. 2013. *A Companion to Woody Allen*. Chichester, UK: Wiley-Blackwell.

Baker, Aaron, and Juliann Vitullo. 2001. "Screening the Italian-American Male." In *Masculinity: Bodies, Movies, Culture*, edited by Peter Lehman, 214–25. New York: Routledge.

Baker, Houston. 1993. "Spike Lee and the Commerce of Culture." In *Black American Cinema*, edited by Manthia Diawara, 154–76. New York: Routledge.

———, and K. Merinda Simmons, eds. 2015. *The Trouble with Post-Blackness*. New York: Columbia University Press.

Baraka, Amiri. 1993, "Spike Lee at the Movies." In *Black American Cinema*, edited by Manthia Diawara, 145–53. New York: Routledge.

Barlowe, Jamie. 2003. "'You Must Never Be a Misrepresented People': Spike Lee's *Bamboozled*." *Canadian Review of American Studies* 33, no. 1 (Spring): 1–16.

Barrett, James. 2012. *The Irish Way: Becoming American in the Multiethnic City*. New York: Penguin Press.

Barthes, Roland. 1999. "Myth Today." In *Visual Culture: The Reader*, edited by Jessica Evans and Stuart Hall, 51–58. London: Sage Publications.

Bauman, Zygmunt. 1998. "Allosemitism: Premodern, Modern, Postmodern." In *Modernity, Culture, and "the Jew,"* edited by Bryan Cheyette and Laura Marcus, 146–56. Stanford, CA: Stanford University Press.

Becker, Ernest. 1973. *The Denial of Death*. New York: Simon and Schuster.

Belfort, Jordan. 2007. *The Wolf of Wall Street*. New York: Random House.

———. 2009. *Catching the Wolf of Wall Street*. New York: Random House.

Beltran, Mary. 2008. "Mixed Race Latinowood: Latino Stardom and Ethnic Ambiguity in the Era of *Dark Angels*." In *Mixed Race Hollywood*, edited by Beltran and Camilla Fojas, 249–68. New York: New York University Press.

Bergmann, Martin S. 1987. *The Anatomy of Loving: The Story of Man's Quest to Know What Love Is*. New York: Columbia University Press.

Berkowitz, Edward D. 2010. *Mass Appeal: The Formative Age of the Movies, Radio, and TV*. New York: Cambridge University Press.

Blake, Richard. 2005. *Street Smart: The New York of Lumet, Allen, Scorsese, and Lee*. Lexington: Kentucky University Press.

———. 2013. "Allen's Random Universe in the European Cycle: Morality, Marriage, Magic." In *A Companion to Woody Allen*, edited by Peter Bailey and Sam Girgus, 539–58. Chichester, UK: Wiley-Blackwell.

Bowman, Cara, Nazli Kibria, and Megan O'Leary. 2014. *Race and Immigration*. Cambridge, UK: Polity Press.

Bridges, Tylor. 1994. *The Rise of David Duke*. Jackson: Mississippi University Press.

Brodkin, Karen. 1998. *How Jews Became White Folks and What That Says about Race in America*. New Brunswick, NJ: Rutgers University Press.

Brunette, Peter, ed. 1999. *Martin Scorsese: Interviews*. Jackson: Mississippi University Press.

Campbell, Neil. 2008. *The Rhizomatic West: Representing the American West in a Transnational, Global, Media Age*. Lincoln: Nebraska University Press.

Carpenter, Faedra. 2013. "Spectacles of Whiteness from Adrienne Kennedy to Suzan-Lori Parks." In *Cambridge Companion to African American Theatre*, edited by Harvey Young, 174–95. New York: Cambridge University Press.

———. 2014. *Coloring Whiteness: Acts of Critique in Black Performance*. Ann Arbor: Michigan University Press.

Carroll, Bret, ed. 2003. *American Masculinities: A Historial Encyclopedia*. Thousand Oaks, CA: Sage Publications, 2003.

Carr, Steven. 2001. *Hollywood and Anti-Semitism: A Cultural History up to World War II*. New York: Cambridge University Press.

Cashmore, Ellen. 2009. *Martin Scorsese's America*. Cambridge, UK: Polity Press.

Casillo, Robert. 2006. *Gangster Priest: The Italian American Cinema of Martin Scorsese*. Toronto: University of Toronto Press.

"Cate Blanchett Finds Humor in the Painfully Absurd." Interview, "All Things Considered," National Public Radio, January 10, 2014. http://www.npr.org/2014/01/10/26138089/cate-blanchett-finds-humor-in-the-painfully-absurd.

Cazenave, Noel A. 2011. *The Urban Racial State: Managing Race Relations in American Cities*. Lanham, MD: Rowman & Littlefield.

Chalom, Adam. 2009. "Beyond Apicorsut: A Judaism for Secular Jews." In *Religion or Ethnicity: Jewish Identities in Evolution*, edited by Zvi Gitelman, 286–302. New Brunswick, NJ: Rutgers University Press.

Cheyette, Bryan, and Laura Marcus, eds. 1998. *Modernity, Culture, and "the Jew."* Stanford, CA: Stanford University Press.

Childs, Erica. 2005. *Navigating Interracial Borders: Black–White Couples and their Social Worlds*. New Brunswick, NJ: Rutgers University Press.

Christie, Ian, and David Thompson, eds. 2003. *Scorsese on Scorsese*. London: Faber and Faber.

Codde, Philippe. 2007. *The Jewish American Novel*. West Lafayette, IN: Purdue University Press.

Conard, Mark, ed. 2008. *The Philosophy of Martin Scorsese*. Lexington: Kentucky University Press.

Connor, J. D. 2015. *The Studios after the Studios: Neoclassical Hollywood (1970–2010)*. Stanford, CA: Stanford University Press, 2015.

Cook, David. 1990. *Lost Illusions: American Cinema in the Shadow of Vietnam and Watergate*. New York: Charles Scribner and Sons.

Corkin, Stanley. 2011. *Starring New York: Filming the Grime and Glamour of the Long 1970s*. New York: Oxford University Press.

Covington, Jeanette. 2010. *Crime and Racial Constructions: Cultural Misinformation about African Americans in Media and Academia*. New York: Lexington Books.

Curry, Renee. 2013. "Woody Allen's Grand Scheme: The Whitening of Manhattan, London, and Barcelona." In *A Companion to Woody Allen*, edited by Peter Bailey and Sam Girgus, 277–93. Chichester, UK: Wiley-Blackwell.

Daileader, Celia. 2005. *Racism, Misogyny, and the Othello Myth: Interracial Couples from Shakespeare to Spike Lee*. Cambridge, UK: Cambridge University Press.

Davis, Mike. 1998. "Las Vegas Versus Nature." In *Reopening the American West*, edited by Hal Rothman, 53–76. Tucson: Arizona University Press.

Delgado, Celestino. 1994. "The Narrator and the Narrative: The Evolution of Woody Allen's Film Comedies." *Film Criticism* 19, no. 2 (December): 40–54.

Dershowitz, Alan. 1998. *The Vanishing Jew: In Search of Jewish Identity for the Next Century*. New York: Simon and Schuster.

Diawara, Manthia, ed. 1993. *Black American Cinema*. New York: Routledge.

Di Donato, Pietro. 1939. *Christ in Concrete: A Novel*. New York: Bobbs-Merrill.

DiGirolamo, Vincent. 2004. "Such, Such Were the B'hoys." *Radical History Review* 90 (Fall): 123–41.

Douglas, Susan J. 1999. *Listening In: Radio and the American Imagination*. New York: Random House.

Dreier, Peter, John Mollenkopf, and Todd Swanstrom. 2014. *Place Matters: Metropolitics for the Twenty First Century*. 3rd ed. Lawrence: Kansas University Press.

Dunne, Michael. 1991. "Metaleptical Hijinks in Woody Allen's *Stardust Memories*." *Literature/Film Quarterly* 19, no. 2 (April): 114–18.

Dyson, Michael. 1995. *Making Malcolm: The Myth and Meaning of Malcolm X*. Oxford: Oxford University Press.

Eilberg-Schwartz, ed. 1992. *People of the Body: Jews and Judaism from an Embodied Perspective*. Albany: State University of New York Press.

Embry, Jessie, and Brian Cannon, eds. 2015. *Immigrants in the Far West: Historical Identities and Experiences*. Salt Lake City: Utah University Press.

Esolen, Gary. 1992. "More than a Pretty Face: David Duke's Use of Television as a Political Tool." In *The Emergence of David Duke and the Politics of Race*, edited by Douglas Rose, 136–155, Chapel Hill, NC: North Carolina University Press.

Evanier, David. 2015. *Woody: The Biography*. New York: St. Martin's Press.

Evans, Jessica, and Stuart Hall, eds. 1999. *Visual Culture: The Reader*. London: Sage Publications.

Everett, Anna. 2008. "Spike, Don't Mess Malcolm Up: Courting Controversy and Control in *Malcolm X*." In *The Spike Lee Reader*, edited by Paula Massood, 91–114. Philadelphia: Temple University Press.

Fernandez, Ronald. 2007. *America Beyond Black and White: How Immigrants and Fusions Are Helping Us Overcome the Racial Divide*. Ann Arbor: Michigan University Press.

Ferraro, Thomas. 2005. *Feeling Italian: The Art of Ethnicity in America*. New York: New York University Press.

Feuer, Menachem. 2013. "The Schlemiel in Woody Allen's Later Films." In *A Companion to Woody Allen*, edited by Peter Bailey and Sam Girgus, 403–23. Chichester, UK: Wiley-Blackwell.

Fine, Michelle, ed. 2004. *Off White: Readings on Power, Privilege, and Resistance*. New York: Routledge.

Flanagan, Martin. 2009. *Bakhtin and the Movies: New Ways of Understanding Hollywood Film*. New York: Palgrave Macmillan.

Foster, Gwendolyn. 2003. *Performing Whiteness: Postmodern Re/Constructions in the Cinema*. Albany: State University of New York Press.

Foster, Verna. 2015. "White Woods and Blue Jasmine: Woody Allen Rewrites *Streetcar Named Desire*." *Literature/Film Quarterly* 43, no. 3 (January): 188–201.

Frey, William. 2015. *Diversity Explosion: How New Racial Demographics Are Remaking America*. Washington, DC: Brookings Institution Press.

Friedman, Lester. 1982. *Hollywood's Image of the Jew*. New York: Frederick Ungar Publishing Co.

Fuchs, Cynthia, ed. 2002. *Spike Lee Interviews*. Jackson: Mississippi University Press.

Gabbard, Krin. 2004. *Black Magic: White Hollywood and African American Culture*. New Brunswick, NJ: Rutgers University Press.

Gabler, Neal. 1988. *An Empire of Their Own: How the Jews Invented Hollywood*. New York: Crown Publishers.

Gardaphe, Fred. 2006. *From Wiseguys to Wise Men: The Gangster and Italian American Masculinities*. New York: Routledge.

Gates, Henry Louis, Jr., and Spike Lee. 1992. "Film: Just Whose 'Malcolm' Is It, Anyway." *New York Times*. May 31, 1992. http://www.nytimes.com/1992/05/31/movies/film-just-whose-malcolm-is-it-anyway.html.

Gates, Philippa. 2003. "Buddy Films." In *American Masculinities: A Historical Encyclopedia*, edited by Brett Carroll, 73–75. Thousand Oaks, CA: Sage Publications.

Gjelton, Thomas. 2015. *A Nation of Nations: A Great American Immigration Story*. New York: Simon and Schuster.

Gilman, Sander. 1991. *The Jew's Body*. New York: Routledge.

———. 2013. "Foreword." In *Race, Color, Identity: Rethinking Discourses about "Jews" in the Twenty-First Century*, edited by Efraim Sicher, x–xvii. New York: Berghahn Books.

Gitelman, Zvi, ed. 2009. *Religion or Ethnicity: Jewish Identities in Evolution*. New Brunswick, NJ: Rutgers University Press.

Glazer, Nathan, and David P. Moynihan. 1963. *Beyond the Melting Pot: The Negroes, Puerto Ricans, Jews, Italians, and Irish of New York City*. Cambridge, MA: MIT Press.

Goldberg, Robert A. 1992. "Denver: Queen City of the Colorado Realm." In *The Invisible Empire in the West: Toward a New Historical Appraisal of the Ku Klux Klan in the 1920s*, edited by Shawn Lay, 39–66. Chicago: Illinois University Press.

Goldscheider, Calvin. 2009. "Judaism, Community, and Jewish Culture in American Life: Continuities and Transformations." In *Religion or Ethnicity: Jewish Identities in Evolution*, edited by Zvi Gitelman, 267–85. New Brunswick, NJ: Rutgers University Press.

Goldstein, Eric. 2006. *The Price of Whiteness: Jews, Race, and American Identity*. Princeton, NJ: Princeton University Press.

Gordon, Milton. 1964. *Assimilation in American Life: The Role of Race, Religion and National Origin*. Oxford: Oxford University Press.

Grant, Madison. 1921. *The Passing of the Great Race: The Racial Basis of European History*. 4th rev. ed. New York: Scribner's and Sons.

Grant, William. 1997. "Reflecting the Times: *Do the Right Thing* Revisited." In *Spike Lee's Do the Right Thing*, edited by Mark Reid, 16–30. New York: Cambridge University Press.

Graziano, William, Justin Lehmiller, and Laura VanderDrift. 2014. "Peer Influence and Attraction to Interracial Relationships." *Social Science* 3, no. 1: 115–27.

Greenberg, Cheryl. 2013. "I'm Not White, I'm Jewish: The Racial Politics of American Jews." In *Race, Color, Identity: Rethinking Discourses about the Jews in the Twenty-First Century*, edited by Efraim Sicher, 36–55. New York: Berghahn Books.

Guerrero, Ed. 1993. *Framing Blackness: The African American Image in Film*. Philadelphia: Temple University Press.

———. 2012. "*Bamboozled*: In the Mirror of Abjection." In *Contemporary Black American Cinema: Race, Gender, and Sexuality at the Movies*, edited by Mia Mask, 109–27. New York: Routledge.

Guglielmo, Jennifer, and Salvatore Salerno. 2003. *Are Italians White? How Race Is Made in America*. New York: Routledge.

Guida, George. 2010. "Prospero's Muccs: The Meaning of Martin Scorsese's Italian-American Dialect." *Italian America* 28, no. 1 (Winter): 5–17.

Haley, Alex. 1993. *The Autobiography of Malcolm X*. New York: Random House.

Hall, Stuart. 1996. "Cultural Studies: Two Paradigms." In *What Is Cultural Studies? A Reader*, edited by John Storey, 31–49. New York: St. Martin's Press.

Heinze, Andrew. 2004. *Jews and the American Soul: Human Nature in the Twentieth Century*. Princeton, NJ: Princeton University Press.

Herzog, Herta. 1944. "What Do We Really Know about Daytime Serial Listeners?" In *Radio Research, 1942–1943*, edited by Paul Lazerfeld and Frank Stanton, 3–33. New York: Duell, Sloan, and Pearce.

Hill, Jason D. 2009. *Beyond Blood Ties: Posthumanity in the Twenty-First Century*. Lanham, MD: Rowman & Littlefield.

Hill, Mike, ed. 1997. *Whiteness: A Critical Reader*. New York: New York University Press.

Hoare, Carol. 2003. "Psychosocial Development in United States Society: Its Role in Fostering Exclusion of Cultural Others." In *Race, Ethnicity and Self: Identity in Multicultural Perspective*, edited by Diane Koslow and Elizabeth Salett, 17–36. Washington, DC: National Multicultural Institute.

Ignatiev, Noel. 1995. *How the Irish Became White*. New York: Routledge.

Jacobson, Matthew. 1998. *Whiteness of a Different Color: European Immigrants and the Alchemy of Race*. Cambridge, MA: Harvard University Press.

———. 2006. *Roots Too: White Ethnic Revival in the Post Civil Rights Era*. Cambridge, MA: Harvard University Press.

Jewish Telegraphic Agency. 1959. "Numerous Sports Clubs Are Closed to Jews and Negroes." July 14, 1959. https://www.jta.org/1959/07/14/archive/numerous-sport-clubs-in-new-york-are-closed-to-jews-and-negroes.

Johnson, Siri. 1994. "Constructing Machismo in *Mean Streets* and *Raging Bull*." In *Perspectives on Raging Bull*, edited by Stephen Kellman, 95–105. New York: Macmillan.

Joyce, James. 1993. *A Portrait of the Artist as a Young Man*. Edited by R. B. Kershner. Boston: St. Martin's Press.

Kaba, Amadu J. 2011. "Inter-Ethnic/Interracial Romantic Relationships in the United States: Factors Responsible for the Low Rates of Marriages Between Blacks and Whites." *Sociology Mind* 1, no. 3: 121–29.

Kalmar, Ivan. 2013. "Race by the Grace of God: Race, Religion and the Construction of 'Jew' and 'Arab.'" In *Race, Color, Identity: Rethinking Discourses about the*

Jews in the Twenty-First Century, edited by Efraim Sicher, 324–43. New York: Berghahn Books.

Kaplan, Erin Aubrey. 2015. "The Long Road Home." In *The Trouble with Post-Blackness*, edited by Houston Baker and K. Merinda Simmons, 188–93. New York: Columbia University Press.

Kapsis, Robert, ed. 2016. *Woody Allen: Interviews*. Jackson: Mississippi University Press.

Karger, David. 2014. "Conversations with Cate Blanchett of *Blue Jasmine*." *Screen Actors Guild Foundation*. January 10, 2014. https://www.youtube.com/watch?v=qGJv7qFn4JU.

Kellman, Stephen, ed. 1994. *Perspectives on Raging Bull*. New York: Macmillan.

Khatchatourian, Maane. 2014. "Cate Blanchett Talks Woody Allen, 'Blue Jasmine' at Variety Screening Series." *Variety*. January 10, 2014. http://variety.com/2014/scene/awards/cate-blanchett-on-woody-allen-blue-jasmine-97-percent-of-his-direction-is-in-the-writing-1201043248/.

Kimmel, Michael, and Abby Ferber, eds. 2003. *Privilege: A Reader*. Boulder, CO: Westview Press.

King, Geoffrey. 2005. *American Independent Cinema*. Bloomington: Indiana University Press.

Kleinmann, James. 2013. "Woody Allen: Interview." *HeyUGuys*. September 27, 2013. https://www.youtube.com/watch?v=jdoDlfWk5Xw.

Knight, Christopher. 2004. "Woody Allen's *Annie Hall*: The Triumph of Galatea over Pygmalion." *Literature/Film Quarterly* 32, no. 3: 213–24.

———. 2006. "Woody Allen's *Manhattan* and the Ethnicity of Narrative." In *The Films of Woody Allen: Critical Essays*, edited by Charles L. P. Silet, 145–55. Lanham, MD: Scarecrow Press.

———. 2013. "'Raging in the Dark': Late Style in Woody Allen's Films." In *A Companion to Woody Allen*, edited by Peter Bailey and Sam Girgus, 73–94. Chichester, UK: Wiley-Blackwell.

Kolin, Philip, and Harvey Young, eds. 2014. *Suzan-Lori Parks in Person: Interviews and Commentaries*. New York: Routledge.

Konow, David, and Nicholas Pileggi. 2014. "Humanizing Criminals: *GoodFellas* and *Casino*." *Creative Screenwriting*. December 8, 2014. https://creativescreenwriting.com/humanizing-criminals-goodfellas-and-casino/.

Koslow, Diane. 2006. "*Manhattan* and the Ethnicity of Narrative." In *The Films of Woody Allen: Critical Essays*, edited by Charles L. P. Silet, 145–55. Lanham, MD: Scarecrow Press.

Koslow, Diane, and Elizabeth Salett, eds. 2003. *Race, Ethnicity and Self: Identity in Multicultural Perspective*. Washington, DC: National Multicultural Institute.

LaMotta, Jake, with Joseph Carter and Peter Savage. 1970. *Raging Bull: My Story*. Englewood Cliffs, NJ: Prentice Hall.

Larson, Jennifer. 2012. *Understanding Suzan-Lori Parks*. Columbia: South Carolina University Press.

Lay, Shawn, ed. 1994. *The Invisible Empire in the West: Toward a New Historical Appraisal of the KuKlux Klan in the 1920s*. Chicago: Illinois University Press.

Lazerfeld, Paul, and Frank Stanton, eds. 1944. *Radio Research, 1942–1943*. New York: Duell, Sloan, and Pearce.

Lee, Emily, ed. 2014. *Living Alterities: Phenomenology, Embodiment, and Race*. Albany: State University of New York Press.

Lee, Sander. 1997. *Woody Allen's Angst*. New York: McFarland & Co.

———. 2013. "Love, Meaning, and God in the Late Films of Woody Allen." In *A Companion to Woody Allen*, edited by Peter Bailey and Sam Girgus, 504–19. Chichester, UK: Wiley-Blackwell.

Lee, Spike, dir. 1996a. *Get on the Bus*. DVD Video. Columbia Pictures.

———, dir. 1996b. *Girl 6*. DVD Video. Fox Searchlight Pictures. Forty Acres and a Mule Filmworks.

———, dir. 1996c. *Jungle Fever*. DVD Video. Universal Home Video.

———, dir. 1998. *Do the Right Thing*. DVD Video. Universal Home Video.

———, dir. 2000a. *Bamboozled*. DVD Video. New Line Home Entertainment. Platinum Series.

———, dir. 2000b. *Malcolm X*. DVD Video. Warner Brothers Home Video.

———, dir. 2003. *25th Hour*. DVD Video. Home Entertainment, Inc.

———, dir. 2018. *BlacKkKlansman*. DVD Video. Universal Pictures Home Entertainment.

———, with Ralph Wiley. 1992. *By Any Means Necessary: The Trials and Tribulations of the Making of Malcolm X*. New York: Hyperion Press.

Lehman, Peter, ed. 2001. *Masculinity: Bodies, Movies, Culture*. New York: Routledge.

Lehr, Dick, and Girard O'Neill. 2000. *Black Mass: The Irish Mob, the FBI, and a Devil's Deal*. New York: Public Affairs Press.

Letort, Delphine. 2015. *The Spike Lee Brand: A Study of Documentary Filmmaking*. Albany: State University of New York Press.

Lewis, Jon. 1995. *Whom God Wishes to Destroy: Francis Coppola and the New Hollywood*. Durham, NC: Duke University Press.

Levinson, Julian. 2009. "People of the (Secular) Book: Literary Anthologies and the Making of Jewish Identity in Postwar America." In *Religion or Ethnicity: Jewish Identities in Evolution*, edited by Zvi Gitelman, 131–48. New Brunswick, NJ: Rutgers University Press.

Limerick, Patricia Nelson. 1987. *The Legacy of Conquest: The Unbroken Past of the American West*. New York: W. W. Norton.

Litman, Barry, ed. 1998. *The Motion Picture Mega-Industry*. Boston: Allyn and Bacon.

Littlejohn, David, ed. 1999. *The Real Las Vegas: Life Beyond the Strip*. New York: Oxford University Press.

LoBrutto, Vincent. 2008. *Martin Scorsese: A Biography*. Westport, CT: Praeger Publishers.

Lubiano, Wahneema. 2008. "But Compared to What? Reading Realism, Representation, and Essentialism in *School Daze*, *Do the Right Thing* and the Spike Lee Discourse." In *The Spike Lee Reader*, edited by Paula Massood, 30–57. Philadelphia: Temple University Press.

Macready, John. 2013. "A Difficult Redemption: Facing the 'Other' in Woody Allen's Exilic Period." In *A Companion to Woody Allen*, edited by Peter Bailey and Sam Girgus, 95–115. Chichester, UK: Wiley-Blackwell.

Markowitz, Fran. 2013. "Blood, Soul, Race, and Suffering: Full Bodied Ethnography and Expressions of Jewish Belonging." In *Race, Color, Identity: Rethinking*

Discourses about the Jews in the Twenty-First Century, edited by Efraim Sicher, 261–80. New York: Berghahn Books.

"Martin Scorsese: *Wolf of Wall Street* Interview." 2013. YouTube. December 13, 2013. https://www.youtube.com/watch?v=kTCyZoaORao.

Martinez, Zavala. 2003. "Quien Soy? Who Am I? Identity Issues for Puerto Rican Adolescents." In *Race, Identity, and Self: Identity in Multicultural Perspective*, edited by Diane Koslow and Elizabeth Salett, 89–116. Washington, DC: National Multicultural Institute.

Mask, Mia, ed. 2012. *Contemporary Black American Cinema: Race, Gender, and Sexuality at the Movies*. New York: Routledge.

Massood, Paula. 2003. *Black City Cinema: African American Urban Experience in Film*. Philadelphia: Temple University Press.

———, ed. 2008. *The Spike Lee Reader*. Philadelphia: Temple University Press.

McGowan, Todd. 2014. *Spike Lee*. Urbana: Illinois University Press.

McIntosh, Peggy. 2003. "White Privilege and Male Privilege: A Personal Account of Coming to See Correspondences through Work in Women's Studies." In *Privilege: A Reader*, edited by Michael Kimmel and Abby L. Ferber, 147–60. Boulder, CO: Westview Press.

McIvor, David. 2016. *Mourning in America: Race and the Politics of Loss*. Ithaca, NY: Cornell University Press.

McKelly, James. 2008. "The Double Truth, Ruth: *Do the Right Thing* and the Culture of Ambiguity." In *The Spike Lee Reader*, edited by Paula Massood, 58–76. Philadelphia: Temple University Press.

McNary, Dave. 2014. "Martin Scorsese on 'The Wolf of Wall Street': I Wanted to Make a Ferocious Film." *Variety*. January 25, 2014. http://variety.com/2014/film/news/martin-scorsese-on-wolf-of-wall-street-i-wanted-to-make-a-ferocious-film-1201070801/.

Mills, Charles. 2014. "Materializing Race." In *Living Alterities: Phenomenology, Embodiment, and Race*, edited by Emily Lee, 19–41. Albany: State University of New York Press.

Mitchell, W. J. T. 1997. "The Violence of Public Art: *Do the Right Thing*." In *Spike Lee's Do the Right Thing*, edited by Mark Reid, 107–28. New York: Cambridge University Press.

Molina, Natalia. 2014. *How Race Is Made in America: Immigration, Citizenship, and the Historical Power of Racial Scripts*. Berkeley: University of California Press.

Mollenkopf, John. 1992. *A Phoenix in the Ashes: The Rise and Fall of the Koch Coalition*. Princeton, NJ: Princeton University Press.

Newman, Katherine. 1999. *Falling from Grace: Downward Mobility in the Age of Affluence*. Berkeley: University of California Press.

Newman, Michael. 2011. *Indie: An American Film Culture*. New York: Columbia University Press.

Nicholls, Mark. 2004. *Scorsese's Men: Melancholia and the Mob*. North Melbourne, Australia: Pluto Press.

Nichols, Bill. 1994. *Blurred Boundaries: Questions of Meaning in Contemporary America*. Bloomington: Indiana University Press.

Nichols, Mary. 1998. *Reconstructing Woody: Art, Love and Life in the Films of Woody Allen*. New York: Rowman & Littlefield.

Nyce, Ben. 2004. *Scorsese Up Close*. Lanham, MD: Scarecrow Press.

Nyong'o, Tavia. 2008. "Racial Kitsch and Black Performance." In *The Spike Lee Reader*, edited by Paula Massood, 212–27. Philadelphia: Temple University Press.

O'Brien, Eileen. 2008. *The Racial Middle: Latinos and Asian Americans Living Beyond the Racial Divide*. New York: New York University Press.

Omi, Michael, and Howard Winant. 1994. *Racial Formation in the United States: From the 1960s to the 1980s*. New York: Routledge & Kegan Paul.

Osborne, Monica. 2013. "Hollywood Rabbi: The Never Ending Questions of Woody Allen." In *A Companion to Woody Allen*, edited by Peter Bailey and Sam Girgus, 520–38. Chichester, UK: Wiley-Blackwell.

O'Toole, James. 1985. "Prelates and Politicos: Catholics and Politics in Massachusetts, 1900–1970." In *Catholic Boston: Studies in Religion and Community, 1870–1970*, edited by James O'Toole and Robert E. Sullivan, 15–65. Boston: Boston Archdiocese Press.

———, and Robert E. Sullivan, eds. 1985. *Catholic Boston: Studies in Religion and Community 1870–1970*. Boston: Boston Archdiocese Press.

Painter, Nell. 2010. *The History of White People*. New York: W. W. Norton.

Palmer, Bryan. 2003. "The Hands That Built America: A Class-Politics Appreciation of Martin Scorsese's *Gangs of New York*." *Historical Materialism* 11, no. 4: 317–45. https://edisciplinas.usp.br/pluginfile.php/159553/mod_resource/content/1/Palmer%20on%20Scorcese.pdf.

Peatman, John Gray. 1944. "Radio and Popular Music." In *Radio Research, 1942–1943*, edited by Paul Lazerfeld and Frank Stanton, 335–96. New York: Duell, Sloan, and Pearce.

Phillips, Steve. 2015. *Brown Is the New White: How the Demographic Revolution Has Created a New American Majority*. New York: The New Press.

Pinsker, Sanford. 2006. "Woody Allen's Lovable Anxious Schlemiels." In *The Films of Woody Allen: Critical Essays*, edited by Charles L. P. Silet, 1–12. Lanham, MD: Scarecrow Press.

Polhemus, Robert. 2013. "Comic Faith and Its Discontents: Death and the Late Woody Allen." In *A Companion to Woody Allen*, edited by Peter Bailey and Sam Girgus, 116–44. Chichester, UK: Wiley-Blackwell.

Pouzoulet, Catherine. 1997. "The Cinema of Spike Lee: Images of a Mosaic City." In *Spike Lee's Do the Right Thing*, edited by Mark Reid, 31–49. New York: Cambridge University Press.

Primeggia, Salvatore. 2004. "La Via Vecchia and Italian Folk Religiosity." In *Models and Images of Italian American Catholicism: Academy and Society*, edited by Joseph Varacalli, Salvatore Primeggia, Salvatore LaGumina, and Donald D'Elia, 15–39. Stony Brook, NY: Forum Italicum.

Rabinowitz, David and Charlie Wachtel, 2018. "*BlacKkKlansman* Writers on Handing our Baby to Spike Lee." *IndieWire*. http://cs.entertainmentcareers.net/blogs/indie/archive/2018/08/10/blackkklansman.

Rapf, Joanna. 2013. "It's Complicated Really': Women in the Films of Woody Allen." In *A Companion to Woody Allen*, edited by Peter Bailey and Sam Girgus, 257–76. Chichester, UK: Wiley-Blackwell.

Reid, Mark. 1993. *Redefining Black Film*. Berkeley: University of California Press.

———, ed. 1997. *Spike Lee's Do the Right Thing*. New York: Cambridge University Press.

———. 2005. *Black Lenses, Black Voices: African American Film Now*. Lanham: Rowman & Littlefield.

Rice, Tom. 2015. *White Robes Silver Screens: Movies and the Making of the Ku Klux Klan*. Bloomington: Indiana University Press.

Roche, Mark W. 2006. "Justice and the Withdrawal of God in Woody Allen's *Crimes and Misdemeanors*." In *The Films of Woody Allen: Critical Essays*, edited by Charles L. P. Silet, 268–83. Lanham, MD: Scarecrow Press.

Roediger, David. 1997. "White Looks, Hairy Apes, True Stories, and Limbaugh's Laughs." In *Whiteness: A Critical Reader*, edited by Mike Hill, 35–46. New York: New York University Press.

Rogin, Michael. 1996. *Blackface, White Noise: Jewish Immigrants in the Hollywood Melting Pot*. Berkeley: University of California Press.

Roland, Alan. 2003. "Identity, Self, and Individualism in a Multicultural Perspective." In *Race, Ethnicity and Self: Identity in a Multicultural Perspective*, edited by Diane Koslow and Elizabeth Salett, 3–16. Washington, DC: National Multicultural Institute.

Rosenblatt, Paul, Terri Karis, and Richard Powell. 1995. *Multiracial Couples: Black and White Voices*. London: Sage Publications.

Roth, Wendy. 2012. *Race Migrations: Latinos and the Cultural Transformation of Race*. Stanford: Stanford University Press.

Rothman, Hal, ed. 1998. *Reopening the American West*. Tucson: Arizona University Press.

———. 2002. *Neon Metropolis: How Las Vegas Started the Twenty-First Century*. New York: Routledge.

Rubin-Dorsky, Jeffrey. 2003. "Woody Allen After the Fall: Literary Gold from Amoral Alchemy." *Shofar: An Interdisciplinary Journal of Jewish Studies* 22, no. 1 (Fall): 1–16.

Sanders, James. 1985. "Catholics and the School Question in Boston: The Cardinal O'Connell Years." In *Catholic Boston: Studies in Religion and Community, 1870–1970*, edited by Roger Sullivan and James O'Toole, 121–69. Boston: Archdiocese of Boston.

Santo, Avi. 2008. "Para Television and Discourses of Distinction: The Culture of Production at HBO." In *It's Not TV: Watching HBO in the Post-Television Era*, edited by Cara Buckley, Marc Leverette, and Brian Ott, 19–45. New York: Routledge.

Saval, Malina. 2013. "Why Is Hollywood Making Big Budget Movies about Sleazy Jewish Crooks?" *Haaritz*. December 29, 2013. http://www.haaetz.com/jewish/features/. premium-1.566089.

Schickel, Richard, ed. 2011. *Conversations with Scorsese*. New York: Alfred A. Knopf.

Schrag, Peter. 2010. *Not Fit for Our Society: Nativism and Immigration*. Berkeley: University of California Press.

Schumacher, Michael. 1999. *Francis Ford Coppola: A Filmmaker's Life*. New York: Crown Publishers.

Scorsese, Martin, dir. 1989. *Taxi Driver*. DVD Video. Columbia TriStar Home Video.

———, dir. 1995. *4 Westerns: A Personal Journey Through American Movies*. YouTube. https://www.youtube.com/watch?v=pUcgI9jwhlA.

———, dir. 1998. *Raging Bull*. DVD Video. MGM Home Entertainment.

———, dir. 2003. *Gangs of New York*. DVD Video. Buena Vista Home Entertainment. Discs 1 and 2.

———, dir. 2004a. *GoodFellas*. DVD Video. Warner Brothers Home Entertainment.

———, dir. 2004b. *Mean Streets*. DVD Video. Warner Brothers Home Entertainment.

———, dir. 2005. *Casino*. *Casino* Anniversary Edition DVD Video. Universal Studios Home Entertainment.

———, dir. 2006. *The Departed*. DVD Video. Warner Brothers Home Entertainment.

———, dir. 2014. *The Wolf of Wall Street*. DVD Video. Paramount Pictures.

Shoard, Catherine. 2016. "Woody Allen: 'There are traumas in life that weaken us. That's what's happened to me.'" *The Guardian*. August 25, 2016. https://www.theguardian.com/film/2016/aug/25/woody-allen-traumas-in-life-weaken-us-cafe-society-amazon.

Sicher, Efraim, ed. 2013. *Race, Color, Identity: Rethinking Discourses about the Jews in the Twenty-First Century*. New York: Berghahn Books.

Siegal, Mark. 1985. "Ozymandias Melancholia: The Nature of Parody in *Stardust Memories*." *Literature/Film Quarterly* 13, no. 2 (June): 77–84.

Siegel, Robert. 2014. "Cate Blanchett Finds Humor in the Painfully Absurd." Interview. *National Public Radio*. "All Things Considered." January 10, 2014. http://www.npr.org/2014/01/10/261398089/cate-blanchett-finds-humor-in-the-painfully-absurd.

Silet, Charles. L. P. 2006. *The Films of Woody Allen: Critical Essays*. Lanham, MD: Scarecrow Press.

Simmons, K. Merinda. 2015. "The Dubious Stage of Post-Blackness—Performing Otherness, Conserving Dominance." In *The Trouble with Post-Blackness*, edited by Houston Baker and K. Merinda Simmons, 1–20. New York: Columbia University Press.

Sinclair, Upton. 2003. *The Jungle: The Uncensored Original Edition*. Tucson, AZ: Sharp Press.

Smith, Derik. 2012. "True Terror: The Haunting of Spike Lee's *25th Hour*." *African American Review* 45, no. 1/2 (Spring/Summer): 1–16.

Smith, Gavin, ed., and Martin Scorsese. 1998. "Street Smart: Excerpts from Three Martin Scorsese Interviews." *Film Comment* 34, no. 3 (May–June): 1–15.

Smith, Judith. 2004. *Visions of Belonging: Family Stories, Popular Culture, and Postwar Democracy, 1940–1960*. New York: Columbia University Press.

Smith-Shomade, Beretta. 2008. "I Be Smackin' My Hoes: Paradox and Authenticity in *Bamboozled*." In *The Spike Lee Reader*, edited by Paula Massood, 228–42. Philadelphia: Temple University Press.

Sollors, Werner. 1986. *Beyond Ethnicity: Consent and Descent in American Culture*. New York: Oxford University Press.

Sotiropoulos, Karen. 2006. *Staging Race: Black Performers in Turn of the Century America*. Cambridge, MA: Harvard University Press.

Stallworth, Ron. 2014. *Black Klansman: Race, Hate, and the Undercover Investigation of a Lifetime*. New York: Flatiron Books.

Stam, Robert. 1989. *Subversive Pleasures: Bakhtin, Culture Criticism, and Film*. Baltimore: Johns Hopkins University Press.

Stern, Leslie. 1995. *The Scorsese Connection*. Bloomington: Indiana University Press.

Sterritt, David. 2013. *Spike Lee's America*. Cambridge, UK: Polity Press.

Storey, John, ed. 1996. *What Is Cultural Studies? A Reader*. New York: St. Martin's Press.

Sullivan, Robert, and James O'Toole, eds. 1985. *Catholic Boston: Studies in Religion and Community, 1870–1970*. Boston: Archdiocese of Boston.

Swensen, Andrew. 2001. "The Anguish of God's Lonely Man: Dostoevsky's Underground Man and Scorsese's Travis Bickle." *Renaissance* 53, no. 4 (Summer): 267–86.

Tehranian, John. 2009. *Whitewashed: America's Invisible Middle Eastern Minority*. New York: New York University Press.

Tesler, Michael. 2016. *Post Racial or Most Racial? Race and Politics in the Obama Era*. Chicago: Chicago University Press.

Thompson, Anne. 2018. "With Spike Lee's *BlacKkKlansman* Focus Features' Strategy to Reinvent its Roster Becomes Clear," *IndieWire*. https://www.indiewire.com/2018/05/spike-lee-blackkklansman-cannes-focus-features-1201964701/.

Thompson, Jennifer. 2014. *Jewish on Their Own Terms*. New Brunswick, NJ: Rutgers University Press.

Turner, Frederick Jackson. 1893. "The Significance of the Frontier in American History." http://xroads.virginia.edu/~hyper/turner/chapter1.

Turner, Victor, ed. 1982. *Celebration: Studies in Festivity and Ritual*. Washington, DC: Smithsonian Press.

———, ed. 1988. *The Anthropology of Performance*. Baltimore: Johns Hopkins University Press.

Tzioumakas, Yannis. 2006. *American Independent Cinema*. Edinburgh: Edinburgh University Press.

US Immigration Legislation Online. "1790 Naturalization Act." http://library.uwb.edu/Static/USimmigration/1790_naturalization_act.html.

Vest, Jason. 2014. *Spike Lee: Finding the Story and Forcing the Issue*. Santa Barbara, CA: Praeger Press.

Wilhelm, Elliot, ed. 1999. "The Sorrow and the Pity." *VideoHound's World Cinema*. http://www.oocities.org/resistancehistory/sorrowpity.pdf.

Williams, Raymond. 1996. "The Future of Cultural Studies." In *What Is Cultural Studies? A Reader*, edited by John Storey, 168–77. New York: St. Martin's Press.

Wilson, Karen. 2015. "Social Capital and Frontier Community Building: The Case of Immigrant Jews in Nineteenth Century Los Angeles." In *Immigrants in the Far West: Historical Identities and Experiences*, edited by Jessie Embry and Brian Cannon, 263–93. Salt Lake City: Utah University Press.

Yacowar, Maurice. 2006. "The Religion of *Radio Days*." In *The Films of Woody Allen: Critical Essays*, edited by Charles L. P. Silet, 250–55. Lanham, MD: Scarecrow Press.

Young, Harvey, ed. 2013. *Cambridge Companion to African American Theatre*. New York: Cambridge University Press.

Zangwill, Israel. (1921). *The Melting Pot*. Baltimore, MD: Macmillan Company. Project Gutenberg E-Book. https://www.gutenberg.org/files/23893/23893-h/23893-h.html.

Index

Abd Azzam, 227
Abernathy, Graeme, 218
Abraham, 158
Abrams, Roger, 32
Ace Rothstein (character), 82, 91–92, 95–102
advertising industry, 25
affirmative action, 84, 277
African Americans: assimilation of, 18–19; culture, 198, 218–19, 240, 255; disadvantages of, 3; homeowners, 6; identity of, 220; internal migration of, 69; Jews and, 36–37, 275; Mafia and, 67–68; in *Mean Streets*, 36; stereotypes, 205–6
Agent Cunningham (character), 265
Agent Flood (character), 263, 264, 265
Al (character), 182
Alba, Richard, 5–6
Ali, Muhammad, 201
alienation, 25, 35, 41–42, *44*, 120, 155–56, 189
Allah, 224, 225, 226
Allen, Woody, 284, 286; as actor, 176; aesthetic of, 171; on anti-Semitism, 194; associates and collaborations of, 114, 135; child abuse scandal of, 165; comic signature of, 117; death and, 118–19; ethnic culture and, 113, *132*; exilic period of, 175; Farrow and, 165–66; Fellini and, 157; female desire and, 176; filmmaking career of, 113–14; Friedman on, 195; Harry Block

and, 171; influences of, 118; Jewish culture and, 113, *132*, 135, 175–76; Judaism and, 129; late style of, 166; parents of, 135; protagonists of, 128, 175–76, 194; screenwriting of, 177; stoicism, 194. *See also specific films*
Allison Portchnik (character), 117
All the President's Men, 270
Alvy Singer (character), 115–26, 191, 194
American dream, 57, 60, 188
Americanism, 93, 136
The American Jewish Novel (Codde), 156
American Masculinities (Gates), 271
The American Play, 239–40
Amsterdam Vallon (character), 71–72, 75–76, 78–82, 91
anarchism, 166
The Anatomy of Loving, 150, 154
Anbinder, Tyler, 4, 186
ancestry, 2, 13
Angela King (character), 246
Angela Tucci (character), 211–16
Angelou, Maya, 231, 236
Animal House, 106
Annie (character), 117, 118, 121–26, 194
Annie Hall (Allen), 23, 191; Becker and, 150; Coppola and, 117; dramatic logic of, 118; ending of, 124–25; ethnicity of, 117; imagery of, 115; literature and, 116; Los Angeles in, 124, 126; marginality in, 120; New York City in, 128. *See also specific characters*

Womack (character). *See* Sleep'n Eat
women, 120, 179–80, 214–15, 244
Wonder, Stevie, 249
Wonder Wheel, 284
"Woody Allen After the Fall," 165–66
World War I, 186
World War II, 35, 55, 122, 142, 166, 257, 273
Wrangle, Theresa, 238, 246

Xavier (character), 233, 234, 236, 237
xenophobia, 67–68, 269

Yisroel, Chaim (Rabbi), 113
"You Must Never Be a Misrepresented People," 237

Zangwill, Israel, 1, 2, 19–20, 94
Zelig (Allen), 284

About the Author

James F. Scott is a lifelong academic who divides his time between teaching, scholarship, and video production. A long-term member of the Saint Louis University faculty, he served from 2008 to 2014 as Director of the Film and Media Studies program. Scott's scholarly contributions to cultural studies include publications in *American Quarterly*, *Film and History*, and *Literature/Film Quarterly*, as well as contributions to several anthologies. He is also the author of *Film: The Medium and the Maker* (1975), an introduction to Film Studies. For the past three decades he has been continuously involved in film and television production for PBS and the Higher Education Network, scripting and producing more than twenty programs of an educational nature.

CPSIA information can be obtained
at www.ICGtesting.com
Printed in the USA
LVHW081918160721
692904LV00011B/220